THE TROUBLESOME HELPMATE

A History of Misogyny in Literature

The
Troublesome
Helpmate

*A History
of Misogyny in
Literature*

BY KATHARINE M. ROGERS

*University
of Washington
Press*

Seattle and London

To My Mother

✺ ACKNOWLEDGMENTS

I deeply appreciate the generosity of my colleagues who have contributed their time and expert knowledge to the improvement of this book—Dean Marjorie Coogan Downing of Scripps College and Professors Gloria Glikin, Norman Harrington, Margaret Marshall, and Ruth Temple of Brooklyn College. I am especially grateful for the advice and encouragement of Professor James L. Clifford of Columbia University.

Much of the discussion of Swift in Chapter V originally appeared in my article on Swift's attitude toward women in the Autumn, 1959, issue of *Texas Studies in Literature and Language*.

ᝂ PREFACE

> And the Lord God said, It is not good that the man should be alone; I will make him an help meet for him. . . . And the rib, which the Lord God had taken from man, made he a woman, and brought her unto the man.
>
> (Gen. 2:18, 22)

HERE IN two verses is man's traditional view of woman, which — although it assumes her subordinate position — implies that she is his natural companion, essential to his welfare and happiness. It is evident equally from individual biographies, social history, and literature that most men have shared this positive view. But at the same time, in all periods of history, there has been a dark stream of attacks on women.

Walter Map compared woman to a chimera, "beautified with the face of a noble lion, yet . . . blemished with the belly of a reeking kid and . . . beweaponed with the virulent tail of a viper." The hero of *Gawain and the Green Knight*, presented as a model of chivalry, suddenly exclaimed that women have brought to ruin the noblest of men, Adam and Samson, David and Solomon. John Donne, deriding the so-called alchemy of love, said it is useless to hope for mind in women, who are "but *Mummy*, possest." The Chorus of John Milton's *Samson Agonistes* wondered whether it is woman's defective judgment or her incapacity for love that makes her such a thorn in the side of a good man, and explained that God has given the male "despotic power" as the only means to prevent his ruin by women. The Earl of Rochester said that man is an ass to love women, "The idlest part of *Gods Creation*." Jonathan Swift prided himself on "perpetually" reproaching the ladies "for their ignorance, affectation, impertinence," as well as their "sour un-savoury Streams," their flabby breasts, and their extravagant adornment of "a nauseous unwholesom living Carcase." Douglas Jerrold elaborated, through his Mrs. Caudle's thirty-five curtain lectures, on the miseries of a husband. *The Saturday Review*, a prominent Liberal magazine of the nineteenth century, soberly declared that "All the nobler avenues of intellectual distinction" are closed to women because of their incapacity for rational thought. D. H. Lawrence inveighed against "The colossal evil of the united spirit of Woman."

Misogyny, a prominent theme through all periods of English and American literature, can be traced back to the ancient myths of the Jews and the Greeks. In this book I shall describe and try to explain its varying manifestations in our literature — the perennial themes and lasting conventions, the historical variations in the intensity of misogyny and the ways it is expressed, and the distinctive or extreme misogyny of certain writers. While a full account of the cultural factors which encourage hostility to women would require a work of many volumes, I shall indicate the influence of such religious factors as the early Christian denigration of sex, such social ones as anxiety resulting from attempts to maintain a patriarchal system, such economic ones as the reduction of women to complete financial dependence on men.

One of the most significant cultural influences in the twentieth century has been Sigmund Freud's exploration of the unconscious. By pointing out the crucial importance of a child's earliest years and developing his theory of the Oedipus complex, Freud focused attention on the importance of the mother and her enormous potential influence for good or evil. In the beginning, the child perceives his mother as the source of all power — of food, security, and love; of frustration and punishment. Later, she is her son's first erotic object and thus becomes for him the prototype of all women he might love. Although Freud was not the first to apprehend these insights, he and his followers clarified them and made them part of general awareness. As a result, in recent years fear of maternal power has been more explicitly and generally expressed than ever before; in a sense, psychoanalysis has provided material for the misogynists by giving them a new scapegoat in the form of the all-powerful and potentially destructive mother.

Apart from contributing to its subject matter, psychoanalysis helps to clarify the motives for misogyny. The original apparent omnipotence of the mother probably accounts for the fear of female dominance which has haunted men, even in strongly patriarchal societies; indeed, it is usually the most vociferous patriarchs who express it. The boy's initial erotic attachment to his mother, an attachment which she inevitably frustrates in favor of another male, helps to explain why men have so often reproached women for faithlessness, for failure to respond to their love. If, in addition to this inevitable strain on the relationship, the mother should be cold, sadistic, irrational, possessive, or inadequate, the boy is apt to feel her deficiences so deeply that he will generalize them to all women and will never be able to free himself of hostility in his relationships with them.

To trace the expression of misogyny in literature entails an endless series of questions of definition. When Tertullian preaches that woman is the Devil's gateway and ought to go about in squalid mourning, the misogyny is clear. But when Swift describes a typical belle as an ugly, ill-smelling animal, is he reviling women or merely satirizing undue idealization of them? When Adam denounces women in *Paradise Lost*, is he expressing Milton's views or the purposely distorted cries of a man just fallen into sin? When Milton elaborates on female subjection, is he revealing personal fear and dislike of women or simply paraphrasing Holy Writ? When Geoffrey Chaucer has the Wife of Bath confess her many conjugal sins, is he holding her up as a horrible type of wifehood or simply creating a comic character? Should attacks on women be discounted completely if they spring from a particular comic situation or character, such as Truewit's horrifying picture of marriage in *Epicoene* or Henry Higgins' outbursts in *My Fair Lady*? Can jokes be taken as evidence of hostility, or should they be dismissed as innocent fun?

I believe that all the references listed here are significant. Not equally significant, of course. Sometimes the author is more concerned with satirizing a vice found in women than women themselves, or with being funny than satirizing at all. Sometimes he dissociates the misogynistic sentiments from his own point of view. Sometimes his criticism is so lightly hostile that it is compatible with general respect and liking for women. These modifying factors must of course be taken into account in interpreting antifeminist statements found in literary works. But they do not cause the antifeminism to evaporate. Even jokes are frequently significant: as Freud demonstrated, wit is often an indirect means of expressing drives which cannot be directly expressed. Just as obscene wit is a substitute for overt sexual activity, hostile wit is a substitute for direct physical or verbal expressions of hostility. Since most writers have not felt free to express misogyny directly — it is an unnatural attitude, considered shocking in most periods — they have found it necessary to conceal it in some way, both from others and from themselves. Misogyny, therefore, is more apt than not to appear in disguised form. Sometimes the hostility is displaced, so that the hostile feelings for wife or mother, about which a man usually feels guilty, are transferred to the whore, who *should* be vilified. Sometimes it is projected, so that the man who callously exploits women insists that it is they who are exploitative and incapable of love. Sometimes it is rationalized, so that a man insists that keeping women in subjection is necessary protection for their weakness. Sometimes it is made light of, so that the writer claims to be only joking when he represents suffering as the usual condition of married men.

In the seventeenth century a man could harangue against whores in terms readily applicable to women in general; in the nineteenth, when such attacks would have been considered intolerably harsh and crude, a writer could joke merrily about a poor husband's attempts to escape from his wife. Antiwife jokes, which have been a humorous staple from the beginnings of literature, derive their perennial appeal from the hostility which all men (I suppose) occasionally feel toward their wives. (There has also been hostility in the other direction, but misandry is outside the scope of this book.) Now, of course, to hate women is not the same thing as to relish a joke at the expense of one's wife. I simply maintain that the latter reaction involves at least slight and temporary hostility, and that this is on the same continuum as full-fledged misogyny.

I include among the manifestations of misogyny in literature not only direct expressions of hatred, fear, or contempt of womankind, but such indirect expressions as misogynistic speeches by dramatic characters who are definitely speaking for the author and condemnations of one woman or type of woman which spread, implicitly or explicitly, to the whole sex. The tirades against the heroine of John Marston's *The Insatiate Countess*, although ostensibly directed against lustful women only, actually recognize no clear distinction between evil women and women in general. I also include attacks on human follies or vices which focus inappropriately or disproportionately on women, as when Philip Wylie and John Osborne blame the prosperous matrons of England and America for modern materialism, as if the male sex were unanimously struggling to maintain idealism. The view that women are inferior to men and therefore should be subordinated to them is not in itself misogynistic, because it was almost universally held until modern times. But when an author insists on this view to an extent unusually harsh for his period, as Milton and Lawrence did, he is surely revealing misogyny.

Lastly, I have included as evidence of misogyny jokes against women which, because of lengthy elaboration, bitter tone, or consonance with the author's general views, seem to reveal an undertone of seriousness. I have, however, ruled out very light antifeminist jokes as insignificant. For example, it would be unduly ponderous to label as misogynistic Allen Dodd, Jr.'s, "The Permutation of the Proper Place" (*Saturday Review*, March 21, 1964), a small fantasy on women's alleged compulsion to put things away in inappropriate and constantly shifting places, even though it clearly derives from the old charges that women are irrational and untiringly find ways to bedevil their husbands.

I have also ruled out — arbitrarily, since one must set limits somewhere — misogyny outside the English language, apart from the religious and classical backgrounds needed to understand English and American writers. While it is true that misogynistic works such as the second part of *The Romance of the Rose* were widely read and imitated in certain periods, no modern foreign literature had nearly so important and lasting an influence on English writers as the Bible and the classics of Greece and Rome.

Although I have generally adopted chronological organization, in order to emphasize the particular forms which misogyny took during different periods, I have occasionally departed from strict chronology so as to bring out the persistence of certain attitudes from one period to another. Because the shrew-taming plays of the 1590's, for instance, are thoroughly medieval in their presentation of and attitude toward their subject, I have dealt with them in Chapter II, on the Middle Ages. My first chapter, dealing with the traditional background on which English and American writers were to draw, is intended to cover broad periods in order to bring out the effects of certain enduring cultural factors on the expression of misogyny.

In addition to describing, through some of their representatives, the major misogynistic conventions in English and American literature, I have tried to discuss the significant authors who were personally misogynistic. There will inevitably be disagreement about my selection. In doubtful cases I have decided on the basis of the one-sidedness of an author's presentation of women, and of his divergence from what was conventional in his day. One might, for example, consider William Wycherley a misogynist because of his cynical jibes at women and marriage and his caustic exposures of female hypocrites. But actually what he said was conventional in his time and social group; if he stated it more forcefully than George Etherege or William Congreve, it was because his satiric method was heavier-handed. One might consider Restoration drama misogynistic, since it is full of female fools and knaves and speeches against women. However, the plays not only present a remarkable degree of sexual equality but generally feature delightful heroines: for every Lady Fidget there is an Alithea.

Similarly, William Makepeace Thackeray's exposure of the possessiveness and jealousy behind apparent maternal devotion would seem to anticipate the modern attacks on Mom had he not laid far more emphasis on the constructive and inspiring effects of a mother's love. Some critics feel that Henry James revealed misogyny in the form of fear of women, pointing to his succession of male protagonists who shy away from passionate involvement with women and to female characters such as the formidable matriarch Mrs. Newsome in *The Ambassadors* and the vampire wife Mrs. Brissenden in *The Sacred Fount*. But surely this misogynistic undertone is less significant than the charm and goodness with which James endowed his typical heroines — Isabel Archer, Maggie Verver, Milly Theale.

In Ben Jonson, on the other hand, there are no attractive female characters to counterbalance many unpleasant ones. Lady Politick Would-Bee, lustful, charmless, and stupidly pretentious, is a typical example of womanhood as presented in his plays. In Swift, too, one finds a definitely one-sided presentation of woman—not so much of her mental and moral, but of her physical deficiencies. Again and again Swift exposed what he considered the illusions of woman's beauty and romantic love, to a degree unique in his period, without ever presenting a positive view of the feminine roles of mistress, wife, and mother. Of course, both men were Juvenalian satirists whose major subject was human follies and vices, but their particular stress on female failings betrays a definite misogynistic animus. In deciding whether an author who conspicuously presents unadmirable female characters is misogynistic, one must particularly consider whether these are types or individuals: an odious type character such as Jonson's Lady Politick is an expression of hostility against the group so typed, but an odious individual is not. Thus Thackeray's bad women—Becky Sharp and so forth—are no more expressions of misogyny than male villains are expressions of misandry. Dickens' shrews and career women, on the other hand, are invidious type characters: in joining his contemporaries who ruthlessly attacked any attempts at self-assertion by women, and the long line of satirists of bad wives, Dickens was expressing misogyny in the forms characteristic of his period.

Necessarily, a history of misogyny presents a one-sided picture, since it is confined by definition to the negative side of men's attitude toward women. It must be remembered that some expressions of misogyny, where it is a direct reaction against idealization of women, would not exist without that original idealization. More important, in most periods misogynistic writings were decidedly outweighed by expressions of love and praise for women. Renaissance playwrights and audiences enjoyed misogynistic diatribes, and Renaissance sonnet sequences regularly included hostile poems; but the period was mainly characterized by exaltation both of women and romantic love. Donne's savage attacks on women are greatly outnumbered by poems of passionate praise. Even a man like Swift, whose writings incline to misogyny, deeply loved two women and showed in his life and works higher esteem for the sex than was usual in his time. Obviously, men's prevailing attitude toward women, in their writings as well as their lives, has been positive: this is the natural result of human biology and nurture; it is equally necessary for the happiness of the individual and the continuance of society. Men's love and respect for women, however, have always been accompanied — in the culture as a whole and sometimes within a single individual — by some degree of fear, dislike, or contempt. It is the expression of these feelings in literature that I propose to analyze in this book.

CONTENTS

I   Introduction: Eve, Xanthippe, and Clodia   3

II   Medieval Attitudes Toward Love and Marriage   56

III   The Court Wanton, The Bossy Bourgeoise, and the Insatiable Strumpet: The Renaissance   100

IV   St. Paul with a Difference: The Puritans   135

V   Reason vs. Folly and Romantic Illusion: The Restoration and the Eighteenth Century   160

VI   The Drooping Lily: The Nineteenth Century   189

VII   The Fear of Mom: The Twentieth Century   226

VIII   The Reason Why   265

Index   279

THE TROUBLESOME HELPMATE

A History of Misogyny in Literature

Chapter 1 ❦ INTRODUCTION:
EVE, XANTHIPPE, AND CLODIA

1. The Devil's Gateway

I T IS perhaps misleading to start a history of misogyny with the
Bible, since the Old Testament writers generally assumed that
marriage is the proper destiny of man and a good wife a blessing
from God. Yet it must start here, for the Bible contains many texts
which misogynists have appropriated or misappropriated for their
purposes. To the student of misogyny in English literature, it matters
little whether the staple texts were originally intended to be misogynistic or simply became so through generations of misogynistic interpretation. Since the Bible has been accepted for centuries as the
word of God, anything in it acquires great significance: thus a casual
comment, an isolated example, or even a metaphor can easily be mis-
interpreted into a formal condemnation of the female sex. A brief
reference to a particular woman may become highly significant in
the light of later commentary. The episode in which Job's wife tells
her husband to curse God and die — minor in the original book —
has been magnified by later writers into a general indictment of
wives. Her speech, intended to show poor Job failed even by the person who should have been closest to him, has been used as evidence
that women never miss an opportunity to increase their husband's
misery or to lead them into sin.

Early in Genesis, however, comes a story which is unquestionably
misogynistic. After the Elohist's story of God's creating man male
and female in His own image — which implies not only that the two
sexes were created simultaneously as necessary complements to each
other, but that they existed in God as well as in man — comes the
Jahvist's contrasting version, in which Eve was made from Adam's

3

rib as an afterthought.[1] This implies first that woman was created almost reluctantly, when no other creature could satisfy man's needs. Secondly, there is the more significant implication that to this day she exists not in her own right, but only as a "help meet," an accessory to man. Lastly, she was not even created in the divine image, but only in man's; hence she is further removed from God than man is, and as a consequence more prone to folly and vice. This second account has made far more impression on succeeding generations than the first: it appears and reappears in homiletic literature, from St. Paul's epistles to the *Catholic Encyclopedia* of 1912,[2] while the first account is ignored when possible or else explained away. Thus for many centuries women's appeals for rights have been denied on the ground that humans created only as helpers were not entitled to rights: they could live only through their male relatives.

The Jahvist's story of the creation of woman implies that she is inherently a more imperfect creature than man. His story of the Fall serves to prove her moral weakness and her ruinous influence. The serpent misled the woman, as the less intelligent and virtuous human; and then she misled her husband. If she had not yielded, he would not have yielded and thus brought misery on all his posterity. Adam's primary fault, indeed, was hearkening to the voice of his wife. He was punished by the necessity of toil and struggle with recalcitrant nature — a punishment which of course afflicted Eve as well. But she, as the greater sinner, was in addition punished with labor pains and subjection to the man. This story justified the subjection of women both explicitly and implicitly (by showing what happens when a man listens to his wife) and provided divinely inspired "proof" of their natural depravity and inability to control their impulses. Its influence on the Judaeo-Christian tradition can hardly be overemphasized. Although later commentators were to darken its misogynistic implications — changing a myth explaining the bio-

[1] Gen. 1:27, 2:18–22. It is agreed by Biblical scholars that Genesis was written by several authors. The writers of the contrasting accounts of woman are distinguished as "Elohist" and "Jahvist" because the first referred to God as "Elohim," the second as "Jahveh."

[2] This still appears to be the Roman Catholic view, although it is no longer expressed unequivocally. Usually the subject is discreetly avoided, but see *The Origins of Man*, No. 29 of *The Twentieth-Century Encyclopedia of Catholicism* (New York: Hawthorn Books, 1958), by Nicolas Corte (pseud.).

logical fact of labor pains and the social fact of wifely subjection into a divine condemnation of the female sex — they did not have to distort the original to do so.

In all other cases, the commentators did have to distort Old Testament stories in order to make them really misogynistic. They often interpreted a particular case as a generalization about the human condition. Thus they saw Samson not just as an individual ruined by unfortunate encounters with evil women, but rather as a type, placed in the Bible to prove man's defenselessness before female wiles and woman's incapacity for love. Since Samson is represented as a heroic figure, the writer of his story naturally emphasized the women's falsity rather than his mental and moral weakness. The same was done for David, not by the Old Testament writer but by subsequent commentators. David committed his single great sin, adultery with Bathsheba and indirect murder of her husband, because he accidentally saw her naked body. In the Biblical account the emphasis is entirely on David's lust. But Christian preachers were to use the tale as a misogynistic text: obviously a holy man like David could not have committed mortal sin unless seduced, so Bathsheba must have seduced him.

David's son Solomon was more obviously vulnerable to female influence. Contrary to the Lord's commandment, he "loved many strange women"; "his wives turned away his heart after other gods: and his heart was not perfect with the Lord his God, as was the heart of David his father." Under the influence of these women, Solomon sacrificed to Ashtoreth and Milcom, Chemosh and Molech, and thereby caused the ruin of his kingdom. This is a clear case of female seduction, although again the Biblical author was more interested in the guilt of his protagonist, Solomon, than in the wickedness of the women. The story is significant because of the emphasis placed upon it by later writers, who delighted in pointing out that a man "beloved of God" was caused to sin by "outlandish women." [3]

[3] I Kings 11:1–12; Neh. 13:26. Evil foreign queens who seduced their husbands into unrighteousness and the worship of false gods were conspicuous in Jewish history; painted Jezebel is the most famous example. Queen Athaliah, a relative of Jezebel's, had a similar career, but did not make so strong an impression upon English writers. Herodias, in the New Testament, fills a similar role. Other bad women in the Bible occasionally used to point a misogynistic

Undoubtedly, the traditional picture of Solomon as a wise man seduced by women was reinforced by a conspicuous theme in Proverbs, as well as a few references in Ecclesiastes, since he is supposed to have written both books. Neither book is misogynistic as a whole; the last chapter of Proverbs asks: "Who can find a virtuous woman? for her price is far above rubies." (The question, it is true, seems to imply that such a woman is indeed rare; and the loftiest female virtue appears to consist of domestic industry.) Young men are repeatedly urged to avoid loose women, but not to avoid women altogether: "Whoso findeth a wife findeth a good thing, and obtaineth favour of the Lord."

Nevertheless, both books show a keen awareness of the dangers of association with evil women, giving them much more attention than the virtuous. Of the recurrent themes in Proverbs, by far the most conspicuous and most vividly developed is the importance of avoiding "strange women," that is harlots or any women other than one's wife, a warning which is repeated ten times. Hence the book has proved a rich mine for people who wished to attack harlots or even women in general. It was easy to pervert a striking metaphor like "a whore is a deep ditch; and a strange woman is a narrow pit" into an indictment of all women.[4]

Proverbs characteristically presents the erring woman as more guilty than the man: while he is only weak, she has deeply sinister designs upon him. A seductive adulteress brings a man to a piece of bread, that is, to destitution, and "will hunt for the precious life," while the poor credulous man "goeth after her straightway, as an ox goeth to the slaughter." "Many strong men have been slain" by such women. The author of Ecclesiastes expressed similar views on the power of seductive women, colored by his characteristic pessimism. Through diligent search he has found one righteous man among a thousand; "but a woman among all those have I not found."[5] Apart from the story of the Fall, this is the only expression of generalized misogyny in the Old Testament.

---

moral are Potiphar's wife, David's wife Michal, Lot's wife and daughters. Judith and Jael were sometimes interpreted as types of female treacherousness, although in the Bible they are presented as patriotic heroines.

[4] Prov. 18:22, 23:27, 31:10.

[5] *Ibid.*, 6:26, 7:22, 26; Eccles. 7:26, 28.

Proverbs and Ecclesiastes do seem to lay disproportionate stress on the misery caused by bad women, not only harlots but brawling wives. "An odious woman when she is married" is one of the four things which the earth cannot bear. "It is better to dwell in the wilderness, than with a contentious and an angry woman." However, the predominant attitude expressed is what would be expected in a culture which, like traditional Judaism, valued women as wives and mothers. "A virtuous woman is a crown to her husband," even though "she that maketh ashamed is as rottenness in his bones."[6] Like the Romans after them, the ancient Jews sometimes expressed harsh antifeminism; but their basically positive attitude toward women caused this to be directed only at obviously bad ones, harlots and shrews. Correctly interpreted, these attacks on bad women are not misogynistic: it *is* better to dwell in the wilderness than with a quarrelsome woman. But later preachers were to take them out of context and use them to represent the married condition in general.

2

The Old Testament warned men against feminine wiles, presented examples of evil women, and occasionally suggested that wives were more apt to be trials than helpmates. In the New Testament a new note appeared, which was to be greatly intensified by later genera-

[6] Prov. 12:4, 21:19, 30:21–23. Other passages in the Old Testament which were sometimes used by later writers against women are Isa. 3:16–4:1, an attack on Jewish women for their wantonness and luxury, and many passages in Ezekiel which vividly compare erring Jerusalem to a whore. The passages in Ezekiel (16:25–40, 23:2–49) are not in themselves misogynistic: if Jerusalem (or Israel) is to be personified as a virgin or wife, as was traditional, it is only logical to personify erring Jerusalem as a whore. But because the metaphor is often developed with much realistic detail, ascetic or misogynistic readers could easily interpret a figurative attack upon the Jews for worshiping Baalim as a literal attack upon harlots and then use it as evidence of the iniquitous propensities of woman. The Great Whore of Revelation (Chapters 17–19), a symbol of Babylon, the worldly city, has also been interpreted misogynistically, although the writer of Revelation used her as a symbol only and used females to personify good things (the holy Jerusalem, the bride of the Lamb) as well as evil. Misogynistic interpreters, however, ignore the good female symbols in favor of the Great Whore and tend to assume that a woman is an all too appropriate symbol for the worst of abominations. Spenser's Duessa, in Book I of *The Faerie Queene*, becomes an avatar of the Great Whore; but she is counterbalanced by the good female figure, Una.

tions of Christians: disparagement of sexual relations and the married state. This feeling was prevalent throughout the Greco-Roman world in the first century, appearing among the pagan Neoplatonists and Jewish Essenes as well as the Christians. While a condemnation of sex does not necessarily entail misogyny, there is an obvious connection between them: abhorrence of sex leads to abhorrence of the sexual object, while guilt feelings about desire are conveniently projected as female lust and seductiveness. (If women had written the books, the condemnation would no doubt have been associated with misandry instead.)

To Christ himself are attributed two sayings which imply a preference of celibacy over marriage. After Christ said that a man might divorce his wife only for adultery, the disciples concluded that men would be better off not to marry at all, to do without a wife altogether rather than be permanently tied to a vexatious one. They would be, Jesus replied, except that not everyone is capable of living as a celibate. He went on to commend those men "which have made themselves eunuchs for the kingdom of heaven's sake. He that is able to receive" the recommendation to celibacy, "let him receive it." Christ's only other comment on the subject occurs in his description of his second coming, which includes the verse: "woe unto them that are with child, and to them that give suck in those days." [7] The meaning seems to be that such people will suffer more in the general distress, or else are necessarily too cumbered with earthly concerns to respond properly to the occasion. But taken out of context, as many commentators were to take it, the verse seems to imply a divine condemnation of pregnant and lactating women, that is of women fulfilling their natural role.

St. Paul's depreciation of marriage was far more emphatic and definite. Indeed, condemnation of sex, along with pure misogyny, is more pronounced in St. Paul than in any other writer in the Bible. On the question of marriage he wrote:

> It is good for a man not to touch a woman.
>
> . . . .
>
> I would that all men were even as I myself. But every man hath his proper gift of God, one after this manner, and another after that.

[7] Matt. 19:9–12, 24:19; Mark 13:17; Luke 21:23. Cf. the vision in Revelation of 144,000 virgin males, "not defiled with women" (14:4).

I say therefore to the unmarried and widows, It is good for them if they abide even as I.

But if they cannot contain, let them marry: for it is better to marry than to burn.

Thus the institution of marriage is no more than a reluctant concession to human frailty, merely a preferable alternative to burning with unsatisfied lust here or burning for fornication in the fires of Hell. While marriage is not sinful (forbidding to marry he condemned as a heresy), and while people should take care not to aim at a continence they cannot attain, celibacy is unquestionably the better way: married people "have trouble in the flesh" and are overconcerned with worldly things.[8]

The connection between moral condemnation of sex and the consequent necessity to repress sexual desire, and the belief that women are particularly sinful and must therefore be kept in subjection, is very apparent in St. Paul. He was the first Biblical writer to emphasize the misogynistic implications of the Jahvist's account of the Creation and Fall. He gave unprecedented emphasis to the Fall, in part no doubt because the story gave support to his natural misogyny, in part because it was the cornerstone of his theology: without the Fall there would have been no need for redemption by Christ, and hence no need for his own mission. The more catastrophic the Fall was, the more important it became to exonerate Adam as much as possible by placing the major guilt on Eve. So St. Paul, developing his doctrine of strict subjection of women, made the most both of the Jahvistic account of woman's creation merely as an accessory to man and of her responsibility for the Fall:

Let the woman learn in silence with all subjection.

But I suffer not a woman to teach, nor to usurp authority over the man, but to be in silence.

For Adam was first formed, then Eve.

And Adam was not deceived, but the woman being deceived was in the transgression.

Women must "keep silence in the churches":

[8] I Cor. 7:1, 7–9; I Tim. 4:3; I Cor. 7:28, 32–34. This is still the doctrine of the Roman Catholic church: see R. F. Trevett, *The Church and Sex* (New York: Hawthorn Books, 1961), a volume of *The Twentieth-Century Encyclopedia of Catholicism*, pp. 41–45.

And if they will learn any thing, let them ask their husbands at home: for it is a shame for women to speak in the church.

After all, the word of God did not come out from them. He supported his position by referring to "the law" (Gen. 3:16), although the law did not command silence, only obedience. In all places women must submit to their husbands "as unto the Lord":

For the husband is the head of the wife, even as Christ is the head of the church: and he is the saviour of the body.

Therefore as the church is subject unto Christ, so let the wives be to their own husbands in every thing.

Even when St. Paul was not insisting on the subservient position of women, his phrasing could be revealing. His ideal of marriage was that everyone should "possess his vessel in sanctification and honour."[9] "Possessing one's vessel" unfortunately remained for many Bible readers an adequate formulation of the husband's relationship to his wife: she is a passive object, providing only necessary relief of his physical desires.

St. Paul interpreted women's long hair as the natural sign of their need to be covered, that is of the subjection proper to them. He further insisted that they veil their heads in church as an additional sign of subjection:

For a man indeed ought not to cover his head, forasmuch as he is the image and glory of God: but the woman is the glory of the man.

For the man is not of the woman; but the woman of the man.

Neither was the man created for the woman; but the woman for the man.

Women should also veil themselves "because of the angels," that is, the mysterious "sons of God" mentioned in Genesis 6:2–6, who fell in love with mortal women and begot on them children so wicked that they provoked God to send the Deluge.[10] Evidently St. Paul

[9] I Tim. 2:11–14; I Cor. 14:34–36; Eph. 5:22–24; I Thess. 4:4. Apocryphal works such as the Books of Adam and Eve carried to an almost ludicrous extreme the emphasis which St. Paul had laid on Eve's guilt.

[10] I Cor. 11:7–10, 15. St. Paul and later Christian commentators, including St. Augustine and Milton, gave a strongly misogynistic interpretation to the puzzling passage in Genesis about the union of the "sons of God" with the "daughters of men." The original passage is not clearly directed against women. The writer of I Peter was as insistent on female subjection as St. Paul was

interpreted this story as proof of women's dangerous seductive powers, which can cause even angels to sin.

St. Paul's doctrines wielded an enormous influence on Christian culture. He was the first to state explicitly that marriage was morally inferior to virginity. He repeatedly insisted that women must be subject to their husbands in everything and that they had no spiritual authority, and he originated the analogy that a man is to his wife as Christ is to the Church, which of course implies that any deviation of a wife's will from her husband's is sinful. He demonstrated the antifeminist implications of the Jahvistic account of creation, and above all he focused Christian attention upon the Fall and upon the fact that the serpent seduced Adam through his wife. The foundations of early Christian misogyny — its guilt about sex, its insistence on female subjection, its dread of female seduction — are all in St. Paul's epistles. They provided a convenient supply of divinely inspired misogynistic texts for any Christian writer who chose to use them; his statements on female subjection were still being quoted in the twentieth century by opponents of equality for women.

3

While the Apocrypha were less influential, lacking the divine sanction of the Bible itself, they were widely read and often cited as authorities. Ecclesiasticus, indeed, is accepted as canonical by the Roman Catholic church. Many of these books express in more extreme form sentiments present in the canonical books. Ecclesiasticus, for example, resembles Proverbs in its praise of the good wife and warnings against harlots and contentious wives. But the writer extended his specific criticism of bad women to a generalized sour misogyny of which Proverbs is free. He had the typical misogynistic suspicion of all women and intense awareness of their power to destroy men:

> Give not thyself to a woman,
> So as to let her trample down thy manhood.

. . . .

(3:1–7). Although the subjection of women was implicit in the traditional Jewish social structure, it is less conspicuously emphasized in the Old Testament than in the New; but see Esther 1:10–22 and Isa. 3:12.

> On a maiden fix not thy gaze,
>> Lest thou be entrapped in penalties with her.
>
> . . . .
>
> Hide thine eye from a lovely woman,
>> And gaze not upon beauty which is not thine;
> By the comeliness of a woman many have been ruined,
>> And this way passion flameth like fire.
> With a married woman sit not at table,
>> And [mingle not] wine in her company.

His only feeling about women was a wish to escape being hurt by them, and this could be assured only by avoiding them altogether. A man must refrain from seducing a maiden not because she would lose her virtue and good fame, but because he would be forced to pay a penalty.

This exploitative attitude — the feeling that a man's relationships with women should be determined by the practical need to minimize the inevitable penalties to himself — is frequent among misogynists. It is characteristically accompanied by the pessimistic conviction that somehow a woman always does manage to be an affliction to her male relatives, try as they may to escape unscathed. "A daughter," says the writer of Ecclesiasticus, "is to a father a treasure of sleeplessness":

> In her youth, lest she pass the flower of her age,
>> And when she is married, lest she be hated;
> In her virginity, lest she be seduced,
>> And in the house of her husband, lest she prove unfaithful;
> In her father's house, lest she become pregnant,
>> And in her husband's house, lest she be barren.
> Over thy daughter keep a strict watch,
>> Lest she make thee a name of evil odour —
> A byword in the city and accursed of the people —
>> And shame thee in the assembly of the gate.

Your only hope is to lodge her in a room without a window, keep her from showing herself to any male and from talking with wives:

> For from the garment issueth the moth,
>> And from a woman a woman's wickedness.
> Better is the wickedness of a man than the goodness of a woman.

The writer's almost paranoid suspiciousness of woman, his view of her as a singularly troublesome though necessary domestic animal, is closer to the attitude of Greeks like Hesiod than to the Jewish tradition: in general the Jews valued marriage too highly to see women merely as dangerous animals which had to be controlled.[11]

His awareness of the ruinous power which women can exercise over men, however, fits right into the Jewish tradition. A famous story in I Esdras makes the point that woman is the strongest force in the world: man labors for woman, and steals for her as well, "and when he hath stolen, spoiled, and robbed, he bringeth it to his love. . . . Yea, many there be that have run out of their wits for women, and become bondmen for their sakes. Many also have perished, have stumbled, have sinned for women."[12] The influence of the story of the Fall is apparent in the writer's assumption that women's influence is generally exerted for destructive ends; they drive man to crime and madness rather than inspiring him to achievement and virtue.

The Testaments of the Twelve Patriarchs, a Jewish apocryphal book with Christian interpolations, places the distinctively Christian condemnation of sex incongruously into the mouths of Jewish patriarchs. The work, which purports to be deathbed exhortations made by each of Jacob's sons, is shot through with misogyny: belief that sexual intercourse is defiling, conviction of women's sinister power, advice that the only way to avoid harm from women is to stay away from them. Judah describes a divine revelation in which he saw that "women bear rule over king and beggar alike; and from the king they take away his glory, and from the valiant man his strength, and from the beggar even that little which is the stay of his poverty"; Benjamin urges his hearers against impure desire; Issachar says the man of simple goodness "cannot allow within his mind a thought of female beauty, that he should not pollute his mind in corruption";

[11] *The Apocrypha and Pseudepigrapha of the Old Testament*, ed. R. H. Charles *et al.* (Oxford: Clarendon Press, 1913), I, 345–46, 470–71. See the *Jewish Encyclopedia*, under "Sirach," for the strong Greek influence on this book. Similarly, the Hellenizing Jew Philo Judaeus shows the baneful effects of Greek misogyny on Jewish thought. See his *Works*, trans. C. D. Yonge (London: Bohn, 1854), I, 45; IV, 301–7.

[12] *Apocrypha and Pseudepigrapha*, I, 29–31. Thomas Hardy's use of this quotation as the epigraph to Part First of *Jude the Obscure* is a broad hint that Jude's sufferings may be attributed to the ruinous influence of women, Arabella and Sue, on his life.

and Joseph relates at length the machinations of Potiphar's wife. Reuben, as the only one of the sons to have committed a sexual sin (he had slept with his father's concubine), is of course the most aware of women's wicked seductiveness: the sin is neatly transferred from the man, the sinner in the Biblical account, to the woman. Reuben explains the dangers of associating with women:

Hurtful are women, my children; because, since they have no power or strength over the man, they act subtilly through outward guise how they may draw him to themselves; and whom they cannot overcome by strength, him they overcome by craft . . . women are overcome by the spirit of fornication more than men, and they devise in their heart against men; and by means of their adornment they deceive first their minds, and instil the poison by the glance of their eye, and then they take them captive by their doings, for a woman cannot overcome a man by force.[13]

The misogynistic perversion of the Old Testament found in this book was to become ever stronger among Christian writers in the next few centuries. Virtually all the major patristic writers from the first century to the sixth insisted that virginity was a state greatly superior to marriage and emphasized the propriety of keeping women in subjection; most of them repeatedly expressed dread of women's seductiveness and contempt for their mental or moral frailty. They recurred to the Fall again and again, and managed to interpret many other Biblical texts as divine condemnations of the female sex.

4

By the time of Tertullian (160–230), the Christian aversion to sex had hardened into universally accepted dogma. Although in youth Tertullian had made the unfortunate mistake of getting married, he later felt deep remorse for his lapse and ultimately joined the Montanists, a sect even harsher in sexual matters than the orthodox Christians. (Some of his views are now considered heretical, but he is still recognized as an important authority.) His three treatises against remarriage, which show progressively more rigor as he moved into the Montanist camp, are primarily a repudiation of sex, but also of women. Even in the first treatise, he assumed that

---

[13] *The Testaments of the Twelve Patriarchs*, in *The Ante-Nicene Fathers*, ed. A. C. Coxe (New York: Charles Scribner's Sons, 1925), VIII, 10, 19, 22.

women were ruled by unworthy motives and did not consider the possibility of loving companionship in marriage. Dissuading his wife from remarriage if he should predecease her, he listed as her only possible motives lust and the desire to rule another man's household and spend his hard-earned money. If she longs for children she should remember that only the childless, those with "no burdensome fruit of marriage heaving in the womb, none in the bosom," will be able to serve the Lord at his second coming.[14]

In his tracts on women's dress, Tertullian's condemnation of the female sex became explicit. Although addressed to his "best beloved sisters," "On the Apparel of Women" soon abandons any pretense of gentleness. Any woman who realized her (that is, woman's) condition, he says, would "affect meanness of appearance, walking about as Eve mourning and repentant, in order that by every garb of penitence she might the more fully expiate that which she derives from Eve, — the ignominy . . . of the first sin and the odium of . . . human perdition." The judgment of God upon women, that is, labor pains and subjection to men, endures even today; and so does their guilt:

You are the devil's gateway . . . *you* are the first deserter of the divine law; *you* are she who persuaded him whom the devil was not valiant enough to attack. *You* destroyed so easily God's image, man. On account of *your* desert — that is, death — even the Son of God had to die.

A woman must not only refrain from enhancing her appearance, but also "by concealment and negligence" erase the signs of natural beauty as "equally dangerous" to anyone she meets. While physical beauty is not actually a crime, "it is to be *feared*, just on account of the injuriousness and violence of suitors." Every woman must wear a veil — a mother for her sons' sakes, a sister for her brothers', a daughter for her father's — since "All ages are perilled" in her person.[15]

While Tertullian's attitude toward women was unusually vindictive, all of its elements — a low conception of woman's motives

[14] Tertullian, *Ante-Nicene Fathers*, IV, 41, 42. Cf. p. 72. Matt. 24:19 is the basis of his reference to the second coming.

[15] Tertullian, "On the Apparel of Women" and "On the Veiling of Virgins," in *Ante-Nicene Fathers*, IV, 14, 19, 37.

and functions, disparagement of motherhood, dread of female attractiveness, heavy emphasis on woman's responsibility for the Fall — may be found in his contemporaries and successors among the Fathers. All of them followed to the letter St. Paul's dictates on the subjection of women. St. Augustine quoted with approval what his sainted mother, Monica, said to women who criticized their husbands in her presence: that they should consider their matrimonial contracts "as legal forms by which they had become slaves," and should conduct themselves accordingly.[16]

All the Church Fathers accepted as axiomatic that marriage was a state morally inferior to virginity and that sexual intercourse could be justified only by the obligation to procreate. The unique excellence of virginity was a favorite subject for moral tracts; at least one discourse on this subject appears in the works of almost every prolific writer. St. Augustine ingeniously proved that the Old Testament patriarchs had sexual intercourse solely because they were obliged to procreate; Jacob, indeed, would have preferred to abstain from begetting children, and only did so because his wives insisted.[17]

---

[16] St. Augustine, *Confessions*, trans. Vernon J. Bourke (New York: Fathers of the Church [XXI], 1953), p. 248. St. John Chrysostom, preaching on a relevant text in I Corinthians, painstakingly explained that man has four superiorities over woman: ". . . the first being, that Christ is the head of us, and we of the woman; a second, that we are the glory of God, but the woman of us; a third, that we are not of the woman, but she of us; a fourth, that we are not for her, but she for us" ("Homily 26 on I Corinthians"). Cf. "Homily 9 on I Timothy," *A Select Library of the Nicene and Post-Nicene Fathers of the Christian Church*, ed. Philip Schaff (New York: Christian Literature Co., 1889), Ser. 1, XII, 153; XIII, 436. One of the Fathers' most cogent arguments against paganism was the worship of goddesses, which they considered revolting because of the inferiority of woman's mind and the repulsiveness of her physical functions. E.g., see Athanasius, "Against the Heathen," *Nicene Fathers*, Ser. 2, IV, 9, and Arnobius, *Seven Books Against the Heathen*, in *Ante-Nicene Fathers*, VI, 466, 483.

[17] St. Augustine, *City of God*, trans. Gerald G. Walsh and Grace Monahan (New York: Fathers of the Church [XIV], 1952), pp. 557–58. At least, however, St. Augustine admitted that sexual intercourse (without passion or excitement) existed before the Fall. Gregory of Nyssa insisted that there would have been no sexual intercourse, but rather some form of angelic reproduction, without the Fall ("On the Making of Man," *Nicene Fathers*, Ser. 2, V, 406–7). Among the various Biblical texts which the Fathers twisted to support their denigration of marriage, a favorite was Matt. 13:8, from Christ's parable of

The connection between condemnation of sex and misogyny becomes obvious in an anecdote which St. Augustine related in his "Soliloquies." One day his reason convinced him "How vile, how detestable, how shameful, how dreadful" was "the embrace of a woman." That very night, he admitted, he indulged in sensual fantasies; but the following day he was again convinced that there is "nothing which brings the manly mind down from the heights more than a woman's caresses and that joining of bodies without which one cannot have a wife."[18] Although they believed theoretically that sexual relations were equally defiling for both sexes, the Fathers naturally, as men, emphasized women's corrupting influence on men rather than men's on women.

St. John Chrysostom, a mild and gentle man whose writings consist mainly of sermons addressed to a worldly flock at Antioch, did not indulge in excoriations of women. But he shared the general belief in their degrading influence: "How often do we, from beholding a woman, suffer a thousand evils; returning home, and entertaining an inordinate desire, and experiencing anguish for many days. . . . The beauty of woman is the greatest snare." A son, he advised, should be kept away from all women, except possibly some charmless old maidservant; "from a young woman shield him as from fire."[19] This is no young monk, it is important to realize, but a boy

the sower and his seed. See the interpretations by St. Jerome ("Against Jovinianus," *Nicene Fathers*, Ser. 2, VI, 347), St. Augustine (*City of God*, p. 479), etc.

[18] St. Augustine, *Soliloquies*, trans. Thomas F. Gilligan (New York: Cima Publishing Co. [Fathers of the Church, I], 1948), pp. 365, 376. For a more extreme statement of this position, see the directions to celibate men in "Two Epistles Concerning Virginity," ascribed to St. Clement of Rome, in *Ante-Nicene Fathers*, VIII, 61–65. Cf. *Stories of the Holy Fathers*, trans. Ernest A. Budge (Oxford: Oxford University Press, 1934), p. 228, and "The Sayings of the Fathers," *Western Asceticism*, ed. and trans. O. Chadwick (Philadelphia: Westminster Press, 1958), p. 54. Although Clement of Alexandria is conventionally praised for his gentle tone and relatively moderate attitude toward sex, he also solemnly warned men against looking at women. See *Christ the Educator*, trans. Simon Wood (New York: Fathers of the Church [XXIII], 1954), pp. 202–3, 205, 259, 262.

[19] St. John Chrysostom, "Homily 15 Concerning the Statues," *Nicene Fathers*, Ser. 1, IX, 441–42, "Address on Vainglory and the Right Way for Parents to Bring Up Their Children," in M. Laistner, *Christianity and Pagan Culture in the Later Roman Empire* (Ithaca, N.Y.: Cornell University Press, 1951), pp. 109–12.

who is to marry and lead an ordinarily virtuous life in this world; and the whole treatise, far from displaying rancor, is a gentle exhortation.

When St. John was concerned with monks' relationships with women he used far stronger language. Although he had adapted himself to the world, he was ascetic by nature and believed virginity to be the only really good life. So when a young man abandoned his monastic vocation and became engaged to be married, St. John was moved to write "An Exhortation to Theodore After His Fall." Theodore should think carefully about the probable consequences of association with women, about David's adultery and Solomon's apostasy. And he should consider the true nature of that female beauty for which he is about to cast off his virtue:

. . . if you consider what is stored up inside those beautiful eyes, and that straight nose, and the mouth and the cheeks, you will affirm the well-shaped body to be nothing else than a whited sepulchre; the parts within are full of so much uncleanness. Moreover when you see a rag with any of these things on it, such as phlegm, or spittle you cannot bear to touch it with even the tips of your fingers, nay you cannot even endure looking at it; and yet are you in a flutter of excitement about the storehouses and depositories of these things?

So why not "release yourself from your accursed bondage, and return to your former freedom?"[20]

In some ways St. Jerome was more favorably disposed toward women than any other Father of the Church. He enjoyed teaching women and found his closest friends, such as Paula and her daughter Eustochium, among them. He stoutly defended his friendships with women on the ground that there was no cause for shame in associating with that sex from which the Virgin Mary had come. Yet, as a fanatical advocate of virginity, he attacked married life in withering terms and warned men against women's seductive powers. He himself, even while starving as an ascetic in the desert, was often tormented by visions of dancing girls. He warned a clergyman against allowing a woman to enter his house or sitting alone

[20] St. John Chrysostom, "An Exhortation to Theodore After His Fall," *Nicene Fathers*, Ser. 1, IX, 104, 112. Gregory of Nyssa expressed similar views in "On Virginity," *Nicene Fathers*, Ser. 2, V, 346. Cf. St. John's alarming pictures of the probable miseries of husbands in "Homily 52 on Matthew" and "Homily 15 on Ephesians," *Nicene Fathers*, Ser. 1, X, 383, XIII, 124.

with one in a quiet place: "You cannot be a man more saintly than David, or more wise than Solomon. Remember always that a woman drove the tiller of Paradise from the garden that had been given him." [21] St. Jerome reveals a curious split between real admiration for virgins and widows who abstained from remarriage — women seen as spiritual companions — and distaste for them as sexual objects.

When a man named Helvidius dared to take literally the Biblical reference to Jesus' brothers, concluding that Mary must have had relations with Joseph after the virgin birth, St. Jerome was moved to fury by the obscene blasphemy: ". . . you have defiled the sanctuary of the Holy Spirit from which you are determined to make a team of four brethren and a heap of sisters come forth." How inexpressibly disgusting to think of Mary behaving like an ordinary wife, being agreeable to her husband and having about her "children watching for her word and waiting for her kiss"! St. Jerome saw nothing in the least attractive in motherhood: pregnant women he considered "a revolting sight," and he could not imagine why anyone would want progeny, "a brat . . . to crawl upon his breast and soil his neck with nastiness." [22]

Thus, while St. Jerome esteemed certain women, he exalted them at the expense of their sex. His violent depreciation of women's most important and most prized biological function is at least an indirect expression of strong hostility. It took furious indignation against Jovinian, who had dared to maintain that marriage was as virtuous a state as virginity, to bring St. Jerome's latent misogyny into the open. After overwhelming Jovinian with Biblical arguments proving that marriage is a defilement resulting from the Fall, St. Jerome appealed to the authority of Solomon, as one thoroughly experienced in conjugal affairs. And he then proceeded to misinterpret texts from Proverbs so as to show through the experiences of a man "who suffered through them, what a wife or woman is." He justified his citing of three texts about whores and one about a termagant as general characterizations of wives by this argument:

[21] St. Jerome, Letters 22, 52, *Select Letters*, trans. F. A. Wright (London: Heinemann, 1933), pp. 67, 203.
[22] St. Jerome, "Against Helvidius," *Nicene Fathers*, Ser. 2, VI, 343–45; St. Jerome, Letters 54, 107, *Letters*, pp. 233, 363. Cf. *Letters*, p. 93.

"What necessity rests upon me to run the risk of the wife I marry proving good or bad? . . . How seldom we find a wife without these faults [contentiousness and passion], he knows who is married." Where Proverbs mentions the insatiability of the barren womb, obviously referring to a barren woman's longing for children, St. Jerome read that woman's sexual desire is never satisfied. Where Proverbs lists an odious wife among the four things which the earth cannot bear, St. Jerome interpreted that "a wife is classed with the greatest evils." Then, after quoting at length from Theophrastus' lost book on the disadvantages of marriage, a book "worth its weight in gold," he triumphantly drew up a long list of bad wives, including Terentia who married three times, railing Xanthippe who emptied dirty water on Socrates' head, Metella who was openly unchaste, drunken Actoria Paula who defied her husband Cato, Olympias who shut Philip of Macedon out of his own bedroom.[23]

Because they were following in the tradition of St. Paul and were all overconcerned with woman as a potential seducer, even the gentlest of the Fathers could not resist an occasional reference to Eve's responsibility for the Fall, which passed as a hereditary taint to all her daughters. St. Augustine's account of the Fall in the *City of God* was typical in exonerating Adam as much as possible. Just like Solomon, who was not "deceived into believing in the worship of idols, but was merely won over to this sacrilege by feminine flattery," "Adam transgressed the law of God, not because he was deceived into believing that the lie was true, but because in obedience to a social compulsion he yielded to Eve, as husband to wife, as the only man in the world to the only woman." It was because of Eve's guilt that Christ was born of a woman, an otherwise inexplicable fact. If he had not been:

. . . women might have despaired of themselves, as mindful of their first sin, because by a woman was the first man deceived, and would have thought that they had no hope at all in Christ. . . . The poison to deceive man was presented him by woman, through woman let salvation for man's recovery be presented; so let the woman make amends for the sin by which she deceived the man, by giving birth to Christ.

[23] St. Jerome, "Against Jovinianus," *Nicene Fathers*, Ser. 2, VI, 367, 383-85.

It went without saying that Christ had to be male, but woman was allowed to make some small contribution to the redemption of humanity. Besides, Christ, being divine, could not be defiled by contact with the female sex.[24]

While the Fathers were by no means all Tertullians, most of them not only enthusiastically followed St. Paul's teaching on man's Fall and the consequent subjection of women, but accentuated and elaborated the Biblical material on their own. Every one of the major Christian writers from the first century through the sixth assumed the mental and moral frailty of women, dwelt upon the vexations of marriage, and reviled the body and sexual desire. This attitude was to pervade the medieval Church and persists into religious writings even today.

It is unfortunate that the exponents of Christian thought during these early centuries were clerical celibates, men whose attitude toward women would almost necessarily be distorted. Even those who could bring themselves to associate with women insisted that they desexualize themselves, branding any distinctively feminine characteristics as degrading and polluting. Under the guidance of the Fathers, Christian literature became misogynistic to a degree unequaled in the Western world before or since. It had reached the point where Christ's association with women had to be explained away on the ground that otherwise the sin-laden female sex could not even hope for redemption.

Although the Fathers may have derived from Jewish tradition their fear of woman's seductive influence and their belief that she is frailer than man and should be kept subject to him, the major cause of their misogyny was undoubtedly their condemnation of

[24] St. Augustine, *City of God*, p. 378; *Sermons on New Testament Lessons*, in *Nicene Fathers*, Ser. 1, VI, 246. St. Cyril of Alexandria even found ammunition against women in a part of the Bible which seems to be, if anything, favorable to the sex. See his interpretation of John, Chapter 20, in *Commentary on the Gospel According to St. John* (Oxford: Library of the Fathers, 1874), II, 654, 656, 662. In extenuation of the Fathers' diatribes, it must be borne in mind that some of them, such as St. John Chrysostom's denunciations of the luxury-loving matrons of Antioch, were undoubtedly justified. Moreover, many of the Fathers had both friendship and esteem for particular women who met their exacting moral standards. St. Augustine idolized his mother, and St. Jerome greatly valued his women friends.

sexual desire. From the myth of the Fall, from the stories of Samson, David, and Solomon, from a number of apparently neutral Biblical texts, they derived the conviction that woman's attractiveness is the greatest possible peril to man's soul.[25] In an effort to nullify her pernicious influence, they repeatedly insisted that the female body is not really an attractive object, but a vessel of filth, and that the production of children is not a joyful and rewarding experience, but a degradation.

And at the same time that they denigrated woman's sexual functions, they tended to reduce her to an exclusively sexual being, existing solely to fulfill these functions. The Fathers generally assumed that a man cannot look at a woman except lustfully, and they saw every woman, no matter who she was or how behaving, as a seductress. This overpreoccupation with sex was of course an indirect effect of their attempt to repress their own physical natures, and their extreme sexual guilt caused them to project their forbidden sexual desires onto women. This projection in turn reinforced their belief that women were particularly sexual, and hence particularly sinful, and intensified their constant warnings against the dangers of associating with them. If femininity is equated with sexuality and sexuality with sin, woman is naturally seen as a degraded being whose only hope for salvation is through suppressing herself as much as her frailty permits.

5. *Patriarchy in Greece and Rome*

About three centuries before the Jahvist recorded his story of Eve and the apple, Hesiod, a sour Greek farmer, wrote down a remarkably similar one. It tells how Pandora, the first woman, brought innumerable evils upon men through her disobedient curiosity. After Prometheus has stolen and given to men the fire which Zeus intended to withhold from them, Zeus plots in revenge: "I will give men as the price for fire an evil thing in which they may all be glad of heart while they embrace their own destruction." So he gets each of the gods to contribute some charm or skill or piece of finery to

---

[25] The idea that sexual experience degrades man may be latent in the story of the Fall itself, where the first explicit statement that Adam knew his wife (Gen. 4:1) comes after they have eaten the forbidden fruit. However, I believe this is a misogynistic perversion of the text.

make the first woman completely irresistible — including, from Hermes, "a shameless mind and a deceitful nature." Finally, "the sheer, hopeless snare" is finished, and Hermes takes her, along with a large jar supposedly containing bridal gifts from all the gods but never to be opened, as a present to Epimetheus, who makes the mistake of accepting her. Shortly after her arrival Pandora opens the jar, so that the evils inside come swarming out; and since that moment men have been afflicted with heavy labor and diseases and premature old age.[26]

The original tale ran very differently. Pandora, whose name means "all-giving," had given real gifts instead of evils; for she was the matriarchal Great Goddess. This was the all-powerful mother-deity who, under various names, ruled over gods and men alike before the advent of patriarchy. At that time she naturally had to yield precedence to a male-dominated pantheon, and myths were perverted accordingly.[27] Hesiod may have invented this version; in any event he liked it so much that he retold it in his *Theogony*, underlining its point yet more darkly: from Pandora "is the deadly race and tribe of women who live amongst mortal men to their great trouble, no helpmeets in hateful poverty, but only in wealth." And, as if this were not enough, women make miserable even men who have nothing to do with them: ". . . whoever avoids marriage and the sorrows that women cause, and will not wed, reaches deadly old age without anyone to tend his years, and though he at least has no lack of livelihood while he lives, yet, when he is dead, his kinsfolk divide his possessions amongst them."[28]

[26] Hesiod, *The Homeric Hymns and Homerica*, trans. Hugh Evelyn-White (London: Heinemann, 1943), pp. 7, 9.

[27] Robert Graves, *The Greek Myths* (Harmondsworth, Middlesex: Penguin Books, 1955), I, 148. Graves, the leading contemporary proponent of this view, has developed it also in *The White Goddess*. While I am not convinced of its historical soundness — the evidence is scanty and often ambiguous — there seems to be no question that it is psychologically valid. No matter how patriarchal a society may be, the infant first perceives it as a matriarchy, because for him his mother is the all-important, all-powerful figure. As he is socialized he comes to accept the standards of his society — in a patriarchy, the superior power and capacity of men. It is certainly plausible to reason by analogy that the development of human society, like that of the individual, went from matriarchy to patriarchy.

[28] Hesiod, *Homeric Hymns*, p. 123.

Hesiod's picture of the disadvantages of celibacy reveals an unpleasantly low conception of the function of woman: to nurse a man in senility and to bear children so that he need not leave money to distant relatives. Besides being a product of misogyny, such a conception would tend to increase it, obscuring whatever higher qualities women might have, and scarcely calculated to elicit amiable or generous behavior from them. Hesiod, a true peasant, thought of a wife primarily as an expense — at best a constant drain on her husband's income, at worst a financial calamity: "Do not let a flaunting woman coax and cozen and deceive you: she is after your barn. The man who trusts womankind trusts deceivers." When you start out in life get yourself a house and an ox and a woman, but be sure it is a slave woman so she will plough with the oxen as well as providing for you sexually. And see that she has no children to distract her from ministering to you. At thirty you may marry, but choose your wife carefully, so that "your marriage will not be a joke to your neighbours." [29] Although Hesiod ungraciously accepts marriage as a necessity, he accepts it on the baldest utilitarian grounds, regarding a wife as hardly more than an expensive though essential piece of livestock.

This jaundiced attitude toward married life prevailed through most of ancient Greek literature. Greek opinion on the subject is conveniently summarized in "On Marriage," a treatise ascribed to Theophrastus, a student of Aristotle's. This work, with its memorable antithetical style, became a handy text for succeeding generations of misogynists — including St. Jerome in the fourth century, John of Salisbury in the twelfth, Chaucer in the fourteenth, George Gascoigne in the sixteenth, and Joseph Swetnam in the seventeenth. Besides distracting a man from his study of philosophy, a wife will squander his money and spoil his sleep with curtain lectures. Unlike any other piece of livestock, she may not be thoroughly examined before she is acquired, "for fear she may not give satisfaction." A woman is vain and jealous and insistent on her perquisites: you must call her my lady, keep her birthday, and respect all her hangers-on, including those who minister to her lust. You cannot possibly live happily with a wife:

[29] *Ibid.*, pp. 31, 33, 47, 53, 55.

If you give her the management of the whole house, you must yourself be her slave. If you reserve something for yourself, she will not think you are loyal to her; but she will turn to strife and hatred, and unless you quickly take care, she will have the poison ready. If you introduce old women, and soothsayers, and prophets, and vendors of jewels and silken clothing, you imperil her chastity; if you shut the door upon them, she is injured and fancies you suspect her,

as in fact you do. A wife is equally troublesome whether rich or poor, beautiful or ugly: "To support a poor wife is hard: to put up with a rich one, is torture." A beautiful woman attracts lovers, while an ugly one is all the more easily seduced. "It is difficult to guard what many long for. It is annoying to have what no one thinks worth possessing." A man may marry "to get a manager for the house, to solace weariness, to banish solitude"; but he would do better to buy a faithful slave, who would be more industrious, submissive, and obedient. Even if a man's wife is good and agreeable — a rare bird, indeed — he has to "share her groans in childbirth, and suffer torments when she is in danger." (Children, also, give more trouble than they are worth.)[30]

This negative attitude toward marriage would naturally be expected in a strongly patriarchal culture which, emphasizing the limitations of woman's mind and character, minimized her potentiality for contributing to man's solace, mental stimulation, and emotional support. Since at most she was a breeder of children and a housekeeper, the only virtues possible to her were the humble ones of industry, thrift, and quietness. The Greeks emphasized the expensiveness of a wife in part because they saw her essentially as a servant: a servant represents a drain on rather than a sharer in the master's income.

Since the virtues expected of her were largely negative, the wife who displayed any positive qualities at all was apt to be considered

[30] Quoted at length by St. Jerome, "Against Jovinianus," *Nicene Library* (New York: Christian Literature Co., 1893), Ser. 2, VI, 383–84. The equation of women with livestock was almost explicit in Semonides of Amorgos' neat catalogue of the ten types of wife, nine of whom are household afflictions. See Fragment 7, *Elegy and Iambus*, ed. and trans. J. M. Edmonds (London: Heinemann, 1931), II, 217–25. See also many epigrams in *The Greek Anthology*, trans. W. R. Paton (London: Heinemann, 1916), especially those by Palladas of Alexandria: e.g., III, 87, IV, 31, 205, 253.

troublesome. Furthermore, the narrow restrictions on the wife's role must necessarily have frustrated women of intelligence and spirit to the point of rebellion, so that many doubtless reacted against patriarchal suppression by being disagreeable or insubordinate.

The woman who stands out as the typical Greek wife — Socrates' Xanthippe — shows the rebelliousness and perversity which naturally resulted from Greek opinions on marriage and women. Perhaps the most egregious shrew in history, she constantly tried even the exceptional fortitude of her saintly husband. Indeed, according to Diogenes Laertius, that is why Socrates continued to live with her: in the society of Xanthippe he could learn to adapt himself to the rest of the world. Moved by his experiences with his wife, Socrates is supposed to have answered a young man who asked whether he should marry:

On the one hand loneliness, childlessness, the dying out of your stock, and an outsider as your heir will be your destiny; on the other eternal worry, one quarrel after another, her dower cast in your face, the haughty disdain of her family, the garrulous tongue of your mother-in-law, the lurking paramour, and worry as to how the children will turn out.[31]

Jibes against marriage and shrewish wives became humorous staples in Greek Middle and New Comedy, which bristle with speeches like this Theophrastian catalogue:

Who thinks of marrying, thinks wrong, you know,
Because his thinking ends in doing so.
A tale of woe begins with married life.
If a man's poor, what's given him with his wife
Makes her not mate but master; if he's not
And dowry isn't included in the lot,
The same thing — two to feed instead of one;
If she's *bad*-looking, life for him is done,
There's no more going out at night; if *good*,
He shares her favours with the neighbourhood.

---

[31] Diogenes Laertius, *Lives of Eminent Philosophers*, trans. R. D. Hicks (London: Heinemann, 1959), I, 167; Valerius Maximus, *Factorum et Dictorum Memorabilium Libri*, ed. Karl F. Kempf, trans. Pike (Leipzig: Teubner, 1888), p. 327. Diogenes Laertius told another tale which was constantly repeated and elaborated: "When Xanthippe first scolded him and then drenched him with water, his rejoinder was 'Did I not say that Xanthippe's thunder would end in rain?'"

The moral is, that he who thinks to wed,
Aims at the fair but hits the foul instead.[32]

While this comedy survives only in the form of fragments taken out
of context, its constantly recurring attacks on marriage suggest that
these expressed a prevalent attitude. In any case, it was the fragments, not the whole plays, which endured to influence later
literature.

Roman comedy presents marriage in the same way, principally
it seems because the Roman dramatists closely followed the conventions of Greek New Comedy. Although Plautus' satire is good-
humored and obviously reflects antifeminine folklore rather than
personal misogyny, the fact remains that none of his male characters are shown to be happy with their wives and most are definitely
unhappy; they flee the shrews who dominate their homes and find
pleasure only with courtesans. The situation in *The Twin Menaechmi* is typical: Menaechmus I, the local man, is forever trying
to escape from his shrewish wife. When he first appears, he has just
managed to scold her away from the front door so he can get away
with one of her dresses to give his mistress: ". . . a fine way to
cheat this clever guardian of mine. . . . I got the spoils from the
enemy and didn't lose a man." After vigorously upbraiding her husband, the wife sends for her father to defend her rights, only to be
rebuked for trying to make a slave of her husband. To object to his
keeping a mistress, her father tells her, is just as outrageous as to
insist that he "sit with the maids and card wool." As long as he keeps
her properly clothed, fed, and served, she has nothing to complain
about, though if he really does steal her dresses he must change his
ways.[33] Menaechmus is not criticized by anyone but his wife: the
other characters assume without question that he can behave as he
likes and should not be afflicted by her protests, and their sympathy
and that of the audience is plainly directed toward him. In the end
his property is to be auctioned off, including, if anyone should want
her, his wife.

While this attitude obviously appealed to the Roman audience —

[32] Anaxandrides, *The Fragments of Attic Comedy*, ed. and trans. J. M. Edmonds (Leiden: E. J. Brill, 1959), II, 75.
[33] Plautus, *The Twin Menaechmi*, in *The Complete Roman Drama*, ed.
George E. Duckworth (New York: Random House, 1942), I, 443, 471.

otherwise Plautus would not have been popular — it expressed superficial jocularity rather than deep resentment. The Roman matron was not generally treated like Menaechmus' wife: she enjoyed much higher status than her Greek counterpart, and thus was able to make a greater contribution to her husband's happiness and was more apt to be loved and respected by him. Apart from a few flippant epigrams and scattered roars of outraged patriarchy, there are no attacks on respectable women in Roman literature.

Of course, many Greeks had a more benign attitude toward women than these attacks on marriage would suggest, considering the wife a helpmate rather than a necessary evil. But almost all of them believed that she should be narrowly restricted. Plutarch, writing at the end of the classical period, thought that girls should be married very young so that "their bodies alike and minds would be delivered to the future husband pure and undefiled." Although he rose above the narrowly utilitarian views of Hesiod, he assigned woman a limited sphere which would necessarily stunt her personality. In "Advice to Bride and Groom," he said, "The wife ought to have no feeling of her own," but should follow her husband's changing moods. Nor should she have preferences, friends, property, or even a religion of her own, but follow her husband in everything. His attitude on the subjection of women is strikingly like St. Paul's, although free of the hostility produced by Paul's sexual distrust: "A woman ought to do her talking either to her husband or through her husband," and the man should control her "as the soul controls the body." This subjection is proper because women cannot be trusted to achieve virtue and reason by themselves: on their own, unguided by their husbands, they "conceive many untoward ideas and low designs and emotions."[34] This assumption of woman's

---

[34] Plutarch, *The Lives of the Noble Grecians and Romans*, trans. John Dryden and A. H. Clough (New York: Random House, n.d.), p. 96; Plutarch, *Moralia*, trans. Frank Babbitt (London: Heinemann, 1928), II, 309–11, 323, 339, 341. Cf. Xenophon's opinions on marriage, found in *Memorabilia and Oeconomicus* (London: Heinemann, 1953), pp. 107, 387, 415, 451; the often quoted statement attributed to Pericles by Thucydides that "The greatest glory of a woman is to be least talked about by men" (*History of the Peloponnesian War*, trans. Rex Warner [Harmondsworth, Middlesex: Penguin Books, 1954], p. 122), and an equally famous quotation from Demosthenes: "Mistresses we keep for . . . pleasure, concubines for the daily care of our persons, but wives

frailty, common in Jewish as well as Greek writers, is an invaluable rationalization for a patriarchal system. Through the whole classical period the Greeks insisted on woman's destructive and immoral potentialities, using these to justify the subjection in which they kept her.

6

Just as Pandora was degraded from the giver of all gifts to the bringer of all evils, Here, originally another avatar of the Great Goddess, declined to the mere consort of the major deity and finally degenerated into a shrewish nuisance, forever trying to exert a power which she did not have and to hold a husband bent on the pursuit of more attractive females. Although she was the goddess of marriage, she aroused dislike rather than affection in her husband; and even as a mother she was unfeeling and destructive. She threw her own child, Hephaestus, out of heaven because his lameness made her ashamed; and her other offspring range from Ares, the odious god of war, down to the monster Typhaon, "a plague to men."[35] Homer, while otherwise free of misogyny, made a point of showing Here as unloved and troublesome. In Homer's representation, the Father of Men and Gods complained about Here's habitual prying, scolding, and defiance of his will, and ultimately he wished her into the bottomless pit — in short, he regarded his marriage as a galling yoke, just like the ordinary Greek.

In Virgil this animus against Here (Juno) is more clearly marked, although never — because of Virgil's piety — quite made explicit. On the very first page of the *Aeneid*, he ascribes the afflictions of the noble hero and his long-suffering band of Trojans to ruthless, vindictive Juno and comments: "It is hard to believe Gods in Heaven capable of such rancour." Virgil shows Juno tirelessly persecuting righteous Aeneas, in defiance of her husband, who has

---

to bear us legitimate children and to be faithful guardians of our households" ("Against Neaera," *Private Orations*, trans. A. T. Murray [London: Heinemann, 1939], III, 445, 447).

[35] Hesiod, *Homeric Hymns*, pp. 103, 347, 349. Here's relentless persecution of Hercules is particularly significant because, as he was usually represented as a great benefactor of humanity, it is evidence of her hostility to all mankind. Thomas Heywood — in *The Generall History of Women* (London: W. H., 1657), p. 9 — made a particular point of the deformities of Juno's offspring.

granted the Trojans success and endless dominion. Her only regret is that other gods' malice is usually more effective than her own. Finally Jupiter tells his wife that she must suppress her vindictiveness, since she has already driven "the Trojans in torment over lands or over waves," kindled a horrible war, and brought "ugly shame on a home." [36] So at last she yields, ineffectual as usual. Juno, unquestionably the villainess of the *Aeneid*, is depicted with a hostility not shown toward any other divine or even human character. Apart from its darker emphasis (to some extent the result of Juno's being on the "wrong" side here, on the "right" in the *Iliad*), Virgil's hostile portrait is more significant than Homer's because Homer's gods all act discreditably at times, while Virgil's tone is uniformly serious, and because Virgil's all-righteous Jupiter, whom Juno constantly defies, is far more loftily conceived than Homer's Zeus.

The decline of matriarchy in Greek religion and ethics, with its consequent disparagement of women, is brought out clearly in the plays of Aeschylus. At the close of *The Eumenides* he actually represented Patriarchy Triumphant on the stage. Orestes, pursued by the Furies because of his matricide, defends himself on the ground that his victim's murder of her husband was an equally bad or worse crime than his. When the leader of the Furies points out that a woman is not blood kin to her husband, Orestes contends that a child is not blood kin to his mother either. He calls on Apollo to defend his point of view, which naturally outrages the Furies, the representatives of the old order. Apollo, who claims to be voicing the opinions of Zeus, makes his case. The mother:

> . . . doth but nurse the seed
> New-sown: the male is parent; she for him,
> As stranger for a stranger, hoards the germ
> Of life.

As proof he cites the birth of Athene, who is acting as judge:

> Never within the darkness of the womb
> Fostered nor fashioned, but a bud more bright
> Than any goddess in her breast might bear.

Finally Athene decides in favor of Orestes:

[36] Virgil, *The Aeneid*, trans. W. F. Jackson Knight (Harmondsworth, Middlesex: Penguin Books, 1956), pp. 27, 184, 334.

For me no mother bore within her womb,
And, save for wedlock evermore eschewed,
I vouch myself the champion of the man,
Not of the woman, yea, with all my soul, —
In heart, as birth, a father's child alone.[37]

Of course, one cannot be sure how closely this scene expresses Aeschylus' own views. The Greeks must have believed that a child's mother had some importance, since they were very concerned that their children be the offspring of Athenian women; and Apollo's speech for the defense is obvious special pleading, complete with a shameless personal appeal to the judge. Yet Aeschylus would hardly have ended his major trilogy on a quibble, so it seems that this climactic scene should be taken as representing a serious and fundamental shift in loyalty. The idea that a child's mother functions only as incubator was a completely respectable one in Greek times, as is shown by Aristotle's scientific works a century later.

It is difficult to understand why Aeschylus' successor Euripides acquired his reputation for misogyny — a reputation which was hilariously dramatized by his contemporary Aristophanes and is accepted by so perceptive a modern critic as H. D. F. Kitto. Actually, Euripides' empathy with women was remarkable: his awareness of the wretched helplessness of women in Greek society, his picture of the agonizing jealousy of a barren woman, his recognition that the supposedly weaker sex manages to endure repeated childbirth are just a few examples. His attitude toward women, like most of his attitudes, was both unconventional and progressive.

This is clearly shown in Euripides' treatments of the legends of Medea and Phaedra, two of the stock villainesses in Greek tradi-

---

[37] Aeschylus, *The Eumenides*, in *The Complete Greek Drama*, ed. Whitney J. Oates and Eugene O'Neill, Jr. (New York: Random House, 1938), I, 294, 297. Aeschylus' first extant play, *The Suppliants*, which deals with the descendants of Io, shows a marked bias in favor of Zeus at Here's expense, as he shifted the blame for Io's undeserved sufferings from Zeus to Here. Athene's speech in *The Eumenides* reveals incidentally how she, once the Great Goddess in another guise, was fitted into a patriarchal pantheon. First, she was born parthenogenetically from a god instead of from a goddess (Metis) as in the original myth. Then, like Artemis, yet another personification of the Great Goddess, she developed from an unmarried matriarch into a man-like virgin, becoming identified with men more than women. Both remained independent of men, but forfeited sexual life and children as the price of their independence.

tion. Without sentimentalizing either of these ladies, he presents them with understanding and shows that their adversaries were not innocuous victims. Medea's entering speech wins her the sympathy of the audience, as she laments the helplessness of a woman absolutely subjected to her husband's whims and confined to what may be a miserable home. The Chorus, which is thoroughly sympathetic to Medea, points out that if women had the gift of song they could tell as long a tale of men's treachery as men do of women's.[38] Jason, who takes a consistently superior attitude toward women, appears as an unprincipled, self-indulgent coxcomb. Thus Euripides pointedly discredits the conventional Greek view of women by associating it with Jason, a selfish weakling and a fool. Medea is ruthless and dangerous, but she comes off far better than her complacent husband.

In *Hippolytus* Euripides does not so clearly direct sympathy toward the heroine, although he does make her more than an uncontrolled creature driven mad by desire. His Hippolytus, however, is not a lamb-like innocent but a harsh ascetic, who dies not through mere misfortune but through his arrogant attempt to repress a part of his own nature: the fanatical devotee of virginity (Artemis) is destroyed when he rejects love (Aphrodite). Hippolytus is a misogynist for the same reason that the early Christians were. Of course, taken out of context, his speech on women when he first hears of his stepmother's passion for him, is blistering:

Great Zeus, why didst thou, to man's sorrow, put woman, evil counterfeit, to dwell where shines the sun? If thou wert minded that the human race should multiply, it was not from women they should have drawn their stock, but in thy temples they should have paid gold or iron or ponderous bronze and bought a family . . . and so in independence dwelt, from women free. But now as soon as ever we would bring this plague into our home we bring its fortune to the ground . . . the husband, who takes the noxious weed into his home, fondly decks his sorry idol in fine raiment and tricks her out in robes, squandering by degrees, unhappy wight! his house's wealth. [The economic argument, again.] . . . it is easiest for him who has settled in his house as wife a mere cipher, incapable from simplicity. I hate a clever woman; never may she set foot in *my* house who aims at knowing more than women need; for in these clever women Cypris implants a larger store

38 Euripides, *Medea*, in *Complete Greek Drama*, I, 728, 732.

of villainy, while the artless woman is by her shallow wit from levity debarred.[39]

Clearly this is meant to be an extreme, distorted statement, and not to be identified with Euripides' own views. In fact, he is masterfully portraying a misogynist in full malignancy, including his suspicious hatred of all women, his particular distrust of intelligent ones, and his conviction that they are simply parasites on men. Euripides is exposing a type which a conventional Greek would have been apt to admire.

The significance of Euripides' treatment of these legends is brought out by contrasting it with the conventional interpretations, as dramatized by Seneca five centuries later. In his plays on Medea and Phaedra, Seneca seems to be mainly interested in displaying the heroines' wickedness. He says nothing about injustice toward women in his *Medea*, suggests nothing wrong with Hippolytus' excessive purity in his *Phaedra*. Seneca's Medea is accurately characterized by Creon as a "cursèd pestilence": her past crimes are frequently mentioned and her witchcraft emphasized in a long, gruesome incantation scene; she wishes she had, like Niobe, seven sons to kill instead of only two; and no sympathy for her is expressed anywhere in the play. Jason, on the other hand, is a reasonable and altruistic man.

If Jason is whitewashed, Hippolytus becomes a stoic saint, even though he is capable of an utterly unreasonable tirade against woman:

> . . . She with her wicked arts
> Besets the minds of men; and all for her
> And her vile, lustful ways, unnumbered towns
> Lie low in smoking heaps; whole nations rush
> To arms; and kingdoms, utterly o'erthrown,
> Drag down their ruined peoples in their fall.[40]

Seneca never suggests that Hippolytus' views are not entirely correct, since he is practically uncriticized in the play.

[39] Euripides, *Hippolytus*, in *Complete Greek Drama*, I, 780. Jason also wished that men could reproduce without women; see I, 735.

[40] Seneca, *Phaedra*, in *Complete Roman Drama*, II, 642. Cf. his *Hercules on Oeta*.

Euripides' reputation for misogyny rests not only on his choice of subject — passionate heroines who create havoc in their surroundings — but also on statements of women's power for evil which are scattered through his plays. While some of these sentiments are discredited by the base or prejudiced characters who utter them, others do seem to be presented as correct. For example, Medea declares that "We women, though by nature little apt for virtuous deeds, are most expert to fashion any mischief." Virtuous Andromache, provoked by Hermione's abusive threats, exclaims, "How strange it is, that though some god hath devised cures for mortals against the venom of reptiles, no man ever yet hath discovered aught to cure a woman's venom, which is far worse than viper's sting or scorching flame; so terrible a curse are we to mankind." And Hermione herself, when she has seen the error of her ways, complains that she was seduced by other women: "Oh! never, never . . . should men of sense, who have wives, allow womenfolk to visit them in their homes, for they teach them evil." [41] I believe, however, that Euripides included these remarks not to express hostility to women, but to protect himself against a charge of sentimentalizing them, to which his sympathy even with villainesses could easily expose him. Insisting that women were not brainless weaklings, he naturally admitted their power for evil as well as for good. He believed that many women were evil and few were wise, but his opinion of the human race in general was low; men emerge just as unfavorably from his plays.

Actually, then, Euripides systematically attacked the misogynistic platitudes of his time: by portraying women as intelligent and forceful, with rights and wishes of their own, he undermined the complacent assumption that it was proper to subject them utterly to men, to treat them like small children; by representing Hesiod-type misogynists as base or distorted people, he worked to discredit these views. Why, then, did he himself acquire a reputation for misogyny? First, a society which expected women to be passive and inconspicuous found Euripides' strong-willed heroines libels on

[41] Euripides, *Complete Greek Drama*, I, 732, 854, 870. Some critics consider *The Bacchae* a misogynistic play, but I see it as a presentation of the disastrous results of trying to repress one's own irrational nature, rather than of the destructiveness of women.

their sex. Secondly, in order to preserve their prejudices intact, they took his misogynistic comments out of context and ignored his feminist points, thereby willfully misinterpreting him. This type of reaction to his ideas indicates misogyny in the reader rather than the writer.[42]

Aristotle's opinions on women, on the other hand, never required distortion to harmonize with conventional thought: he was an eminently solid upholder of the status quo. His *Politics*, in part an answer to Plato's relatively feminist *Republic*, defends the treatment of women in contemporary Greek society essentially through the cherished conservative doctrine that "Whatever is, is right." Because women occupy an inferior position they must be naturally inferior, and because they are naturally inferior they should occupy an inferior position. The idea of a natural hierarchy which sanctifies the social hierarchy pervades Aristotle's political thought: "It is natural and expedient" for the soul to govern the body, the intellect the emotions, man the lower animals, and the male the female, since "the male is by nature superior and the female inferior."

Aristotle must deal with the question of whether his natural subjects — slaves, children, and women — possess reason and moral virtue, for if they do it is hard to justify their natural subjection. He concludes that they do, but only "in such measure as is proper to each in relation to his own function . . . the temperance of a woman and that of a man are not the same, nor their courage and justice, as Socrates thought, but the one is the courage of command, and the other that of subordination."[43] Characters in drama should

---

[42] Aristophanes' *Thesmophoriazusae* is a willful misreading of Euripides, resulting from Aristophanes' dislike for Euripides' radical ideas on women and other subjects. The action of the play, the women's trial of Euripides for libel, naturally affords ample opportunity to rake up all the stock misogynistic charges, although the satire is too exuberantly good-humored to be taken as a serious attack on womankind. Aristophanes enjoyed satirizing the traditional Greek female failings of lust and bibulousness; see *The Thesmophoriazusae*, *Lysistrata*, and *The Ecclesiazusae*. The latter play is a burlesque of the radical feminist views propounded in Plato's *Republic*: that there should be community of wives and political equality for women. In both *The Republic* and *The Laws*, Plato showed, for an ancient Greek, an exceptionally high opinion of women.

[43] Aristotle, *The Politics*, trans. H. Rackham (London: Heinemann, 1932), pp. 21, 63.

be both good and accurately portrayed; nevertheless, Aristotle graciously admits that women and slaves may be represented, since "Even a woman is 'good' and so is a slave, although it may be said that a woman is an inferior thing and a slave beneath consideration." But although a woman may be "good" in her own way, it is not appropriate for her "to be manly or clever."[44]

Even if women are mentally and morally inferior to men, even if they rightly should occupy a subordinate position in society and the family, there is one sphere in which they necessarily dominate: the production of children. Or so one would think if he had not read Aristotle's *Generation of Animals.* Unable to admit that women play the major role in so deeply important an activity as the creation of offspring, Aristotle reduces them to mere incubators. A summary of his views cannot convey the insistence with which he iterates and reiterates his theory that woman plays a passive, almost negligible, role in reproduction. The female contributes only matter, identified with menstrual blood, to the process of generation. Hence she provides only her child's body, its soul coming from its father. Because the female role is passive, a child is formed from a man and a woman "only in the sense in which a bedstead is formed from the carpenter and the wood."

Since the male provides the form of the child, it seems strange that all human offspring are not boys. What happens is that in the act of generation the male principle, from excessive youth or age or some other cause, unfortunately fails to gain the mastery. While the norm is that the male will produce its like, there can be all degrees of deviation from it, the most extreme being monsters that do not appear human at all. "The first beginning of this deviation is when a female is formed instead of a male," although "this indeed is a necessity required by Nature." Females are obviously necessary for human reproduction, and the human system of reproduction (that is, one requiring two sexes) is the best possible type since it separates the superior Form principle from the inferior

[44] Aristotle, *The Poetics,* trans. W. H. Fyfe (London: Heinemann, 1953), p. 55. Cf. *Nicomachean Ethics* and *The History of Animals,* in *The Basic Works of Aristotle,* ed. Richard McKeon (New York: Random House, 1941), pp. 637, 1065–66, and *The Generation of Animals,* trans. A. L. Peck (London: Heinemann, 1943), pp. 335–39.

Matter. Nonetheless, the offspring is deficient in whatever "faculty" (sex or some other characteristic) the male has not dominated. A woman is an "infertile male"; the female is female because of her inability to produce semen. In short, "we should look upon the female state as being as it were a deformity, though one which occurs in the ordinary course of nature."[45]

Aristotle's discussion of reproduction shows with particular clarity a motive for the disparagement of women that is apt to develop in patriarchal societies. His repeated insistence on woman's unimportance reveals a compulsion to deny her actual power and significance. If the male members of a patriarchal society were altogether confident of their superior power and capacity, they would feel no anxiety about their status and — on this ground at least — no hostility to women. But of course they cannot: the patriarch always has the haunting memory of his original dependence on his mother. Hence he must keep reassuring himself that woman is really weak and insignificant.

Insistence on the deficiencies of women also serves to justify keeping them in subjection: a man can more comfortably enjoy his male prerogatives when he is convinced he ought to have them. Although Aristotle's depreciation of women is so elaborate and insistent that it seems to reveal particular hostility, he was typical insofar as he was rationalizing the opinions of his culture. He had a profound influence on the misogynistic tradition because his seemingly dispassionate and logical pronouncements provided contemporaries and successors with a plausible rationalization for patriarchal disparagement of women.

7

Although the code of Numa was extremely patriarchal, the defense of patriarchy was not nearly so conspicuous a theme in Roman as in Greek literature. In Republican times there is an occasional patriarchal diatribe, such as the Elder Cato's reaction to mild political agitation by the matrons. His speech reveals the characteristic intense fear of woman's dominance and power, as he warns men against making any concessions to women on the

[45] Aristotle, *Generation of Animals*, pp. 103, 113, 131–33, 391, 401, 403, 461.

grounds that "The moment they begin to be your equals, they will be your superiors." [46] The more attached a man is to his patriarchal status, the more worried he is about losing it; and the resulting anxiety is apt to make him overestimate woman's power.

Despite Cato's warning, by imperial times the Roman matrons approached *de facto* equality, and, paradoxically, outbursts against their insubordination became rarer. Most men, it seems, had ceased to worry so much about threats to their status. But a few ardent patriarchs remained, notably Juvenal.

Juvenal's Sixth Satire is probably the most horrifying of all catalogues of female vices. His main theme is lust, which opens the poem and recurs insistently in varying forms. There is Hiberina, who would as soon be satisfied with one eye as with one man; the mother-in-law who relives her own lustful delights by assisting with her daughter's affairs; the green-eyed adulteress who defends herself with defiant insolence even when caught in her lover's arms; the female devotees from whose orgies even a mouse scuttles away conscious of his sex; Eppia, who runs off cheerfully to Egypt with a broken-down gladiator, although if her husband were to take her on a sea voyage she would vomit all over him; the Empress Messalina, who would slink out to a brothel, joyfully receive all comers in her cell reeking of unwashed bedding, and after working till the last possible moment return to the palace "exhausted by men but unsatisfied." Women's adultery is aggravated by their poor taste in lovers — gladiators, actors, even transvestites. Be glad your wife refuses to have children, for otherwise "you might perhaps find yourself the father of an Ethiopian."

And, as a culminating insult, the matron applies beauty aids for the greater delectation of her lovers, stuffing her cheeks with lumps of dough and plastering her face with smelly unguents. For her lover "she discloses her face; she removes the first layer of plaster, and begins to be recognizable." But her husband, seeing her "coated over . . . with all those layers of medicaments," cannot tell whether her face is a face or a sore. Although Juvenal claimed to be satirizing the vicious Roman ladies of his time, he did not limit this monstrous lust particularly to them. In her religious orgies,

---

[46] *Livy*, trans. E. T. Sage (London: Heinemann, 1935), IX, 419.

"woman shows herself as she is." And all women are the same, the barefooted slave as well as the lady riding in her litter.

Juvenal's exaggerated insistence that all women are lustful is found in almost all misogynists; he also shows the patriarch's outrage at any attempt by women to move out of the limited sphere allotted them. Without extenuating the revolting behavior he describes, I might point out that in part it resulted from women's desire to assert themselves, to share the sexual rights of men. The woman who marries and divorces eight husbands in five autumns is obviously lustful and self-indulgent, but she is also exercising the right of divorce which had once been the prerogative of the Roman male.

Some of Juvenal's other charges are more definitely directed against women who do not know their place. Since conjugal love is, for Juvenal, synonymous with uxoriousness, it necessarily leads to henpecking: "If you are honestly uxorious, and devoted to one woman, then bow your head and submit your neck ready to bear the yoke. Never will you find a woman who spares the man who loves her; for though she be herself aflame, she delights to torment and plunder him." You will give no presents if she objects, nor buy or sell anything without her consent. She will choose your acquaintances for you and turn your oldest friend away from your door. Finally, "you will have to write down among your heirs more than one rival of your own."

Besides tyrannizing over their husbands, as — according to the misogynists — wives have always done, women in Juvenal's day were displaying mannishness by entering traditionally masculine preserves. Women plan their legal cases and advise the lawyers (and "There never was a case in court in which the quarrel was not started by a woman"), practice fencing, attend political meetings and boldly speak to public officials, and, worst of all, affect learning:

But most intolerable of all is the woman who as soon as she has sat down to dinner commends Virgil, pardons the dying Dido, and pits the poets against each other, putting Virgil in the one scale and Homer in the other. The grammarians make way before her; the rhetoricians give in; the whole crowd is silenced: no lawyer, no auctioneer will get a word in, no, nor any other woman. . . . She lays down definitions, and discourses on morals, like a philosopher; thirsting to be deemed both wise and eloquent.

A woman should not be able to understand everything she reads.

I hate a woman who is for ever consulting and poring over the "Grammar" of Palaemon, who observes all the rules and laws of language, who like an antiquary quotes verses that I never heard of, and corrects her unlettered female friends for slips of speech that no man need trouble about: let husbands at least be permitted to make slips in grammar!

By the end of this description it is clear that what Juvenal really cannot stand is superiority in a woman. This is even more obvious when he admits that a wife can be *too* virtuous; although Juvenal feels free to castigate women for their faults, he is equally hostile to the faultless. Let a wife be beautiful, charming, rich, fertile, nobly descended, and chaste — "a prodigy as rare upon the earth as a black swan! yet who could endure a wife that possessed all perfections?" He would rather marry a country wench than Cornelia, mother of the Gracchi, if she was aware of her virtues: ". . . who was ever so enamoured as not to shrink from the woman whom he praises to the skies, and to hate her for seven hours out of every twelve?"[47] This dislike of virtues in women is typical of the patriarchal misogynist, who cannot tolerate qualities which weaken his sense of masculine superiority. The misogynist must be able to dislike women; the patriarch must be able to feel superior to them.

The attitudes toward women of these Greeks and Romans demonstrate the pernicious influence of an extremely patriarchal social system. Whenever the patriarch feels the need to justify his subjugation of women, as he usually does, he must rationalize his position by disparaging them. Although a man might admit, as Juvenal did, that he actually disliked good qualities in women (which made it more difficult to look down on them), patriarchal writers were more apt simply to insist that women are weak in mind and character, and therefore incapable of directing themselves. Woman's

---

[47] *Juvenal and Persius*, trans. G. G. Ramsay (London: Heinemann, 1940), pp. 93, 97, 99, 101, 103, 109, 119, 121, 123, 133. Although Juvenal's comprehensiveness is unparalleled in Roman literature, both his themes and the epigrammatic style and striking exaggeration which give them force were anticipated by Seneca: e.g., Seneca charged that in his time noble ladies married only in order to be divorced, chastity was simply a proof of ugliness, and ladies called living with one paramour "marriage"— *On Benefits*, in *Moral Essays*, trans. John W. Basore (London: Heinemann, 1932), III, 155–57.

inability to control her baser impulses was so common an assumption in Greek culture that it appears even in the relatively feminist Euripides, whose favorite theme was the horrors of her unleashed passions.

On a deeper level, the patriarch may allay his fear that woman is naturally more powerful than man (derived probably from the original dependence of every child upon his mother and necessarily anxiety-provoking to one who insists upon male dominance) by reassuring himself of her unimportance in all human affairs. This would explain why Aeschylus and Aristotle belittled woman's role in reproduction. Cato, confronted by more independent women who were making their wishes felt in public life, openly expressed his dread of female power.

It seems strange that the Jews, whose culture was as patriarchal as the Greeks', showed little of their bitterness toward women and in fact generally exalted the good wife and mother. (The obvious exceptions, St. Paul and the writer of Ecclesiasticus, were influenced by Greek thought.) One probable reason is that patriarchy was so securely established in Jewish culture before the writing of the Bible that men no longer felt an acute need to defend themselves against women or to justify their position, and were thus free to appreciate the pleasures of female society and family life. In early Greek culture, on the other hand, traces of matriarchy are still apparent, and the reaction against women is consequently more bitter. Thus Hesiod, one of the earliest Greek writers, is also the most rancorous against women. While Aristotle's extreme and insistent belittlement of women reveals definite hostility, he did not feel the need to attack them overtly.

The originally strong patriarchy of Roman culture seems to have been gradually and painlessly abandoned as the Roman matron acquired increasing freedom in her family and society. Evidently most Roman men, if they were aware of the change, were able to accept it without alarm. Juvenal, however, out of tune with his time and personally misogynistic, reacted savagely against the emancipated matrons of his day, much as insecure Greek patriarchs had done long before him. Woman's relative independence under the Roman Empire also contributed to the antifeminism of St. Paul and other early Christian writers, who found it alarming because of their inheritance of Jewish patriarchy and their ascetic conviction that woman must be kept under control because of her sexuality.

Carried to its logical extreme, the patriarchal rationale deprives woman of any admirable qualities beyond innocuousness: as a mother she is an incubator; as a wife she does the housework without giving trouble. She is supposed to be so deficient in mental and moral virtues that she can contribute little to the welfare of her husband or society at large, and, of course, any independent action she might take is bound to be disastrous. The wife who rebels against her role brands herself and her sex as termagants and troublemakers; the one who accepts it is disparaged for her limited capacity and generally ignored in literature. Moreover, a man who thinks of his wife as a slave more than as a companion and partner will probably expect hostility from her, and fear and dislike her accordingly. The result is the overwhelmingly negative picture of marriage that emerges from Greek literature.

8. Odi et Amo — The Classical Attitude Toward Love

In addition to degrading the position of women in general by assuming them incapable of intellectual companionship or exalted love, an extremely patriarchal system tends to divide the sex into two stereotypes, probably in life and certainly in literature. On the one hand there is the wife, who adds nothing to her husband's pleasure and is all too apt to detract from it by failing to fulfill her household duties or resisting his authority. On the other hand is the mistress, who does provide sensual pleasure but cannot be a worthy object for a man's love because her intrinsic deficiencies as a woman are aggravated by her low character. The wife might be insufficiently eager to please,[48] but the prostitute had her typical professional vices of rapacity and deceitfulness. Shrewish wives

---

[48] See an epigram quoted in Athenaeus, *The Sages at Dinner*, trans. Charles Gulick (London: Heinemann, 1927), VI, 21–23: "No wonder there is a shrine to the Companion everywhere, but nowhere in all Greece is there one to the Wife." For the wife can behave as she likes [*sic!*], secure of her place as mistress of the house unless her husband wants to forfeit her dowry. The kept mistress, on the other hand, knows that she must continually buy her man with sweetness and fascination unless she wants to be thrown out.

or mercenary courtesans — women were an affliction to men either way.

For some Greeks the only solution was homosexual love: they confined idealistic love to boys, reducing women to mere breeders or objects of lust. There is a full statement of this point of view in Plato's *Symposium*, although the frequent citation of this work as evidence that Plato exalted homosexual over heterosexual love rests on a fundamental misinterpretation. It is true that Pausanias, one of the early speakers in the dialogue, has no doubt that love for young men is nobler and purer than love for women. Only those who "turn to the male, and delight in him who is the more valiant and intelligent nature" are loving the soul, rather than lusting after the body. Societies which condemn homosexual love do so because it is "inimical to tyranny," developing spirit and self-respect and encouraging strong bonds of friendship. Pausanias assumes of course that love of women must be sensual only, that the communication of virtue and wisdom, the noblest aim of love, is impossible to women, and that no strong bond of friendship can develop with a woman.

There is, however, no indication in the dialogue that Pausanias' views are to be accepted as correct. Socrates, who as usual presents the only dependably "correct" view, maintains that the highest love is that which transcends the sexual completely, being directed toward absolute beauty (God). Although Socrates himself loves youths, he claims to have learned about love from a woman. No one explicitly condemns Pausanias' speech, but no one approves it or makes such invidious statements about women or heterosexual love. Pausanias' views, a logical development of patriarchal disparagement of women, were prevalent in his time and generally acceptable; but they were not Plato's. In *The Laws* Plato made his attitude indisputably clear through his mouthpiece, the Athenian Stranger: homosexual intercourse in either sex "is contrary to nature, and . . . originally due to unbridled lust." [49]

Even after homosexual love was generally condemned, as it was

---

[49] Plato, *The Symposium*, in *Dialogues*, trans. Benjamin Jowett (New York: Random House, 1937), I, 309–10; *The Laws*, in *Dialogues*, II, 418. While Aristophanes also seems to praise homosexual love, his speech is certainly burlesque in part, perhaps altogether.

in later Greek and Roman society, heterosexual love continued to be disparaged. Righteous Aeneas, for example, is noticeably impervious to female charms. He cannot be said to have loved any of the three women with whom he is involved, although Virgil tried to dramatize his devotion to Creusa and Dido. It is obvious that Aeneas values his father and son far more than his wife, especially when he avoidably loses her in Troy;[50] and he resists Dido's entreaties with a firmness uncomfortably close to insensibility. Lavinia is not a person at all, merely the visible sign of empire. The only romance in the *Aeneid* which is clearly two-sided and favorably presented is the homosexual relationship between Nisus and Euryalus. Whether Aeneas' resistance to women was an unintentional product of Virgil's own emotional limitations or a consciously planned mark of lofty character, it illustrates the classical disparagement of passion between men and women.

Apart from the late Greek romances one finds no idealization of heterosexual romantic love in classical literature: the general assumption was that such love was at best sensual gratification, and that if it had profound effects on the lover, it tormented or degraded rather than ennobling him. It did not seem to occur to the Greeks and Romans that a passionate attachment to a woman could offer satisfaction to the mind and spirit as well as to the body, could provide lifelong happiness as well as transitory sensual pleasure. The idealization which was gradually stripped from homosexual love was not attached to heterosexual love until medieval times.

When they rejected homosexual love, the Greeks were apt to conclude that *all* types of love are unsatisfactory, as did an anonymous writer in *The Greek Anthology*:

By what road shall one go to the Land of Love? If you seek him in the streets, you will repent the courtesan's greed for gold and luxury. If you approach a maiden's bed, it must end in lawful wedlock or punishment for seduction. Who would endure to awake reluctant desire for his lawful wife, forced to do a duty? Adulterous intercourse is the worst of all and has no part in love, and unnatural sin should be ranked with it.

[50] A medieval misogynist, John of Salisbury, commended Virgil for wisely expressing "the proper order of affection" in Aeneas' flight from Troy: first the father, then the son, and lastly the wife. See *The Statesman's Book of John of Salisbury*, trans. John Dickinson (New York: Knopf, 1927), p. 51.

A wanton widow, the writer continues, is as bad as a harlot, while a chaste one continually bothers you with her remorse. If you sleep with your own servant, she will become your mistress; if with another man's, you will be legally prosecuted.[51] The author assumes that a man's proper relationship with a woman is to get from her the maximum of sexual enjoyment for the minimum of expense; he therefore sees women exclusively in terms of what they might contribute to his gratification and obviously disapproves of their having any wishes whatever of their own.

Greek Middle and New Comedy, which regularly represented wives as nagging and unattractive, were often even harder on prostitutes. Of course, prostitutes, operating outside the moral scheme and to some extent outside organized society, are fair game for the most vitriolic attacks. This colorful catalogue by Anaxilas is typical:

> Lives there the man who's really loved a whore?
> Vicious? what living creatures could be more?
> Take fire-breathing Chimaera, lone Great Snake,
> Charybdis, triple sea-hound Scylla, take
> Sphinx, Hydra, lioness, Harpy, asp, and say
> If these surpass such loathsome things as they.
> The whores win every time. First Plangon; she
> Burns, like Chimaera, gents from oversea —
> . . . .
> Phryne's Charybdis to the life; she nips
> And gulps not only shipmasters but ships.
> . . . .
> And Sphinxes? All; they don't say straight, this lot,
> They'd like to kiss and cuddle and what not,
> But "I wish a four-legged couch" or "sofa," say,
> Or "a three-legged pot-hanger, would come my way,"
> Or "a two-legged lady's maid." A few of us
> Twig, turn blind eyes, and flee like Oedipus,
> And so, half-heartedly, escape; but most
> Of the lookers-out for love at once get tossed
> Sky-high. No; of all beasts of sea or shore
> There's none so pestilential as your whore.[52]

[51] Agathias Scholasticus, *The Greek Anthology*, I, 291.

[52] *Fragments of Attic Comedy*, II, 341–43. Cf. Alexis on the numerous beauty aids used "to fit young ladies out as slimy snakes," *ibid.*, II, 417–19. Plautus

Martial, who imitated the Greeks both in his epigrams and his love preferences — boys and prostitutes — delighted in turning on the latter when they became old and unappetizing. Of his many epigrams modeled on *Greek Anthology* attacks on aging prostitutes, this one was to echo and re-echo through the misogynistic tradition:

Although . . . your tresses, Galla, are manufactured far away, and you lay aside your teeth at night, just as you do your silk dresses, and you lie stored away in a hundred caskets, and your face does not sleep with you — yet you wink with that eyebrow which has been brought out for you in the morning, and no respect moves you for your outworn carcass — which you may now count as one of your ancestors. Nevertheless you offer me an infinity of delights. But Nature is deaf, and although she may be one-eyed, she sees you anyhow.[53]

Although Martial jibed at marriage in the Greek manner, the Romans in general had a high conception of marriage; and their epigrams against wives appear to be idle flippancies rather than expressions of emotional conviction.[54] On the other hand, their feelings about women as mistresses were almost always ambivalent. Catullus' *odi et amo*, "I hate and I love," accurately describes their usual attitude. They may have loved their wives, but their erotic objects were generally courtesans or adulteresses, for whom they felt contempt and hostility along with sexual passion. Catullus' Clodia, hugging close her hundreds of lovers, not loving them but leaving their loins limp nevertheless, is a typical Roman mistress.[55]

---

followed his Greek predecessors in his representation of courtesans, as he did in most matters. See particularly his *Truculentus*.

[53] Martial, *Epigrams*, trans. Walter Ker (London: Heinemann, 1920), II, 97–99. Cf. I, 233, II, 213.

[54] This poem attributed to Petronius is typical: "A wife is a burden imposed by law, and should be loved like one's fortune. But I do not wish to love even my fortune for ever" — *Petronius*, trans. Michael Heseltine (London: Heinemann, 1951), p. 343. Cf. Martial's epigrams against adulterous, dominant, or learned wives — *Epigrams*, I, 381, II, 13, 253.

[55] *Catullus, Tibullus, and Pervigilium Veneris*, trans. F. W. Cornish (London: Heinemann, 1950), pp. 17, 163. Gilbert Highet's interpretation of Catullus' poem on Attis (LXIII), in which Attis repents of his self-castration and tries, frantically but vainly, to escape from the mother-mistress goddess Cybele, is sound and illuminating: Highet sees the poem as an allegory of Catullus' relationship with Clodia — hopelessly tied to her despite his awareness that she is ruining him. (*Poets in a Landscape* [New York: Knopf, 1957], pp. 25–27.) The same poem also suggests the connection between feelings of helplessness before the mother and the mistress, since Cybele represented both.

Hostility to the mistress is actually more intense and striking in Roman literature than in Greek, despite the Romans' generally more favorable attitude toward women. This results from the greater importance of heterosexual passion in Roman society (which of course was made possible by the better position of women): since most of the Roman erotic poets seem really to have cared about their mistresses and really suffered from their unworthiness, the reader is strongly impressed by the misery which their loves made them undergo.

Because every one of the major Roman erotic poets fell in love with and hence wrote about unworthy women, they naturally had much to say about female inconstancy, lust, and venality. While their mistresses may have deserved these reproaches, it remains a question why the poets chose such women as objects of their devotion. I suspect a tinge of sadism in their love, a need to despise women, as well as a masochistic compulsion to suffer in erotic relationships. There was certainly some masochism in Catullus, Tibullus, and Propertius, all of whom loved whores, suffered acutely in their passion, apparently felt that love entailed abject slavery to the mistress, and yet gloried in their subjection to her. Even if these sentiments were to some extent dictated by convention, why should convention require a lover to be the victim of an unworthy woman? Very likely because such an arrangement permitted an expression of sexual hostility in passionate relationships which was not acceptable in respectable marriage. This hostility was seldom overt, although it comes close to the surface in Propertius and Ovid.

Propertius, with as miserable a love and as unworthy a mistress as Catullus' Clodia and Tibullus' Nemesis, came the closest of the three to overt misogyny. He berated his Cynthia for her faults, generalized from her to her sex, and indignantly proclaimed the ignominy of subjection to women. Cynthia, unable to "forego the joys of even one night," easily covers her unfaithfulness with deceit, the only art that woman has never failed to learn. She has the typical prostitute's vices of greed and cold insincerity, which she shares with all her female contemporaries. If only Roman matrons would imitate Indian widows, who compete to die on their husband's bier: "The victors burn and offer their breasts to the flame and lay charred faces upon their husband's body." Here the sadism latent in Propertius' conception of love becomes almost explicit. Although he

sometimes willingly accepted his slavery to Cynthia, he occasionally protested with true patriarchal outrage against the humiliation
of sexual subjection to women.[56]

Obviously these erotic poets could not be called misogynists,
since they devoted so much of their lives and their art to the cele-
bration of women. But they established a tradition of ambivalence
which was to persist through western European love poetry: love
is ecstasy, but it is wretched slavery as well; the mistress is adored,
but she is all too often unworthy of that adoration. Thus even the most
ardent love poets may be found reviling or repudiating their mistresses, or women in general.

9

Austere, philosophical Lucretius, writing at about the same time
as these erotic poets, shared their conception of love as an altogether sensual passion that inevitably brings misery with it. But
because he was a rationalistic moralist, it was obvious to him that
love should be eradicated, and he proceeded to give advice to this
end. Since what is disastrous is overwhelming devotion to one love
object, you should dissipate this emotion by promiscuous attach-
ments — "lance the first wound with new incisions." Even a prosperous *grande passion* is a wretched business, entailing "waves of
delusion and incertitude," an element of sadism, pangs which cannot be satiated, and obsessive dependence on another person. To
free yourself from this curse, you should first concentrate on your
mistress' failings of mind and body, to destroy your romantic
overestimation of her. This generally means no more than stripping
away the usual lover's illusions — for a lover acclaims his sallow
wench as a nut-brown maid, praises the modesty of a girl dumb as
a fish, declares that a fiery scold "burns with a gem-like flame," and
calls a swollen-breasted woman "Ceres suckling Bacchus."

In the rare case that your mistress is faultless, you can still free
yourself by reflecting that "in her physical nature she is no different . . . from the plainest of her sex. She is driven to use foul-
smelling fumigants. Her maids keep well away from her and snigger

[56] *Propertius*, trans. H. E. Butler (London: Heinemann, 1952), pp. 89,
213–17, 223. Tibullus' masochism is almost overt in Poem IV of Book II.

behind her back." Often enough, were the tearful lover who pleads at the door of her dressing room actually admitted, "one whiff would promptly make him cast round for some decent pretext to take his leave. His fond complaint, long-pondered and far-fetched, would fall dismally flat. He would curse himself for a fool to have endowed her with qualities above mortal imperfection." Since women are well aware of this, they take pains to hide their back-stage activities from their lovers. "But their pains are wasted, since your mind has power to drag all these mysteries into the daylight." Still, he ends with unexpected charity: "Then, if the lady is good-hearted and void of malice, it is up to you in your turn to accept unpleasant facts and make allowance for human imperfection." [57] This seems to be the first appearance of the lady's dressing room theme, which was to be perennially useful to misogynists. Lucretius' conviction that, since romantic love is irrational, *no* woman's attractiveness can survive a keen analysis by reason, was also to reappear often, particularly in the Age of Reason.

The first imitator of this advice was, of all people, the immoralist instructor in the art of illicit love, Ovid, in his *Remedies of Love*. In this work, which undoes the lessons of *The Art of Love* by showing lovers how to break off unsatisfactory affairs, the ambivalence implicit in the other Roman erotic poets becomes explicit. Having built up the charms of love and women in *The Art of Love*, Ovid strips them away in *The Remedies*; he shows how to counteract the attractions of a mistress, however lovely she may be. While he does on the whole wish to preserve the illusion of women's beauty so as to preserve the delights of love, *The Remedies* reveals delight in ridiculing and degrading women. First Ovid uses Lucretius' idea that the same quality can be seen as a fault or a virtue depending on one's point of view, although what is presented as truth in Lucretius is presented as sour grapes in Ovid: "Where you can, turn to the worse your girl's attractions. . . . Call her fat, if she is full-breasted, black, if dark-complexioned. . . . If she is not simple, she can be called pert: if she is honest, she can be called simple." Induce her to display whatever talent she lacks — to sing if she has

---

[57] Lucretius, *The Nature of the Universe*, trans. R. E. Latham (Harmondsworth, Middlesex: Penguin Books, 1951), pp. 163–67.

no voice, to dance if she trips over her feet, and so forth. It will further help you fall out of love to visit your mistress when she is making up her face: the smell of women's cosmetics has often made him queasy. Or you could even lurk "in hiding while the girl performed her obscenities." But "Heaven forfend I should give anyone such counsel! tho it may help, 'twere better not to use it."

While Ovid's attitude to love is ambivalent, his evaluation of women is entirely consistent: attractive as they may be, they are frail, foolish, and greedy. If Ovid never said anything very bitter about women, it was probably because he never seriously cared about one. His loves, whether real or fictitious, were of the same type as those of the more earnest erotic poets; but the conclusions about female nature which he drew from them, however cynical, were presented lightly. Still, his entertaining disparagements of women and exposures of female arts contributed vastly to the misogynistic tradition: his ironic advice to women urges them to do the very things for which moralists attacked them, and his advice to men develops a derisive picture of women's weaknesses. His warning about courtesans' greed is typical of his amused cynicism: "But hold in awful dread your lady's birthday; let that be a black day whereon a present must be given. Shun it as you may, yet she will carry off the spoil; a woman knows the way to fleece an eager lover of his wealth." She will ask for a gift to buy a birthday cake, having birthdays "as often as she requires." She will claim to have lost a jewel, which of course must be replaced. She will borrow things, never to return them. "Ten months and as many tongues would not suffice me to tell the unholy ruses of the fair."

Ovid found women as foolish as they are frail, regarding them as charming toys easily won by pretenses. You must admire your mistress incessantly — her dress, the part she has put in her hair, her arms, her voice — "Only while so talking take care not to show you are feigning." "Counterfeit heartache with words: her belief in that you must win by any device. Nor is it hard to be believed: each woman thinks herself lovable; hideous though she be, there is none her own looks do not please." Tears are particularly useful — natural if possible, otherwise simulated by touching your eyes with a wet hand. If you are planning to free a slave or spare him from punishment, let your mistress think you do it at her intercession: ". . . let her play the powerful lady . . . be sure she thinks you spellbound by her beauty."

Ovid's conception of love as a mutually predatory relationship, while not morally weighted, was hardly conducive to idealization of women and again hints at the sado-masochism latent in all these poets' conceptions of love. In advising girls to display themselves, he uses a series of hunting metaphors: "The wolf draws nigh to many sheep that she may prey on one . . . ever let your hook be hanging; where you least believe it, there will be a fish in the stream." The most apparently unpromising situation may prove fruitful: "Often a husband is sought for at a husband's funeral; it is becoming to go with dishevelled hair, and to mourn without restraint."

Although it is often said that Ovid wrote only about courtesans, this particular illustration clearly refers to respectable women; and his development of the point that "all women can be caught" similarly indicates that he was talking about women in general. Although woman "conceals desire better" than man, her lust is uncontrollable — think of the incestuous passions of Byblis and Myrrha, the bestiality of Pasiphaë, the adultery of Aerope with Thyestes, the betrayal of her father by Scylla, the murder of Agamemnon by Clytemnestra, the double infanticide of Medea, the gory death of Hippolytus, and the blinding of Phineus' innocent sons. "In us desire is weaker and not so frantic: the manly flame knows a lawful bound." "Come then," he concludes, "doubt not that you may win all women"; "Only persevere; you will overcome Penelope herself." Even force is welcomed: women "often wish to give unwillingly what they like to give." [58]

The same cheerful cynicism about womankind appears in the famous tale of the Widow of Ephesus in Petronius' *Satyricon;* for Petronius as for Ovid, all women could be caught. A certain Widow

---

[58] Ovid, *The Art of Love and Other Poems*, trans. J. H. Mozley (London: Heinemann, 1947), pp. 31–37, 41–43, 45, 55, 59, 87, 149, 201–3, 207–9. Like all the Roman erotic poets, Horace suffered from the inconstancy of his mistresses; but his sufferings are hardly to be taken seriously. Pyrrha might be false, or other girls greedy (Odes I.5, III.16); but Horace was never bitter or heartsick. Horace came closest to misogyny in his derision of old women, either hags who persisted in acting like belles (e.g., Epodes 8, 12) or witches like Canidia (e.g., Epodes 5, 17).

of Ephesus, not satisfied with the usual rites of mourning for her husband, insisted on weeping over his body in its tomb until she should die also. "There was but one opinion throughout the city, every class of person admitting this was the one true and brilliant example of chastity and love." But nearby there was a soldier, guarding the bodies of some executed robbers. Seeing a light in the tomb and hearing the lady's groans, he went to investigate, and on understanding the situation, brought his supper into the tomb and tried to console her with the usual platitudes. At last she consented to share his supper, and after further persuasion "the conquering hero won her over entire." After they had slept together for three nights the parents of one of the crucified men took advantage of the soldier's absence to steal their son's body; and he prepared to kill himself to avoid punishment. But, as "The lady's heart was tender as well as pure," she suggested that her husband's body fill the vacancy; and accordingly the dead man was put to use and the live man saved.[59]

Despite the sourness of some of their satirists, the Romans on the whole were less misogynistic than the Greeks. They seldom vilified respectable women, their wives and the mothers of their children, or the female sex in general. One reason seems to be the greater freedom the Roman matron attained, which meant that, being less limited and frustrated, she was less apt to turn into a shrewish affliction, and so men could find greater satisfaction in marriage. Furthermore, the more patriarchal the system, the more worried the patriarch is about maintaining his prerogatives; and anxiety generates hostility. Although the Romans did often express hostility toward disreputable women — their mistresses — this was qualified by positive feelings at least as strong as the negative ones on the part of the serious erotic poets, by obvious lightness of tone in writers like Ovid and Petronius.

Nevertheless, the Romans' ambivalence toward their mistresses was to have profound effects on later Western tradition. First, in choosing for their mistresses women who displayed the typical prostitute's faults, the Romans focused attention on unworthy representatives of the female sex. The recurrent charges that woman

[59] *Petronius*, pp. 229–35.

is rapacious, deceitful, fickle, and incapable of responding to true love may all be traced to the faults of Clodia and her ilk, as publicized by the Roman erotic poets. Secondly, the painful and humiliating affairs of these men suggested that romantic love was inevitably degrading; and their inability to escape from those affairs, that woman is irresistibly powerful. The idea that the wise man should avoid romantic love, derivable from the Christian denigration of sex, was reinforced for the Middle Ages by the Romans' descriptions of their sufferings under bondage to women. Ovid, whose amused contempt for the female mind and character has perennially appealed to similar temperaments since, formalized Roman ambivalence toward love in his sequence of *The Art of Love* and *The Remedies of Love*. This set the pattern for innumerable lovers' recantations of love in the Middle Ages and the Renaissance.

Two elements in Roman culture contributed to this disparagement of the erotic love object. In the first place, the Romans inherited from the Greeks and from their own early ancestors a patriarchal tendency to disparage the female mind and character: if a man sees woman as intrinsically foolish, frail, and incapable of controlling her lower impulses, he neither expects nor is likely to get lofty devotion from her. And then the Roman splitting off of sexual from conjugal love further encouraged a tendency to look down upon the mistress. Necessarily she was disreputable — a prostitute or an adulteress — and she could be vilified not only for what she actually was, but as a substitute for the respectable matron who was not considered a proper target for abuse.

However, a deeper psychological explanation for ambivalence toward the erotic love object must be sought, since it is also found under quite different cultural conditions, in fact in all cultures in which romantic love is an important ideal. There seems always to be an impulse to tear down what has been elevated, so that the very worshiper who has proclaimed love an ecstasy and his mistress a goddess may in a mood of reaction call love a degrading dependence and his mistress a worthless coquette. The more intense the relationship, the more apt it is to engender ambivalence. The underlying reasons for man's tendency to react against his own intense passion can probably be traced to the complex development of the human libido, as Freud analyzed it. He showed that sado-masoch-ism, although it seems to be the antithesis of love, is normal in the erotic life of children and may persist into adult relationships. Furthermore, the prototype of a man's erotic relationships with women is his childish love for his mother, which necessarily in-cludes some elements of frustration: the child's absolute depend-ence on her and her inevitable preference for another male may account for the adult lover's feeling of helplessness before women and constant charges that they are faithless and unresponsive to devotion. Usually the angry complaints against the mother are displaced onto a less venerated woman, such as the mistress.

Roman ambivalence toward the female love object, Greek patri-archal disparagement of woman's character and importance, and early Christian hostility to her as a sexual temptation laid the foundations for the mass of misogynistic writing which has ap-peared in every period of English literature. Of course, these causes often operated simultaneously, and one cannot always discriminate among the various motives for some traditional charge. Jewish and Roman society were patriarchal as well as Greek, and in St. Paul's insistence on the subjection of women can be seen the effects both of sexual distrust and the traditional patriarchy of his culture. Simi-larly, Propertius' sexual hostility against Cynthia was aggravated by the patriarch's mortification at seeing that woman may have the upper hand. The charge that woman is more lustful than man, per-haps the most prominent in the whole arsenal of misogyny, can be traced to all three of the underlying motives: a sexual ascetic is likely to project his own lustful feelings upon women; an ambiva-lent lover will accuse his mistress of unfaithfulness or sexual insa-tiability which make her unworthy to be the object of a man's love; and a patriarch is apt to worry constantly that the wife he owns may rebel against his sovereignty by giving her body to other men.

Naturally, the intensity and volume of the charges have varied with different writers and changing social conditions; but the under-lying motives remain constant. In the Middle Ages the influence of early Christian asceticism appears in priests' warnings against women and denigration of marriage, and even occasionally in the romances. The ambivalence shown in the romances and courtly love literature in general can also be traced to the ambivalence toward erotic love found in Roman literature, which also offered many precedents for medieval poems on woman's treachery, fickleness, and rapacity. And the motive behind attacks on the insubordinate wife, a favorite medieval subject, was clearly patriarchal indignation at women who refused to accept their subject status.

Chapter II ❧ MEDIEVAL ATTITUDES TOWARD
LOVE AND MARRIAGE

1. *"Flee Wisely Women"*

ROMAN cynicism about women was taken up enthusiastically in the Middle Ages, when misogyny became increasingly prominent as a theme in literature. Although the most intense medieval attacks on women were prompted by fear of their seductive powers inherited from the early Christian ascetics, the classical tradition contributed not only much illustrative material but precedents for attacks on marriage and especially for the ambivalence found in the courtly love tradition. Medieval men, with their love of authorities and ancient examples, drew almost as heavily from the classical storehouse of misogyny as they did from the Bible and the Church Fathers. Critics of courtly love deflated chivalric romantic idealism by borrowing Ovid's exposures of woman's frailty, greed, and wiles; and it was medieval writers against marriage who gave Xanthippe her permanent notoriety as a shrew. Both Geoffrey Chaucer and John Gower elaborated one of Diogenes Laertius' tales showing Socrates' unshakable patience with his wife.[1]

Medieval writers, however, unlike the typical Greeks and Ro-

[1] One cold day, returning home from the well with a pot of water, Xanthippe started to berate him for idleness as he sat by the fire reading. When her prolonged scolding provoked no response, she finally emptied the water pot on his head. He merely remarked that this was to be expected, since storm winds always blow loud and bring a rain. John Gower, *The Complete Works*, ed. G. C. Macaulay (Oxford: Clarendon Press, 1899), II, 243–44. Cf. Chaucer's more vulgar version of the story: *The Poetical Works*, ed. F. N. Robinson (Boston: Houghton Mifflin, 1933), p. 99 ("The Wife of Bath's Prologue," lines 727–32). According to a medieval tradition, based probably on the disparagement of women in their writings, both Aristotle and Virgil had been victimized by women. In "My Love Was False and Full of Flattery," in *The Bannatyne MS*, ed. W. Tod Ritchie (Edinburgh: Scottish Text Society [New Ser., 22, 23, 26, and Third Ser., 5], 1928, 1930, 1934), IV, 28–29, a poet, probably Weddirburne,

mans, were apt to spread their attack from harlots and shrews to all women. Influenced by early Christian asceticism, they often maintained that all women were like Ovid's courtesans and dragged their lovers or husbands into misery and ruin. John of Salisbury, a prominent twelfth-century ecclesiastic, illustrates this tendency in his *Policraticus*, a miscellany intended as joyous entertainment. Collecting every possible example against women from classical myth, history, and literature, he starts with Diana, goddess of hunting. Since John considered the sport self-indulgent and vicious, he found it natural that it was presided over by a goddess: no doubt "the people did not wish to degrade their gods." "The inferior sex excels in the hunting of birds," he goes on, because "inferior creatures are always more prone to rapine." He proceeds to the more traditional example of Cleopatra, closing a hostile account of her career with this epitaph. Suicide was:

A worthy death for a poisonous courtesan created to corrupt character and assail the virtue of noble men. She had formerly dominated kings; afterward not to be pitied despite her pitiable plight, she made her exit — a tragedy perhaps for her, but a comedy for the Roman Empire that she had been striving to overthrow. The fact that he remained invincible in his encounter with the notorious woman is especially counted among Augustus' most distinguished titles to renown.

The example of Dido proves the disastrous consequences of female rule. The "careless and irresponsible levity," the ill-considered favor with which she received Aeneas, led ultimately to the destruction of her city. "This was the end of the effeminate rule of a woman, which, though it had a beginning and basis in virtue, could not find an issue into subsequent prosperity." Further, "because vice took root in the rulership of a woman, the citizens became effeminate," and their commonwealth rotten.[2]

---

complains how his mistress joined his rival in making fun of him. The shame and scorn she made him suffer exceeded that of Absolon in Chaucer's "Miller's Tale," of Virgil hung in a cage by his love, of Aristotle bridled by his, of Troilus seeing Diomedes with the love tokens he had given Cressida.

[2] John of Salisbury, *Frivolities of Courtiers and Footprints of Philosophers*, trans. J. B. Pike (London: Oxford University Press, 1938), pp. 14, 17, 181–82; *The Statesman's Book of John of Salisbury*, trans. John Dickinson (New York: Knopf, 1927), pp. 248, 251. (Both *Frivolities* and *The Statesman's Book* are partial translations of *Policraticus*.)

Misogynistic feeling in the Middle Ages was, of course, much mitigated by the cult of courtly love, which not only held that the love of woman was free of sin, but exalted it to a degree unprecedented in earlier periods, insisting that the love of woman was the root of all virtue. Cleopatra and Dido, attacked by clerical writers for their immoderate passions and ruinous influence on men, appear in Chaucer's *Legend of Good Women* as Cupid's saints and martyrs; and John Lydgate wrote a poem glorifying Dido's wholehearted passion and constancy.[3]

Nevertheless, a reaction against courtly love seems to have been inherent in the system, so that misogyny crept into even the chivalric romances. As in Ovid, the art of love was succeeded by its remedies, although the remedies were apt to become more bitter as the art was more exalted. It appears that even the ardent courtly lover occasionally suspected that he had overidealized love and women, and was moved to bitter rejection or at least to a wish to right the scales with a portrayal of what woman "really" is — often a cynical portrayal. This tendency may have been intensified by the fact that the object of courtly love was necessarily an adulteress, even though marriage was not so sacred an institution in the Middle Ages as it had been in Rome and was to be after the Reformation.

More obviously, the ascetic Christian ideals, which were in such sharp conflict with those of courtly love, were never entirely forgotten. In the Grail legends, indeed, they overshadow all others. Sir Thomas Malory repeatedly emphasizes in *Le Morte D'Arthur* (1469–70) that virginity is essential for success in the Grail quest. Early in the search, Sir Gawaine dreams of a herd of 150 bulls — two white, one white with a black spot, and the rest black — which go off to seek better pasture, the black ones returning weak and lean. As this dream is later interpreted, the herd represents the fellowship of the Round Table, "which for their sin and their wickedness be black." Their sin, it is made clear, is desire for women: the two white bulls signify "Sir Galahad and Sir Percivale, for they be maidens clean and without spot"; and the spotted one, "Sir Bors de Ganis, which trespassed but once in his virginity,

[3] "The Moral of the Legend of Dido," in John Lydgate, *A Selection from the Minor Poems*, ed. J. O. Halliwell (London: Percy Society, 1840), pp. 69–71.

but sithen he kept himself so well in chastity that all is forgiven him." The search for better pasture represents of course the search for the Grail, and the surviving black bulls come back weak because sinners — that is, men with sexual desires — cannot attain it. In the course of the quest, two of the successful knights, Percivale and Bors, are tempted by devils in the guise of beautiful women; and Percivale punishes himself for almost yielding by stabbing himself deeply in the thigh. Galahad is not even tempted, presumably because he is so holy as to be altogether immune to sexual attraction. In the end, after the destruction of the Round Table, all the surviving knights become hermits. This may imply a rejection of earthly love, although, of course, by this time there is not much else for them to do.

Although Malory does not emphasize women's guilt as seductresses, he often shows them ruining men. Morgan le Fay continually tries to destroy her virtuous and devoted brother King Arthur, as well as to undermine virtue in general: she hates him beyond all men because he is the most eminent of her kin; she steals his sword, replacing it with a brittle replica, and sends him a mantle intended to burn him to coals; she tries to lead Launcelot and Tristram, the best of the knights, into fatal ambushes; and so forth.[4] The ultimate ruin of the Round Table itself is brought about mainly by Guinevere's childish, spiteful behavior to Launcelot.

On a lower social level, Robin Hood, who was as chivalrous as any knight in romance, died because he was betrayed by a woman. In the ballad of "Robin Hood's Death," Robin went to Kirkly Abbey to be let blood by his cousin, the Prioress. After greeting him cordially, she took him into a secluded room and bled him "While

---

[4] Sir Thomas Malory, *Le Morte D'Arthur* (London: J. M. Dent, 1953), I, 100–101, 104, 110–11, 338, II, 203–4, 214, 217, 227. On an occasion when the Christian ideal of marital chastity incongruously intrudes into the adulterous society of the *Morte D'Arthur*, Malory implies a scathing comment on female unfaithfulness. Intent on mischief as usual, Morgan le Fay sent to court a drinking horn from which only a faithful wife could drink without spilling. Of the one hundred ladies who are forced to drink from the horn, only four pass the test (*ibid.*, I, 286–87). While Malory was sympathetic to the exposed lovers, "The Boy and the Mantle," a ballad on the same theme, flatly condemned the unfaithful wives. (*English and Scottish Popular Ballads*, ed. H. C. Sargent and G. L. Kittredge [Boston: Houghton Mifflin, 1904].)

one drop of blood would run down." Then she left him, locking the door. By the time he realized what had happened, he was too weak to get out of the window and could only blow three weak blasts on his horn. Little John came running and begged for permission to burn down the whole nunnery, but Robin Hood forbade this, having never hurt a woman in all his life.[5]

The most startling illustration of the clerical misogyny that often lurked in the minds of romance writers emerges in *Gawain and the Green Knight* (fourteenth century). Gawain, who here appears as the ideal knight, has on the whole triumphantly passed a series of tests of his courage and chastity; but, although his host and adversary congratulates him on his success, Gawain is remorseful for having dishonorably concealed the gift of a life-saving girdle from his host's wife. (Under her husband's directions, she has three successive days tempted Gawain to sexual intimacy.) So he declines an invitation to stay longer, sends his compliments to the lady, and then, without a word of warning, bursts into the following misogynistic invective:

> But no marvel it is for a fool to act madly,
> Through woman's wiles to be brought to woe.
> So for certain was Adam deceived by some woman,
> By several Solomon, Samson besides;
> Delilah dealt him his doom; and David
> Was duped by Bath-sheba, enduring much sorrow.
> Since these were grieved by their guile, 'twould be great gain
> To love them yet never believe them, if knights could.
> For formerly these [Adam, etc.] were most noble and fortunate,
> More than all others who lived on the earth.[6]

Not only does the chivalrous Gawain blame the lady unjustifiably, since she was only executing her husband's plan to prove his virtue; but he supports his attack with the stock medieval examples of men ruined by women.

That ambivalence was inherent in the courtly love tradition is clearly shown by Andreas Capellanus' classic handbook, *The Art of Courtly Love* (late twelfth century), where elaborate instructions

[5] "Robin Hood's Death," *English and Scottish Popular Ballads*, pp. 288–89. Cf. "A Gest of Robin Hood," *ibid.*

[6] *Gawain and the Green Knight*, trans. T. H. Banks, in *The Age of Chaucer*, ed. William Frost (Englewood Cliffs, N.J.: Prentice-Hall, 1950), p. 317.

on the conduct of a courtly love affair are followed by a section on
"The Rejection of Love," which is an extravagant diatribe against
women. Just as the structure of Andreas' work derives unmistakably
from Ovid's *Art* and *Remedies of Love*, his representation of women
as greedy, shallow, and foolish is a heavy-handed version of Ovid's.[7]

Much more pleasantly, John Lydgate used the same combination
of Ovidian satire on women and courtly love background in *Reason
and Sensuality*, his expanded adaptation of the romantic allegory
Les Échecs amoureux. Describing the lovers' chess game at the end,
he commented ironically on the nature of woman: although the
girl's first pawn, signifying Youth, bears a crescent moon on his
shield, this by no means suggests that women are inconstant; their
hearts never change. Her third pawn, Simplicity, has a lamb on his
shield, showing that women are exactly as meek as lambs. He went
on to hit in the same way at women's unbridled passions, inability
to keep secrets, weakness for flattery, greed, extravagant dress,
pride, duplicity, and shrewishness.[8]

2

Often poets relieved the strain of writing courtly love lyrics by
writing poems mocking women. The Bannatyne Manuscript (compiled in 1568 but medieval in spirit) divides its love poems into
four groups: love songs; songs in contempt of love and evil women;
songs in contempt of false, vicious men; and songs "detesting of
love and lechery."[9] Antiwoman poems became as formalized as love

[7] Although *The Art of Courtly Love* was written by a Frenchman in Latin, I
include it here because it shows so clearly the ambivalence which was latent or
less obvious in English works in the courtly love tradition.

[8] John Lydgate, *Reson and Sensuallyte*, ed. E. Sieper (London: Early English Text Society [Ex. Ser. LXXXIV], 1901), pp. 161ff. *The Romance of the
Rose* also combines satire on women's artifice, folly, and greed with a framework of courtly love, although in this case the two elements were contributed
by different authors. It is still significant that the cynical misogynist Jean de
Meun chose to express his ideas in a continuation of a romantic allegory and
that he generally followed the framework of the original.

[9] *The Bannatyne MS*. The misogynistic poems in this collection include,
among many others, "Ane ballat of the creatioun of the warld man his fall and
redemption" (II, 31), "Tho^t all þe wod under the hevin þat growis" (IV, 23),
"Devyce proves and eik humilitie" (IV, 34–35), "Aganis mariage of evill wyvis"
(IV, 36–37), three "ballads of impossibilities compared to the truth of women
in love" (IV, 40–45).

poems and like them frequently expressed virtuosity rather than genuine feeling or serious opinion. Apparently fervent misogynistic attacks occur in the works of Chaucer, Lydgate, William Dunbar, and most of the lesser writers; but there are also poems praising love and women with equal fervor. Often the poems actually took the form of debates on the worth of women: is it a good thing that she was taken out of Adam's side or is it not? In "The Clerk and the Nightingale," the nightingale, supporting the negative position, compares woman to a delicious-looking apple rotten at the core. When the clerk asks him how to recognize a true and good woman, he answers that every true woman wears a robe of gray marble stone: that is, is dead. Every good woman can do miracles: she can reach the sky with her foot and cover all England with the skirt of her tunic. At this point the clerk tells the nightingale he had better fly away fast. Off he goes, with the parting shot: love whatever woman you like, and she will laugh you to scorn.[10]

Another popular device typically used against women was the undercutting refrain. One clever popular song, taken from a minstrel collection, begins:

> In every place ye may well see,
> That women be true as turtle [turtledove] on tree,
> Not liberal [licentious] in language, but ever in secree [secret],
> And great joy among them is for to be.
> Cuius contrarium verum est. [Of which the contrary is true.]

> The steadfastness of women will never be done,
> So gentle, so courteous they be every one,
> Meek as a lamb, still as a stone,
> Crooked nor crabbed find ye none!
> Cuius contrarium verum est.

The poem goes on to praise women's steadfast keeping of secrets, love of peace, submissiveness to their husbands, sobriety, and thrift —*Cuius contrarium verum est.*

A *jeu d'esprit* in the Maitland Folio is feminist if read according to line division, antifeminist if read according to punctuation:

[10] "The Clerk and the Nightingale, II," *Secular Lyrics of the XIVth and XVth Centuries*, ed. R. H. Robbins (Oxford: Clarendon Press, 1952), pp. 176–79.

All women are good, noble and excellent
Who can say that x they do offend
Daily x they serve their God with good intent
Seldom x they displease their husbands to their lives' end
Always x to please them they do intend
Never x man can find in them bruikilnes [instability].[11]

Sometimes it is not so easy to distinguish between literary jokes like these and expressions of real hostility. One poem advising lovers to "Look well about," while very rhetorical, is heavier-handed and more sober in tone than the preceding examples. The poet warns men not to be blindly enamored with appearances; remember that even Samson and Solomon were deceived by women, and "Beware, therefore: the blind eat many a fly." Be sure not to trust women too much: although they can paint the fairest outward appearance, "Their steadfastness endureth but a season; / For they feign friendliness and work treason." Whoever trusts them will get the reward he deserves, "for women can shave nearer than razors or shears." They have three natural gifts — deceitfulness, spinning, and the capacity to weep at will, even when all is cheerful. The poet concludes with a favorite medieval figure:

> In sooth to say, though all the earth so wan
>   Were parchment smooth, white, and scribable,
> And the great sea that called is the ocean
>   Were turned into ink, blacker than sable,
>   Every stick a pen, each man a scrivener able,
>   Not could they then write woman's treachery;
>   Beware, therefore: the blind eat many a fly.[12]

A popular song of the late fifteenth century not only makes the same warning but advises a sadistic retaliation. Let your mistress be fair and white as whalebone and tell you she is constant as stone;

[11] "Abuse of Women," *ibid.*, pp. 35–36. *The Maitland Folio MS*, ed. W. A. Craigie (Edinburgh: Scottish Text Society [New. Ser., 7], 1919), p. 433. A similar trick poem appeared in *Harper's Magazine* in 1855: feminist if the lines of its quatrains are read consecutively, antifeminist if read 1-3-2-4, etc. It is quoted in William Wasserstrom's *Heiress of All the Ages* (Minneapolis: University of Minnesota Press, 1959), p. 12. Cf. "When to Trust Women," a poem from the same collection as "Abuse of Women," which uses the popular "When nettles in winter bear roses red" figure to prove that you should never put your trust and confidence in a woman (*Secular Lyrics*, p. 103).

[12] "Scorn of Women," *Secular Lyrics*, pp. 224–25.

you still must not trust her. I have tried them one by one, and my best advice is "Pluck off her bells, and let her fly." (That is, let her go, like an errant hawk; but there is probably also an obscene double meaning.) If you are poor, she will complain that other women dress better than she; and then she will play you false unless you let her fly first. If you are rich, she still will not be satisfied with her share; and again you had better let her fly. Women betray with their kisses just like Judas; all you can do is outgo them in inconstancy. Beat her black and blue and before too long send her on her way. Watch carefully to see when her fancy begins to wander; then act cordially until you are ready to let her fly.[13]

The author of this poem would no doubt have justified the excessive cynicism of his advice to mistreat women by claiming that he wrote of bad women only. The weakness of this recurrent excuse is that such authors frequently draw so blurry a line between bad women and all women that the reader can hardly be expected to see it. For example, "Against Evil Women," supposedly a warning against whores, is clearly directed against the sex in general. As so often when men become bitter against women, the author — perhaps William Dunbar — emphasizes and re-emphasizes their lust, beginning:

> The beastly lust, the furious appetite,
> The hasty woe, the very great defame,
> The blind descretioun [power of discernment] and the foul delight
> Of womankind that dreads for no shame
> Setting at nought God nor man's blame
> Their lusts have them nourished so but dread [without doubt]
> That all their trust is in their God Cupid.

Just as a pedigreed bitch in heat takes a mongrel to assuage her lust, a lady, no matter how many proper suitors she may have, will suddenly give herself to some crooked cripple — such is woman's beastly lust and appetite. Wise old clerks have written to warn us against women's malice and wiles, to show us what injuries they have done by their deceitful eloquence: Solomon's wisdom, Aristotle's

---

[13] *Reliquiae Antiquae: Scraps from Ancient Manuscripts*, ed. Thomas Wright and J. O. Halliwell (London: W. Pickering, 1841–43), I, 28–29. Cf. "Turne up hur halter and let hur go," a popular song of the same period which expresses essentially the same attitude, I, 76–77.

learning, Samson's strength, and Hector's prowess helped them not at all against women's subtle tricks and their deceitful tales (tails).[14]

3

Although these misogynistic poems were primarily expressions of the seamy side of the courtly love tradition, they often expressed clerical antifeminism as well. The medieval clergy were, as Chaucer's Wife of Bath and others noted, a traditionally misogynistic class. Being celibate, they emphasized the dangers of female seduction and the trials of marriage. Although exhortations to avoid women were not apt to be quite so violent in the Middle Ages as in early Christian times, the Church officially maintained the position that virginity is preferable to marriage and that women are inferior to men.

St. Thomas Aquinas refuted the error of "holding virginity not to be preferable to marriage" by Biblical examples (Christ and St. Paul) and by reason, which shows us that virginity, "directed to the good of the soul," is superior to marriage, "directed to the good of the body" (procreation). He went on to say that "Venereal pleasures above all debauch a man's mind," twice quoting St. Augustine's statement "that nothing so casts down the manly mind from its height as the fondling of a woman." To love a woman too ardently, even if she is one's own wife, is adultery.[15] Chaucer's Parson, whose tale is a convenient assemblage of conventional fourteenth-century moral ideas, likewise condemned married "adulterers" who have intercourse only for fleshly delight, thus giving themselves "to all ordure." Ideally, sexual intercourse between married people was not a mortal sin, only a venial one.[16] In other words, sexual rela-

---

[14] "Against Evil Women," *Maitland Folio,* pp. 391–92. Cf. "The Remedy of Love," a poem wrongly attributed to Chaucer, found in *Works of the English Poets from Chaucer to Cowper,* ed. A. Chalmers (London: J. Johnson *et al.,* 1810), I, 539–40.

[15] St. Thomas Aquinas, *The Summa Theologica,* trans. by the Fathers of the English Dominican Province (London: Burns Oates & Washbourne, 1920–29), Part II, Second Part, Qu. 152, Art. 4; Qu. 153, Art. 1, 2; Qu. 154, Art. 8.

[16] Chaucer, *Poetical Works,* pp. 306–7. Cf. Richard Rolle, *The Fire of Love,* trans. Richard Misyn, ed. R. Harvey (London: Early English Text Society [Orig. Ser., 106], 1896), p. 53, and *Hali Meidenhad,* ed. F. J. Furnivall (London: Early English Text Society [18], 1922), pp. 12, 28.

tionships were considered sinful under any circumstances; and full acceptance of woman as a physical being became a mortal sin. Thus medieval theory remained uncompromisingly ascetic, although, as popular literature shows, practice had become more human and natural.

The Church's official attitude to women is best illustrated by St. Thomas Aquinas' discussion of the creation of woman in *Summa Theologica*, in which he felt compelled to begin by justifying her existence. Perhaps she should not have been created at all, since according to Aristotle she "is a misbegotten male," and "nothing misbegotten or defective should have been in the first production of things." Again, since there was no subjection before sin, how could woman, a natural subject because as the passive sexual partner she had "less strength and dignity than man," have existed before sin? Thirdly, "occasions of sin should be cut off," and "God foresaw that woman would be an occasion of sin to man." It is reassuring to see that St. Thomas found good answers to all three objections. First, woman had to be made as a helper to man — "not, indeed, as a helpmate in other works . . . since man can be more efficiently helped by another man in other works; but as a helper in the work of generation." She is necessary there in order to free the male for a higher aim than generation, namely, "intellectual operation." Although females are defective and misbegotten when considered from the individual point of view, they are (as Aristotle explained) essential and desirable as part of the human species. Secondly, while servile subjection of women and others came as a result of sin, civil subjection was necessary from the beginning to maintain "the good of order"; by this subjection woman is and always was "naturally subject to man, because in man the discernment of reason predominates." Thirdly, without "those things which proved an occasion of sin, the universe would have been imperfect."

St. Thomas had to overcome a serious stumbling block in adapting Aristotle's biology to Christian theology: Aristotle had said that the father provides a child's soul while the mother supplies only formless matter. As Christians believe that the soul comes from God, the superior father is left making no contribution at all. St. Thomas' solution is ingenious: while the soul comes from God, the father supplies the formative power without which the female matter could not receive it. For this reason a child should love his father more than his mother, since the father is principle of his natural origin "in a more excellent way than the mother, because he is the active principle, while the mother is a passive and material principle."[17]

The belief that woman is morally weaker than man and was created only to fulfill her sexual function, together with sexual guilt resulting from the asceticism of the Church, naturally led to a strong emphasis in medieval religious manuals and sermons on woman's dangerous seductive propensities. Medieval clerics, like the patristic writers, often supplemented their warnings by inconsistently declaring that the female body is really not attractive at all. The author of the early thirteenth-century *Ancren Riwle* (*Rule for Anchoresses*), writing in a gentle paternal tone to three young anchoresses of whom he was evidently fond, compares a woman who lets herself be seen by men to a person who uncovers a pit for people to fall into. "The pit is her fair face, and her white neck, and her light eye, and her hand, if she stretch it forth in his sight . . . all that belongs to her, whatsoever it be, through which sinful love might the sooner be excited." If a woman does anything, even unawares, by which a man is tempted, if she only arouses his desire or occasions a sin with another woman, she will be held responsible for his lost soul on the day of judgment. Yet if the body is rightly considered, it is hardly enticing:

There cometh out of a vessel such things as it contains. What cometh out of the vessel of thy flesh? Doth the smell of spices or of sweet balsam come thereof? . . . Man, what fruit doth thy flesh bear in all its apertures? Amidst the greatest ornament of thy face; that is, the fairest part between the taste of mouth and smell of nose, hast thou not two holes, as if they were two privy holes? Art thou not formed of foul slime? Art thou not always full of uncleanness? Shalt thou not be food for worms?[18]

---

[17] St. Thomas Aquinas, *The Basic Writings*, ed. Anton C. Pegis (New York: Random House, 1945), I, 879–81. *Summa Theologica*, Part II, Second Part, Qu. 26, Art. 10. St. Thomas consistently assumed that a woman is her husband's property; e.g., he said that the male adulterer is worse than the fornicator because he commits injustice as well as unchastity "in so far as he usurps another's property" (*Basic Writings*, II, 594).

[18] *The Ancren Riwle*, ed. and trans. James Morton (London: Camden Society [LVII], 1853), pp. 59, 277.

The great fourteenth-century mystic Richard Rolle, like the author of *The Ancren Riwle*, was neither harsh nor misogynistic by temperament, but was equally apprehensive of woman as a sexual being. Although he said that virtuous Platonic friendship between men and women was not only lawful but praiseworthy (especially, it is true, because women's natural frailty makes them need the guidance of good men), he felt that a truly good woman would conceal herself from men so as to avoid the responsibility of tempting them. He told how a woman spent her life enclosed in a tomb, taking her food through a small hole to avoid seeing or being seen by anyone. After many years someone asked her why, and she answered that once a young man's soul had been hurt by looking at her beauty, and since then she has hid herself; she had rather stay in the tomb as long as she lives than that any soul made in the likeness of God should perish because of her. Rolle eulogized, "Lo, so perfectly a woman lived."

Rolle's zeal to turn men from love of women to the higher love of God led him to declare that nothing is more perilous, fouler, and more stinking in a man than to set his mind on woman's love. For when a woman feels that a man loves her immoderately, she beguiles him with blandishments and thus draws him on to whatever deeds are conceived in her wicked will. Remember how the wisest of men, Solomon, was led by immoderate love for women into unfaithfulness to God. Woman's love distracts the wit, perverts and overturns reason, changes wisdom to folly, withdraws the heart from God, and enthralls the soul to fiends. In conclusion, "Flee wisely women, and thy thoughts always from them keep far"; for even if a woman should be good, by the spurring of the fiend you may be overdelighted by her beauty. If you find this difficult, only think what the flesh is: ". . . dost thou not know that fleshly fairness is a covering of filth and the dregs of corruption, and often the cause of damnation?" [19] If a man had the eyes of a lynx, to see the insides as

[19] Rolle, *The Fire of Love*, p. 92; *Yorkshire Writers: Richard Rolle of Hampole . . . and His Followers*, ed. Carl Horstman (London: Swan Sonnenschein, 1895), I, 194; *Fire of Love*, pp. 53–54, 65–66; *The Amending of Life, Selected Works*, ed. and trans. G. C. Heseltine (London: Longmans, Green, 1930), p. 115. Cf. "The Beginning of Man's Life," a poem attributed to Rolle, which attempts to abate human pride by pointing out that before birth man dwells in a

well as the out, elaborated the author of *The Ayenbite of Inwyt* (*The Prick of Conscience, ca.* 1340) in a popular medieval expression, he would see that a fair body is no more than a white sack full of stinking dung, like a dunghill covered with snow.[20]

Robert of Brunne's *Handlyng Synne* (1303) is a conventional manual of moral instructions addressed not to hermits but to the general public of both sexes. Although Robert does not single out women for attack, his manual again illustrates the distrust of the female sex standard in medieval preachers. Whoever remains alone with a woman will soon fall to lechery, no matter how chaste or distant he may be. A man should not even look at women too much: the sight of them makes men's thoughts deceitful, and in such sight there is much guilt.[21] As another preacher put it, "If thou wilt be Christ's clean child, flee as Christ's coward the company of foolish [wanton] women, nor be none too familiar with any manner of women."[22]

Sometimes the preachers expressed their hostile fear of women's seductiveness in terms of a moral attack on their vanity, a perennial grievance. Typically they preached against overelaborate dress on the grounds that it wantonly endangered the souls of men. John Bromyard, a prominent fourteenth-century Dominican, provides an especially full analysis:

In the woman wantonly adorned to capture souls, the garland upon her head is as a single coal or firebrand of Hell to kindle men with that fire; so too the horns of another, so the bare neck, so the brooch upon the breast, so with all the curious finery of the whole of their body. What else does it seem or could be said of it save that each is a spark breathing out hell-fire,

---

corrupt dungeon, where he finds no other food "But loathsome slime and clotted blood / And stink and filth" (*Yorkshire Writers*, I, 372). While in general medieval people did not follow the extravagantly misogynistic ways of the Desert Fathers in the early centuries of Christianity, they continued to admire them. The last few chapters of *The Golden Legend*, an enormously influential collection of saints' lives, are devoted to hermits like St. Pastor, who refused to see his aged mother.

[20] Dan Michel's *Ayenbite of Inwyt, or Remorse of Conscience*, ed. Richard Morris (London: Early English Text Society [23], 1866), p. 81.

[21] Robert of Brunne, *Handlyng Synne*, ed. F. J. Furnivall (London: Early English Text Society [119, 123], 1901), pp. 240, 258.

[22] Quoted by Gerald R. Owst, *Literature and Pulpit in Medieval England* (Cambridge: Cambridge University Press, 1933), p. 384.

which this wretched incendiary of the Devil breathes so effectually . . . that, in a single day, by her dancing or her perambulation through the town, she inflames with the fire of lust — it may be — twenty of those who behold her, damning the souls whom God has created and redeemed at such a cost for their salvation. For this very purpose the Devil thus adorns these females, sending them forth through the town as his apostles, replete with every iniquity, malice, fornication.

Elsewhere he compares such women to the painted tombstone that conceals a rotting corpse.[23]

4

The baneful effects of woman's influence were reinforced by every possible example from the Bible, already familiar from the writings of the early Fathers. Eve's responsibility for her husband's fall is heavily underlined, for example, in three of the four major cycles of mystery plays. In the Chester play of "The Creation and Fall," the Devil is shown plotting to destroy Adam through Eve by appealing to her feminine lechery and eagerness to do whatever is forbidden. Once Adam has eaten the fruit, he curses Eve and exclaims:

> Yea, sooth said I in prophecy,
> When thou was taken of my body,
> Man's woe thou would be witterlye [certainly],
> Therefore thou was so named.

Eve accepts these reproaches without a word of protest. Adam goes on "movingly" to draw the moral:

> Now all my kind by me is kente [taught],
> To flee women's enticement;
> Who trusteth them in any intent,
> Truly he is deceived.
> My lecherous wife hath been my foe,
> The devil's envy hath shente [injured] me also:
> These two together well may go,
> The sister and the brother.[24]

23 Quoted *ibid.*, pp. 395–96.
24 *The Chester Plays*, ed. Thomas Wright (London: Shakespeare Society [17, 35], 1843), I, 29, 32. Cf. *York Plays*, ed. Lucy Toulmin Smith (Oxford: Clarendon Press, 1885), pp. 33–34, and *Ludus Coventriae*, ed. J. O. Halliwell (London: Shakespeare Society [4], 1841), pp. 31–32.

Even women who were the innocent occasions of men's sins were seducers in the eyes of medieval clergymen. The author of *The Ancren Riwle* shows that because Jacob's daughter, Dinah, walked out to see the country she was raped; and because she was raped, a great city was burned, its prince and people were slain, and her father and brothers, "high patriarchs," broke a truce and became outlaws. Then he moralizes: ". . . this evil . . . came of Dinah . . . not from her seeing Sichem . . . with whom she sinned [*sic!*], but . . . from her letting him set his eyes upon her." "Likewise Bathsheba," he goes on, "by unclothing herself in David's sight, caused him to sin with her, though he was so holy a king and God's prophet."[25]

While these references reveal definite hostility to women — an avid desire to find evidence against the sex — authors sometimes used the standard examples almost as a formula, simply to add the touch an occasion called for. The most usual form runs like this: "Who was stronger than Samson, wiser than Solomon, holier than David? And yet they were all overcome by the queyntise [finery] and wiles of women."[26] Lydgate's "Examples Against Women," while as exhaustive as the sermons of the most industrious preacher, appears to be a literary exercise rather than an arraignment. Of course, by his time — the fifteenth century — the examples had been worn very thin. To begin with, predictably, there is Eve, who "first began / Death to devise and poison to man." Then there are Solomon's wives, who seduced him into idolatry, and Rachel, who insubordinately stole her father's gods and deceived him. And look what happened to Holofernes, who made the mistake of loving and

---

[25] *Ancren Riwle*, pp. 55, 57. The most curious bad example is an apocryphal sister of Judas, invented presumably to provide the necessary feminine influence behind the most heinous of all betrayals. See a thirteenth-century poem, "The Bargain of Judas," in *English Lyrics of the XIIIth Century*, ed. C. Brown (Oxford: Clarendon Press, 1932), p. 38. Cf. the ancient Coptic *Gospel of the Twelve Apostles*, in which Judas is provided with a wife for the sole purpose of making a woman responsible for his treachery. The *Gospel* is found in *Patrologia Orientalis* (Paris: Firmin-Didot, 1907), Vol. II.

[26] Quoted in *Literature and Pulpit*, p. 385. Cf. *Ayenbite of Inwyt*, p. 204, and Chaucer's "The Parson's Tale," p. 309 (the same examples), John of Salisbury's *Statesman's Book*, p. 20 (David and Solomon), and *Middle English Sermons*, ed. W. O. Ross (London: Early English Text Society [Orig. Ser., 209], 1940), p. 235 (David and Holofernes), etc.

trusting Judith. And was it not piteous that when Job was at his most miserable, "His wife him rebuked and on a dunghill left him lie?" Delilah requited Samson's truth and love with duplicity and betrayal. Finally Lydgate draws the moral: these old examples ought to be enough to warn men, even if there were no new ones; but whoever refuses to learn from the example of others will be a horrible example himself when he has come to repentance.[27]

On the other hand, since medieval men were influenced by the cult of the Virgin and the theory of courtly love as well as by patristic and classical misogyny, they were as fond of finding examples for women as against them. While patristic writers dwelt morbidly on the sin of Eve, their medieval counterparts never tired of insisting that the sanctity of Mary more than made up for it. In a thirteenth-century poem, "The Thrush and the Nightingale," the thrush contends that women always deceive men, that they will all sell themselves for a little gold, that the experiences of Adam and Samson show women's effect on those who love them. The thrush is unimpressed by the nightingale's arguments that women are virtuous and sweet until he cites the example of the Virgin Mary; then the thrush has no alternative but to concede abjectly: he was crazy to enter the debate, he will never again say a word against women, and he will fly out of the country in disgrace.[28]

5

Despite the chivalrous devotion inspired by the Virgin, however, clerical feeling in the Middle Ages definitely inclined toward antifeminism. Early in the period the clergy amused themselves with variations of this sort of formula, written in Latin:

What is woman? Hurtful friendship; inescapable punishment; necessary evil; natural temptation; desirable calamity; domestic danger; delightful injury; born an evil, painted with good color; gate of the devil; road to iniquity. . . . From the beginning sin was taken from them.[29]

[27] John Lydgate, *The Minor Poems*, ed. H. N. MacCracken (London: Early English Text Society [Orig. Ser., 192], 1934), II, 443–45.

[28] "The Thrush and the Nightingale," *English Lyrics of the XIIIth Century*, pp. 101–7.

[29] *Reliquiae Antiquae*, I, 168.

Although such a string of epithets looks better in Latin than in English, it set the pattern for many vernacular poems. For example, there is this piece of abuse, which also illustrates the early English overfondness for alliteration:

> O wicked women, wilful, and variable,
>> Right false, fickle, fell [fierce], and frivolous,
> Dowgit [obstinate], dispytfull [malicious], dour, and dissavable,
>> Unkind [unnatural], cruel, curst, and covetous,
>> Overlight of laitis [manners], unleill [disloyal], and lecherous,
>>> Turned from truth, and taiclit with [entangled in] treachery,
>>> Unfirm of faith, filled with felony! [30]

This goes on for two more stanzas.

The most comprehensive medieval assaults on women were two attacks on the institution of marriage which proceed directly from the early Christian tradition. Although the authors were to some extent indulging in rhetoric for its own sake, they seem to have been convinced of the truth of what they wrote. John of Salisbury's eloquent description of "The Annoyance and Burdens of Wedlock" in *Policraticus* appears to be heartfelt. Although he concedes that matrimony does excuse lustful pleasure, which is otherwise vile, he goes on to say that "it is more fecund in worry than in joy," supporting this view with a lengthy quotation from Theophrastus and Socrates' supposed opinion that marriage is even more irksome than single loneliness. John supplies no evidence for his allegation of woman's frivolity, ungoverned passions, and cruelty; but for her lechery — "there is no female so modest that she will not be stirred with passion at the advances of a stranger" — he finds the excellent authority of the tragic writer Eumolpus, a fictitious character in Petronius' *Satyricon!* John then tells, essentially verbatim, Eumolpus' story of the Widow of Ephesus, adding to it with satisfaction that she "paid the penalty both of her impiety and of her traitorous crime." The clerical bias comes out clearly as he proceeds: since marriage, although it must be good because it was instituted by God, is vexatious, "who except one bereft of sense would approve sensual pleasure itself, which is illicit, wallows in filthiness, is something that men censure, and that God without doubt condemns?" Philosophers

[30] "Abuse of Women," *Secular Lyrics*, pp. 225–26.

and clerics who cannot keep from the embraces of women "seem hardly human."[31]

According to Richard de Bury in his *Philobiblon* (fourteenth century), clerks were taught by their books to flee a certain "biped beast," namely woman, "more than the asp and the basilisk." Women revile books, he went on, condemn them as superfluous, and wish to exchange them for expensive clothes. And well they might, if they consider the contents of such books as Ecclesiasticus, Theophrastus' treatise on marriage, and Valerius' letter.[32] Walter Map's "Letter from Valerius to Ruffinus," found in his *De Nugis Curialium* (*Courtiers' Trifles*, a satirical miscellany of about 1200), was the most famous medieval attack on marriage. It was, for example, an important source for Chaucer. Although Map's rhetorical artfulness seems to suggest a more literary purpose than John of Salisbury's, the two works are quite similar in substance and tone. Map tells how he found a formerly philosophical friend sad and unsociable, guessed that he must be in love, and, in the hope "that he would rise again after his fall," wrote him a letter of dissuasion. "Being ensnared by the beauty of a lovely person," he wrote:

thou knowest not, poor wretch, that what thou seekest is a chimera. But thou art doomed to know that this triform monster, although it is beautified with the face of a noble lion, yet is blemished with the belly of a reeking kid and is beweaponed with the virulent tail of a viper.

You should imitate the virtue of Ulysses shunning Circe and the sirens and be warned by the example of Adam: "Disobedience . . . until the end of the world will never cease from assailing women and rendering them ever unwearied in carrying to the fell consequences their chief inheritance from their mother. O friend, a man's highest reproach is a disobedient wife. Beware!"

Love even for a good woman — and good women are rarer than the phoenix — is invariably accompanied by worry and unhappiness; and bad women "punish bitterly the bestowal of love, and devote themselves utterly to dealing distress." Therefore, "fear all the sex." Jupiter became a bull for Europa: ". . . lo, him whom

[31] John of Salisbury, *Frivolities*, pp. 355, 358, 360, 363.
[32] Richard de Bury, *The Philobiblon* (New York: P. C. Duschnes, 1945), pp. 23–24.

worth lifted above the heavens, a woman hath lowered to the level
of brutes! A woman will have the power to compel thee to bellow
unless thou art greater than Jupiter." It is better to have a succession of amours than to marry, since "many maladies interrupted
by the alternation of health are less painful than one illness which
affecteth us with incurable pangs." The advice, which comes from
Lucretius and is obviously more appropriate to a pagan philosopher
than a Christian archdeacon, reveals the typical medieval cleric's
low conception of *all* relationships with women. Among other classical anecdotes, Map told one especially popular in the Middle
Ages: a man named Pacuvius, bursting into tears, told his neighbor
Arrius, "I have in my garden a barren tree on which my first wife
hanged herself, and then my second, and just now my third." Arrius
answered, "I marvel that thou hast found cause for tears in such a
run of good luck," and again, "Great heavens, what heavy costs to
thee hang from that tree!" And thirdly: "My friend, give me of that
tree some branches to plant."

After asserting, not very convincingly, that no one curses women
except from painful experience, Map worked up to a crescendo.
Livia intentionally poisoned her husband, Drusus, for hate; Lucilia,
the fictitious wife of Lucretius, accidentally poisoned hers with a
love potion: though they strove "with opposite intent," neither was
"cheated of the goal of women's wiles, that is, her own natural
evil." Women are adept at hurting, which is their general disposition; but when they wish to help, they harm instead. Map concluded,
apparently with deep seriousness, "My friend, may the omnipotent
God grant thee power not to be deceived by the deceit of the omnipotent female, and may He illuminate thy heart, that thou wilt not,
with eyes bespelled, continue on the way I fear. But, that I may not
seem to thee the author of *Orestes* [Euripides], farewell!"[33]

This letter is the quintessence of medieval misogyny — displaying as it does ingenuity at finding evidence against women, the
patriarchal view that a woman's disobedience to her husband is the
greatest possible reproach both to her and him, the assumption that

[33] Walter Map, *De Nugis Curialium*, trans. F. Tupper and M. B. Ogle (London: Chatto and Windus, 1924), pp. 182–87, 190–93, 196–97. Cf. the venomous
poem "Golias de Conjuge Non Ducenda," probably by Map; it was translated
by Lydgate as "The Pain and Sorrow of Evil Marriage."

all relationships with women are degrading, and a dread of female influence, aggravated by the fear that woman is omnipotent as well as inevitably vicious. While it expresses only one trend of a period which also indulged in courtly love and adoration of the Virgin, it is a typical expression of ecclesiastical opinion. Walter Map was a prominent clergyman, and his work was widely read and quoted. The conception of woman as the ruin of man remained lively among all classes during the Middle Ages, in part because the Church officially condemned sex and depreciated marriage. In theory the Middle Ages accepted the misogynistic views of the early Christian Fathers on woman's dangerous seductiveness and the consequent necessity of keeping her in subjection.

But tirades like the "Letter from Valerius" also owed something to the medieval love of extreme statements for and against, and of accumulating large collections of authorities to support a position. Misogyny was a popular theme for rhetorical exercises, much as courtly love was, partly because of the ambivalence inherent in courtly love as in any system which greatly overidealizes women. Medieval writers' reliance on authority and example meant that the arguments of Theophrastus and Ovid, the examples of Eve and Xanthippe, were passed from work to work to work. When the writers wished to make use of contemporary life instead of traditional views, as they increasingly did in the later Middle Ages, they generally concentrated on one female villain: the insubordinate wife.

The medieval valuation of love was both higher and lower than the classical one — elevated by the cult of courtly love, lowered and embittered by the passionate asceticism of many churchmen. The negative medieval view of love was inconsistent, furthermore, because derived from two disparate sources: the Church's official doctrine that sexuality was always sinful, and the Roman writers' presentation of erotic love as a rapturous and indispensable part of life, frequently painful but not to be avoided on grounds of sinfulness. The only point on which the two views agreed was that erotic love was always or frequently degrading — and this attitude was countered by the theory of courtly love, which held that love was the force that improved man's character and elevated his spirit even to Heaven. Nevertheless, medieval writers, steeped in Roman erotic literature, wrote poem after poem to demonstrate woman's faithlessness, rapacity, and indiscriminate lust. And ascetic church-men, some at least moved by genuine conviction more than conven-tion, continued through the Middle Ages to warn men to avoid women, to denigrate all sexual relationships, and to harp upon the ruinous influence of Eve and her daughters.

6. The Wife of Bath versus Patient Grisilde

The medieval wife, despite her theoretical subjection, achieved considerable *de facto* equality in everyday life. It is true that the Church instructed her to obey her husband in everything and never ceased to remind her of the sinful nature she had inherited from Eve, that her marriage was usually made without regard to her (or her bridegroom's) wishes, that her husband was entitled to beat her, and that socially and economically she was completely under his power. Indeed, wives were virtually devoid of legal rights until the later nineteenth century; until the Married Woman's Property Act of 1857, for example, the husband owned all of his wife's prop-erty, including anything she might have, be given, or earn. Never-theless, the medieval wife seems in general to have shared her hus-band's life and enjoyed his affection and respect. Medieval men did not usually relegate their wives to the position of household drudges and seek all pleasure from prostitutes, attacking both types with equal enthusiasm.

Satire on wives is for the most part good-natured and humorous; in some cases, such as Chaucer's Dame Alice of Bath, the bad wife even becomes a likable figure. The most important motive for the medieval attacks seems to have been the impulse to rebel against marriage, which is almost inherent in the institution: since two people can rarely live together in eternal harmony, it is natural that men will complain of various faults in the women with whom they must spend their lives and wistfully envision a happier state with a continuously endearing spouse or perhaps with no restrictions at all. (If women had written books, as the Wife of Bath points out, the accusations would be directed the other way.) Nevertheless, the attacks do seem to be unusually numerous in this period, the bad wife appearing as typical; and patriarchal influence is notice-able in the main charge against wives — insubordination — and in the ideal of the perfect wife — Patient Grisilde.

The story of Grisilde, which carries patriarchal wish-fulfillment to its furthest possible extreme, was beloved by the Middle Ages — admired by Petrarch, told by Boccaccio[34] and by Chaucer's Clerk (a member, it is true, of a traditionally misogynistic class). Not only is the saintly heroine subject, but the slavishness of her subjection is underlined at every point. A nobleman, having reluctantly agreed to marry, takes one of his serfs, Grisilde, as his wife. His reason for choosing a serf is made apparent in his proposal: he will marry her if she will cheerfully comply with his every wish, never showing the slightest dissatisfaction. She agrees and becomes a model wife, not only in pleasing him but in fulfilling all the functions of a great lady. But when she bears a daughter, her husband decides to test her submissiveness by telling her that he must have the child killed. Without a single sign of grief or protest, Grisilde answers that nothing he wills could displease her and that she has no attachment to anything but himself. He will not gratify her by revealing his pleasure in this answer, but merely sends an officer to take the infant away; Grisilde does not so much as sigh, although she does beg the man to bury the little body, unless her lord objects. When her next child, a son, reaches the age of two, he takes that one away from her too. She responds as she had before, and as the years go by:

> She showed well, for no worldly unrest
> A wife, as of herself, nothing ne should
> Will in effect [fact], but [except] as her husband would.

Finally he tells her that she must go, since he is marrying a new wife. Of course, she returns cheerfully to her father's hut, only to be recalled to prepare the house for her husband's bride. At last he reveals that this bride is really her daughter, that her son is also alive, and that she remains and always will be his wife; he has only been testing her womanhood. She humbly thanks him for sparing her children and says she would be willing to die on the spot now that she knows she has his love and favor; and they all live happily

---

[34] Petrarch did not care for *The Decameron*, which Boccaccio, his friend, sent him; but he was so taken with the story of Grisilde, which Boccaccio placed last in the collection in order to end on an exalted note, that he translated it into Latin in order to give it the immortality he felt it deserved.

ever after. Apart from the explicit emphasis on wifely subjection in this tale, it seems significant that Grisilde willingly sacrifices her maternal ties, the ones most important to a woman, to her duty to men: wholehearted devotion to a father is followed by wholehearted devotion to a husband. And not only does patriarchy triumph in the story, but insistence on female submission is surely carried to the point of sadism.

Although modern Chaucerian critics tend to read this tale exclusively as an allegory of the Christian's proper patience under trials imposed by God, I cannot accept their view that the substance of the narrative should be ignored. On one level — and this is the level relevant to my discussion — the tale is certainly about the relationship between a husband and a wife. There is no evidence that medieval readers saw any incongruity in the presentation of the relationship — Grisilde's wifely behavior is held up for admiration, and Walter's acts, however harsh, were apparently within his rights. Of course, the Church preached that all men should submit to the will of God, but it also preached to wives that they should submit cheerfully and unquestioningly to the will of their husbands. Furthermore, the Clerk's lament that "Grisilde is dead, and eek [also] her patience," while lighter in tone than his exhortation to fortitude under affliction from God (lines 1142–62), seems to express genuine regret that women nowadays are incapable of living up to the ideal represented by Grisilde. His delightful ironic song in praise of modern archwives, who disdain humility, fight their husbands on every occasion, and bring them to heel through "crabbed eloquence" or jealousy, drives home the point: Grisilde provided the ideal for contrast with the deplorable behavior of a woman like the Wife of Bath.[35]

[35] Chaucer, *Poetical Works*, pp. 131, 137–38. Cf. the saintly Constance's exclamation as she goes off to an unwanted marriage in a heathen country: "Women are born to thraldom and penance, / And to been [be] under man's governance" (*ibid.*, p. 78). The ballad of "Child Waters" tells a story of female abjectness rewarded, much like that of Grisilde. D. W. Robertson, Jr., in *A Preface to Chaucer* (Princeton, N.J.: Princeton University Press, 1963), has most recently and eloquently presented the view that "The Clerk's Tale" is to be read as an allegory, not as a conventional narrative; indeed, he sees the entire "marriage group" of *The Canterbury Tales* as dealing with the relationship between the soul and God, not with marriage at all (pp. 272, 274–75,

The Clerk was by no means alone in his regrets for dead Grisilde, which were shared by the Host and the Merchant in *The Canterbury Tales*, as well as many of Chaucer's followers. The reality that brazenly defied their ideal is represented by Chaucer's Wife of Bath, incomparably the best of numerous presentations of the traditional bad wife, many of which show how the old material could be vitalized by fresh observation and clever variations in technique. The Wife of Bath has not only had five husbands — "Thanked be God" — but she has mastered them all; that is, she combines the insatiable lust that the Church reprehended in her sex with the insubordination that was even more frequently condemned. She is also an extravagant dresser, a drinker, a gossip, and a babbler of secrets, especially her husband's. Her first three husbands, who were good, and rich, and old, were easy conquests. Having gained their love and, more important, their property, she no longer bothered to be nice to them; in fact, they were happy to bring her pretty things from the fair in order to get pleasant words from her for a change. When straight-

---

376–77). As I stated in the text, this position seems to me too extreme. The fact that Petrarch and Chaucer read an allegorical moral into the tale (a favorite medieval habit) does not invalidate the obvious moral which emerges from the narrative as a whole. Both morals are intended, though only the teaching on wifely submission is relevant to this discussion. I might add that Robertson himself once uses the narrative matter of "The Clerk's Tale" as evidence of medieval attitudes (p. 82).

Other possible objections to my interpretation of "The Clerk's Tale" are that (1) Chaucer in no way endorses the attitude toward wifely subjection presented in this tale, which represents not his views but those of an ascetic clerk who would be expected to be hostile to women, and (2) the tale is meant to be a fantastic elaboration on the virtue of patience, not in any way a recommendation for behavior in the real world. For statements of these opinions, see G. L. Kittredge, "Chaucer's Discussion of Marriage," and James Sledd, "The *Clerk's Tale*: The Monsters and the Critics," *Chaucer Criticism: The Canterbury Tales*, ed. R. J. Schoeck and J. Taylor (Notre Dame, Ind.: University of Notre Dame Press, 1960), pp. 130–33, 141–42, 168–69. I believe that first, although Chaucer purposely gave this eulogy of wifely subjection to a pious clerk who would be particularly offended by the Wife of Bath's unorthodox arguments and unabashed insubordination, this is not meant to undercut the tale: the Clerk is presented as an admirable figure, the ideas of the tale are generally consistent with medieval moral views, and when Chaucer did intend to show that the character of the teller distorted the tale he made it very obvious, as in "The Merchant's Tale." Secondly, there is no reason to suppose that the tale exists in a social and moral vacuum: like most ideals, Grisilde is an extension of reality.

forward chiding was not effective enough, she would make up a long tale of the dreadful things they had said about women when drunk (an incidental opportunity to recite the usual charges against the sex), after which tirade the poor men were happy to make peace, overlooking any of her little failings. Although she was reluctant enough to pay her bodily debt to her husbands, indeed paying it only when rewarded with a handsome present, she conscientiously paid them back for every harsh word they said to her. Her fourth husband was a rake — but only at first. She soon fixed him — not by cuckolding him (interestingly, she never is actually unfaithful to her husbands), but by making him seethe with jealousy. She hopes he is now in heaven, having been put through his purgatory on earth.

Initially, the fifth husband, Jankyn, seemed too much even for the Wife of Bath to tame. She had started courting him one Lent while her husband was in London and she was improving her time by seeking new friends — diligently attending sermons and pilgrimages in her gay scarlet gown. When her fourth husband died, she wept for him — "As wives mooten [must], for it is usage"[36] — but not very much, being provided with a replacement. Following the bier she noticed the beautiful shape of Jankyn's legs, and at that point gave him her heart altogether. Inconveniently, she remained in love with him (mostly from female perversity, since he had been stand-offish with her), so she could not deny him his bodily debt even after he had beaten her black and blue. Furthermore, he set up as a spouse-tamer himself, lecturing her from a book of misogyny called "Valerius and Theophrastus"; her summary of its contents provides yet another run-through of misogynistic charges. One night, when she thought he would never stop reading, she ripped three leaves out of his book and shoved him into the fire. He hit her back, very hard; and at last she found the opportunity to tame him. Pretending to be dying, she said she loved him anyway; and he was so remorseful he promised never to hit her again. After this and a few more storms, he agreed to let her rule house and land, his tongue and himself; and he burned his book.

Having developed the Wife's shameless defiance of orthodox

---

[36] Chaucer, *Poetical Works*, pp. 91, 98, 138.

views of her proper position and behavior, Chaucer raises an interesting possibility at the end of her prologue: after getting the mastery, she was kind and true to her husband all his life. Thus he seems to suggest that a marriage might succeed even if the wife, the "body" in St. Paul's metaphor, ruled the husband, her "head." "The Wife of Bath's Tale" makes the same point. A young knight who must find out on pain of death what women most desire discovers that it is "sovereynetee," supremacy. The hag who supplies this information forces him to marry her, naturally much against his will; but when he agrees to yield to her in everything, she becomes young and beautiful and promises to be a good and true wife, and they have a happy marriage. In the course of the tale, Chaucer lists all the things that women particularly value — riches, prestige, fun, expensive clothes, sexual pleasure, repeated marriages, and flattery, especially if undeserved. Love and virtue and anything that women ought to desire are conspicuously absent. Thus he gets in a third battery of misogynistic charges in the Wife of Bath's Prologue and Tale, apart from her own character and career.

Even though she is a composite of all the qualities a woman was not supposed to have, and Chaucer drew much of his material from earlier misogynistic sources, the Wife of Bath is not only a fresh but an engaging character. Her cheerfulness, vitality, and frankness make her attractive. She defends her behavior very shrewdly indeed, turning to her purpose texts even from misogynistic St. Paul. For example, she makes good use of St. Paul's grudging admission that wives and husbands owe each other a bodily debt, that is, have the use of each other's bodies to avoid fornication; his warning that married people "shall have trouble in the flesh"; and his exhortation to husbands to love their wives (naturally, she ignores completely his more emphatic command to wives to obey their husbands):

> A husband I will have, I will not lette [conceal],
> Which shall be both my debtor and my thrall,
> And have his tribulation withal
> Upon his flesh, while that I am his wife.
> I have the power during all my life
> Upon his proper [own] body, and not he.
> Right thus the Apostle told it unto me;

> And bade our husbands for to love us well
> All this sentence me liketh every deel. [This whole opinion
> pleases me every bit.][37]

Chaucer makes her defense so plausible at times that he seems to be raising questions about orthodox views on marriage: was the Church too contemptuous of those who followed God's commandment to increase and multiply? Could a marriage possibly succeed if the husband yielded sovereignty to the wife? (Perhaps Chaucer's own opinion is most closely approximated in "The Franklin's Tale," told after the Wife of Bath has made a case for the husband's subjection and the Clerk for the wife's. In this story of an ideal marriage, each partner yields in all things to the other, although the husband keeps nominal sovereignty in deference to social convention.) Further, the Wife of Bath is not only an object but a penetrating critic of misogyny, pointing out that "clerks" (clergymen and scholars) habitually speak ill of women, often because they are too old to appreciate them, and that we hear so much of women's sins because it is men who write the books.[38] Chaucer was probably making fun of misogynists as much as of women in this character and her tale.

Although there is no real bitterness against women in Chaucer's works, only the sort of gay burlesque he directs against the Wife of Bath, he made extensive use of misogynistic charges. The Merchant, who is miserably married — his shrewish wife would outmatch the Devil himself — tells a bitter tale of a wife's deception of her old husband, starting with a savagely ironic encomium on wives and the joys of marriage. (The condemnation of women is mitigated, however, by the repulsive selfishness of the cuckolded husband.) The Host comments that although his wife is not deceitful, as most women are, she is such a shrew that he sorely rues being tied to her. The Nun's Priest indulges in some sly thrusts at women, partly because of his clerical outlook, but also no doubt because, working for the Prioress, he is professionally subordinate to women. His hero Chauntecleer, soothing Pertelote after an argu-

---

[37] *Ibid.*, p. 93. She is perverting texts which recur in St. Paul, such as I Cor. 7:4, 28; Eph. 5:25, 28.

[38] *Ibid.*, p. 99.

ment, quotes sweetly to her, "Mulier est hominis confusio," which he misleadingly translates, "Woman is man's joy and all his bliss." Then, after Chauntecleer has followed his wife's advice and thereby exposed himself to the fox, the Priest comments slyly:

> Women's counsels been ful ofte colde [are very often disastrous];
> Woman's counsel brought us first to woe,
> And made Adam from Paradise to go,
> There as he was full merry and well at ease.
> But for I noot [don't know] to whom it might displease,
> If I counsel of women would blame,
> Pass over, for I said it in my game.
> Read authors, where they treat of swich [such] matter,
> And what they say of women ye may hear.
> These been the cock's words, and not mine;
> I can no harm of no woman divine.[39]

The person he fears to displease is doubtless the Prioress, his employer.

In general Chaucer puts his attacks on women into the mouths of appropriate characters like the celibate Priest and the embittered Merchant. His "Envoy to Bukton," while written in his own person, is clearly no more than a literary joke at the expense of bachelors who get caught. On the occasion of Bukton's approaching marriage, Chaucer warns: you will have sorrow in your flesh for your life and be your wife's thrall; if the authority of the Bible is not enough for you, you will probably learn by experience that you would have been better off taken prisoner in Frisia than fallen into the trap of marriage. Do read the Wife of Bath on this subject before you get caught.

The device Chaucer used to open his *Legend of Good Women,* a book glorifying "Cupid's saints" — women like Thisbe and Dido who died for love — reinforces the view that his interest in the woman question was literary rather than personal, that he expressed misogynistic charges mainly because they are entertaining.

---

[39] *Ibid.,* pp. 138–40, 153, 242–43. Cf. the Guildsmen's wives in the Prologue, who are socially pushing like the Wife of Bath (p. 23); the wife in "The Shipman's Tale," who betrayed her husband for money to buy clothes; the wife in "The Manciple's Tale," who betrays her husband for a far inferior man, since like the she-wolf woman seeks the rudest mate she can find (p. 269); and the Miller's implication that most wives cuckold their husbands (p. 57).

In the Prologue to the *Legend*, the God of Love condemns Chaucer for writing against love and women, in *Troilus and Criseyde* (which tells the story of a famous jilt and in the end exhorts people to follow heavenly rather than earthly love) and in his translation of *The Romance of the Rose*, and accordingly sentences him to write a book in praise of women, from the viewpoint of the religion of love. It is a graceful way to introduce his book, and clearly no more than that.

7

John Lydgate, a close follower of Chaucer who also wrote on both sides of the woman question with apparently equal enthusiasm, often presented men who were like the Wife of Bath's five husbands. While some of his poems are effective in phrasing and detail, all seem to be conventional, merely the expression of contemporary fashionable themes. His "Bycorne and Chichevache" is a pageant portraying two famous mythical beasts of the Middle Ages: Bycorne, who grows fat on patient husbands, and Chichevache, who starves for lack of good wives. Poor Chichevache is so emaciated she is ashamed to show herself; in more than thirty years of searching she has found but one Grisilde, who is long since dead. Now women are too prudent to be patient. Modern husbands are in a sad plight, since, afraid to stand up to their wives, they will necessarily fall prey to Bycorne. "A Mumming at Hertford" presents the same pitiful picture: a group of rustics appear before the King to complain of the hard lives they lead because their wives are so fierce. Robin the Reeve comes home weary from the plough to sour looks and cold soup. His wife, who has spent the day out drinking, finds no time to cook him anything nice; and if he dares to say a word of complaint, she will hit him with her distaff. Bartholomew the butcher has killed bulls and boars, but he never dares to quarrel with his wife, who, like the Wife of Bath, prides herself on repaying her husband for every harsh word or blow. So the poor men petition the King to modify the old custom of rule by wives. The women, however, remain defiant, citing as their precedent the worthy Wife of Bath's demonstration that wives make their husbands win heaven despite the Fiend, by putting them through their purgatory on earth. Wifely patience died with Grisilde;

it is now a wife's part to chatter incessantly, revealing every secret, and, if she is prudent, to have an answer ready to every charge. The King abstains from giving a definitive sentence on the grounds that, despite his sympathy with the unfortunate husbands, he must recognize the vested right of the women, based on custom and confirmed precedent.

"Advice to an Old Gentleman Who Wished for a Young Wife," probably by Lydgate, redevelops the January and May theme of "The Merchant's Tale," indeed with specific reference to Chaucer's story. Not only will your proposed wife be sexually insatiable, dominate you completely, and scold you morning, noon, and night, a wise friend advises the man; but she will be just like the wife in the story who had seven husbands and mourned for none of them except the seventh. When the astonished neighbors asked why, she answered that when each of his predecessors had been on his bier, she was already provided with a new husband; but this time she has no one and is destitute.[40]

Although William Dunbar's "The Two Married Women and the Widow" (about 1508) closely derives from the Wife of Bath's Prologue, it is a colorful poem in its own right, with a highly amusing, if inconsistent, characterization of the widow. Like most imitations of Chaucer, however, it is heavier-handed and lacks the sympathy which Chaucer showed for his disreputable protagonist. The poem is set in an ironically romantic frame, opening with a glowing description of three beautiful and richly dressed ladies in an arbor on a spring morning. Then the widow asks the wives what joy they have found in marriage. The first wife, after bewailing as unnatural the law that makes marriage permanent, complains that her present husband is a dotard, impotent and jealous besides. The second woman's husband is handsome enough to look at but too worn out in Venus' works to be good in bed any more. Both, it goes without saying, have thoroughly tamed their men. The widow, from her wider experience, then preaches so as to "pierce your perverse hearts / And make you meeker to men."

The point of her lecture is that, while any "wise" woman exploits her husband, the really "wise" one does this while appearing pious

---

[40] Lydgate, *Minor Poems*, II, 434–38, 675–81. "Advice to an Old Gentleman" is found in John Lydgate, *A Selection from the Minor Poems*, pp. 27–45.

and devoted. Of course she was always a shrew — stubborn, haughty, spiteful, and bold — but she always appeared sober, sweet, and guileless. My first husband, she tells them, was a hoary old creature that spit out phlegm, yet I kissed him avidly, laughing at him to myself. Meanwhile I had a lustier lad to slake my lust. Then I married a rich merchant, by no means my equal in breeding, bearing, or beauty. The fool kept forgetting this, but I would remind him: I'd raise my voice and call him pedlar. After a while I made him obey and treat me with due respect. Once I had gained control of his property, I crowed over him like a victorious cock. I'd have ridden him to Rome with a bridle if it weren't for my reputation and people's talk. He bought me beautiful rich clothes, but I've kept them unworn, for his successor. I banished his family from our house and always held his friends my foes. He's dead now, and with him all my sorrow and dreary thoughts, although I still weep and dress in mourning. When I go to church I pull my cloak around my face — so as better to look which young man is broadest in the shoulders, or which will furnish the best banquet in Venus' chamber. But if any of my husband's friends are watching, I have a sponge ready to wet my cheeks, so everyone admires my wifely devotion and pities me. I love to go on pilgrimages, more for the company than for the pardon; but even more I enjoy entertaining my suitors. I can comfort a host of them at the same time: I nip on the finger of the one next to me, and serve the one on the other side in the same way. I lean back hard against the one behind me, step on the foot of the one in front, and cast sweet looks at the ones a distance away. I speak some words particularly to every man, so wisely and womanly that it warms their hearts.

Thus, like the Wife of Bath, the widow prides herself on her "wisdom." As she says:

> Faith has a fair name but falset [falsehood] fares better
> Fie on her that can not feign her own fame to save
> Yet am I wise in such work and was all my time
> Though I want wit in worldliness I wiles have in love
> As any happy woman has that is of high blood.[41]

The irony is that preachers constantly exhorted women to be wise, in the sense of discreet, while women like the Wife of Bath and the

[41] *Maitland Folio*, pp. 98–115.

widow use *wisdom* as the key word in their program of deceit and
exploitation of men. The appalling thing about both women is that
they can see nothing in wisdom but worldly wisdom, nothing in love
but self-advancement through sex. Both are too "wise" ever really
to love. While this type of person is always with us, it may be noted
that medieval social conditions, which essentially deprived women
of legal and economic rights, encouraged an exploitative attitude
in them.

8

Bad wives have always been a favorite subject in popular literature. In the amusing ballad "The Farmer's Curst Wife," Satan tells
a farmer he must have his wife, to whom the farmer says he is
most welcome. So Satan takes her off to Hell, but she behaves so
frightfully that the devils turn her out in panic. Satan finally brings
her back to her husband, saying that he has more than met his
match as a tormentor.

The husband in "At the town's end" complains that "this is a
heavy life" when his wife makes a scene because he has given
something away. His wife shook her fist and berated him:

> "Thou knave, thou churl," gan [began] she [to] say,
> "In the twenty devils way,
> Who bade thee give my good [property] away
> At the town's end?"

In this period, all the family property belonged to the husband:
as the man told his wife, everything she had was from him, while
he had nothing from her but chiding and brawling. Unable to for-
bear longer, he hit her on the ear, at which she pretended to be
dying, although there was no blood visible.

A favorite form for this subject matter was a henpecked husband's complaint. One poor husband warns young men against
marrying an older woman, as he has done. When he comes from
the plough at noon, his wife throws him his food in a cracked dish.
He dares not ask her for a spoon or for bread, meat, or cheese:

> If I ask [from] our dame fleych [meat],
> She brekit [breaks] my head with a dish:
> "Boy, thou art not worth a reych! [rush]"
> I dare not seyn [say anything] when she says "Peace!"

Another poem of the same type opens:

> All that I may swynk [labor] or sweat,
> My wife it will both drink and eat;
> And [if] I say aught she will me beat —
> Careful is my heart therefor! [42]

In medieval drama, also, the shrew — who is by all odds the most conspicuous type of female character — is a stock source of humor. In the Towneley play of Noah, after Noah has been ordered to build the ark, he is terrified to tell his wife, who can be counted on to make a scene. When he meets her and asks how she is, she retorts: The worse for seeing you — tell me at once where you have been all this time; you don't care if we all die of want; while we sweat and slave, you do whatever you like. When he tries to tell her about the flood, she berates him for always dreading something: "Thou speakest ever of sorrow; / God send thee once thy fill!" Finally he tells her to hold her tongue or he will make her hold it; they exchange blows until she cries out as if dying. Noah comments, "Thou can both bite and whine" — that is, like the Wife of Bath and the woman in "At the town's end," she starts fist fights and then shrieks piteously if she loses. He then stops the quarrel, having work to do. She is only too happy to see him go: everyone can do without him very well.

After Noah has built the ark he gets his family to go into it — all except his wife. She sees no reason to do so — certainly not because her husband tells her to. She is frightened into compliance when she hears about the flood, but then she dislikes the look of the ark and insists on sitting outside until she has spun all the wool on her spindle. Neither the pleas of her family nor the increasingly threatening weather can move her until she actually feels the water, at

[42] "The Farmer's Curst Wife," *English and Scottish Popular Ballads*, p. 605. "'Alas,' said the goodman," *Songs, Carols and Other Miscellaneous Poems from Richard Hill's Commonplace-Book*, ed. R. Dyboski (London: Early English Text Society [Ex. Ser., 101], 1907), pp. 110–11. Two "Henpecked Husband's Laments," *Secular Lyrics of the XIVth and XVth Centuries*, pp. 38–39. Cf. "Our Goodman," "The Wife Wrapt in Wether's Skin" (*English and Scottish Popular Ballads*, pp. 597–98, 603–4), "In villa, in villa" (*Songs, Carols*, p. 109), "A Paraphrase of the Ten Commandments" (*Reliquiae Antiquae*, II, 27–28), "Off Ladies Bewties," "God gif I wer wedo now" (*Maitland Folio*, pp. 66–67, 244–45).

which point she rushes into the ark. When Noah mildly points out that her delaying has been dangerous, she retorts that she would not go a single step at his bidding. Finally he beats her, she tells the women in the audience that she would like to be a widow, and he warns the men to tame their wives before it is too late.[43] In the York and Chester plays, Noah's wife delays not only from sheer perversity but because she insists that every one of her female drinking companions must come into the ark too; they are more important than her family.[44]

In *The Second Shepherds' Play*, a shepherd complains that his wife is "As sharp as thistle, as rough as a briar," with "a gallon of gall," prefixing his lament with advice to the young men in the audience not to marry. Another's wife is good at three things only — eating, drinking, and breeding. He would give everything he has as an offering for her soul, that is, to see her dead.[45] Despite their complaints, however, the husbands in medieval drama get along quite well with their shrews; and the authors' treatment of this material is comic rather than caustic.

The shrew remained a popular character in drama well into the Renaissance, often becoming the central interest in a play as drama became secular. At first she was just like Noah's wife; afterwards, because of late sixteenth-century social conditions, she was more apt to appear as a City Madam.[46] In the anonymous *Tom Tyler and His Wife* (mid-sixteenth century) the hero enters lamenting that the eight pence a day he earns with hard labor is immediately squandered by his wife. Furthermore:

> The more that I please her, the worse she doth like me,
> The more I forbear her, the more she doth strike me,
> The more that I get her the more she doth glike [gibe at] me.[47]

[43] *The Wakefield Pageants in the Towneley Cycle*, ed. A. C. Cawley (Manchester: Manchester University Press, 1958), pp. 18–24.

[44] *York Plays*, pp. 47–50, *Chester Plays*, pp. 48–49, 52–54. In the Newcastle *Noah's Ark*, of which only a brief fragment is extant, Noah's wife is inspired by the Devil to scheme deliberately to frustrate Noah's building of the Ark. (Millicent Carey, *The Wakefield Group in the Towneley Cycle* [Göttingen: Vandenhoeck & Ruprecht, 1930], p. 69.)

[45] *Wakefield Pageants*, pp. 45–46, 49. Cf, the third shepherd's lament in the "Play of the Shepherds," *Chester Plays*, p. 121.

[46] See Chapter III, pp. 125–27.

[47] *Tom Tyler and His Wife*, ed. G. C. Moore Smith and W. W. Greg (Ox-

After he sneaks out for fear she will find him and start to brawl, his wife, who is appropriately named Strife, appears and tells the audience how she enjoys life by making her husband drudge for her. She then has a drinking party with her female friends, but when poor Tom Tyler comes in, thirsty from labor, she berates him for idleness and drives him off to make more money for her. Tom Taylor takes pity on him, disguises himself in Tyler's clothes, and, when Strife comes in to abuse him, beats her well. She is completely subdued, thinking that her husband has finally asserted himself, and promises to be a good and submissive wife in the future. But that night when they are in bed together she groans with anguish and reproaches him for beating her so unmercifully: half his blows would have won her over, but now she cannot love him any more. Moved to misguided pity, Tom Tyler protests that he was not the one who beat her. Immediately she turns on him, promising him three blows for every one that Taylor gave her. She beats him so long that even her female friends remonstrate. In the end Patience appears to reconcile the couple — precisely how, is not specified.

The continued popularity of the shrew as a dramatic character is shown by the shrew-taming plays of the end of the sixteenth century, in which an unruly woman is taught to yield instant obedience to her husband's commands, however unreasonable, and in the end preaches what is no doubt supposed to be an edifying sermon on wifely obedience. The crudity with which the shrew is character-ized and the attitude she inspires — for the authors clearly direct the audience's sympathy at the man who starves and exhausts his wife into submission — are characteristically medieval. Further, the heroine of the anonymous *Taming of a Shrew* bases her sermon on the old argument of Eve's turpitude:

> Then to His image did He make a man,
> Old Adam, and from his side asleep
> A rib was taken, of which the Lord did make
> The woe of man, so termed by Adam then
> "Wo-man," for that by her came sin to us;

---

ford: Malone Society, 1910), p. 3. Other plays of the same period which are primarily concerned with dramatizing the miseries a shrew inflicts on her husband are John Heywood's *A Mery Play betwene John Johan the husband Tyb his wife and syr Jhān the preest* and Thomas Ingelend's *The Disobedient Child*.

> And for her sin was Adam doomed to die.
> As Sarah to her husband, so should we
> Obey them, love them, keep, and nourish them,
> If they by any means do want our helps;
> Laying our hands under their feet to tread,
> If that by that we might procure their ease;
> And for a precedent I'll first begin
> And lay my hand under my husband's feet.

This she proceeds to do.[48]

Shakespeare's adaptation of this play, *The Taming of the Shrew*, seems patriarchal and antifeminist until we compare it with its predecessor; but actually, in accordance with what appear to be his general views on women, he considerably mitigated the misogyny. His Kate's sermon avoids the Biblical arguments and makes at least some appeal to reason: it is only right for a wife to pay her husband, who labors for her, the small tribute of "love, fair looks, and true obedience." Women's bodies were made soft and weak to suggest that their hearts and tempers should be too. How foolish for women to try to fight men when their "lances are but straws." She concludes:

> Then vail your stomachs, for it is no boot,
> And place your hands below your husband's foot:
> In token of which duty, if he please,
> My hand is ready; may it do him ease.

But she only offers to make the servile gesture which her predecessor actually performed. It is possible that Shakespeare, who was hardly so foolish as to think women powerless, wrote this concluding speech tongue-in-cheek; but it seems unlikely that he cared enough about this play to do more than change it so as to provide some plausible reasons for wifely subjection, a doctrine which he probably approved in theory.[49] About thirty years later John

---

[48] *The Taming of a Shrew*, ed. F. S. Boas (London: Chatto and Windus, 1908), pp. 62–63.

[49] William Shakespeare, *The Comedies*, ed. W. J. Craig (London: Oxford University Press, 1946), pp. 822–23. For a general discussion of Shakespeare's attitude toward women, see Chapter III, pp. 118–21. That Shakespeare accepted the doctrine of wifely subjection is suggested by his presentation of the relationship between Othello and Desdemona and, more important, by the fact that he never expressed disapproval of this doctrine, which was generally held in his day.

Fletcher wrote a play on the taming of Petruchio, *The Woman's Prize*, leading to the conclusion that neither party should tyrannize over the other in marriage. But at about the same time he wrote his own taming of the shrew play, *Rule a Wife and Have a Wife*, in which again a woman who foolishly plans to master her husband is thoroughly chastened.

9

Medieval authors show that wives were not only disobedient when their wishes differed from their husbands', but also for the sheer joy of disobedience. As the author of "The Remedy of Love" put it:

> Forbid her not, that thou noldest [dost not wish to] have done,
> For look what [whatever] thing she is forbod [forbidden],
> To that of all things she is most prone,
> Namely [especially] if it be ill and no good,
> Till it be executed she is nigh wood [crazy].[50]

Thus the favorite attack on women in the Middle Ages was for insubordination—disobedience, scolding, verbal or physical resistance, struggling for the mastery—no doubt because patriarchy was still so strong in Church teaching and social practice. What the patriarch most resents in women is self-assertion, and he is hypersensitive to signs of this. Furthermore, a patriarchal system is apt to provoke women into struggling against it. One form of the struggle was the traditionally feminine love of talk which, especially when indulged with female cronies in the alehouse, was often an expression of independence of home and husband. Wives are constantly shown chattering in church, gossiping in the alehouse, babbling out all their husband's secrets, pressing fatal advice on him,

---

[50] "The Remedy of Love," in *Works of the English Poets*, ed. Chalmers, I, 542. One of the best of many medieval tales illustrating this point appears in *An Alphabet of Tales*, a fifteenth-century translation of a Latin collection. Once there was a knight's wife, a good woman, who utterly scorned Eve for her disobedience to Adam. Her husband told her this scorn was unwise, and to settle the argument ordered her on pain of a fine not to go barefoot into the ditch on the day she bathed. After this she absolutely could not resist the temptation to do so. *An Alphabet of Tales: An English Fifteenth-Century Translation of the Alphabetum Narrationum of Etienne de Besançon*, ed. M. M. Banks (London: Early English Text Society [Orig. Ser., 126, 127], 1904–5), II, 384.

and in general, in the contemporary phrase, clattering like a mill. There was a special devil, Tutivillus, who wrote down the names of women who talked in church.[51] Not only did the idea persist from classical times that women loved drinking, but they were supposed to spend their days in the local tavern, swilling the best ale or wine with their female cronies, "gossips." With these gossips, who were much dearer to them than husband or children, they exchanged every secret they knew, as well as hints for getting the better of men. In "How, gossip mine, gossip mine," a group of women gather at the tavern, two by two so no one will realize it is a party, each bringing something good to eat. When one complains that her husband beats her unmercifully, the others are scornful: Alice, who dreads no man, wishes short life to any man that strikes a woman; and "Margaret meek" swears she knows no man alive "that giveth me two strokes, but [unless] he have five." Having enjoyed themselves all they like they go home. Some women do this once a week, some three times, some every day.[52]

The most effective poem on gossips in the alehouse is John Skelton's "The Tunnyng [brewing] of Elynour Rummyng," in which no opportunity for disgusting detail is missed. Elinor herself, the keeper of the tavern, is scurfy and lousy, her face bloated with drink and bristled like a sow's ear, her nose ever dripping, her back crooked, and her joints stiff — though she considers herself very spruce when on holidays she puts on her best pleated dress, her red kirtle, and her enormous turban. To her tavern come all the sluts of the neighborhood, bringing dishes, shoes, or their wedding rings to pawn to her for drink: a thirsty housewife does not concern herself about thrift. They are in such a hurry that many come half-dressed:

> With their naked paps,
> That flips and flaps;

---

[51] "On Chattering in Church," *Religious Lyrics of the XVth Century*, ed. C. Brown (Oxford: Clarendon Press, 1939), p. 277. Robert of Brunne told how a deacon once burst into laughter while reading the gospel, because he saw two women chattering, and behind them a fiend with pen and parchment writing down all they said (*Handlyng Synne*, pp. 290–91).

[52] *Songs, Carols*, pp. 106–8.

> It wigs and it wags,
> Like tawny saffron bags;
> A sorte [company] of foul drabs
> All scurfy with scabs.[53]

The dispenser and the drinkers of the ale are equally and memorably repulsive.

The Precepts of Alfred, an ancient collection of proverbial wisdom, flatly expresses the generally held medieval conviction that it is fatal for a man to tell his secrets to his wife. For if she should happen to become angry with her husband, even if his enemies are by, nothing will silence her:

> Word-mad is woman, I ween,
> Her tongue aye too swift hath been,
> And rule it, she never may.[54]

A tale in the *Gesta Romanorum,* a popular collection of *exempla* for preachers probably compiled in England at the turn of the fourteenth century, neatly illustrates this point. An erring knight obtains pardon from the king on condition that he appear at the senate-house with his most devoted friend, his best jester, and his most deadly foe. In preparation the knight proposes to his wife that he kill a guest of theirs for his money. She readily consents, and the knight, after sending the guest on his way, kills a calf, puts its dismembered body in a sack, and gives the sack supposedly containing the man's remains to his wife to hide. Then, on the appointed day, he appears at the senate-house with his dog, his year-old child, and his wife. Required to produce his best friend, the knight strikes his dog so it flees howling away, returning however when he calls it back; thus he demonstrates that it is "the most faithful of all friends." The best jester turns out to be his baby. To reveal his worst enemy, he suddenly turns to his wife, strikes her, and accuses her of ogling the king. Furious, she shrieks that he is a murderer and, as the quarrel becomes hotter, that she will show the king the

---

[53] John Skelton, *The Poetical Works,* ed. A. Dyce (London: Thomas Rodd, 1843), I, 95–97, 99–100, 103–4.

[54] *The Chief Middle English Poets,* trans. and ed. Jessie L. Weston (Boston: Houghton Mifflin, 1914), p. 292.

body of the man he has murdered. Of course they find the calf's body instead, and everyone praises the man's wit.[55]

It was also a medieval commonplace that a man must not heed the advice of his wife:

> And 't was said by the folk of old:
> "Women's counsel is counsel cold [fatal]."
> And that man doth come to ill
> Who is led by a woman's will.[56]

The Seven Sages of Rome, a vastly popular collection of Eastern tales translated into English in the early fourteenth century, which is also a useful anthology of misogyny, lays particular emphasis on the fatality of woman's advice and the wickedness of wives. The framework of the collection is that the Empress of Rome, after unsuccessfully trying to seduce her stepson, falsely accuses him of trying to ravish her. The Emperor believes her tale, especially as his son must keep silence for seven days; and she then tells a story to persuade him to hang the youth. He is about to do so when the first of the seven sages who have brought up his son appears and tells a tale against trusting women. The Emperor agrees to spare his son, and then the Empress tells another tale; then the second sage speaks, and so forth through the seven. When the Emperor's son can speak again, he explains everything and further demonstrates that the Empress' "bower-maiden" is really her lover in disguise, so in the end she is burned for adultery and attempted murder. While the Empress is given the chance to tell stories against heirs and counselors, it is clearly those against women which are designed to win the reader's sympathy.

The first sage tells how a knight's baby son, left alone, was threatened by a snake but saved by his father's favorite greyhound. However, in the struggle the child's cradle was overturned on top of him and much blood was spilled. Coming home, his mother found the blood and no child, assumed the hound had killed him, and insisted that her husband kill it. After killing the hound when it came to meet him, the knight found the child unharmed under his cradle

---

[55] *Gesta Romanorum,* trans. Charles Swan (New York: J. W. Bouton, 1872), II, 164–67.

[56] *The Precepts of Alfred,* in *Chief Middle English Poets,* p. 293.

and the remains of the snake. Overwhelmed with remorse, he left his family and went off to be a crusader. The obvious moral, never trust your wife, is emphasized and re-emphasized at the end of the tale: the knight thrice mentioned in his repentance speech that he had done ill because he listened to his wife, and the author adds six more statements of the sentiment.

The second sage, proving the infinite craft of woman, tells how a young wife, locked out when she returned home late from a rendezvous, managed to get in and lock out her old husband instead, while she reviled him for whoring in tones that the whole neighborhood could hear. The third sage likewise undertakes to prove:

> That women are the fountain and the flood,
> The very root, and special invention [source]
> Of all falset [falsity], lesings [lies] and deception.

In his tale a merchant's pet magpie told him every time his young wife cuckolded him, until finally the woman, after enjoying her lover as usual, made the magpie believe there had been a terrible storm by pouring water and pebbles (counterfeit rain and hailstones) on her head through a hole in the roof. The bird told her master the whole story, but since there had been no storm, he thought she was lying and killed her as a troublemaker. Then he discovered the hole in the roof, repented, and gave up business to become a pilgrim — all because he believed his wife.

The fourth and fifth sages' stories are not misogynistic, but the sixth returns to the old theme, telling how a knight was shamefully hanged because he followed his wife's advice. Having persuaded her husband to murder her three young suitors for their money, she then betrayed the crime when she became angry at him. This story proves woman's cruelty, her covetousness, her love of seducing men, her shrewishness (in quarreling with her husband), and her inability to keep secrets. The seventh sage tells the story of the Widow of Ephesus with some significant modifications. First, the woman's husband died because of her, at the shock of seeing her bleed from a minor cut. Secondly, the soldier (here a sheriff) told her that her husband's body would only pass for that of the stolen thief if it were mutilated by the removal of its front teeth, ears, and sex; and when he declared that he could not injure a corpse because of his knighthood, she did it herself. Thirdly, the sheriff in the end reviled her for shameless callousness and rightfully cut off her head. As would be expected, the author who so darkened the woman's guilt was outraged rather than amused by her behavior: adding medieval moral indignation to Roman cynicism about woman's nature, he turned an old jest into a misogynistic indictment. As if *The Seven Sages of Rome* did not already contain enough misogyny for anyone, the sixteenth-century editor added "outcryings" after each example of female villainy, which are even more abusive than the tales themselves.[57]

Despite the fact that medieval satire on wives was frequently lightened by humor, clerical influence remained evident in the form of a generally negative attitude toward marriage: more often than not, a wife was shown to be making her husband's life miserable. Wives who fight their husbands constantly, with "arrows of crabbed eloquence" or even fists, wives who bring their husbands to heel through jealousy, wives who drive their husbands to drudge ceaselessly for them and give nothing in return, wives who neglect their families to gossip all day in the alehouse, wives who ruin their husbands by betraying their most intimate secrets, are among the most persistently popular subjects in medieval literature. Thus early was set the stereotype of the noisy, expensive, henpecking wife: she was to appear regularly in literary works such as Ben Jonson's plays and Charles Dickens' novels, and has continuously to this day been a staple of popular humor.

With the increased secularism of the Renaissance, however, and especially with the Protestant shift from an ideal of celibacy to one of monogamy, came a generally less biased picture of marriage. Although, as *The Seven Sages* demonstrates, sweeping indictments of wives, and of women in general, remained acceptable even into the Renaissance, they were gradually disappearing from

[57] *The Sevin Seages* [of Rome], trans. Johne Rolland "with ane Moralitie efter everie Doctouris Tale, and siclike efter the Emprice Tale, togidder with ane loving and laude to everie Doctour efter his awin Tale, & ane Exclamation and outcrying upon the Empreouris wife efter hir fals construsit Tale," ed. G. F. Black (Edinburgh: Scottish Text Society [Third Ser., 3], 1932), pp. 67ff., 100–101, 211–13. The third Sage's story of the maligned magpie is referred to in "The Wife of Bath's Prologue," p. 93.

the mainstream of literature. The sixteenth-century editor of *The Seven Sages* was a hack, as were his contemporaries who indulged in similar diatribes. Major medieval writers like Chaucer made extensive use of the stock misogynistic charges, though they often presented them lightly; but by Shakespeare's time the important writers devoted less space to misogyny and expressed it indirectly.

1

THE HUMANISM and enlightenment of the Renaissance, its emphasis on maximum development of the individual, its rebellion
against medieval asceticism, should have produced decisive changes
in the prevailing attitude toward women. Actually, however, the old
ideas continued to appear in popular pamphlets and even, to a
lesser extent, in sophisticated sonnet sequences. Journalists still
wrote comprehensive indictments of women from Eve onward or
vividly described the spiritual descendants of the Wife of Bath;
erotic poets still turned on their mistresses or rejected love in the
name of higher things. Indeed, mainly because of the invention of
printing, works both for and against women became even more
numerous than in the Middle Ages.

There is little difference in content and tone between the medieval
and the Renaissance indictments of womankind, although the latter
are, on the whole, more secular. Renaissance pamphleteers wrote
independently of the celibate tradition of the medieval church and,
despite their moral professions, were obviously inspired more by
the profit motive than by religious fervor. These misogynistic attacks must have satisfied popular demands which persisted from
the Middle Ages: rebellion against marriage, expressed in the form
of complaints that wives bring far more woe than pleasure, and
the impulse to tear down overexaltation of love and women which
was inherited from the ambivalent courtly love tradition. The nature and frequency of the sixteenth- and seventeenth-century charges
against women suggest that the motives which prompted them are
constant, that there is a strong current of hostility toward women

even when it is opposed to the prevailing atmosphere of a period. The tone of the charges indicates that it was still not considered necessary to soften attacks on women; the idea that women are too delicate to be harshly or openly criticized was a development of the eighteenth and nineteenth centuries.

That most of the misogynistic tracts of the sixteenth and seventeenth centuries were hack works appears transparently in the several pamphlet wars about women that were waged during the period. In 1541 *The Schole house of Women* started a thirty-year controversy. *The Schole house* is thoroughly medieval in content, method, and compendiousness; and yet despite, perhaps even because of, its lack of originality, it was extremely popular. The author, probably Edward Gosynhill, is confident that all married men will confirm his opinion that women "Been evel to please, and wors to trust." They always insist on having the last word, although their opinions are worthless; and "Malice is so rooted in their hart" that a man seldom hears one good word from them in a whole year. Whatever they once finger they cannot be restrained from acquiring, and in general they crave much and give nothing in return. If you "intend to use them oft," you must support them in luxury; and even so they will take lovers once your back is turned. They refuse to do a stroke of work for fear of spoiling their beauty and will feign sickness once or twice a week as an excuse to lie in bed all day receiving visits from their gossips. A man might as well throw stones into the wind as try to thwart a woman's will: "To prattle to them of reason or lawe" or to try "to keep them under awe" are equally ineffectual. What they lack in physical strength they make up in malice; they all, like Jezebel and Herodias, like to incite men to discord and cruelty; Peter denied Christ because of a maid's persistent questions. Woman's lust is amply demonstrated by Biblis, Mirrha, the daughters of Lot, Messalina, and Helen; her willfulness by Eve, Lot's wife, and Queen Athaliah; her treachery by Samson's wives; her general unhelpfulness by Job's wife, who mocked her husband in his misery and derided his appeals to God:

> Thy prating leve, foule thee befall,
> Trust me [God] wil thee never heale;
> Thy beasts, thy goods and thy children all

> Be dead and brent [burnt] now every deale [bit],
> And thou liest heer with many a bile [boil]
> Prating and praying to the devine,
> And wurse thou stinkest than a dead swine.

A remarkable expansion of Job 2:9–10. The author concludes that women might well be glorified were it not for two venial faults: "They neither doo, nor yet say wel." [1]

The vertuous schole-hous of ungracious women, a dialogue in which a godly widow instructs a wayward wife, tried through its title to capitalize on the popularity of the original *Schole house*. Charles Bansley's *Treatyse shewing and declaring the Pryde and Abuse of Women Now a Dayes*, a dull ballad-sermon against women's love of new fashions and extravagant dress, was supposedly occasioned by the failure of *The Schole house* to reform the female sex. *The Schole house of Women* also provoked three refutations. The fact that the first of these was by Gosynhill, the probable author of *The Schole house* itself, illustrates the factitious nature of these popular denunciations or defenses of women. [2]

Much the most entertaining of the potboiling attacks on women, although it too is depressingly long, is Thomas Dekker's *The Batchelars Banquet* (1603, based on La Sale's *Quinze Joyes de Mariage*). This work, an alarming Progress of Marriage beginning with the newlywed's training of her husband, is enlivened by dramatic dialogues which catch very realistically such things as the mealy-mouthed shrewdness of a woman who gets what she wants by play-

---

[1] *The Schole house of Women*, in *Remains of the Early Popular Poetry of England*, ed. W. C. Hazlitt (London: J. Russell Smith, 1864–66), IV, 106, 108–12, 129, 131–36, 144. Francis Lee Utley's *The Crooked Rib: An Analytical Index to the Argument about Women in English and Scots Literature to the End of the Year 1568* (Columbus: Ohio State University Press, 1944) lists the innumerable misogynistic works produced in the Middle Ages, suggests the traditions which influenced them, and points out that they continued to pour forth even when the Renaissance was fully established in England.

[2] Bansley's poem is included in *Early Popular Poetry*, IV, 231ff. The three refutations of *The Schole house* were *The prayse of all women*, called *Mulierum Pean* (1542?), *A Dyalogue defensyve for women agaynst malycyous detractoures* (1542), *A Lytle and bryefe treatyse, called the defence of women . . . made agynst the Schole howse of women* (1560). For further description of these works for and against women, see Carroll Camden, *The Elizabethan Woman* (Houston, Tex.: Elsevier Press, 1952), pp. 241–52.

ing on her husband's pity and guilt. Seeing any woman with more expensive or fashionable clothes than hers, she resolves that she will have the same and unerringly finds the best opportunity for taking advantage of her husband, that is, in bed: ". . . when therefore this lustie gallant would prosecute his desired pleasures, for which cause he chiefly ran wilfully into the perill of Lobs pound, then squeamishly she begins thus, saying; I pray you husband let me alone . . . for I am not well at ease." The reason for her suffering, she is persuaded to reveal with pretended reluctance, is that she has been to a party and found herself less fashionably dressed than any other woman there.

When her husband points out that they need their money to pay the rent, she immediately bristles — not from anger, of course, only from regret that she married him instead of a man who would have loved her. She refuses his overtures at night, gets up especially early the next morning, and sulks the whole day. That night, unable to hold out longer, he promises her a new dress; but she persists in ungraciousness. He lies awake the whole night thinking how to please her, being so besotted as to believe her a good wife, and the next morning rushes off to buy her cloth on credit. She joyfully flaunts her new dress everywhere, but the poor husband finds himself seized for debt. Now his wife, forced to economize and do the housework herself, makes his life miserable by scolding: "Was ever woman of my degree and birth brought to this beggery?" Since she has conveniently forgotten that her pride caused their fall and has made him forget it too, his misery is doubled by worrying about her troubles. Yet, wretched as he is, the silly man is "wrapt in a kind of pleasing woe, out of the which he hath neither power nor will to wind himself, but therein doth consume the remnant of his languishing life, and miserably ends his dayes." This chapter ending, emphasizing not only the miseries of marriage but the miraculous power of undeserving women to retain men's affection, becomes a sort of refrain in the book. Dekker harps not only on men's powerlessness before women, but on men's enjoyment of their servitude — which of course makes women even more dangerous.

The next chapter tells how a wife, once having acquired clothes which please her, shows them off everywhere to attract gallants, thereby torturing her husband with jealousy. Then she becomes pregnant, probably with some other man's help; and her poor husband must "trot up & down day & night, far, & neere, to get with great cost that his wife longs for: if she lets fall but a pin, he is diligent to take it up, least she by stouping should hurt her selfe." Meanwhile she does nothing but complain. When the child is finally born, he must entertain all her gossips from far and wide. If he is lavish, they will consume his substance in eating and drinking; if not, they will condole with his wife on account of his cruelty and advise her how to tame him.

After nine or ten years of marriage the wife is still fresh and strong (the vicissitudes of childbearing being negligible), while her poor husband is utterly worn out with business and family cares. To provide clothes for his wife and daughters so as to "enjoy an easie bondage," he must slave continuously; yet when he comes home exhausted, his wife chides, the servants ignore him, and no one will get him any dinner. Even when he goes to bed he gets no peace, since his wife and the nurse purposely set the children crying to torment him. Finally, when the poor man has become sick from his hard work for the family, his wife leaves him alone in his room, spends all her time complaining to the neighbors, and at last conspires with her eldest son to rule him absolutely, keeping all his friends away on the pretext that he has become senile.

While *The Batchelars Banquet* is obviously a humorous work, probably inspired by the salability of books on women, and furthermore scores justified points against certain types of wife, it also reveals some signs of real misogyny in Dekker's conviction that all women are fighting for power and his dread of their supremacy. It is "a generall imperfection of women, bee they never so honest, never so kindly used . . . to strive for the breeches" and practice perversity on purpose to keep their husbands "in continuall thought and care how to please" them. The consequences of female sovereignty are appalling:

The honestest woman, and most modest of that sexe, if shee weare the breeches, is so out of reason in taunting and controuling her husband, for this is their common fault, and be she never so wise, yet, because a woman, scarce able to govern her self, much lesse her husbande, and all his affaires, for were it not so, God would have made her the head; which sith it is other wise, what can bee more preposterous, then that the head should be governed by the foote? if then a wise and honest womans superioritie bee unseemely, and breede great inconvenience, how is he drest, thinke you, if hee light on a fond wanton, and malicious dame? [3]

This shows the usual patriarchal insistence that even the best women must be kept subject because they are incapable of governing their own dangerous passions and a common misogynistic perversion of the Biblical account of Creation which has woman drawn from man's foot instead of his rib, which signifies equality. The patriarch's haunting fear that woman is more powerful than man, and hence that she will enslave him completely given the slightest opportunity, is seen constantly in the book.

A far less entertaining tract, Joseph Swetnam's *The Araignment of Lewde, idle, froward, and unconstant women*, made considerably more stir. It went into ten editions between 1615 and 1637, as well as editions in 1690, 1702, 1707, 1733, and 1807; and provoked not only three replies but a comedy called *Swetnam, the Woman-hater*. Swetnam's book is repetitious and filled with such original gems as the "if all the world were paper" figure applied to women's wiles; the horrible examples of Samson, David, Solomon, and Hercules; and the saying that women have only two faults, that they neither say well nor do well. He opened with a familiar conciliatory gesture, which is even less convincing than usual: he was writing

to better the good by the naughty examples of the badd . . . women are all necessary evils [he later attributed this epithet to God!] and yet not all given to wickedness, and yet many be so bad, that in my conceit if I should speake the worst that I know by some women . . . my tongue would blister to report it.

His account of the Creation and Fall is typical of his approach, his charges, and his triteness:

Moses describeth a woman thus: At the first beginning (saith he) a woman was made to be a helper unto man, and so they are indeede, for she helpeth to spend & consume that which man painefully getteth. He also saith that

---

[3] Thomas Dekker, *The Batchelars Banquet*, in *The Non-Dramatic Works*, ed. A. Grosart (London: Huth Library, 1884), I, 155–66, 173–78, 191–97, 210, 234–41, 255–56. Some scholars question Dekker's authorship of *The Batchelars Banquet*, but the *Short Title Catalogue* attributes it to him.

they were made of the ribbe of a man, and that their froward nature sheweth; for a ribbe is a crooked thing good for nothing else, and women are crooked by nature, for small occasion will cause them to be angry. Againe . . . she was no sooner made but straight way her minde was set upon mischiefe, for by her aspiring minde and wanton will she quickly procured mans fall, and therefore ever since they are & have been a woe unto man, and follow the line of their first leader.

This Biblical foundation (however perverted in the interests of misogyny) and emphasis on woman's frowardness and extravagance with her husband's hard-earned money persist throughout the tract and help to account for its enormous popularity with the middle class. Money spent on your wife is pure waste, Swetnam charged. While all man's other livestock repay the trouble he takes to care for them, "what labour or cost thou bestowest on a woman is all cast away, for she will yeelde thee no profite at all." If you marry a good woman she will be quickly spoiled by your good treatment; if a bad one, her behavior will be insupportable; if a beautiful one, she will be vain; if an ugly, you cannot love her; if a rich one, you must defer to her; if a poor, you must maintain her.[4]

These attacks on wives show that antifeminism of the medieval type continued to flourish until well into the seventeenth century. Indeed, as late as 1716 Ned Ward produced *Female Policy Detected,* which starts out to warn men against prostitutes but soon turns into a medieval-style misogynistic tirade meant to dissuade them from marriage. It is a collection of ancient jokes, aphorisms, and charges, many of them plagiarized from Swetnam. Ward's book is unusual, however; by and large in his time such

---

[4] Joseph Swetnam, *The Araignment of Lewde, idle, froward, and unconstant women* (London: J. Smeeton, 1807), pp. A2, 1, 10, 28, 29, 33, 36. Swetnam also denounced women's ungovernable will and passions, vindictiveness, dissimulation, pride, incessant talk, lewdness, inconstancy, inability to keep secrets, vanity, and extravagance in dress. On the Swetnam controversy, see Camden, *The Elizabethan Woman,* pp. 258–63.

Gosynhill, not finding enough room for misogynistic interpretation in the Biblical story of woman's creation from man's rib, repeated the traditional scurrilous tale that she was created from a dog's rib instead, and drew appropriate conclusions (pp. 122–24). With Gosynhill's version compare the equally scurrilous tale that she was made from man's tail. This appears as late as the nineteenth century, in a poem by Thomas Moore called "The Rabbinical Origin of Women."

attacks were considered too crude and extreme, and were replaced by more subtle ones.

Debates on woman's worth also persisted in the Renaissance, not only in the form of pamphlet wars, but in the popular anthologies of quotations (*Politeuphia*, 1597; *Englands Parnassus*, 1600; and so forth), which always included a section full of extreme statements for and against women. The traditional charges of deceitfulness and ungovernable passion were printed and reprinted: "Women's sorrows are either too extreem, not to be redressed; or else tricked up with dissimulation, not to be beleeved." "Being moved to anger, they become more envious then a serpent, more malicious then a tyrant, and more deceitful then the devill."[5]

Although most of the Renaissance attacks on woman's finery were concerned more with her extravagance than her seductiveness,[6] even

---

[5] *Politeuphia, Wits Common-wealth,* ed. Nicholas Ling (London: G. Badger, 1647), pp. 28, 30. Ling's is the most misogynistic of the Renaissance anthologies of quotations: of his fifty-one aphorisms about women, forty are definitely hostile. Cf. *Englands Parnassus,* ed. Robert Allott (London: Longman, 1814), pp. 21–22, 242, 377–82, and *Belvedére: or, The Garden of the Muses* (Manchester: Spenser Society [17], 1875), pp. 104–7. While it would be tedious to list many more of the examples of medieval-type misogynistic works appearing in the Renaissance, I might mention the popular joke books of the period. In *Shakespeare's Jest-Books: Reprints of the Early . . . Jest-Books Supposed to Have Been Used by Shakespeare,* ed. W. C. Hazlitt (London: Willis & Sotheran, 1864), 3 vols., there are not only many jokes which depend on the medieval charges against women, but repetitions of the old stories: e.g., that of Socrates' remark when drenched by Xanthippe (I, 65). Besides the authors represented in *Early Popular Poetry,* many poets kept up the old misogynistic themes: e.g., Samuel Rowlands in his gossips in the alehouse poems, *Tis Merrie when Gossips meete* (1602) and *A whole crew of kind Gossips, all met to be merry* (1609), both in *The Complete Works* (Glasgow: The Hunterian Club [2–4], 1880), 3 vols. Robert Greene, a fertile writer in all the fashionable genres of the late sixteenth century, clearly shows the persistence of the old emphasis on female subjection, even though he was noted mainly as a writer of romances. See his *Life and Complete Works,* ed. A. Grosart (London: Huth Library, 1881–86), V, 162, VII, 231, 284, 290, VIII, 24.

[6] The Renaissance satirists' particular emphasis on women's extravagance and finery came partly because women were indulging in more elaborate makeup and more fantastic fashions in the later sixteenth century than they had before, partly because their flaunting of expensive new fashions typified the increasing social climbing and ostentation which conservatives deplored. See, for example, Stephen Gosson's *Quippes for Upstart Newfangled Gentlewomen*

a popular writer like Thomas Nashe could occasionally revert to medieval denigration of the body and threats of hell fire. In *Christs Teares Over Jerusalem* (1593) he denounced women's pride, their "naturall sin," just like a celibate preacher of the Middle Ages:

Nothing els is garish apparraile, but Prydes ulcer broken forth. . . . As many jagges, blysters, and scarres, shall Toades, Cankers, and Serpents, make on your pure skinnes in the grave, as nowe you have cuts, jagges, or raysings, upon your garments. . . . Your morne-like christall countenaunces shall be netted over and (Masker-like) cawle-visarded with crawling venomous wormes. Your orient teeth toades shall steale into their heads for pearle; of the jelly of your decayed eyes shall they engender them young. . . . O, what is beauty more then a wind-blowne bladder, that it should forget whereto it is borne? It is the foode of cloying-concupiscence, lyving, and the substaunce of the most noysome infection, beeing dead.

At the Judgment Day God will hand over these painted sepulchres to Satan, who will pour boiling pitch over their painted faces, soak their pampered skins in bubbling lead, and replace their jewels with clinging scorpions and their luxuriant wigs with snakes. Unless women reform, their "paines in hell (above mens) shal be doubled, for millions have you tempted, millions of men (both in soule and substance) have you devoured. To you, halfe your husbands damnation (as to *Evah*) will be imputed." Since *Christs Teares* shows every sign of being a straightforward moral work, these reversions to medieval attacks on women must have been meant seriously.

The Anatomie of Absurditie (1589), a gay, irresponsible attack on the many things which struck Nashe as absurd, is a work far more characteristic of him. It includes an attack on women, as his ridicule of contemporary love poetry slipped into a medieval-style rejection of love; but this is modified by his generally flippant tone. Love poets never remember "that as there was a loyall *Lucretia*, so there was a light a love *Lais*, that as there was a modest *Medullina*, so there was a mischievous *Medea*," and so forth. But why should he spend his ink

in painting forth theyr ugly imperfections, and perverse peevishnesse, when as howe many hayres they have on their heads, so many snares they will

---

(1595), in *Early Popular Poetry*, IV, 250–51, and "The Invincible Pride of Women," in *Humor, Wit & Satire of the Seventeenth Century*, ed. John Ashton (London: Chatto and Windus, 1883), pp. 40–41.

find for a neede to snarle men in; how many voices all of them have, so many vices each one of them hath; how many tongues, so many tales; how many eyes, so many allurements. . . . What pride have they left un-practised, what enticement to lust have they not tried?

He concluded the subject by praising the wisdom of the Essenes, "who abhorre the company of women." [7] Although Nashe's state-ments could hardly be more sweeping, the prevailing lightness of *The Anatomie* suggests that he did not take them with complete seriousness nor expect his readers to. However, the very appearance of these sentiments proves that they remained acceptable to the so-phisticated sixteenth-century reader.

The Elizabethan formal satirists joined Nashe in deriding the extravagancies of contemporary love poetry, and occasionally in attacking the women idolized. John Marston, who seems to have been genuinely indignant about lovers' foolishness, described women as "Glowe wormes bright / That soile our soules, and dampe our reasons light." (The glowworm comparison was popular, since a glowworm, bright and pretty from a distance, is seen in the hand to be an ugly black bug.) In another poem he ridiculed Curio, heartbroken at the death of his mistress' monkey and brought to the point of suicide by an unresponsive lady: How can a man let his mortal soul be enslaved by "craftie natures paint?" and "Be underling to such a vile controule?" Grieved at "the base dishon-ors" of his sex in adoring "female painted puppetry," he even revived the illustration used by Walter Map four centuries before: "The sonne of *Saturne* is become a Bull, / To crop the beauties of some female trull." It must be that our souls have deserted us in scorn, leaving only our bodies to wallow in slime "Such as [is] wont to stop port Esqueline," the public privy. He closed with an impassioned appeal to the souls to return and thus free men from the polluting mud of involvement with women (*The Scourge of Villanie*, VII, VIII, 1598). [8] The intensity of Marston's exclamations

[7] Thomas Nashe, *The Works*, ed. R. B. McKerrow (London: Sidgwick & Jackson, 1910), I, 11, 16–17, 19, II, 138–40.

[8] John Marston, *The Poems*, ed. Arnold Davenport (Liverpool: Liverpool University Press, 1961), pp. 146, 153–56. The glowworm comparison was used by Swetnam (*The Araignment*, p. 12), among others. Joseph Hall derided contemporary love poetry in *Virgidemiarum*, Book I, Satires I and VII, and Book VI, Satire I. Most of the formal satirists of this period devoted one

against desire for women indicates that he was not merely following a convention, but seriously meant what he wrote. His works
reveal an obsessive concern with sexual vice, which apparently led
him to misogyny as it led the Church Fathers, although his attack
differs from theirs in being secular: he emphasized the moral ignominy of lust rather than the charge that the daughters of Eve
seduce man from godliness.

2

Rejection of love and women is found not only in the satirists
of love poetry, but in the erotic writers themselves, most of whom —
like their medieval predecessors — occasionally reacted against the
courtly idolization of women, protesting against the degrading bondage of love or denouncing the unworthiness of womankind. The
ambivalence toward love which persisted through the Renaissance
is well illustrated in Robert Burton's lengthy discussion of its good
and bad points in his *Anatomy of Melancholy* (1621). He drew his
arguments for the negative mainly from Ovid's *Remedies of Love*,
but strengthened them with an appropriate paraphrase from St.
John Chrysostom's "Exhortation to Theodore After His Fall."[9]

"A cooling Carde for Philautus and all fond lovers," at the end
of John Lyly's *Euphues* (1578), is similar to the palinode which
followed Andreas Capellanus' *Art of Courtly Love*. *Euphues* (Part
I) seems to be a typical romance, in which the most important,
indeed perhaps the only, business of life is elaborately conducted
love affairs. But in the end, after Euphues has seduced his best
friend's mistress and in turn been jilted by her, he becomes very
moral and writes a letter of advice to his friend. Supposedly he is
warning both sexes against the follies of love, but the letter soon

---

satire out of six to women's vices, emphasizing lust and beauty aids, pride
and extravagant dress. See, for example, Henry Hutton's *Follie's Anatomie*
(1619), the last satire; *Micro-Cynicon* (1599), possibly by Thomas Middleton, Satire III; Everard Guilpin's *Skialetheia* (1598), Satire II. Sixteenth- and
seventeenth-century attacks on women's extravagant dress and beauty aids,
found in formal satires, epigrams, plays, and moral tracts, are far too numerous to list.

[9] Robert Burton, *The Anatomy of Melancholy*, ed. F. Dell and P. Jordan-
Smith (New York: Farrar and Rinehart, 1927), pp. 251–52, 737–38, 780–81,
785–86.

turns into an attack on women, "the gate to perdition." In breaking off a love affair:

Lette neyther their amyable countenances, neyther their painted protestacions, neyther their deceitfull promises, allure thee to delaies. . . . *Hiena*, when she speaketh lyke a man deviseth most mischiefe . . . women when they be most pleasaunt, pretend most trecherie. . . . Hee that toucheth pitche shall be defiled, the sore eye infecteth the sounde, the societie with women breedeth securitie in the soule, and maketh all the sences sencelesse.

So use your God-given talents worthily, that is, for your own advancement, rather than degrading them in the courtship of ladies: "Is it not folly to shew wit to women which are neither able nor willinge to receyve fruite thereoff?" Think of your lady's tricks and deceits, her greed and malice. Turn her good qualities against hei and induce her to reveal her deficiencies — call her good complex·ion a painted wall and make her laugh if her teeth are bad. Then there is the last Ovidian remedy, the trip to the lady's dressing room:

. . . the sleeking of theire faces, and all their slibber sawces . . . bring quesiness to the stomacke, and disquyet to the minde. Take from them their periwiggs, their payntings, their Jewells, their rowles, their boulsterings, and thou shalt soone perceive that a woman is the least parte of hir selfe. When they be once robbed of their robes, then will they appeare so odious, so ugly, so monstrous, that thou wilt rather thinke them Serpents then Saynts, & so lyke Hags, that thou wilt feare rather to be enchanted then enamoured.

"Let every one loath his Ladye," Euphues (and Lyly) concluded, "and bee ashamed to bee hir servaunt . . . flye women." [10] After all this, the postscript in which he claimed to be speaking only of bad women, having always honored good ones, scarcely carries conviction.

In *Euphues*, as in Lyly's work as a whole, this is simply the negative side of the ambivalence toward love and women which recurs in erotic literature. But the Earl of Northumberland seems to have repudiated love altogether, although — as is characteristic of his period — he repudiated it in the name of philosophy rather than religion. In about 1596 the Earl, who was married to Dorothy Rich, the sister of Sidney's Stella, wrote an essay to explain to a lady,

[10] John Lyly, *Euphues*, in *The Complete Works*, ed. R. W. Bond (Oxford: Clarendon Press, 1902), I, 247, 250, 252, 254–57.

evidently his wife, why his passion for her had cooled. At first, the Earl began, he had been an avid wooer of ladies. This means, it soon becomes apparent, that he had exerted himself to get as much from them as possible without giving anything in return. He had devoted much thought to methods for seducing ladies — professions of honorable love to the young and inexperienced, sophistry to the religiously scrupulous, insidious familiarities to the virtuous and honorable, flattery to the proud, promises of money to the needy (only promises, of course — "otherwise she will pray uppon thee"). But one day, looking for the *Arcadia,* he happened on a physics book instead. After reading a few pages, he realized that learning was constant and his mistress fickle; that "it treated of hidden misteries" and "shee of vulger trifles"; that it produced perpetual contentment and she merely post-coital sadness. Although she was not ugly among women, compared to learning she was positively deformed.

[In love] there is, myndes disquiet, attendant servitude, flatteringe observance, losse of tyme, passion without reason, observing base creatures, torture of jealowsie, allowance of tryfles, toyle of body, hazard of person, decrease of health, losse of reputation, prodigall expence, slackinge of good actions, scornefull disgraces, feare of future reward.

In the pursuit of learning, on the other hand, there are peace, happiness, understanding, good deeds, and consciousness of virtue.[11]

Generally, rejection of love in the Renaissance was not a permanent repudiation, as Northumberland's appears to have been, but rather an occasional mood. The poet's adoring attitude toward his (real or fictitious) mistress wavers because of her unfeeling behavior or his own human variability, and he expresses bitterness against her or women in general. These poems form a small proportion of the total Renaissance output, far less than in the Middle Ages or the Restoration. Furthermore, the bitterness expressed rarely seems passionately sincere; it seems that if the poet's mistress were to treat him kindly, his misogyny would soon disappear. Nevertheless, medieval-type misgivings about love and women do appear

---

[11] Frances A. Yates, *A Study of "Love's Labour's Lost"* (Cambridge: Cambridge University Press, 1936), pp. 208, 210–11.

in the works of nearly every love poet of the sixteenth and seventeenth centuries.

Poems of reaction against their lady, or women in general, or the tyranny of erotic love, became a conventional feature in the sonnet sequences. However, although all the sonnet sequences reveal some hostility, they express at most only indirect misogyny: the poet complains with bitter disgust of a woman's incapacity to appreciate love (Sir Thomas Wyatt's "What vaileth trouth"), or he chooses to write about a conspicuously unworthy woman (Shakespeare's sonnets to the dark lady), or he gloats about the future hideousness of his unfeeling mistress (Michael Drayton's "There's nothing grieves me, but that Age should haste / That in my dayes I may not see thee old"), or he wonders whether love for a woman is really only lust, whether the only aspiration worthy of a man is heavenly love (Sir Philip Sidney's "Leave me ô Love, which reaches but to dust, / And thou my mind aspire to higher things").[12]

Edward de Vere, Earl of Oxford, was an unusually rebellious lover for his period: in his works sincere rejection of women clearly predominates over conventional adoration. His most famous poem, "If women could be fair and yet not fond" (i.e., foolishly credulous or doting), is no routine accusation of cruelty or inconstancy, but a serious expression of contempt for women. The Earl wonders how men can "forget themselves so far" as to enslave themselves to creatures so frail as women. Seeing how they range like haggard hawks, "How oft from Phoebus do they flee to Pan" (or, in Hamlet's words, how they go from Hyperion to a satyr), "Who would not

[12] The works of George Gascoigne, written earlier, in the 1570's, show the clear-cut medieval cleavage between poems in praise of women and love and poems rejecting both as absolutely unworthy: see, for example, his formal recantation, "The Recantation of a Lover," in *Complete Works*, ed. J. W. Cunliffe (Cambridge: Cambridge University Press, 1907–10), I, 51–52. George Turbervile, another mercilessly prolific rejecter as well as adorer of women, dispraised "Women that Allure and Love Not," craved pardon for his "Forepassed Follies" as a lover, and lamented "That His Ladie Is Matched with Another" because of the fickleness native to women. Although love poems predominate in *Tottel's Miscellany*, it contains many which complain of the inconstancy, wiles, and hardheartedness of women. Louis Salomon lists many of the Renaissance lovers' protests in his *The Devil Take Her! A Study of the Rebellious Lover in English Poetry* (New York: A. S. Barnes & Co., 1961).

scorn and shake them from the fist / And let them fly fair fools which way they list." Yet we flatter them to amuse ourselves in times of boredom; we "train them to our lure with subtle oath" until — "weary of *their* wiles" (my italics) — we ease ourselves by slipping away.[13]

The cynically exploitative attitude expressed here is characteristic of misogynists who reject women as unworthy. In the same spirit, the author of *The Schole house* referred casually to using women often, Dekker assumed that a man marries merely to get his sex conveniently, Swetnam complained that a woman "will yeelde . . . no profite at all," Lyly warned men against showing any mercy when breaking off a love affair, and Northumberland boasted of getting poor women by promising them money but giving them nothing. At the same time that these men were exhausting their ingenuity to cheat women, they complained of female wiles; while they regarded women as vessels to be used at minimum expense, they complained of female incapacity to give love.

John Donne, the most passionate of the Renaissance love poets, was also the most intensely ambivalent about women. Although he glorified romantic love to unsurpassed heights in poems like "The Extasie" and "A Valediction: Forbidding Mourning," he was equally capable of degrading it and women to unsurpassed depths. With all his capacity for exalted passion, he had moods of ferocious cynicism in which he tore away romantic idealizations and turned on women as savagely as the most embittered misogynist. The outstanding example is "Loves Alchymie," his attack on the idea that love produces an ennobling transformation. Like the alchemist who tries futilely to extract gold from base metals, the lover tries to get something transcendent from his sensual experiences with women. The sensual experience itself is no more than a bubble, or a short summer's night which seems as cold, as barren and devoid of emotional warmth, as a winter's one; and idealizations of this lust are but shadows of the bubble. By describing consummation as enduring "the short scorne of a Bridegroomes play," Donne implied that the

---

[13] Edward de Vere, Earl of Oxford, *The Poems*, ed. J. Thomas Looney (London: Palmer, 1921), p. 37. Benjamin Rudyerd's "On Women," *Memoirs of Sir Benjamin Rudyerd*, ed. J. A. Manning (London: T. & W. Boone, 1841), pp. xxviii-xxix, is equally harsh.

man finds the experience a necessary relief rather than an ecstasy ("endure") and necessarily despises his sexual partner ("scorne"). Any male animal who can endure this gets as much from "love" as anybody else; only an unrealistic fool would expect more. The reason is obvious: "Hope not for minde in women; at their best / Sweetnesse and wit, they'are but *Mummy*, possest." That is, once you have had them, they are nothing but dead meat.

Similar, if not quite so withering, statements are scattered throughout Donne's works. After alluring men, women reject them in the name of conscience or honor — chimeras as empty as the respect they claim from men, or as the women are themselves ("A Valediction: of the Booke"). "Graves have learn'd that woman-head / To be to more than one a Bed" ("The Relique"). It would be pointless to try to meet a woman both true and fair, for even if such a miracle should be heard of somewhere, she would be "False . . . to two, or three" before a man could come to her ("Goe and catche a falling starre"). A man may use women as he likes, discarding them like table scraps: ". . . when hee hath the kernell eate, / Who doth not fling away the shell?" ("Communitie"). After lovers have what they so "Blindly admire, and with such worship wooe," they find in the object of their adoration merely satisfaction for one sense, "And that so lamely, as it leaves behinde / A kinde of sorrowing dulnesse to the minde" ("A Farewell to Love"). And yet both "A Valediction: of the Booke" and "The Relique," taken as wholes, glorify the women and the affairs they describe: Donne felt compelled to tear down even as he was building up. Similarly, his poem of high compliment "To the Countesse of Huntingdon" opens with a reminder that woman is inferior by her creation and rightly barred from office in church or state:

> Man to Gods image, *Eve*, to mans was made,
>   Nor finde wee that God breath'd a soule in her,
> Canons will not Church functions you invade,
>   Nor lawes to civill office you preferre.

Innocence, Donne proceeded, is a rare comet among women, and active good positively a miracle.

Donne's "Paradoxes" are so willfully perverse, so obviously exercises in cleverness for its own sake, that one hesitates to use them as evidence of the author's feelings. Yet the misogynistic commonplaces with which they are filled must not only have been current in his time but have had some appeal for him. The first Paradox, "A Defence of Womens Inconstancy," includes this comparison: "Women are like *Flies*, which feed among us at our Table, or *Fleas* sucking our very blood, who leave not our most retired places free from their familiarity, yet for all their fellowship will they never be tamed nor commanded by us." The second is an ingenious, presumably ironical, case "That Women Ought to Paint." The sixth, "That It Is Possible to Finde Some Vertue in Some Women," repeats the old libels, however humorously it may have been intended: women's justice is proven by their punishing the sins they have occasioned with beggary or disease, their wisdom by their wiles, their fortitude by the valiant men they have overthrown. Their intemperance Donne freely admits — he had not intended to furnish them with all virtues. His answer to the "problem" — "Why hath the Common Opinion Afforded Women Soules?" — strings together a series of traditional misogynistic jibes, the first of which was accepted as scientific fact in Donne's day:

It is agreed that we have not so much from them as any *part* of either our *mortal soules* of *sense* or *growth*; and we deny *soules* to others equall to them in all but in *speech* for which they are beholding to their *bodily instruments*: For perchance an *Oxes* heart, or a *Goates*, or a *Foxes*, or a *Serpents* woulde speake just so, if it were in the *breast*, and could move that *tongue* and *jawes*.[14]

And so on.

Love lyrics continued to show this ambivalence throughout the seventeenth century, with an occasional contemptuous poem appearing among many devoted to worshipful praise of a mistress or women in general. Few poets, however, were as impassioned as Donne, either for or against women. Robert Herrick's works, which consist mainly of innocuous praises of Julia and others, include an occasional warning against maidens' charms as "traps to take fooles in," and one surprisingly bitter remedies-of-love poem. The scathing contempt of "Upon some women" comes as a shock amid the general sweetness of Herrick's verse:

[14] John Donne, *Complete Poetry and Selected Prose*, ed. John Hayward (with Blake's *Complete Poetry*) (New York: Random House, 1941), pp. 4, 20, 21, 26, 42, 48, 144–45, 278, 281, 288.

Thou who wilt not love, doe this;
Learne of me what Woman is.
Something made of thred and Thrumme [fringe or scraps of thread];
A meere Botch of all and some.
Pieces, patches, ropes of haire;
In-laid Garbage ev'ry where.
Out-side silk, and out-side Lawne;
Sceenes to cheat us neatly drawne.
False in legs, and false in thighes;
False in breast, teeth, haire, and eyes:
False in head, and false enough;
Onely true in shreds and stuffe.[15]

Sir John Suckling, also of course a love poet, occasionally reacted against the convention. In "Farewell to Love" he rejoiced that he could now see through the illusion of female beauty:

If I gaze now, 'tis but to see
What manner of death's-head 'twill be,
When it is free
From that fresh upper skin,
The gazer's joy and sin.

The pomatum which the lady uses to set her hair reminds him of a snail's slimy track, and the curls which hang over her ears, of "two master-worms" which have already eaten through the ear-holes. Now that he spies in every woman only "A quick corse," "They mortify, not heighten" him.[16]

Poems such as these were to remain exceptional until the Restoration, during which cynical period the attacks on love and women increased markedly. Nevertheless, the recurrent appearance of antiromantic hostility in sixteenth- and seventeenth-century poetry shows that the ambivalence of the romantic tradition inherited from the Roman erotic poets remained alive even in the period when

[15] Robert Herrick, *The Poetical Works*, ed. F. W. Moorman (London: Oxford University Press, 1921), pp. 53, 76–77.

[16] Sir John Suckling, *The Works*, ed. A. H. Thompson (London: George Routledge, 1910), pp. 37–38. Cf. James Shirley's "Curse," "To the Proud Mistress," and "To a Beautiful Lady," *Dramatic Works and Poems*, ed. A. Dyce (London: John Murray, 1833), VI, 455–57, 459; Dr. John Hall's "Of Beauty," *Caroline Poets*, ed. G. Saintsbury (Oxford: Clarendon Press, 1906), II, 205; Andrew Marvell's "The Garden," *The Poems and Letters*, ed. H. M. Margoliouth (Oxford: Clarendon Press, 1952), I, 49.

English lyric poetry was most dominated by poems in praise of love and women. Although the Renaissance retractations were more secular and generally less virulent, as well as less frequent, than those of the Middle Ages, poets continued to indulge in the medieval charges that women's bodies are really masses of corruption; that women are lustful and undiscriminating; that they offer no more than sensual gratification, which is degrading; and that they are to be used, discarded, and escaped from before they ruin their lovers.

3

It is in drama, the dominant genre in Renaissance England and the one which developed distinctive form in this period, that we see a significant change in the expression of misogyny in the Renaissance. While misogyny remained a topic of lively interest, a reliable staple for comic or melodramatic effects, in drama it was no longer presented as an acceptable attitude. It appears in the works of most of the major dramatists, but for the most part either is attributed to certain characters whose attitudes are carefully dissociated from the author's, or else limited to certain offensive female types. While there are few misogynistic plays, there are numerous set pieces against women, evidently responses to a popular demand. The characters who voice these pieces may be suffering from acute disillusionment, either justified or proceeding from a mistaken belief that their mistresses have been false to them; or they may be clearly presented as cynical extremists.

The misogyny in Shakespeare's plays, I believe, is there equally because Shakespeare was interested in all aspects of human psychology and because he was aware of what his public wanted. It is invariably dissociated from the attitude presented as right in the play. When Hamlet exclaims, "Frailty, thy name is woman!" he is provoked by justified disgust with his mother's behavior; his generalization of his disgust with her to all women is represented as part of his illness. At the same time, although Hamlet's outbursts against women are motivated in terms of his character and situation, they serve also to gratify current interest in misogyny. Hamlet has various motives for his savagery to Ophelia in Act III, Scene i — disgust with women and sex, suspicion of her complicity in the plot to spy on him, a desire to fool the King and Polonius. But in addition to these, Shakespeare probably had the practical motive of enlivening his play with the familiar misogynistic charges. Certainly the accusations in Hamlet's abuse of Ophelia — lust, painting, affectation, and hypocrisy — were conventional and not particularly appropriate to the woman addressed.

King Lear's outburst against women, which also follows a shattering disillusionment, is definitely inappropriate to his situation, since Regan and Goneril do not go in for pretenses of modesty:

> Behold yond simpering dame,
> Whose face between her forks presageth snow;
> That minces virtue, and does shake the head
> To hear of pleasure's name;
> The fitchew nor the soiled horse goes to't
> With a more riotous appetite.
> Down from the waist they are Centaurs,
> Though women all above:
> But to the girdle do the gods inherit,
> Beneath is all the fiends'.

Shakespeare did not mean this to be taken as an exposure of the true nature of woman: Lear is mad, and immediately after this speech asks for "an ounce of civet . . . to sweeten my imagination." Yet it is significant that this particular example of hypocrisy, woman's insatiable lust hidden under a façade of purity, immediately leaps into the minds of both character and author. Such women were stock figures in contemporary satire — for example, Joseph Hall's character who looks like a shrined saint in the daytime and behaves like Messalina at night.[17]

Posthumus, in *Cymbeline* (1610 or 1611), indulges in a more elaborate outburst against women when he is led to believe that his wife has betrayed him. Like Hippolytus, he regrets that men cannot be created without the help of women, and thus remain untainted by feminine influence:

> . . . Could I find out
> The woman's part in me! For there's no motion
> That tends to vice in man but I affirm

[17] William Shakespeare, *The Tragedies*, ed. W. J. Craig (London: Oxford University Press, 1948), p. 817. Cf. Timon's railing in *Timon of Athens*, in *Tragedies*, pp. 440–43. Joseph Hall's character appears in *Virgidemiarum*, Book IV, Satire I.

> It is the woman's part; be it lying, note it,
> The woman's; flattering, hers; deceiving, hers;
> Lust and rank thoughts, hers, hers; revenges, hers;
> Ambitions, covetings, change of prides, disdain,
> Nice longing, slanders, mutability,
> All faults that man may name, nay, that hell knows.[18]

This situation, in which a man's mistaken and indeed practically groundless suspicion of his wife or mistress provokes him to denunciations of the sex, was a stock emotional device, as in Robert Greene's *Orlando Furioso* (1591), Francis Beaumont's and John Fletcher's *Philaster* (1611), and Part II of Dekker's *The Honest Whore* (1630).[19] Its recurrent appearance shows how popular tirades against women must have been with the Jacobean audience. When there was no wicked female character whose behavior could be used to provoke a misogynistic tirade, the playwright made an opportunity by setting up a situation in which the misjudgment of a good woman could provoke one.

The fact that misogynists were among the stock characters of seventeenth-century drama further indicates that people must have enjoyed satire on women. But these misogynists are all shown to be cynical villains like Iago or eccentric fools like Morose. It is hardly necessary to point out that Shakespeare so degraded the character of Iago, his only professional misogynist, and placed him in such an idealistic romantic setting, that his views are stripped of all credibility. The same may be said of the sycophantic fool Parolles in *All's Well That Ends Well* (1602?), who tells a man married to a girl much too good for him, "A young man married is a man that's marred."[20] Bosola in John Webster's *Duchess of Malfi* (1614), a

---

[18] Shakespeare, *Tragedies*, pp. 1092–93. Cf. Leontes' tirades when he suspects Hermione in *The Winter's Tale*, in William Shakespeare, *The Comedies*, ed. W. J. Craig (London: Oxford University Press, 1946), pp. 1002–4.

[19] Greene, *Life and Works*, XIII, 149–50. *Philaster*, in *Six Plays by Contemporaries of Shakespeare*, ed. C. B. Wheeler (London: Oxford University Press, 1946), pp. 349–50. Thomas Dekker, *The Dramatic Works*, ed. Fredson Bowers (Cambridge: Cambridge University Press, 1953–61), II, 170–71. This device remained popular as late as John Dryden's *Aureng-Zebe* (1675). Wrongly suspecting his virtuous Indamora of falsity, Aureng-Zebe storms at her: "Ah, sex, invented first to damn mankind," and so forth. (*John Dryden*, ed. G. Saintsbury [New York: Hill and Wang, n.d.], p. 332.)

[20] Shakespeare, *Comedies*, p. 863.

less unsympathetic villain than Iago, voices misogynistic satire to which the author appears to allow some validity. Again the satire is used to give acid comic relief to a somber tragedy, but Webster did not undercut it as Shakespeare did Iago's.[21]

In George Chapman's *Bussy d'Ambois* (1607) so many characters voice misogynistic sentiments that I suspect they express the author's own attitude. Declarations of woman's falsity, uncontrollable passions, and ruinous power over men are placed in the mouths of both sympathetic and unsympathetic characters, are not contradicted by counterdeclarations, and are supported by the behavior of the women in the play. Repeatedly an action of a female character provokes a wholesale misogynistic condemnation, which is left unchallenged, as if expressing a general truth so obvious that no further evidence is needed. When Monsieur learns that a woman who refused him on grounds of virtue had an adulterous affair with another man, he exclaims:

> O the unsounded sea of women's bloods,
> That when 'tis calmest, is most dangerous!
> Not any wrinkle creaming in their faces,
> When in their hearts are Scylla and Charybdis,
> Which still are hid in dark and standing fogs,
> Where never day shines, nothing ever grows,
> But weeds and poisons that no statesman knows:
> Not Cerberus ever saw the damned nooks
> Hid with the veils of women's virtuous looks.

Monsieur sees in her deception proof of the hellish passions always seething beneath woman's smooth façade and of course has no reservations about generalizing from this one adulteress to her whole sex.[22] He is a villain, it is true; but there is no indication in the play that Chapman did not accept his attitude as correct. The abundance of misogynistic statements in *Bussy*, and the fact that none of them is explicitly or implicitly challenged, suggests that Chapman himself found these sentiments congenial.

[21] See, for example, Bosola's jibes at court ladies' make-up and greed: *Six Plays by Contemporaries of Shakespeare*, pp. 416, 422.

[22] George Chapman, *Tragedies*, ed. T. M. Parrott (New York: Russell & Russell, 1961), I, 40. Cf. pp. 7, 27, 31, 36–37, 60, 62. With Monsieur's speech compare Edgar's in *King Lear*: "O undistinguished space of woman's will!" (Shakespeare, *Tragedies*, p. 821).

This suggestion is supported by Chapman's comedy *The Widow's Tears* (1612). In this dramatization of the Matron of Ephesus story, he intensified the misogyny of the original by aggravating the lady's behavior and definitely implying that it is typical of all women. When Tharsalio aspires to marry the governor's widow, his sister-in-law Cynthia points out that she had solemnly vowed eternal constancy to her late husband. Tharsalio retorts:

. . . do not you wives nod your heads and smile one upon another when ye meet abroad? . . . Do you not brag among yourselves how grossly you abuse [your husbands'] honest credulities? How they adore you for saints, and you believe it, while you adhorn their temples, and they believe it not? How you vow widowhood in their lifetime and they believe you, when even in the sight of their breathless corse, ere they be fully cold, you join embraces with his groom, or his physician, and perhaps his poisoner; or at least, by the next moon (if you can expect so long) solemnly plight new hymeneal bonds, with a wild, confident, untamed ruffian.

Cynthia is naturally indignant at such cynicism, but as the action develops it turns out that he is absolutely right. The heartbroken widow soon agrees to marry him, having heard that he is good in bed.

Cynthia, deeply shocked, makes a point of professing eternal constancy to her husband should he happen to die. He decides to test her fidelity by making her believe that he has. Cynthia entombs herself with his supposed coffin, just like the Widow of Ephesus, to drink nothing but her tears until she dies with him. Her husband comes back, disguised as a strange soldier, and easily seduces her, as in the original tale. The same complication arises about the missing body, and Cynthia too volunteers her husband's to replace it on the cross; but Chapman aggravates her guilt by making the soldier confess to having murdered her husband himself and tell her his last word was "Cynthia!" She is shocked, but as she still wants to marry the soldier, she urges him to hurry and take the body. When her husband, throwing off his disguise, cries out, "What is a woman? What are the worst when the best are so past naming? . . . Paint them, paint them ten parts more than they do themselves, rather than look on them as they are," the audience is no doubt supposed to agree. Being a comedy, the play ends with an unconvincing reconciliation between Cynthia and her husband. But despite his comic form, Chapman managed to be just about as venomous as the author of *The Seven Sages*. On its next reappearance, in Oliver Goldsmith's *Citizen of the World* (1760), the story is again told lightly, as a joke rather than a misogynistic satire, although Goldsmith did kill off his inconstant widow, who commits suicide from shame and disappointment. By the later eighteenth century, misogyny as harsh as Chapman's was no longer acceptable.[23]

For the most part, however, Renaissance dramatists limited the misogyny in their comedies to particular characters, whom they used as satiric butts rather than as mouthpieces for their own point of view. But of course at the same time that the misogynists were being ridiculed, their charges against women could be enjoyed as antifeminist satire. Marston's *Parasitaster, or The Fawn* (1606) displays a gallery of foolish misogynists: two affected cynics who claim to know all about women and a jealous idiot who persists in suspecting his virtuous wife. Naturally, much is said about women's misvaluation of men, vulnerability to sexual temptation, and uncontrollable passions and tongues; but the falsity of these attitudes is a major point of the play.

Ben Jonson's Morose, in *Epicoene* (1609), who finds women so odious that he will marry only a mouselike mute, is obviously a figure of fun. When Truewit tries to persuade Morose not to marry, Jonson makes the most of his opportunity to relate the miseries of conjugal life; but, although Jonson and his audience no doubt enjoyed this extended refurbishing of Juvenal, it is so placed in the dramatic structure of the play that no one can take it seriously. *Epicoene, or The Silent Woman* as a whole is a collection of misogynistic charges: the very subtitle is an indirect jibe at female garrulity; Truewit flippantly disparages women in Ovidian style; Otter describes his wife in terms of a modernized version of Martial's epigram on Galla;[24] and the Collegiate Ladies illustrate the odiousness of female presumption. Yet, since the charges are presented indirectly and farcically, the play cannot be called really misogynistic.

[23] Chapman, *Comedies*, I, 369–70, 421. Goldsmith told his similar story in Letter 18 of *The Citizen of the World*.
[24] Ben Jonson, *Plays* (London: J. M. Dent, 1960), I, 500–502 (Truewit's Juvenalian tirade), 529 (echo of Martial).

4

While the dramatists did not condemn women outright, but only through misogynistic characters who usually represented a distorted point of view, they were very fond of purple passages against whores, which owe something to the recurrent whore metaphor in the Bible. To condemn women had become questionable; to condemn whores was morally righteous. And yet, as the commentaries on Proverbs demonstrate, it is easy to generalize from bad women to all women, to attribute the incontestable sinfulness of the whore to her entire sex. Perhaps the most effective of the tirades is Monticelso's in Webster's *The White Devil* (1608):

> Sweetmeats which rot the eater; in man's nostril
> Poisoned perfumes: they are cozening alchemy;
>
> . . . .
>
> Cold Russian winters, that appear so barren
> As if that nature had forgot the spring:
> They are the true material fire of hell:
>
> . . . .
>
> . . . Your rich whores
> Are only treasuries by extortion filled,
> And emptied by curs'd riot. They are worse,
> Worse than dead bodies which are begged at gallows,
> And wrought upon by surgeons, to teach man
> Wherein he is imperfect. What's a whore?
> She's like the guilty counterfeited coin
> Which, whosoe'er first stamps it, brings in trouble
> All that receive it.[25]

In the scene where Hippolito reforms Bellafront in Dekker's *Honest Whore*, Part I (1604), there is a longer and more literally detailed tirade against whores: they have no souls, their bodies are "like the common shoare, that still receives / All the townes filth," and so on for 101 lines.[26] Such passages are too long and lurid to be interpreted entirely in terms of their dramatic function in the plays or their satiric purpose of reprehending vice.

Furthermore, Marston's *Insatiate Countess* (1613) shows how an attack on a whore can slip into general misogyny, both in the

---

[25] *Six Plays by Contemporaries of Shakespeare*, p. 128.
[26] Dekker, *Works*, II, 53–56.

character of the heroine — a personification of all the vices then charged to woman — and in the comments on her sex which her behavior provokes. At the beginning of the play, Countess Isabella is in mourning for her first husband; during the course of it she seduces four honorable men, three for simple lust and the fourth for revenge. After she has promptly wooed and won the first young man, a courtier comments that he will never again trust a woman mourning nor be pleased with anything done by women, "Nature's step-children, rather her disease." Soon afterward she elopes with a second man, only to abandon him for his best friend. There is no indication in the play that the second man's outburst when she has cast him off is not to be accepted as a correct evaluation of women:

> Farewell, thou private strumpet, worse than common!
> Man were on earth an angel but for woman.
> That sevenfold branch of hell from them doth grow,
> Pride, lust, and murder, they raise from below,
> With all their fellow-sins. Women are made
> Of blood, without souls: when their beauties fade,
> And their lust's past, avarice or bawdry
> Makes them still loved; then they buy venery,
> Bribing damnation, and hire brothel-slaves:
> Shame's their executors, infamy their graves.
> Your painting will wipe off, which art did hide,
> And show your ugly shape in spite of pride.[27]

Infuriated by his lampoons against her lust and dishonesty, Isabella induces her third lover to go out and kill him. When the two friends are reconciled instead, she persuades a fourth man to kill both of them, offering her person as a reward.

The Jacobean dramatists extensively attacked other obnoxious female types besides the whore: the court lady (who, as the dramatists saw her, was not very different), the learned lady (in Jonson), and the rich tradesman's wife or "city-madam." The shrew of medieval drama developed into this specialized type with the increased wealth of the middle class and their resulting eagerness to climb socially. The theme of *Eastward Ho!* (1605), a collaborative effort of Chapman, Jonson, and Marston, is the folly and wickedness of

[27] John Marston, *The Works*, ed. A. H. Bullen (London: John C. Nimmo, 1887), III, 136–37, 199.

trying to rise above one's given place in society; and the most conspicuous bad example is Gertrude, who is, like so many bad women
in literature, abetted by her mother. Gertrude, a middle-class girl
who is to be married to a knight, utterly disdains tradesman's ways;
she "must be a lady, and . . . will be a lady." She likes "some
humours of the city-dames," such as eating cherries only out of season or dying rich scarlet black, but will have none of their mincing
bourgeois manners, such as modesty with men. She rejoices that her
family will have to call her "Madam" after her marriage, but she
has to depend on the tailor to teach her the manners of a lady.[28] In
the end her knightly husband deserts her, and she is forced to ask
her father's pardon for her foolish pride.

The most extensive gallery of proud bourgeoises appears in
Philip Massinger's *The City Madam* (1632). Sir John Frugal's
wife and daughters, who dream of becoming countesses, "take state
/ As they were such already." Indeed, "Few great ladies going to
a mask . . . outshine ours in their every-day habits." Sir John
must permit this exorbitance, "Or there's no peace nor rest for him
at home." Since Lady Frugal, a devotee of astrology, has found out
that the stars guarantee her daughters sovereignty over their husbands, the two girls proceed to lay down conditions to their suitors.
Anne stipulates that her knight grant her will in all things whatsoever without argument and provide her with a retinue of servants
and the newest fashions to attract the gallants from her private box
at the theatre; if he complies with these conditions he will find her
"A most indulgent wife." Mary does not deign to make stipulations;
rather, she will take control of the entire property, allowing her
husband what she thinks fit. The second man, a rich squire, bursts
out that he would rather turn to the next sow-gelder than satisfy his
desire with her; and the knight takes his departure more delicately
but as firmly. Eventually the women's pride is brought down, the
two girls win back their suitors by submission, and Lady Frugal
promises to be a good wife in the future. Sir John tells her to set
a good example to "Our city dames, whom wealth makes proud,
to move / In their own spheres"[29] — that is, to restrict herself to
the middle class and to domestic subordination.

[28] *Ibid.*, pp. 14–16.
[29] Philip Massinger, *Plays*, ed. A. Symons (London: Vizetelly and Co., 1887),

Jonson's version of the city madam is much like those of his contemporaries, although he characteristically emphasized her stupidity more than anything else. Chloe in *The Poetaster* (1601) is
typical. She continually abuses her tradesman husband, fawns on
anyone who is a gentleman born — including Captain Tucca, who
gallantly addresses her as "punk" — and, though she prides herself
on her breeding, is unaware of such elementary mythology as the
connection between Mars and Venus. Fallace in *Every Man Out of
His Humour* (1599), Mistress Otter in *Epicoene*, and Pinnacia Stuff
in *The New Inn* (1629) are of the same type. Yet no matter how
perverse, ungracious, and even unfaithful these women are, Jonson
always shows their husbands doting on them, as did the unfortunate
men in Dekker's *Batchelars Banquet*. Perhaps this implausible addition to the picture results from the misogynist's disgusted apprehension that, no matter how badly they behave, women can always
control men sexually. Or perhaps it is meant to suggest that all
conjugal love is uxoriousness, as Juvenal had implied. Devotion to
these odious women, then, would burlesque devotion even to a good
wife. Macilente in *Every Man Out*, speaking, it seems, for Jonson,
advises a doting husband against being too amorous and obliging:
"When women doubt most of their husbands' loves, / They are
most loving." Therefore you must ration your kindness to your wife,
as you do fodder to your horse. Conceal your desire for her, making
her believe that you are kind only from a sense of duty. In short,
keep her insecure, so that she will continously exert herself to please
you.[30] This is just the treatment that Fallace deserves, but it seems
unduly harsh as general marriage counsel.

Jonson's presentation of the court lady is particularly effective
because he dwells on her mental emptiness more than the lust and
beauty aids emphasized by other dramatists. Saviolina, in *Every
Man Out*, enthralls her foolish admirers and herself with an unceas-
ing flow of pointless and derivative wit. Despite her pose of fashionable sophistication, she is completely unable to distinguish a clown
from a gentleman. In *Cynthia's Revels* (1601) a judicious critic

---

I, 402, 431–35, 496. Cf. Thomas Middleton's *Anything for a Quiet Life*, which
presents two unhappy marriages, one in the upper and one in the middle class,
in each of which a man is made miserable by his proud, shrewish wife.

[30] Jonson, *Plays*, I, 88–89.

neatly sums up the type: ". . . the most proud, witty creatures, all things apprehending, nothing understanding, perpetually laughing."[31] That is, they have all the froth of intellect — liveliness, responsiveness, fluency on all subjects — but utterly lack the solid qualities of sense and understanding.

Jonson's "Epigram on the Court Pucell," a more savage treatment of the same theme, strips the glamor from a lady of apparently dazzling wit and sophistication. She attracts the prime wits of the court to spar for her approval; she writes fashionable poetry; she talks with equally fluent and well-turned phrases on politics, religion, and bawdry. Yet Jonson not only reduces her cleverness to emptiness, but envelops it in unpleasant sexual imagery. The wits fight like cocks in her chamber, her efforts at neat phrasing are lip-thirstiness, she composes "in an Epicoene fury," and her writing is forcing a Muse "with Tribade lust," that is, with the lust of a lesbian playing the male role. Thus Jonson implied that an intellectual woman is usurping a man's role and associated female intellectual pretensions with unchastity. This arbitrary association has always been popular with antifeminists, who would presumably justify it on the grounds that the woman who throws off the mental restrictions imposed on her sex will throw off all others as well, and that female passions unrestricted are necessarily dangerous and sinful. It is an easy way to discredit female intellectuals and to dramatize the "unwomanliness" of their activities.

In other epigrams on court ladies, Jonson emphasized primarily lust, the sin with which the satirists most often charged them. At court, he declared indignantly, it is "civilitie to be a whore," so long as the man in question wears velvet or plush. The ladies spend hours "discoursing with their Glasse, / How they may make some one that day an Asse." "One, whose band sits ill" nauseates them; but they will leap like a bitch in heat upon a fashionable fop.[32]

It is not these attacks on lustful ladies, common in Jacobean

[31] *Ibid.*, I, 207. Cf. Beaumont and Fletcher's Megra, in *Philaster*, Marston's Rossaline in *Antonio and Mellida*, and a whole gallery of vicious court ladies in his *Malcontent*.

[32] Ben Jonson, *Works*, ed. C. H. Herford and P. and E. Simpson (Oxford: Clarendon Press, 1954), VIII, 163–64, 222. Cf. his epigram "To Fine Lady Would-Bee" (p. 46), in which he asked and answered the question why she feared to bear a child since she so loved to make them.

satire, that betray Jonson's misogyny, but rather his unusually pronounced dislike of women who consider themselves witty or learned.
There were many learned ladies in Tudor times, when, under the
influence of Renaissance emancipation and enthusiasm for learning, girls were often given much the same education as boys. Despite
occasional protests that it was dangerous to develop women's minds,
most writers seemed to appreciate intelligent women and to accept
learning for women as a good thing. There are virtually no caricatures of learned ladies in early seventeenth-century drama outside
of Jonson. But these portraits recur in Jonson's plays, in which most
of the women are stupid, with the would-be intellectuals simply
more obnoxious than the others.

The best known, Lady Politick Would-Be, displays — besides
the jealousy and baseless sexual vanity so often attributed to women
and the dishonesty that infects almost everyone in *Volpone* (1606)
— merciless garrulity and egregious intellectual conceit: she is a
self-proclaimed authority on every subject. When she has forced
her way into Volpone's room and asked how he does, he answers:

> Troubled with noise, I cannot sleep; I dreamt
> That a strange fury enter'd, now, my house,
> And, with the dreadful tempest of her breath,
> Did cleave my roof asunder.

All this conveys to her is a hint to tell her own dream. When Volpone claims he has attacks when people tell him dreams, she pours
out a list of fifteen remedies, explaining modestly:

> I have a little studied physic; but now,
> I'm all for music, save, in the forenoons,
> An hour or two for painting [her face as well as canvas,
>   presumably]. I would have
> A lady, indeed, to have all, letters and arts,
> Be able to discourse, to write, to paint,
> But principal, as Plato holds, your music.

Volpone retorts that a poet as old and knowing as Plato says the
"highest female grace is silence." Lady Would-Be, who does not
recognize Sophocles, eagerly inquires who this could be:

> Petrarch, or Tasso, or Dante?
> Guarini? Ariosto? Aretine?
> Cieco di Hadria? I have read them all,

and indeed is carrying two or three of them around with her. She then treats him to a series of critical commonplaces on the Italian poets: Petrarch is passionate, Dante is hard, and so forth. When she at last observes that he is not listening and he tells her his mind is perturbed, she gives him a lecture on philosophy. Nothing can save Volpone until Mosca tells her that Sir Politick is with a courtesan, at which she flies off in a jealous fury. Mosca comments, "They that use themselves most license, / Are still most jealous." [33] Jonson's picture of Lady Would-Be's shallow pedantry, her pride in thread-bare bits of critical wisdom, and her obliviousness to her listeners' boredom is brilliant. But the unchastity referred to here and else-where in the play seems superfluous and out of character. It was brought in, it seems, as an easy way to discredit Lady Would-Be further, and perhaps because Jonson could not resist adding this worst of female sins to the odious character of an intellectual woman.

The Collegiate Ladies in *Epicoene*, who have set themselves up as judges of wit and fashion (about which they know nothing), use "most masculine, or rather hermaphroditical authority." They have tamed their husbands, practice free love, and preserve their non-existent youth and beauty by refusing to bear children. They make a great show of friendship for each other, but — women being sup-posed incapable of friendship — they miss no opportunity to back-bite their fellow-collegiates. In *Catiline* (1611) Jonson displayed to scorn Sempronia, a learned lady who had already become a stock example of the woman with too many talents. Like all Jonson's female intellectuals, she is middle-aged and painted and very gen-erous with her sexual favors. She loves to discourse on public af-fairs, considers herself one of the key politicians in Rome, and has a "very masculine" wit, which means that she is a critic, composes verse, and is adept in repartee. She even thinks that states might sometimes employ women as ambassadors, an idea which is sup-posed to show the extravagance of her feminist presumptuousness. Jonson took the character of Sempronia from Sallust, whose *War with Catiline* he followed closely in this play; but he made her

---

[33] Jonson, *Plays*, I, 439–42. The quotation from Sophocles is from his *Ajax* (*Complete Greek Drama*, ed. Whitney J. Oates and Eugene O'Neill, Jr. [New York: Random House, 1938], I, 325).

unattractive and added her political pretensions and the "masculinity" of her wit.[34] Elaborating on a congenial theme, Jonson made of a woman criticized for her political affiliation a bluestocking odious for her feminism.

Although Jonson's dislike for intellectual women was mainly the result of individual temperament, it also reflected the general trend of his period. When the brilliant Elizabeth I was succeeded by James I, who disliked female intellectuals, there was a reaction against mental development for women. Sir Thomas Overbury's widely admired poem on the ideal wife ("A Wife," 1614) emphasizes the perils of intellect in woman and the limitations of her role. "Give me next *good*, an *understanding* wife," he asked; but "understanding" was to be strictly limited, as too great a supply simply gives women more scope for evil-doing, for expressing their natural tendencies toward mischief:

> A *passive understanding* to conceive,
> And judgment to discerne, I wish to finde:
> Beyond that, all as hazardous I leave;
> *Learning* and *pregnant wit* in woman-kinde,
>   What it findes malleable, makes fraile,
>   And doth not adde more *ballast*, but more saile.

"Domesticke charge doth best that *sex* befit," and serves the additional purpose of keeping women out of trouble: "Their leysure 'tis corrupteth *woman-kind*." Books, of course, "are a part of mans prerogative."[35] Thomas Killigrew's *The Parson's Wedding* (*ca.* 1640) features a learned lady, in this case a "she chirurgeon," characterized much in Jonson's manner. Killigrew represents her as caring for sick men solely for the pleasure of handling their

---

[34] Jonson, *Plays*, I, 492, II, 107–8, 156. Sallust, *The War with Catiline*, trans. J. C. Rolfe (London: Heinemann, 1921), pp. 43–45.

[35] Sir Thomas Overbury, *The Miscellaneous Works in Prose and Verse*, ed. E. F. Rimbault (London: Reeves and Turner, 1890), pp. 40–41. Overbury's argument that mental training for women would simply develop their native capacity for mischief was common among sixteenth- and seventeenth-century opponents of education for women. Those who argued for educating women — and this controversy raged in several countries throughout the Renaissance —insisted that mental training would fortify their virtue. On the whole argument, see Ruth Kelso, *Doctrine for the Lady of the Renaissance* (Urbana: University of Illinois Press, 1956).

naked limbs, calling "the fornication charity." [36] The objection to
her activities is not really on grounds of modesty, however (as is
apparent from the revolting tone of the play), but on grounds of
woman's proper subordination. Lady Freedom conducts her activities independently of her husband, and she is very successful at
curing patients.

Of the major writers of the Renaissance, Jonson comes the closest
to misogyny. His works are conspicuously full of attacks on female
failings and conspicuously deficient in portrayals of good women
and of romantic love. *Epicoene*, his play most concerned with
women, resounds with the classical misogynistic charges. While he
did not indulge in overt diatribes against the sex, no contemporary
dramatist gave such emphasis to obnoxious female types, who figure prominently in over half his plays; and none so pointedly
avoided romantic idealization of women. It might be objected that
Jonson was a misanthropist rather than a misogynist, that he emphasized women's failings more than their virtues because of his
low estimation of mankind in general. But his picture of women is
particularly one-sided: while intelligent and even good male characters appear in Jonson, there are virtually no admirable female
characters to counterbalance the brainless, shrewish, vain, and lustful women in his plays. Jonson's hostility to women is indicated
more definitely by his particular detestation of those who tried to
step out of their allotted sphere by cultivating wit or learning, which
clearly suggests the misogynist's need to keep women subordinate
in order to nullify their power.

A more common sign of fear of women in the Renaissance was
the repeated attack on the whore, which often attributed enormous
powers to her, more than she could possibly in fact have. (Surely
a normal man can escape from the clutches of a whore if he wants
to.) The unrealistic exaggerations of these charges — which represent a common prostitute as capable of ruining millions of men,
who are powerless before her — probably reflect the psychological
reality of fear deriving from the infant's view of the mother as
apparently omnipotent. Of course, these attacks form a tiny part
of the total literary output of the Renaissance, and must always

[36] Thomas Killigrew, *The Parson's Wedding*, in *Dodsley's Select Collection
of Old Plays* (London: Septimus Prowett, 1827), XI, 471.

be distinguished from sweeping condemnations of women, which are not found in the major secular writers of the period.

Nevertheless, it is clear that harsh expressions of misogyny were appreciated well into the seventeenth century. A popular playwright like Dekker wrote an indictment presenting married women as so many Wives of Bath; a university wit like Nashe described in gloating detail the writhings of beautiful women in Hell. Even setting aside hack journalism, we find denunciations of women in most writers of the time: while the total works in which these passages appear are usually not misogynistic, it is obvious that people still enjoyed writing and hearing that women are "Mummy, possesst" or made "Of blood, without souls." Men seem to be prone to conservatism in their attitude toward women even in a period of generally progressive thought, perhaps because their emotions are so deeply involved.

Partly because of this tendency to cling tenaciously to old ideas about women in a changing culture, partly because the Renaissance was a period of transition — between medieval asceticism and modern idealization of conjugal love, between harsh attacks on women's ungovernable passions and moderate criticisms of their weaknesses — the Renaissance attitude toward women was curiously mixed. Popular journalism, in which originality would not be expected, continued the medieval charges against women virtually unchanged in tone and content. Erotic poetry and romances, deriving from the medieval tradition of courtly love, showed a similar ambivalence toward women, although Renaissance literature emphasized the positive side more strongly. In drama, generally speaking, we find the attitude that seems most truly characteristic of the age: frequent expression of misogyny unsoftened by concessions to feminine delicacy, which is not, however, presented as a tenable attitude toward women. Most of the playwrights definitely disavowed misogyny by restricting their attacks to certain types of bad women or by placing generalized denunciations in the mouths of unreliable characters. On the other hand, they showed much ingenuity in bringing misogynistic charges into the plays, often devising characters and situations for this purpose. Misogynists might be regarded as distorted people, but brutal misogyny remained an interesting and acceptable literary staple, so long as it was not advocated outright.

In the religious writings of the sixteenth and seventeenth centuries, we are also apt to find harsh antifeminism reminiscent of the Middle Ages, although it is usually tempered by a high regard for marriage. Neither secular nor religious writers in this period felt any need to moderate their criticism of women by consideration for the supposed fragility of the female sex.

Chapter IV ♋ ST. PAUL WITH A DIFFERENCE:
THE PURITANS

1

WHILE THE subordination of women was accepted almost universally during the sixteenth and seventeenth centuries, the really zealous expressions of this doctrine are to be found among religious writers, especially those of Puritan sympathies. Reacting against the Roman Catholic Church and all its ways, the Puritans reverted to the patriarchy of the Old Testament, specifically as it was expounded by St. Paul. Although they extolled marriage — for they almost never followed St. Paul's sexual asceticism — they condemned the courtly lover's worship of women as disgusting effeminacy.

Naturally, men holding Pauline views were tremendously disturbed by the increased independence which women had been showing during the Renaissance, and their anxiety was aggravated by the chance that in the mid-sixteenth century Catholic queens, Mary Tudor and the Regent Mary of Guise, were ruling England and Scotland. John Knox, exiled in Geneva, perpetrated the most notorious attack on female rulers in his *First Blast of the Trumpet against the Monstrous regiment* [rule] *of women* (1558). "It is the dutie," he opened, "of everie true messager of God" to expose to the world "this monstriferouse empire of women, (which amongest all enormities, that this day do abound upon the face of the hole earth, is most detestable and damnable)," "to the end that some may repent and be saved." In support of his proposition that promoting a woman to rule any nation or city "is repugnant to nature, contumelie to God, a thing most contrarious to his reveled will and approved ordinance, and finallie it is the subversion of good order, of all equitie and justice," he contended first that women are hopelessly lacking in the qualities necessary for rule: ". . . their sight in civile regiment is but blindnes: their strength, weaknes: their counsel, foolishenes: and judgement, phrenesie, if it be rightlie considered . . . experience hath declared them to be unconstant, variable, cruell and lacking the spirit of counsel and regiment."

Secondly, St. Paul took from woman "all power and authoritie, to speake, to reason, to interprete, or to teach, but principallie to rule or to judge in the assemblies of men." The same God, he concluded,

that hath denied power to the hand to speake, to the bely to heare, and to the feet to see, hath denied to woman power to commande man, and hath taken away wisdome to consider, and providence to forsee the thinges, that be profitable to the common welth: yea finallie he hath denied to her in any case to be head to man.

Far from its being a man's duty to obey a female sovereign, "to place a woman in authoritie above a realme, is to pollute and prophane the royall seate, the throne of justice . . . and . . . to maintaine them in the same, is nothing els, but continuallie to rebell against God." Two of Knox's colleagues, John Ponet and Christopher Goodman, wrote tracts in the same vein, liberally besprinkled with references to Queen Jezebel, which are however less impassioned, and motivated by political partisanship more than misogyny.[1]

Knox never blew his projected Second and Third Blasts, because his more prudent colleagues pointed out that a female ruler sympathetic to Protestantism would probably soon ascend the throne of England. But he never recanted his views on women. When, after Elizabeth's accession, he wanted to enter England, he wrote her minister, William Cecil: "For the miraculouse woorke of God's comfortinge his afflicted by an infirme vessell, I doe reverence." Only if Queen Elizabeth would confess "that the extraordinary dis-

---

[1] John Knox, *The First Blast of the Trumpet against the Monstrous regiment of women*, ed. Edward Arber (Westminster: Constable, 1895), pp. 6–7, 11–12, 18, 28, 45. John Ponet wrote *A Short Treatise of Politique Power* (1556); Christopher Goodman, *How Superior Powers Ought to be Obeyed* (1558). Cf. Thomas Becon, *An Humble Supplication unto God*, in *Prayers and Other Pieces*, ed. J. Ayre (Cambridge: Cambridge University Press, 1844), pp. 227–28, 242. James E. Phillips cites other similar opinions in "The Background of Spenser's Attitude Toward Women Rulers," *Huntington Library Quarterly*, V (October, 1941, and July, 1942), 5–32, 211–34.

pensation of Godes great mercy maketh that lawfull unto her, which both nature and Godes lawe denye" to other women, would he be willing to maintain her right to rule.[2]

While the objectors to female rule necessarily scorned women, those who defended it did not necessarily think well of them. John Aylmer's *An Harborough for faithful Subjects* (1559), a refutation of Knox's *Blast*, ardently maintained women's right to rule not because they are fit for it, but because God often chooses to work through weak instruments. If He places in authority "a woman weake in nature, feable in bodie, softe in courage, unskilfull in practise, not terrible to the enemy, no shilde to the frynde," it is because "It is as easy for him to save by fewe as by many, by weake as by strong, by a woman as by a man." Thus God has worked through weak women — Deborah and Judith and Anne Boleyn (who precipitated the Reformation in England) — as well as through Samson's hair and the jawbone of an ass. Typically, women are "fond, folish, wanton, flibbergibbes, tatlers, triflers, wavering, witles, without counsell, feable, careles, rashe, proude, deintie, nise, talebearers, evesdroppers, rumour raisers, evell tonged, worse minded, and in everye wise doltified with the dregges of the Devils dounge hill." Even though women may occasionally rule, they may never join the clergy, where mental and moral virtues are truly indispensable.[3] Aylmer, who had been a Puritan exile, was at the time aspiring toward a career in the Church of England, and his book is filled with fulsome flattery of Queen Elizabeth; it is not hard to see, however, why she kept him waiting a long time for his bishopric.

Edmund Spenser, courtly as he was, maintained essentially the same position with regard to women rulers. His inclusion of this topic in *The Faerie Queene* (1596), where it is unnecessary to the theme and embarrassingly at variance with his glorification of Queen Elizabeth, shows how important he must have considered restrictions upon women. Much as he exalted romantic love and duly feminine women, he made a point of including in his masterpiece a rationale for female subordination. One of the major of-

[2] Phillips, "Spenser's Attitude Toward Women Rulers," pp. 19–20.

[3] S. R. Maitland, *Essays on . . . the Reformation in England* (London: Francis & John Rivington, 1849), pp. 209, 214–15.

fenders against justice, the subject of Book V, is Radigund, an Amazon who fights with, conquers, and rules men. She is proud, cruel, and lustful; indeed, her career of contention with men was motivated by nothing more than frustrated lust, when a knight persistently rebuffed her advances. (This is an interesting anticipation of the Freudian view that women are motivated to compete in "masculine" fields by feelings of sexual inadequacy.) Radigund's pride is shown by her attempt to rise above her place in the scheme of things. Lust and cruelty were generally imputed to masterless women, because of woman's alleged inability to control her passions and even to comprehend justice.

Having conquered men, Radigund forces them to dress and work as women, thus putting into graphic allegorical form the conventional argument that a woman who rules is as much a monster as a man who spins. The obvious degradation of the aproned spinster knights is, Spenser makes clear, an allegory of the degradation of any sort of subordination to women. When Radigund conquers Artegall, it is not through her strength — for she has no strength, properly speaking — but through her good luck and his weakness, his susceptibility to her beauty. Like Milton's Adam, he is "fondly overcome with female charm." Both Spenser and Milton, who held essentially the same views on sex and women, were keenly aware of the dangerous seductiveness of beauty: some men will blame Artegall "For yeelding so himselfe a wretched thrall, / To th'insolent commaund of womens will"; but they should bear in mind that "never yet was wight so well aware, / But he at first or last was trapt in womens snare."

Ultimately Artegall is rescued by his love, the righteous female warrior Britomart, who, after killing Radigund and conquering her city, repeals "The liberty of women . . . Which they had long usurpt" and deals "true Justice" by restoring them "To mens subjection." She hands over the city to the formerly captive knights, whom she makes swear fealty not to her, but to Artegall. Not relying on allegory to make his point, Spenser moralized explicitly on Radigund's treatment of her male captives:

> Such is the crueltie of womenkynd,
>> When they have shaken off the shamefast band,
>> With which wise Nature did them strongly bynd,

T'obay the heasts of mans well ruling hand,
That then all rule and reason they withstand,
To purchase a licentious libertie.
But vertuous women wisely understand,
That they were borne to base humilitie,
Unlesse the heavens them lift to lawfull soveraintie.

Spenser was forced by his political views to make the same exception to female subjection that Aylmer did, but his opinion of women,
while more politely expressed, was not very different. Female rule
may be righteous, but only in the exceptional cases in which God
has endowed a woman with sovereign power, like Gloriana in *The
Faerie Queene* or her prototype, Queen Elizabeth. Earlier in the
poem Spenser made a point of including, "Proud wemen, vaine,
forgetfull of their yoke" — Semiramis, Sthenoboea, and Cleopatra — among the victims of the House of Pride.[4]

With the accession of James I, the right or ability of women to
rule ceased to be a significant question, and this particular controversy died out. But a related grievance persisted: women's outrageous fondness for fashions proper to men (as well as men's for
those of women). Puritan preachers and pamphleteers denounced
these fashions partly on the usual grounds, as evidence of vanity
or lust or newfangledness, but mainly because they jeopardized
the principle of male superiority. As in Spenser, male dress symbolized superiority and female, subjection. Thus William Prynne

[4] Edmund Spenser, *The Poetical Works*, ed. J. C. Smith and E. De Selincourt
(London: Oxford University Press, 1952), pp. 293, 296–98, 301, 309. It might
be objected that an attack on female government could never have escaped
the eye of Queen Elizabeth, to whom *The Faerie Queene* was dedicated; but
I do not see how Spenser's text can be interpreted otherwise than as a rationale
for female subordination. I suppose that his fulsome praise of Gloriana, Britomart, and Mercilla made more impression on the Queen than his condemnation
of Radigund's activities. In any case Elizabeth was a practical woman who was
far more concerned with whether her subjects were loyal to her personally
than with whether they justified her right to rule by the equal capacity of
women or by a special dispensation from God. The latter justification, suggested
in the last line of the stanza I have quoted, was often used by antifeminist Puritan supporters of Elizabeth and was evidently entirely satisfactory to her.
Sir David Lyndesay, in *The Monarche* (1552), similarly attacked the pride
of women who aspired to rule, through the horrible example of masterful, lustful Semiramis: *Works* (London: Early English Text Society [Orig. Ser. 11,
19], 1865–66), pp. 32, 35, 98, 105–6.

opened his preface to *The Unlovelinesse of Love-Lockes* (1628) with the hope that his treatise might be profitable in his time:

. . . wherein as sundry of our Mannish, Impudent, and inconstant female sexe, are Hermophradited, and transformed into men; not onely in their immodest, shamelesse, and audacious carriage . . . but even in the unnaturall Tonsure, and Odious, if not Whorish Cutting, and Crisping of their Haire, their Naturalle vaile, their Feminine glory, and the very badge, and Character of their subjection both to God, and Man: so divers of our Masculine, and more noble race, are wholy degenerated and metamorphosed into women;

not only in manners and dress, but in curling their hair. The purpose for which love-locks are worn is even more outrageous than are the locks themselves: ". . . to please, or Humour, a Vaine, Fantastique, Light, or Whorish Mistress, Dame, or Sweete-heart."

In *Histrio-Mastix* (1632) Prynne renewed his attack on "mens degenerating into women" and "the aspiring of women above the limits of their female sex" by means of masculine hair-styles and dress. English gentlewomen, he exclaimed, persisted in cutting their hair, "as if they all intended, to turne men outright and weare the Breeches, or to become Popish Nonnes."[5] One of the major Puritan objections to Roman Catholicism was the opportunity it offered women to lead an independent religious life, free from direct subjection to men. Of course, Puritan preachers also continued to attack all the usual forms of female finery in the usual terms: Philip Stubbes, for example, excoriated women's cosmetics, elaborate hair styles, ruffs, and so forth in his *Anatomie of Abuses* (1583) and called the decorated female body "a dunghil covered with white & red."[6]

2

The aspect of female subjection which had the most general importance and received the most attention was, naturally, that of

[5] William Prynne, *The Unlovelinesse of Love-Lockes* (London, 1628), first page of preface, p. 38. *Histrio-Mastix: The Players Scourge* (London: Michael Sparke, 1633), pp. 200–201.

[6] Philip Stubbes, *The Anatomie of Abuses*, ed. F. J. Furnivall (London: New Shakespeare Society [Ser. 6, Nos. 4, 6], 1877–79), I, 80. This edition includes many citations from other writers which parallel Stubbes's charges. Cf. also John Donne, *Sermons*, ed. Henry Alford (London: Parker, 1839), IV, 229–31,

the wife to her husband. Misogynistically inclined Protestant preachers delighted in sermons on this topic, since most of them, as Protestants, would not express outright scorn of marriage or of women as sexual objects. Even among Protestants, however, a minority continued to depreciate marriage on into the eighteenth century. William Law, advocating celibacy for the clergy, sneered:

I know very well, that the Reformation has allowed Priests and Bishops not only to look out for Wives, but to have as many as they please, one after another: But this is only to be consider'd as a *bare Allowance*, and perhaps granted upon such a Motive, as *Moses* of old made one to the *Jews*, for *the Hardness of their Hearts*.

A clergyman making love to a woman is a shocking sight. Suppose John the Baptist, after preaching on repentance and the Kingdom of Heaven, had proposed to an accomplished young lady. Should not "those Clergy who date their Mission from Jesus Christ himself . . . look upon *Love-Addresses* to the Sex, as *unbecoming*, as *foreign*, as *opposite* to their Character, as to the *Baptist*'s"? After reading St. Paul, he concluded, "who would imagine . . . there should be any need of Church Authority to restrain any one in Holy Orders, from seeking after a Wife?" [7]

Most Protestant preachers on marriage, however, ignored this aspect of St. Paul's teaching, although they assiduously followed his dicta on wifely subjection. Of course, the belief that women should be subject to men did not mark a man as misogynistic, since it was axiomatic in that period (as indeed it still must be to anyone who accepts the dicta of St. Paul as revealed truth). But misogyny is evident in unnecessarily rigorous interpretations of St. Paul and in rancorous insistence on woman's responsibility for the Original Sin. The liberal view of the time was that man and woman were

---

and Joseph Hall's sermon "The Righteous Mammon" in *Works* (Oxford: D. A. Talboys, 1837–39), V, 114.

[7] William Law, *An Appeal to all that Doubt . . . To which are added, Some Animadversions upon Dr. Trap's Late Reply* (London, 1756), pp. 255, 257, 259–61. Cf. John Colet, *An Exposition of St. Paul's First Epistle to the Corinthians*, trans. J. H. Lupton (London: G. Bell, 1874), pp. 90–91; Richard Hooker, *Of the Laws of Ecclesiastical Polity* (London: J. M. Dent, 1954), II, 391; John Donne, *The Sermons*, ed. G. R. Potter and E. M. Simpson (Berkeley: University of California Press, 1953——), II, 341.

equal before the Fall, women being made subject only afterward; that a wife should obey her husband through love, not fear; and that wife-beating was never permissible to a Christian man.[8] Woman was subject, but not abject. Interpretations of the Biblical texts ranged from this to overt misogyny.

"Of the State of Matrimony," one of a series of twelve sermons which Edward VI had published in 1547 and which he ordered all the clergy in England to read through twice to their congregations (reissued with additions in 1562 by Queen Elizabeth), provides a convenient statement of the official view that a wife must obey her husband, in accordance with Biblical commands; must freely acknowledge her faults, to avoid strife and demonstrate her subjection; and must realize that the cap she wears symbolizes her subjection. The sermon depends not only on Biblical authority, but also on the supposed nature of woman: ". . . a weak creature . . . more prone to all weak affections and dispositions of the mind . . . than men be; and lighter . . . and more vain in their phantasies and opinions."[9] Richard Hooker, in his authoritative *Of the Laws of Ecclesiastical Politie* (1597), pointed out the usefulness of the custom of the bride's father giving her away in marriage: ". . . it putteth women in mind of a duty whereunto the very imbecility of their nature and sex doth bind them, namely to be always directed, guided and ordered by others."[10]

When John Donne developed from a love poet into a preacher, his romantic idealizations of women and his cynical diatribes against them were alike sobered into a strict interpretation of the Pauline doctrine of wifely subjection. The husband who wrote the rapturous "Valediction: Forbidding Mourning" became the preacher who reminded husbands that "There is not a more uncomely, a poorer thing, then to love a Wife like a Mistresse." In one sermon, expounding the wife's role according to the Biblical account of the creation of woman, he cited St. Augustine's argument that two male friends

[8] The liberal view was presented by Jeremy Taylor in "The Marriage Ring," *The Whole Works*, ed. R. Heber (London: Ogle, Duncan, 1822), Vol. V; Owen Feltham, *Resolves: Divine, Moral, Political* (London: H. Seile, 1628), XXX, LXXXV of "A Second Centurie," etc.

[9] Doris Mary Stenton, *The English Woman in History* (London: George Allen and Unwin, 1957), pp. 104–6.

[10] Richard Hooker, *Of the Laws of Ecclesiastical Polity*, II, 393.

might live together "much more conveniently" than a man and a woman and explained that woman was created only to propagate children, to help the man, and (after the Fall) to provide a remedy for lust. Even so, "man might have done well enough alone," had not God preferred the welfare of the race to that of the individual.

Although Donne did not actually call woman a necessary evil, he implied as much by describing her as a "remedy" to supply the defects of the individual man — and an imperfect remedy at that: God, Who is in no way obligated to provide us with the best solution for our problems that we might conceive for ourselves, did not create woman with the care and deliberation that He used for man, so that naturally she is the weaker vessel. Woman must remember this, and also that she was created as an accessory, not a principal, and furthermore that "no body values his staffe, as he does his legges." If a woman thinks herself to be more than a mere helper, she is not even that much: just as God did not join Eve in commission with Adam in naming the creatures, a woman may not be her husband's partner or claim responsibility for his success; she cannot and must not aspire to do more than second him at a respectful distance. To be sure, there are a few wives who are stronger and wiser than their husbands, but they must not reveal this to the world or even "repeat it in their own hearts, with such a dignifying of themselves, as exceeds the quality of a helper." Woman must remember that she was taken not from man's head but from his side, "where she weakens him enough, and therefore should do all she can, to be a Helper." To this end she must have the virtues of chastity, sobriety, taciturnity, and verity; but "wit, learning, eloquence, musick, memory, cunning" are unnecessary, perhaps even undesirable in woman, because they "make her never the fitter" for a helpmate.

Just as Donne gave the most antifeminist possible interpretation to the Biblical account of woman's creation, he emphasized her guilt in the Fall:

Even before there was any Man in the world, to sollicite, or tempt her *chastity*, she could finde another way to be false and treacherous to her husband: both the husband, and the wife offended against God, but the husband offended not towards his wife, but rather eate the Apple . . . lest by refusing to eate, when she had done so, he should deject her into a desperate sense of her sinne.

Milton, too, was to use this traditional interpretation of Adam's motivation, which gilds his sin with amiable weakness while aggravating Eve's. "The Progresse of the Soule" includes another severely misogynistic account of the Fall, although it is lightened by an obscene play on dying or slaying and sexual intercourse. In the Garden of Eden:

> Man all at once was there by woman slaine,
> And one by one we'are here slaine o'er againe
> By them. The mother poison'd the well-head,
> The daughters here corrupt us, Rivolets;
> No smalnesse scapes, no greatnesse breaks their nets;
> She thrust us out, and by them we are led
> Astray, from turning, to whence we are fled [i.e., the metaphorical
> Eden of sexual delight].
> Were prisoners Judges, 'twould seeme rigorous,
> Shee sinn'd, we beare; part of our paine is, thus
> To love them, whose fault to this painfull love yoak'd us.[11]

The combination of sensuality and misogyny, so evident in Donne, was not unusual in his period.

William Whateley, an eminent preacher, was, like Donne, happily married; and he had quite a high view of marriage, insisting in his *Bride-Bush, or, A Direction for Married Persons* (1623) that "a man must love his wife above all the creatures in the world besides" and that he should never stay away from her to disport himself abroad. But Whateley spelled out the wife's subjection even more bluntly than Donne. First, "she must acknowledge her inferioritie: secondly, she must carry her selfe as an inferior." Let anyone who wishes to be a good wife:

. . . set downe this conclusion within her soul: Mine husband is my superiour, my better: he hath authoritie and rule over me, nature hath given it him, having framed our bodies to tendernesse, mens to more hardnesse; God hath given it him. . . . His will I see to bee made by God the tie and tedder, not of mine actions alone, but of my desires and wishes also.

Even if a woman's birth, wealth, wit, or competence are superior to her husband's, she should remember "that a womans chiefest ornament, is lowlinesse of mind"; she wickedly abuses her gifts if she

[11] Donne, *Sermons*, ed. Potter and Simpson, II, 339, 343–46, V, 114–15; John Donne, *Complete Poetry and Selected Prose*, ed. John Hayward (with Blake's *Complete Poetry*) (New York: Random House, 1941), p. 218.

uses them to undermine her husband's superiority. For "She must regard him as Gods deputie," regardless of his personal qualifications. She must fear him, that is, "abhorre and shunne it as the greatest evill that can befall her, next to the breach of Gods commandements, to displease and offend her husband." She must speak to him in such a tone that even someone who did not know them would perceive that an inferior was speaking to her better, and she must never be so disrespectful as to address him by a nickname. She must not only obey her husband's every lawful command, but do so with complete willingness, "even as a well-broken horse, that seems to have but one soul with the rider"; and she must "patiently suffer all his reprehensions and corrections" — including beating, for Whateley sanctioned beating as a method of husbandly correction when words failed. Even if the beating is unjustified, a good wife will take it quietly. She may not leave her husband for harsh treatment, such as cruelty or drunkenness: "If God have made thine house thy dungeon, thine husband thy Jaylor; yet thou must not seeke to make an escape, till he deliver thee out that put thee in." [12]

John Sprint elaborated these points with more rancor in *The Bride-Womans Counseller*, a sermon preached at a wedding in 1699. (Nevertheless, he wondered plaintively in his preface that "some ill-natured Females" — no good wives, of course — had taken offense at it.) He decided to preach on the wife's duty rather than her husband's because it is harder to obey than to rule, because women are less capable of learning than men, and because most of the disturbances which have attended married life and brought so much reproach on that state "are owing to the Indiscretion and Folly, if not to the Obstinacy and Stubbornness of disobedient Wives."

Since woman was responsible for the Fall, he went on, "'tis but fit and just, that she, who hath been so greatly instrumental of so much Mischief and Misery to Man, should be actively engaged to please and comfort him," no matter how difficult this may be. Although even before the Fall she was to have been subject to her husband, her compliance would have been easy and pleasant; "but

---

[12] William Whateley, *A Bride-Bush, or, A Direction for Married Persons* (London: B. Fisher, 1623), pp. 38, 44, 107–8, 189–94, 196, 199, 208–9, 211, 213.

since the Fall, Man is grown more humersome, and hard to be pleased, and Woman less able and willing to do it; which being so thro' her own means, it was but just and righteous with God to impose a Work upon her, which her self made so hard and difficult." Since Eve ruined her good-natured and loving husband, a modern wife has no one but herself to blame that she must now "cast about every way" and use "Art and Skill . . . Diligence and Industry" to please hers.[13]

In some sermons the misogyny which lurked beneath all the markedly rigorous statements on female subjection emerged into the open. Hugh Latimer, preaching before King Edward VI, rejoiced that "Christ limiteth unto us one wife only" and dilated on the difficulties of ruling even that one:

For a woman is frail, and proclive unto all evils: a woman is a very weak vessel, and may soon deceive a man and bring him into evil. Many examples we have in holy scripture. Adam had but one wife . . . and how soon had she brought him to consent unto evil, and to come to destruction! How did wicked Jezebel pervert king Achab's heart from God and all godliness, and finally unto destruction! [14]

In passages like this, the connection between insistence on the subjection of women and misogyny is clearly apparent: keeping women subject is seen as the only means to restrain their natural proclivity to evil, for, weak as they may be morally, they are dangerously strong in their influence upon man.

Henry Smith's *A Preparative to Marriage* (1591) shows the same belief in woman's wickedness and preoccupation with how to control her. Although its ostensible purpose was to advise men how to choose their wives and live happily with them afterward, Smith seems to have been more concerned with warning them against the consequences of unwise marriages: "Such furies do haunt some men . . . as though the devil had put a sword into their hands to kill themselves; therefore choose whom thou mayest enjoy, or live alone still, and thou shalt not repent thee of thy bargain." Indeed, even the best wives "are cumbersome enough." As for evil ones,

[13] John Sprint, *The Bride-Womans Counseller* (London: H. Hills, 1709), pp. 3–4, 6–7.
[14] Hugh Latimer, *Works*, ed. G. E. Corrie (Cambridge: Cambridge University Press, 1844–45), I, 94.

think of Job, who did not curse the day of his birth until after his wife had tempted him to blaspheme ("shewing that wicked women are able to change the stedfast man more than all temptations beside"); think of Samson, ruined by a Philistine woman, and King Jehoram, led astray by his wicked queen, and David, mocked by Michal for his religious zeal. Although Smith gave women the usual exhortations on wifely duties, he feared they would do no good: ". . . this is the quality of that sex, to overthwart, and upbraid, and sue the preeminence of their husbands, therefore the philosophers could not tell how to define a wife, but called her the contrary to a husband, as though nothing were so cross and contrary to a man as a wife."[15]

Misogynistic perversion of Biblical texts might well be expected in a Pauline sermon on marriage, but certainly not in Sir Thomas Browne's *Religio Medici* (1643), a work otherwise characterized by the utmost moderation and charity. After emphasizing the crucial importance of charity and describing himself as unusually humane, Browne suddenly burst into a criticism of remarriage — on grounds not of religious objections to second marriage, but of the deficiencies of woman: "The whole world was made for man, but the twelfth part of man for woman: Man is the whole World, and the Breath of God; Woman the Rib and crooked piece of man." He went on to say in all earnest what dramatists had put into the mouths of notorious misogynists:

I could be content that we might procreate like trees, without conjunction, or that there were any way to perpetuate the World without this trivial and vulgar way of union: it is the foolishest act a wise man commits in all his life; nor is there any thing that will more deject his cool'd imagination, when he shall consider what an odd and unworthy piece of folly he hath committed.

He concluded, with another astonishing reversal: "I speak not in prejudice, nor am averse from that sweet Sex, but naturally amorous of all that is beautiful. I can look a whole day with delight upon a handsome Picture, though it be but of an Horse."[16] Even this re-

---

[15] Henry Smith, *The Works*, ed. T. Fuller (Edinburgh: James Nichol, 1866), I, 12–13, 21, 30.

[16] Sir Thomas Browne, *The Religio Medici and Other Writings* (London: J. M. Dent, 1931), pp. 65, 79. Browne's belief in witchcraft, not generally

mark, of course, is ambiguous: is woman to be valued only as a beautiful object, and how close is the parallel between a handsome woman and a handsome lower animal? The contrast between this whole passage and the rest of the work remains puzzling; one can only note that virulent misogyny lurked in the seventeenth-century religious consciousness even where it would be least expected and that these sentiments, appearing as they do in a serious and moderate religious work, must still have been considered acceptable. Browne was, like Donne, a happily married man (married at the time he published the *Religio Medici*, although not when he wrote it).

Although the prevailing attitude in the eighteenth century was more gallant, views of the Puritan type persisted, for example in William Fleetwood's *The Relative Duties of Parents and Children, Husbands and Wives, Masters and Servants* (1716), originally preached as sermons. After neatly proving women's natural inferiority to men by begging the question — since "It is demonstrably certain" that women are not capable of carrying on business or administering justice, men must perform such functions; therefore men have the necessary capacities, and therefore they are superior to women — he described with sadistic satisfaction women's punishment for the Fall. Like Sprint, he saw this as a subjection purposely made painful:

---

shared by educated people in his time, may be a further indication of misogyny. On one occasion he gave professional medical evidence which helped to convict two women as witches. Although witch crazes were a major expression of misogyny in actual life, they had surprisingly little effect on literature. Historically, accused witches were generally women; and the methods of procedure at witch trials showed the judges' fear of them as women: they were scrupulously to avoid touching a suspected witch or letting her look at them before they looked at her, and the accused were stripped and completely shaved before being dragged backward into court (Jacob Sprenger and Henry Kraemer, *Malleus Maleficarum*, trans. M. Summers [Great Britain: John Rodker, 1928], p. 228). It is true that Sprenger and Kraemer, as well as most English writers on witchcraft, felt called upon to explain that women's particular stupidity and moral weakness made them more prone to witchcraft than men (e.g., King James I, *Daemonologie*, ed. G. B. Harrison [London: John Lane, 1924], pp. 43–44, 69, and William Perkins, *A Discourse of the Damned Art of Witchcraft*, in *The Workes* [London: John Legatt, 1612–13], III, 637). Creative writers, however, did not exploit witchcraft as a means of expressing misogyny; their witches are generally more grotesque than wicked and are seen as *witches* rather than as wicked *women*.

. . . in things difficult and unacceptable, against their Will and Desire, a Subjection to many vain and idle, to many froward and unkind, to many injurious and austere Commands, which the foolish, severe, imperious Humours of the Husbands lay upon them. . . . You shall not be Mistress of your self, nor have any Desire satisfied, but what is approv'd by your Husband; you shall be wholly under his Power and Tutelage, he shall command you many Things that you dislike, and yet you shall obey.[17]

When George Savile, Marquis of Halifax, wrote *The Lady's New Year's Gift: or, Advice to a Daughter* (1688) to prepare his dearly loved twelve-year-old daughter for life, he revealed a cynical secular version of the same view of woman and her role. He started from the premise that a girl could not choose her future husband and did not even have the right of refusal: ". . . their friends' care and experience are thought safer guides to them than their own fancies, and their modesty often forbiddeth them to refuse when their parents recommend." (Despite his apparently sincere professions of paternal devotion, his own "care and experience" were later exerted to marry her to the third Earl of Chesterfield, who was a sullen brute.) Women's lack of freedom was justified because "men, who were to be the law givers, had the larger share of reason bestowed upon them."

Because he was a social writer rather than a preacher inspired by St. Paul, Halifax did offer his daughter a consolation for her position of helpless dependency: actually women are better off than men, he claimed, since by adroit maneuvering they can subdue their masters: "You have more strength in your looks than we have in our laws, and more power by your tears than we have by our arguments." This sop was to become increasingly popular as, in the later eighteenth and nineteenth centuries, moral writers came to avoid harsh references to the sin of Eve, substituting for them some more genteel justification for female subjection.

As a hard-boiled Restoration nobleman, however, Halifax was more explicit than later writers about how this maneuvering was

---

[17] William Fleetwood, *The Relative Duties of Parents and Children, Husbands and Wives, Masters and Servants* (London: J. Hooke, 1716), pp. 134, 137–38. This strictness contrasts with Fleetwood's pussyfooting tolerance toward women's fashions and finery in the two following sermons. Obviously he objected not to women's moral failings but to their challenging of men's privileged position.

to be done in the various situations in which a woman, even one whose marriage was arranged by a devoted father, might be placed. If her husband is unfaithful, she must above all avoid "indecent" complaints; though of course a wife must remain scrupulously faithful, a husband would justifiably resent any expostulations on this ground. If he is a drunkard, she should console herself with the thought that this vice will obscure her faults in his eyes. As "few women can bear the having all they do or say represented in the clear glass of an understanding without faults" — he says in typical Restoration style — they should be grateful when "the errors of [men's] nature make amends for the disadvantages" of women's. When he comes home drunk she must receive him without a storm or even a reproachful look, so that "the wine will naturally work out all in kindness, which a wife must encourage, let it be wrapped up in never so much impertinence." [18] The conjugal scene which emerges here is not attractive. In similar ways a wife is to deal with her husband's savage temper, avarice, or moronic stupidity.

The Lady's New Year's Gift became a classic manual of female conduct. *The Ladies Calling* (1673, generally attributed to Richard Allestree), an even more popular one, presented a softer case for female subjection, of the sort that became increasingly prevalent in the eighteenth century. The author arranged his material in terms of the virtues especially appropriate to women — all of which usefully support a patriarchal system — and then of women's three states of life. After modesty, which among other things involves habitual silence, the leading feminine virtue is meekness. Since women particularly must practice this virtue, and since it is especially hard for them to do so, the writer rejoiced that God and nature have placed them for the most part in states of subjection — to the father in virginity, to the husband in marriage. Their third possible state, widowhood, was "by God himself reckon'd ás a condition the most desolate and deplorable," because it is the condition "when they are most at liberty." (Protestants did not permit women the alternative of sexless independence.)

[18] H. C. Foxcroft, *The Life and Letters of Sir George Savile . . . first marquis of Halifax, with . . . his works* (London: Longmans, Green, 1898), II, 393–97. On the young lady's marriage, see Samuel Shellabarger, *Lord Chesterfield and His World* (Boston: Little Brown, 1951), pp. 16, 18–19.

Moving on to the conduct appropriate to the several stages of woman's life, the author says a virgin has the right to refuse a suitor proposed by her parents, but must never venture to express any positive preference, lest she be suspected of "somewhat too warm desires": ". . . 'tis most agreeable to the Virgin Modesty . . . [to] make Marriage an act rather of their obedience than their choice." A wife's main duties are love, fidelity, and submission, and these must continue unchanged even if she knows her husband to be unfaithful: she must be like the unprotesting lamb under the knife, which moves our pity, rather than the impatiently roaring swine. The only action permitted to her is "to avert his temptations . . . by denying herself even the most innocent liberties, if she see they dissatisfy him." [19] Thus, the author of *The Ladies Calling* assumed women's frailty and advocated their complete subjection, although he avoided the harsh references to the sin of Eve or the sinfulness of women characteristic of the Puritans.

3

John Milton, the greatest of the Puritans, clearly illustrates the nature and limits of their misogyny. While he extolled marriage in the loftiest terms, he insisted with unnecessary emphasis and obvious satisfaction on the wife's inferiority and subjection to her husband. While he was intensely responsive to woman's charm, he was painfully apprehensive of her capacity to seduce and degrade man.

In the "Haile wedded Love" panegyric in *Paradise Lost*, Milton contrasts godly marriage with the other possible forms of sexual relationship, all of them sinful and degrading: prostitution, wanton flirtation, and, most significantly, courtly love, in which man treats

---

[19] *The Ladies Calling*, in *The Works of the Learned and Pious Author of the Whole Duty of Man* (London: George Pawlett, 1687), pp. 2, 4, 12, 16, 29, 59, 64, 65, 67–68. The other requisite feminine virtues are piety, compassion, and affability, which is especially important because of women's naturally violent and ephemeral passions. Some of the many other statements of female inferiority and wifely subjection in the seventeenth century are in Richard Allestree's *The Whole Duty of Man*, in *Works* (London: George Pawlett, 1687), pp. 119–20; William Perkins' *Christian Oeconomie*, in *The Workes*, III, 692; Anthony Horneck's *The Happy Ascetic* (London: Henry Mortlock, 1693), pp. 216–18; Ste. B's *Counsel to the Husband: To the Wife Instruction* (London: Richard Boyle, 1608), pp. 45–49, 56–64, 71–73; Thomas Gataker's *Marriage Duties Briefely Couched togither* (London: William Bladen, 1620), pp. 7–17.

woman as his superior. It is because Adam does not maintain his due authority over Eve that he falls. Eve's inferiority is insisted on from her first appearance: Adam was formed for contemplation and valor, she for softness and grace; "Hee for God only, shee for God in him"; his shoulder-length hair betokens rule, her long golden tresses, "Subjection, but requir'd with gentle sway." This relationship is made apparent in her every speech before the Fall, as Whateley preached it should be. When Adam proposes that they go to bed, she answers:

> My Author and Disposer, what thou bidst
> Unargu'd I obey; so God ordains,
> God is thy Law, thou mine: to know no more
> Is womans happiest knowledge and her praise.

After the Fall, when Adam pleads as extenuation that Eve had misled him, Christ answers:

> . . . was shee made thy guide,
> Superior, or but equal, that to her
> Thou did'st resigne thy Manhood, and the Place
> Wherein God set thee above her made of thee,
> And for thee, whose perfection farr excell'd
> Hers in all real dignitie: Adornd
> She was indeed, and lovely to attract
> Thy Love, not thy Subjection, and her Gifts
> Were such as under Government well seem'd —
> Unseemly to bear rule, which was thy part
> And person, had'st thou known thy self aright.[20]

Milton not only seized all opportunities to emphasize the Jahvist's account of the creation of woman, but in *Tetrachordon* actually rejected the Elohist's statement that man and woman were created equally in the image of God, citing to support this the authority of St. Paul.[21]

Milton expressed his views on marriage directly in his divorce tracts, which were prompted by his experience with his hopelessly

---

[20] John Milton, *Paradise Lost*, IV, 295–308, 635–38, 750–70, X, 146–56, in *Complete Poetry and Selected Prose*, ed. E. H. Visiak (Glasgow: The Nonesuch Press, 1948), pp. 153, 161, 164, 286. Cf. Milton's *Second Defense of the People of England*, ed. E. J. Strittmatter, in *The Works* (New York: Columbia University Press, 1931–33), VIII, 133.

[21] Milton, *Works*, IV (ed. C. L. Powell), 76.

uncongenial first wife. Although, as Allan Gilbert has demonstrated, Milton was defending the right of both parties to escape
from an unhappy marriage, it is apparent that his real concern was
with the suffering of a mismated man. Both parties are entitled to
divorce, but husbands are more entitled than wives. One of Milton's
key points in *The Doctrine and Discipline of Divorce* (1643) is that,
since a wife is defined in Genesis as "a meet help," one "who naturally and perpetually is no meet help, can be no wife" — a point
which obviously could not be used for the benefit of women. More
explicitly, although he conceded that it is right and merciful to
grant divorces to afflicted wives, he condemned the idea that "di
vorce was granted for relief of wives, rather then of husbands" as:

Palpably uxorious! Who can be ignorant that woman was created for
man, and not man for woman; and that a husband may be injur'd as in-
sufferably in marriage as a wife. What an injury is it after wedlock not to
be belov'd, what to be slighted, what to be contended with in point of house-
rule who shall be the head, not for any parity of wisdome, for that were
somthing reasonable, but out of a female pride. *I suffer not* saith S. Paul,
the woman to usurp authority over the man. If the Apostle could not suffer
it, into what mould is he mortify'd that can?

From the familiar texts on bad wives from Proverbs, Milton concluded:

If the Spirit of God wrote such aggravations as these, and as may be guest by
these similitudes, counsels the man rather to divorce then to live with such
a collegue, and yet on the other side expresses nothing of the wives suffering
with a bad husband; is it not most likely that God in his Law had more pitty
towards man thus wedlockt, then towards the woman that was created for
another.

Milton said repeatedly that God has placed the power of divorce
in the hands of the *husband.*[22]

It must be recognized, however, that Milton's view of marriage,
and therefore of women, was much higher than those of many of his
contemporaries. The author of *An Answer to a Book, Intituled, The*

[22] Allan Gilbert, "Milton on the Position of Women," *Modern Language Review*, XV (1920), 7-27, 240-64. Milton, *Works*, III, Part 2 (ed. C. L. Powell
and F. A. Patterson), 458, 474-75, 497-98, 501-2. Cf. *Christian Doctrine*, in
Works, XV (ed. J. H. Hanford and W. H. Dunn), 163, 165, and *Tetrachordon*,
in *Works*, IV, 77.

Doctrine and Discipline of Divorce (1644) refuted Milton's major argument, "That solace and peace are the main benefits of conjugall society," by pointing out that if they were, it would have been much better for Adam, and hence for all men, "to have had another man made to him of his Rib in stead of *Eve*," since experience shows "that man ordinarily exceeds woman in naturall gifts of minde, and in delectablenesse of converse." Hence the solace provided by marriage can only be sexual and the question of mental compatibility in marriage is idle and irrelevant.[23] Milton retorted:

Came this doctrine out of som School, or som stie? . . . mariage . . . is the dearest league of love, and the dearest resemblance of that love which in Christ is dearest to his Church . . . there is one society of grave friendship, and another amiable and attractive society of conjugal love, besides the deed of procreation, which of it self soon cloies, and is despis'd, unless it bee cherisht and re-incited with a pleasing conversation.[24]

While Milton sharply insisted that a wife is more than a sexual vessel, he insisted with equal sharpness that she is less than a man. Adam fell because he allowed himself to become subject to his inferior. Milton's elaborate efforts to explain how this could be, how the mentally and morally weaker being could overcome the stronger, how an inferior being could possibly exert such an influence over even a virtuous man, suggest that he was trying to solve a personal psychological problem as well as one naturally arising from the subjects he chose for his major works.

Before the Fall, Milton's Adam admits to Raphael that the only sensory temptation to which he feels susceptible is that of Eve's beauty, although he understands well that she is his inferior in the distinctively human mental qualities as well as in strength of body; her loveliness and self-possession so impress him that:

> All higher knowledge in her presence falls
> Degraded, Wisdom in discourse with her
> Looses, discount'nanc't, and like folly shewes;
> Authoritie and Reason on her waite,
> As one intended first, not after made
> Occasionally. . . .

---

[23] Anonymous, *An Answer to a Book, Intituled, The Doctrine and Discipline of Divorce* (London: William Lee, 1644), pp. 11–12.

[24] Milton, *Colasterion*, in *Works*, IV, 253–54.

The angel replies sternly that Adam must always bear in mind his superior nature, must love and cherish Eve but never allow her to influence him unduly. Similarly, when Michael shows Adam how the "Sons of God" (of Gen. 6:1–2), whom Milton here identifies with righteous men, will be seduced by beautiful women and under their influence become so wicked as to provoke the Deluge, Adam exclaims:

> O pittie and shame, that they who to live well
> Enterd so faire, should turn aside to tread
> Paths indirect, or in the mid way faint!
> But still I see the tenor of Mans woe
> Holds on the same, from Woman to begin.

Milton did not disdain to make use of the ancient facetious "woe-man" etymology. The angel corrects Adam: "From Mans effeminate slackness it begins . . . who should better hold his place / By wisdome, and superiour gifts receavd."

It may be argued that Adam's excoriation of Eve and her sex immediately after the Fall was intended to express immoderate misogyny: Adam is angry, in a state of sin, and emphatically not under the control of his right reason. On the other hand, it is hard to define where his views diverge from those which Milton elsewhere presented as correct: Adam's expressions are more violent, but do not really differ in content from Milton's own. In the quarrel which follows the Fall, Adam tells Eve, just as the archangels told him, that disaster rightly strikes "Him who to worth in Women overtrusting / Lets her Will rule." When Eve makes her first overture to him afterward, he wishes that she would assume the serpent's shape as well as his falsity, so she could no longer snare her fellow creatures with her beauty. As she was beguiled by the serpent, Adam was by her, since her apparent wisdom and virtue are but a show; her real nature is that of the rib from which she was created — crooked. "Oh, why," he exclaims, did the

> Creator wise, that peopl'd highest Heav'n
> With Spirits masculine, create at last
> This noveltie on Earth, this fair defect [an echo of Aristotle]
> Of Nature, and not fill the World at once
> With men as Angels without Feminine,
> Or find some other way to generate
> Mankind? this mischief had not then befall'n,

> And more that shall befall — innumerable
> Disturbances on Earth through Femal snares,
> And straight conjunction with this Sex: for either
> He never shall find out fit Mate, but such
> As some misfortune brings him, or mistake;
> Or whom he wishes most shall seldom gain
> Through her perverseness, but shall see her gaind
> By a farr worse, or if she love, withheld
> By Parents, or his happiest choice too late
> Shall meet, alreadie linked and Wedlock-bound
> To a fell Adversarie, his hate or shame:
> Which infinite calamitie shall cause
> To Humane life, and houshold peace confound.

With the exception of the wish that women had never been created at all, derived probably from misogynistic set pieces in drama, there is no statement in this speech which could not be matched from those Milton presented as correct. The last ten lines, appropriate to a man who has lived in society rather than to an individual with Adam's limited experience, undoubtedly reflect Milton's personal history. Moreover, Eve humbly — and rightly, we must infer — accepts full responsibility for the Fall: she says she does not deserve the title of Mother of all Mankind, having been Adam's snare instead of help.

The same views are definitely stated by the Chorus in *Samson Agonistes*, which, like most dramatic choruses, expresses the "right" point of view in the play. After Dalila departs in fury, the Chorus generalizes on the nature of woman (again with a covert reference to Milton's experience in his first marriage):

> Is it for that such outward ornament
> Was lavish't on thir Sex, that inward gifts
> Were left for hast unfinish't, judgment scant,
> Capacity not rais'd to apprehend
> Or value what is best
> In choice, but oftest to affect [prefer] the wrong?
> Or was too much of self-love mixt,
> Of constancy no root infixed,
> That either they love nothing, or not long?
>   What e'er it be, to wisest men and best,
> Seeming at first all heavenly under virgin veil,
> Soft, modest, meek, demure,
> Once join'd, the contrary she proves, a thorn

> Intestine [domestic], far within defensive arms
> A cleaving mischief, in his way to vertue
> Adverse and turbulent, or by her charms
> Draws him awry, enslav'd
> With dotage, and his sense deprav'd
> To folly and shameful deeds which ruin ends.
> What Pilot so expert but needs must wreck
> Embarqu'd with such a Stears-mate at the Helm?

Since the virtuous wife who is a genuine helpmate is found very rarely indeed:

> Therefore Gods universal law
> Gave to the man despotic power
> Over his female in due awe,
> Nor from that right to part an hour,
> Smile she or lowre:
> So shall he least confusion draw
> On his whole life, not sway'd
> By female usurpation, nor dismay'd.

Surely it is no accident that two of Milton's three major poems, *Paradise Lost* and *Samson Agonistes*, present two pre-eminent cases of female seduction, which afford ample opportunity for denunciations of women's wiles and falsity and the ignominy of yielding to them. Moreover, in the third, *Paradise Regained*, where no woman appears, Milton made a point of dragging in a reference to female seduction. As Satan is going off to tempt Christ in the wilderness, Belial, "the dissolutest Spirit that fell," advises him to set beautiful women before him:

> Expert in amorous Arts, enchanting tongues
> Perswasive, Virgin majesty with mild
> And sweet allay'd, yet terrible to approach,
> Skill'd to retire, and in retiring draw
> Hearts after them tangl'd in Amorous Nets.
> Such object hath the power to soft'n and tame
> Severest temper, smooth the rugged'st brow,
> Enerve, and with voluptuous hope dissolve,
> Draw out with credulous desire, and lead
> At will the manliest, resolutest brest,
> As the Magnetic hardest Iron draws:
> Women, when nothing else, beguil'd the heart
> Of wisest *Solomon*, and made him build,
> And made him bow to the Gods of his Wives.

Belial, according to Milton's interpretation of Genesis 6:1–2, was one of the falsely titled "sons of God" who coupled with mortal women. Satan must of course reject this advice, since in the Bible he tempted Christ by other means. Milton used this fact to disparage women further, making Satan retort that noble men, unlike Belial, are capable of scorning beauty because intent "on worthier things."

> . . . For Beauty stands
> In the admiration only of weak minds
> Led captive; cease to admire, and all her Plumes
> Fall flat and shrink into a trivial toy,
> At every sudden slighting quite abasht:
> Therefore with manlier objects we must try
> His constancy, with such as have more shew
> Of worth, of honour, glory, and popular praise;
> Rocks whereon greatest men have oftest wreck'd.

Thus Milton managed to have it both ways: women have ruined the best and wisest of men, Solomon and Adam (the poem includes two references to Eve's seduction of Adam); [25] and yet they are too low and trivial a temptation to be used against a man who is truly virtuous. Milton denounces and belittles women simultaneously.

Despite Milton's appreciation of female society and his high conception of marriage, the force and frequency of his insistence on female subjection indicate distrust of and hostility toward women. His assertion that man has "despotic power" over woman places him among the more rigorous interpreters of St. Paul. The fact that he missed no opportunity to insist on her inferiority shows his overpreoccupation with the topic. A more clear-cut manifestation of misogyny, his preoccupation with woman's seductive capacities, her tendency to ruin or degrade man, is shown both by his choice of subjects and the relish with which he developed the attacks

[25] Milton, *Paradise Lost*, VIII, 551–56, IX, 1183–84, X, 889–908, XI, 163–65, 629–36; *Samson Agonistes*, lines 1025–45, 1053–60; *Paradise Regained*, II, 133–34, 150, 158–71, 195, 220–28; IV, 5–6, in *Complete Poetry*, pp. 248, 281, 304–5, 314, 326, 365–68, 386, 430–31. With the lines from *Samson* compare *Doctrine and Discipline*, in *Works*, III, Part 2, 394–95. In his edition of John Milton, *Paradise Regained, the Minor Poems and Samson Agonistes* (New York: Odyssey Press, 1937), Merritt Y. Hughes has pointed out that the "thorn intestine" echoes St. Paul's "thorn in the flesh" and the "cleaving mischief" alludes to the "envenomed robe" given Hercules by his wife (notes on p. 587).

on women naturally suggested by those subjects. It seems clear that Milton was influenced, at least in part by his painful first marriage, to accentuate the misogyny that he found in his culture.

He was, however, typical of many religious seventeenth-century Protestants in his enthusiastic acceptance of sex and marriage and, at the same time, of St. Paul's patriarchal misogyny. While these men assumed that marriage was the proper state of man, they often described women in terms which would encourage male celibacy. This apparently inconsistent attitude is found even in John Knox, who, with all his violent antifeminism, was dependent on women's society and responsive to their charm. Thus the Puritans' misogyny must be evaluated in the light of the positive side of their ambivalent attitude toward women. Nevertheless it remains significant. Numbers of sixteenth- and seventeenth-century preachers delighted in giving the Bible the most antifeminist possible interpretation, self-righteously using Biblical texts as justification for their contempt for and distrust of women. Although they did confine themselves to misogyny which could be sanctioned by the Bible, they demonstrated what virulence could be extracted from it even without the aid of early Christian asceticism. That extreme condemnations of the female sex remained morally and socially acceptable until well into the seventeenth century is shown by their appearance in sermons and in the *Religio Medici.*

Chapter V ♻ REASON VS. FOLLY AND ROMANTIC
ILLUSION: THE RESTORATION AND THE
EIGHTEENTH CENTURY

1

AMONG many changes brought about by the reaction against
Puritanism at the Restoration was a shift in the predominant
attitude toward women. Patriarchal feeling weakened, and sympathetically presented heroines in Restoration drama choose their own
mates, set their own terms of courtship, hold their own in wit com-
bats with men, and clearly do not intend after marriage to make
their husbands' wishes their law. While this departure from the
Miltonic ideal of marriage implied a more independent and equal
status for women, it also encouraged a rivalry between the sexes
which was overtly playful but frequently descended into sadism.
In Restoration literature, sophisticated relationships between men
and women frequently appear as cold-blooded exploitation by the
stronger party, whether man or woman. On the one hand, men were
justified in deceiving and abandoning women; on the other, women
were reviled for doing the same things to men.

Dorimant, the sadistic seducer in George Etherege's *Man of Mode*
(1676), is a representative Restoration hero, held up as a social
ideal. His attitude was often expressed by fashionable poets of the
period, who justified it on the grounds that women are at least as
false and cruel as men. This old charge took on new edge from the
hostility which played a disproportionately large part in sexual
relationships at the time. For example, Etherege's friend the Earl
of Mulgrave wrote:

160

> Since each has in his bosom nurst
> A false, and fawning foe;
> 'Tis just, and wise, by striking first,
> To 'scape the fatal blow.[1]

Alexander Ratcliff's "Satyr Against Love, and Women" expresses the same attitude. Ratcliff set out to prove that a lover is a shame to his sex, dismissed women's beauty as "Worms and Dust in Masquerade," and cynically asked, "What Vertue dwells under a Petty-coat?" Since women were designed by Nature to be enjoyed by men, the way to deal with a reluctant girl is to ravish her, for which she will thank you. Yet, despite his boasted capacity to handle women, Ratcliff will have no more to do with them:

> To spend our precious time 'twixt Hope and Fear,
> And let a Paltry Woman Domineer,
> 'Tis better be a Vassal in Algier.[2]

Wit and Mirth: Or Pills to Purge Melancholy, a large collection of popular songs edited by Thomas D'Urfey (1719–20, but most of the songs are earlier) proves that this sort of thing appealed to all classes at the turn of the eighteenth century; for it includes almost as many anti-love as love poems. In a song from *Orpheus Brittanicus*, for example, a jilted lover crudely reviews the usual charges of embittered lovers:

> When a Woman Love pretends,
> 'Tis but till she gains her Ends,
> And for better and for worse,
> Is for Marrow of the Purse,
> Where she jilts you o'er and o'er,
> Proves a Slattern or a Whore,
> This Hour will tease, will tease and vex,
> And will cuckold you the next;
> They were all contriv'd in Spight,
> To torment us, not delight,
> But to scold, to scold, to scratch and bite,
> And not one of them proves right,

---

[1] John Sheffield, Earl of Mulgrave . . . and Duke of Buckingham, *The Works* (London: John Barber, 1726), I, 18.

[2] George Villiers, Duke of Buckingham, *The Miscellaneous Works* (London: Samuel Briscoe, n.d.), II, 106–8. (This is actually a collection of poems by various writers.)

> But all, all are Witches by this Light,
> And so I fairly bid 'em and the World good night.[3]

In part these attacks on women expressed reaction specifically against Renaissance and Cavalier idealization of love; in part, the reaction against courtly love which has always been essential to the romantic tradition. Visible in the Middle Ages and the Renaissance, the cynical protest became predominant in erotic literature at this period: the proportion of attacks on women in relation to love poems increased, although both types continued to appear in profusion, and poems exalting love and women completely disappeared. The strongest expressions of disgust came from the Earl of Rochester, a great lover in the Restoration style and probably the prototype of Dorimant. At one point he rejected women altogether, finding them inadequate even as sexual objects:

> Love a *Woman!* y'are an *Ass*,
> 'Tis a most insipid Passion,
> To choose out for your happiness
> The idlest part of *Gods Creation*.

> Let the *Porter*, and the *Groome*,
> Things design'd for dirty *Slaves*,
> Drudge in fair *Aurelias Womb*,
> To get supplies for Age, and Graves.

In the future he will console himself with a bottle or, if that fails, "a sweet soft Page" who "Does the trick worth *Forty Wenches*." Rochester was by no means unique in his period, although his outbursts of misogyny are both more effective and more passionate than those of his contemporaries: perhaps because of his own glutted sensuality, he seems really to have felt the sexual disgust which with most was a fashionable pose. The particular intensity of the misogynistic outbursts of men like Rochester and Donne can probably be attributed to their naturally passionate temperaments. The attacks are the counterparts of the authors' equally intense love poems, although Rochester, characteristic of his period and class, was incapable of Donne's idealization of love.

[3] *Wit and Mirth: Or Pills to Purge Melancholy*, ed. Tom D'Urfey (London: J. Tonson, 1719–20), I, 49–50.

There is another influence behind the Restoration cynics' delight in stripping away what they saw as romantic illusions: the neoclassical emphasis on reason as opposed to misleading appearance and sentimental illusion. Rochester's savage "Ramble in St. James's Park" is based on the discrepancy between what women appear to be and what they really are:

> Along these hallow'd Walks it was,
> That I beheld *Corinna* pass;
> Who ever had been by to see,
> The proud disdain she cast on me
> Through charming Eyes, he wou'd have swore,
> She dropt from *Heav'n* that very hour;
> Forsaking the Divine abode,
> In scorn of some despairing *God.*
> But mark what Creatures *Women* are,
> So infinitely vile, and fair.

Rochester could forgive Corinna for being unfaithful to him, but not for making herself "A Passive *Pot* for *Fools* to spend in," for indiscriminately distributing her favors "When neither *Head* nor *Tail* perswade."[4] In cursing her promiscuity he spared no pornographic word or idea.

Rochester's disgust with Corinna for distributing her favors to fools is characteristic of the Restoration not only in its ruthless scorn for sentimental idealization but in its emphasis on want of reason: the Restoration wits often satirized women for preferring fools to intelligent men, and indeed for being less rational than men in every respect. Presenting in terms of irrationality the old charge that woman is less able than man to control her passions, William Wycherley declared that it was vain to seek a mistress or wife who would "steer her Conduct by her Reason," since in women "The Head is always govern'd by the Tail!"[5]

The wits professed to find it natural that women should prefer fools, as the men most like themselves. Besides, only fools could truly admire them:

[4] John Wilmot, Earl of Rochester, *Poems on Several Occasions,* ed. James Thorpe (Princeton, N.J.: Princeton University Press, 1950), pp. 15, 17, 60–61.

[5] William Wycherley, "To His Friend, a Cautious Lover," in *The Complete Works,* ed. M. Summers (London: Nonesuch Press, 1924), IV, 245.

> *Woman*, who is an Arrant *Bird* of Night,
> Bold in the duske, before a Fools dull Sight,
> Must fly, when *Reason* brings the blazing light.[6]

For the wits were sure that woman's attractiveness, however com-
pelling, was an illusion, produced by arts and beauty aids and the
lover's own credulity. As Wycherley put it: "From our own Blindness, not your Brightness, so / Do our too flatt'ring Faith, and
strain'd Devotion grow."[7] Thus love and admiration for women
are opposed to reason — the highest ideal of the age — since they
are based on illusion.

Nevertheless, Wycherley, and even Rochester, were willing to
be taken in by the illusion — not so their contemporary Robert
Gould. In *A Satyr against Wooing* (1698?) he advised men to see
woman as she really is:

> Strip but this Puppet of it's Gay Attire,
> It's — Gauzes, Ribbons, Lace, Commode and Wire,
> And tell me then what 'tis thou dost admire?
>
> . . . .
>
> Open her secret Boxes; Patches here
> You'll horded find, her Paints and Washes there:
> Love's artful Lime twigs, where the chatt'ring Ape
> Sits perch'd, and hasn't the Judgment to Escape;
>
> . . . .
>
> If in her Bed you e'er perceive her fast,
> Mind how her Face is crusted o'er with Past,
> Or nasty Oils us'd nightly to repair
> Her skin, quite spoil'd — with taking of the Air.

The tone of this passage, it is true, is lightened by a flippant touch
at the end; but Gould was capable of proclaiming in deadly seriousness: "Woman! The very name's a crime."[8]

If love was a doubtful blessing, marriage was an undoubted
curse, according to the modish writers of the Restoration. Among
many frivolous expressions of the idea of wife as ball and chain,
Wycherley's "To W. O . . . upon his Offer of a Wife to me, say-

---

[6] Rochester, "A Letter from Artemisa," in *Poems*, p. 23.

[7] Wycherley, "To his Coy Mistress," in *Works*, IV, 213.

[8] Eugene Hulse Sloane, *Robert Gould: Seventeenth Century Satirist* (Philadelphia: University of Pennsylvania Press, 1940), pp. 93, 97.

ing . . . She was Soft-Wax, Virtuous, Pious, and Charitable" is typical:

> What! offer Marriage to me? Yet pretend,
> By such an Offer, to be more my Friend;
>
> . . . .
>
> With Yoke, and Horns, to load my Neck and Head,
> At others Pleasure, to be driv'n, or led.

Her fortune would be too dear at the price of "His Peace, his Honour, and his Liberty"; her title would make her think she had title to "govern him, she shou'd by right, obey"; her wit would make him "her Fool, and Slave, the more"; her good looks would make her vain, and her good nature, accessible to everyone.[9] Of course, many of these attacks on women are simply expressions of the universal cynicism cultivated by the Restoration wits: since cynicism involves a general stripping away of idealization, the conspicuous ideals of love and marriage, the mistress and the wife, were naturally assailed.

Even John Dryden, who was only peripherally associated with the court wits, suddenly interrupted his grave complimentary address "To My Honour'd Kinsman, John Driden" with an invective against women, complete with a reference to Eve's responsibility for the Original Sin. Driden, living a virtuous and peaceful life in

---

[9] Wycherley, *Works*, III, 87–88. Wycherley's attacks on female hypocrites, apparently sanctified prudes who are really lustful and generally vicious (Lady Flippant in *Love in a Wood*, Lady Fidget in *The Country Wife*, Olivia in *The Plain-Dealer*), seem to be harsher even than most of the satire in his plays. However, since his satire is characteristically Juvenalian and since there are attractive and amiable female characters in all the plays, I do not consider this evidence of misogyny.

Cf. Charles Cotton's "The Joys of Marriage," a gay exercise on the theme of Theophrastus: *Poems*, ed. J. Beresford (London: Richard Cobden-Sanderson, 1923), p. 320. Of course attacks on wives continued to appear during the eighteenth century: in D'Urfey's *Wit and Mirth* there are five henpecked husband's laments and a song retelling the old story of the dumb wife cured, Addison and Steele wrote some *Spectators* against shrews, and Robert Burns retold the story of "The Farmer's Curst Wife" and wrote two henpecked husband's laments. However, such works are not very conspicuous during the eighteenth century. One does notice in this period the development of a more subtle treatment of the henpecking wife, as the emphasis shifted from the scold to the woman who dominates her husband by more subtle means, such as tears and hysterics.

the country, was not only free of worldly strife but "uncumber'd with a Wife":

> Where, for a Year, a Month, perhaps a Night,
> Long Penitence succeeds a short Delight:
> Minds are so hardly match'd, that ev'n the first,
> Though pair'd by Heav'n, in Paradise, were curs'd.
> For Man and Woman, though in one they grow,
> Yet, first or last, return again to Two.
> He, to God's Image, She to His was made;
> So, farther from the Fount, the Stream at random stray'd.
>   How cou'd He stand, when, put to double Pain,
> He must a Weaker than himself sustain!

Although Dryden would not "blemish all the Fair," if some are bad it is better to be on the safe side: ". . . better shun the Bait, than struggle in the Snare."

Dryden's Puritan background — an influence that lurks behind many seventeenth- and eighteenth-century writers — broke out in another unexpected reference to Eve in the preface to *Absalom and Achitophel*, where Absalom's yielding to Achitophel is compared to Adam's yielding to "the two Devils, the Serpent and the Woman." His prevailing attitude toward women, however, is better indicated by the preface to his translation of the Sixth Satire of Juvenal. Feeling called upon to apologize for the content of this work, he explicitly dissociated himself from Juvenal's views. It was not generous of him, said Dryden with the patronage which so frequently creeps into protests against treating women harshly, "to attack the weakest as well as the fairest part of the Creation." [10]

2

Most of the neoclassical writers who followed Dryden likewise deprecated harsh satire on women. They carried on the Restoration exposure of women's corrigible and incorrigible deviations from rationality, but rarely flayed them. But there was one conspicuous exception. Jonathan Swift practiced no gallant complaisance to female fools, but excoriated them in such poems as "The Furniture of a Woman's Mind." Not only did he repeatedly attack almost all

[10] John Dryden, *The Poems*, ed. John Sargeaunt (London: Oxford University Press, 1952), pp. 48, 172, 549.

the follies satirized by his contemporaries, but he prided himself on misogyny, referring complacently to his "libels on my Lady [Acheson]," or telling a colleague that he "perpetually" reproached the ladies "for their ignorance, affectation, impertinence, but my paper will not hold all." In his "Letter to a Young Lady on Her Marriage," he spoke of his "little Respect . . . for the Generality" of women and said that he "never yet knew a tolerable Woman to be fond of her own Sex." [11]

Swift's account of "the Annals of a Female Day" in *The Journal of a Modern Lady* (1729) is a good example of his distinctively harsh treatment of a favorite contemporary theme. Eighteenth-century writers, concerned with women's irrational triviality — their misvaluing of men and things, their devotion to foolish fashions, their waste of time in pointless frivolities — often described the lady's day. Alexander Pope's *The Rape of the Lock* (1714) makes fun of the glittering emptiness of a belle's day and her mind. Joseph Addison, quoting the supposed journal of a fashionable lady in *Spectator*, Number 323 (1712), showed how she devoted her days to such occupations as drinking chocolate, giving orders for her lapdog to be washed, and visiting acquaintances whom she knew she would not find at home. The most valuable activity of her whole week was embroidering half a violet leaf on a handkerchief, labor from which a headache soon forced her to desist.

But while Pope's ladies are attractive, however frivolous, and Addison had a clearly constructive purpose — to hold "up Folly to the Light" and show "the Disagreeableness of such Actions as are indifferent in themselves, and blameable only as they proceed from Creatures endow'd with Reason" [12] — Swift's treatment of the theme is almost completely negative. His typical lady rises at noon, suffering from headache and *Weltschmerz* from last night's losses at cards. After spending the afternoon cheapening cloth and getting dressed, she annoys the company through dinner with stale wit and strained politeness. With female friends, she prates, slanders, dis-

[11] Jonathan Swift, *The Correspondence*, ed. F. Elrington Ball (London: G. Bell, 1910–14), III, 102, IV, 58; Jonathan Swift, *The Prose Works*, ed. Herbert Davis (Oxford: Basil Blackwell, 1955), IX, 88, 90.

[12] Joseph Addison *et al.*, *The Spectator*, ed. G. G. Smith (London: J. M. Dent, 1945), III, 6–7.

putes, and talks in *doubles-entendres* over evening tea, after which she must suffer a while alone until friends arrive for cards. Then she plays with feverish rancor until finally, having lost again, she joins her sleeping husband in bed. The tone of this poem is angry. Swift obviously did not find the follies of his heroine engaging or even amusing; he emphasized moral shortcomings such as slandering and ruinous extravagance more than mere errors of judgment, and he made a point of introducing unpleasant details — the cheating at cards, the chatter louder than that of drunken fishwives, and the stinking breath or rank armpits of some of the ladies. Unlike Addison, he berated stupidity and immorality rather than exhorting to constructive activity; and unlike Pope, he was not diverted by levity or charmed by female arts. Where Pope created a mock-heroic fantasy of a combat between the cards, Swift realistically described an ugly squabble over cheating and stupid play. Pope kept his ladies graceful and dainty, however silly and artificial they might be, while Swift treated his empty-headed, ill-natured chatterers with unadorned contempt. The contrast is sharpened when we recall that the inspirer and subject of Swift's poem, Lady Anne Acheson, was not only an intelligent and attractive woman, but a personal friend of his.

The stench of Mopsa's breath and Hircina's armpits in *The Journal of a Modern Lady* [13] are details typical of Swift. Often his satire moves from woman's corrigible follies and vices to her very nature. From his works, in fact, it is possible to collect a comprehensive indictment of the physical aspects of woman. His approach, unique in his period, is evident in his treatment of that ever-popular butt, cosmetics. For most eighteenth-century writers, women's use of beauty aids was a foible, from which at worst they were to be exhorted or gently ridiculed. Richard Steele's *Spectator* on the subject is typical. He told what happened when the beau Will Honeycomb bribed the maid of a beautiful coquette to admit him to her dressing-room. Having seen her work "a full half Hour before he knew her to be the same Woman," he revealed himself when she was half-finished: there she stood, "in the utmost Confusion, with

[13] Jonathan Swift, *The Poems*, ed. Sir Harold Williams (Oxford: Clarendon Press, 1937), II, 449.

the prettiest Smirk imaginable on the finish'd side of her Face, pale as Ashes on the other."[14] Although he was promptly cured of his infatuation for her, what he saw was scarcely horrifying.

Swift's treatment of the lady's dressing-room theme is different indeed. Strephon finds in Celia's room not only tweezers, jars of paint and dry skin cream ("Ointments good for scabby Chops") and puppy's urine, but a besmeared smock and a clogged comb, sweaty towels and stockings, and alum flower "to stop the Steams, / Exhal'd from sour unsavoury Streams." Finally he finds her commode, which — with its contents — is described for forty-six lines. Under her numerous beauty aids, Celia is a hairy, dirty, ill-smelling animal with dry, wrinkled skin. At the end of his tour, Strephon's "foul Imagination links / Each Dame he sees with all her Stinks."[15] Thus Swift shifted his attack from the repulsiveness of make-up to the repulsiveness of what lies beneath, even beneath the make-up of a belle. It was not unusual for satirists to expose the nastiness of certain cosmetics, or for preachers to point out that the most beautiful body would soon come to corruption and stench; but Swift was extraordinary in his insistence that an apparently beautiful female body is really disgusting.

Sometimes the satire leaves beauty aids altogether, being aimed directly at the "beauty." The naked bodies of the maids of honor in Brobdingnag were "very far from being a tempting Sight" to Gulliver, "or from giving . . . any other Motions than those of Horror and Disgust." A passage on relative size in *Gulliver's Travels* (1726) points out that "the fair Skins of our *English* Ladies" only appear so because we do not see them as they really are. Extravagant Irish wives "spend the revenue of a moderate family to adorn a nauseous unwholesom living Carcase."

Often Swift focused on the breast, which he invariably described as disgusting. Aging Corinna, removing her beauty aids, "Pulls out

[14] *The Spectator*, No. 41, I, 125. Cf. Alexander Pope's light allusions to the artificiality of fashionable beauty in *The Rape of the Lock*, I, lines 121ff., and Edward Young's inoffensive moralizing on the superiority of nature to art, *The Love of Fame*, Satire V.

[15] Swift, "The Lady's Dressing Room," *Poems*, II, 526, 529. Cf. "The Progress of Beauty" and "A Beautiful Young Nymph Going to Bed," which was "Written for the Honour of the Fair Sex."

the Rags contriv'd to prop / Her flabby Dugs and down they drop."
"Flabby Dugs," of course, are not peculiar to prostitutes. The two
most revolting things Gulliver saw in Brobdingnag were a nurse's
"monstrous Breast, which . . . stood prominent six Foot," had a
nipple about half the size of his head, and was "so varified with
Spots, Pimples and Freckles, that nothing could appear more nauseous," and "a Woman with a Cancer in her Breast, swelled to a
monstrous Size, full of Holes," in two or three of which he "could
have easily crept," covering his whole body.[16]

This emphasis on the breast suggests an aversion to woman as
mother even more than as sexual partner — a suspicion which is confirmed by the hostile descriptions of motherhood which run through
Swift's work. In addition to many references to maternal folly —
such as soft-headed and ruinous interference with their children's
education — he developed several distasteful mother-and-child pictures, and no attractive ones. The Yahoos, unlike the other races in
Gulliver's Travels, are devoted mothers: the females have kennels
large enough to hold two or three offspring, bring home food to their
young, and carry them "on their Backs, nuzzling with their Face
against the Mother's Shoulders." In "The Battle of the Books"
(1697), Swift carefully built up a family group around the repulsive goddess Criticism, who is very maternal, with seven children
playing about her and many more avidly suckling at her spleen.[17]

Swift's keen sense of smell was particularly sensitive to odors
connected with the female body. Evidently he brooded over the
fact that women perspire and excrete, and felt that these functions
made them disgusting. Chloe, he said with obvious irony, possessed:

> Such Cleanliness from Head to Heel:
> No Humours gross, or frowzy Steams,
> No noisom Whiffs, or sweaty Streams,

[16] Swift, *Works,* XI (1941), 75–76, 96–97, 103; "Answer to Several Letters,"
Works, XII, 80; "A Beautiful Young Nymph Going to Bed," *Poems,* II, 582.

[17] *Ibid.,* XI, 214, 250. See also *A Tale of a Tub,* ed. A. C. Guthkelch and D.
Nichol Smith (Oxford: Clarendon Press, 1920), pp. 240–42. In part the ma-
ternal picture of Criticism travesties Milton's of Sin, in *Paradise Lost.* For
Swift's references to maternal folly, see *Intelligencer,* No. 9, *Letter to a Young
Clergyman, Vindication of Carteret,* "Of the Education of Ladies," "Directions to
Servants." Swift's references to nurses are also invariably unpleasant, except
for Glumdalclitch in *Gulliver's Travels,* who is, of course, not a real nurse but
a little girl.

> Before, behind, above, below,
> Could from her taintless Body flow.

Normal women, presumably, exude all sorts of "Humours gross." The horrifying description of Corinna's undressing and reassembling leads up to the line: "Who sees, will spew; who smells, be poison'd." "A very offensive Smell" came from the skins of the Brobdingnagian maids of honor, and on his final homecoming Gulliver was particularly revolted by his wife's smell, fainting when she embraced him and having to stop up his nose even after he had come to tolerate her presence at dinner. The female Yahoo in heat also had "a most *offensive Smell.*" [18]

For Swift, the fact that women excrete — a fact which obviously had an extraordinary emotional impact on him as well as on the lover-protagonists in his poems — symbolized the falsity of idealizing them. The idea was as old as Ovid's *Remedies of Love*, but Swift seemed almost to recommend what Ovid had mentioned only as a desperate remedy. Certainly he elaborated the idea in unprecedented detail, and more than was necessary to prove his point. Three of Swift's so-called unprintable poems show lovers cured of their infatuation by realizing that women have physical functions. Finding Cassinus in utter despair, the result of bitterly disillusioned love, Peter asks how Celia has exposed her unworthiness. By using the privy, he learns. Strephon's growing disillusionment is completed by finding Celia's commode, a shock which makes him "blind / To all the Charms of Female Kind." In "Strephon and Chloe," romantic love is immediately dissipated when the bride urinates in her husband's presence; after this even decent reticence is no longer practiced between the two. It is explicitly stated that if Strephon had ever seen Chloe on the privy he could not possibly have fallen in love. Apparently the lines:

> Had you but through a Cranny spy'd
> On House of Ease your future Bride,
>
> . . . .
>
> 'Twere better you had lickt her Leavings,
> Than from Experience find too late
> Your Goddess grown a filthy Mate . . .

[18] Swift, "Strephon and Chloe," "A Beautiful Young Nymph," *Poems*, II, 583, 584; *Works*, XI, 102, 248, 273, 279.

mean that one should not enter into intimate relations with a woman at all, since disillusionment like Strephon's is inevitable in the married state. (Earlier in the poem, however, Swift inconsistently ridiculed Chloe's prudery in concealing her natural needs and rebuffing Strephon's overtures on the wedding night.)[19]

Swift's preoccupation with women's "frowzy Steams" and "sweaty Streams" distinguishes him not only from his contemporaries but from previous critics of the body. Where they pointed out what lies beneath the skin or what happens to the flesh after death, Swift emphasized dirt — dirt which could be washed off, and dirt which is inseparable from the animal condition. Typically, his attacks on woman as animal are expressed in anal rather than genital terms: it is not that woman is lustful or tempts to lust, but that she defecates. Where Rochester describing Corinna in St. James's Park disgusts through portraying vicious lust, Swift disgusts through portraying physical defects or excretory necessities.

Nevertheless, the harshness of Swift's misogyny places him back with the Restoration wits, as does his cynicism about beauty and love, his insistence that reason reveals them to be illusory. In "Strephon and Chloe" he implied that the intimacies of married life expose beauty for the illusion that it really is: a handsome wife is "ador'd / By ev'ry Coxcomb, but her Lord," since beauty is as external and deceptive a thing as the fine dress of puppets. Even in the entirely nonsatirical "Letter to a Young Lady," he told a bride that she had "but a very few Years to be young and handsome in the Eyes of the World; and as few Months to be so in the Eyes of a Husband, who is not a Fool."[20]

In contrast to the Restoration rakes, however, who disparaged beauty because they were reacting against glutted sensuality, or sometimes merely persuading women not to be too proud to satisfy them, Swift wrote as a moralist — warning men against overvaluing women and sex. Hence, while appreciations of female beauty abound in the works of the Restoration poets, they are conspicu-

[19] Swift, "Cassinus and Peter," "The Lady's Dressing Room," "Strephon and Chloe," *Poems*, II, 530, 591, 597. The intensity of Swift's disgust with the female body seems to have increased with age: the "unprintable poems" were all published in 1730 and 1731.

[20] Swift, *Poems*, II, 592; *Works*, IX, 89.

ously absent from Swift's. Even in his poems to Stella and Vanessa, his closest approach to love poetry, he said little of the ladies' physical charms. He harped on Stella's age when she was in her thirties, and in the relatively erotic "Cadenus and Vanessa" he barely mentioned Vanessa's beauty, although he described her cleanliness in detail. The contrast between Swift's vague references to women's beauty and his detailed analyses of their physical blemishes is striking.

Similarly, while the Restoration wits wrote both for and against love, Swift's attitude was consistently derisive. Like them in their anti-love moods, he regularly equated love with sexual appetite and often emphasized its degrading effects on man. To fall in love is expressed in "Strephon and Chloe" as to "sell your self to Laughter." Pure romantic love is "that ridiculous Passion which hath no Being, but in Play-Books and Romances," and marriage promptly exposes its illusory nature. While a lover may profess to be interested in the spiritual to the exclusion of the carnal, the "pit" of sexuality is always present. He will inevitably become physically involved with his mistress, or, in Swift's simile, like the philosopher will find "himself seduced by his *lower Parts* into a Ditch." Swift likewise carried on the hardheaded Restoration attitude toward marriage, although his alternative would be celibacy rather than casual affairs. In contrast to contemporary sentimentalizing tendencies, his general references to marriage are uniformly unfavorable. In true Restoration vein he pointed out that matrimony begets "Repentance, Discord, Poverty, Jealousy, Sickness, Spleen, Loathing, &c," or that "no wise man ever married from the dictates of reason." The immortal Struldbruggs' marriages were legally dissolved when they reached eighty, so they would not "have their Misery doubled by the Load of a Wife." [21]

Yet Swift's attitude toward women had a positive side: this

[21] Swift, *Poems*, II, 591; "Letter to a Young Lady," *Works*, IX, 89; "The Mechanical Operation of the Spirit," *Tale*, p. 291; *Works*, ed. T. Scott (London: G. Bell, 1907), I, 286; *Works*, ed. Davis, IX, 263, XI, 196. The source of Swift's comparison of sexual involvement to a pit seems to be Diogenes Laertius' life of Thales Milesius. It was used previously by Nashe in *Christs Teares Over Jerusalem* (*The Works*, ed. R. B. McKerrow [London: Sidgwick & Jackson, 1910], II, 138), and Greene in *Orpharion* (*Life and Complete Works*, ed. A. B. Grosart [London: Huth Library, 1881–86], XII, 23).

"libeller" of the sex genuinely respected their minds and characters. Although he seems to have avoided sexual relationships with
women (that he repressed his sexuality is indicated not only by
what biographical information is available, but by the distaste for
female animality so evident in his works), he relied on female
companionship and thoroughly enjoyed the society of intelligent
women. He never patronized women, but insisted that they be rational and virtuous in the same way that men should be, which
implies of course that they have equal natural capacity. He found
their triviality and empty-headedness disgusting because he saw
no more excuse for these failings in women than in men. Extreme
delicacy, exaggerated modesty, tearfulness, and cowardice, far
from being naturally appropriate to the female sex, were just as
contemptible in women as in men, and also undoubtedly the result
of affectation, although Swift could not imagine why women should
think it attractive to affect fears of nonexistent dangers or harmless
animals. There is "no Quality whereby Women endeavour to distinguish themselves from Men, for which they are not just so much
the worse." [22] He defended women's rights and capacities and in
two of the utopian societies of *Gulliver's Travels* indicated that both
sexes should have essentially the same education. Few of his contemporaries would have admitted as much.

3

Except for Swift, most writers from the early eighteenth century
through the nineteenth apparently felt that the "fair sex" had to
be treated with at least overt gentleness. Accordingly, denunciations
of woman's lust, vindictiveness, or particular propensity toward
evil are largely replaced by paternal guidance or playful ridicule
of her frivolity. Harshness was reserved for the "unfeminine"
woman who dominated her husband, studied Latin, or pursued a
career. That this modulated criticism concealed disparagement of
women is easy to show; occasionally it reveals strong hostility as
well. Addison, Pope, and Steele never excoriated women as Swift

[22] Swift, "Letter to a Young Lady," *Works*, ed. Davis, IX, 93. Cf. his poem
"The Furniture of a Woman's Mind."

did; but on the other hand, their gentle exhortations or ridicule frequently reveal a patronage which Swift eschewed.

Addison specifically concerned himself with women's "little Vanities and Follies," "which are more proper for Ridicule than a serious Censure."[23] The resulting criticism, while undeniably constructive, was that of an indulgent parent correcting a child. Pope's more sparkling satire on female follies, with less obvious constructive lessons, shows the same subtle belittlement. Belinda, the heroine of *The Rape of the Lock*, is exceedingly attractive, but also silly and frivolous: she divides her day among dress, scandalous gossip, and cards; she values lovers and lapdogs at the same rate; she bursts into an outrageous tantrum at the loss of a lock of hair. Much of the poem is devoted to a delicious but telling picture of female triviality. The closest thing Belinda has to a religion seems to be worship of herself. She conducts the elaborate ritual at her dressing table, which holds, indiscriminately, "Puffs, powders, patches, Bibles, billet-doux." Belinda is threatened by some dire disaster, but it is not known

> Whether the nymph shall break Diana's law,
> Or some frail china-jar receive a flaw;
> Or stain her honour or her new brocade;
> Forget her prayers, or miss a masquerade;
> Or lose her heart, or necklace, at a ball.

Obviously Pope was satirizing Belinda's poor judgment in valuing her chastity and a china jar at the same rate, but at the same time he implied that her chastity, honor, prayers, and heart were indeed trivial: the poem shows that virgins' honor *is* as delicate and superficial as a dress. The sylphs manage to preserve it only by diverting their empty minds from one so-called love-object to another:

> With varying vanities, from ev'ry part,
> They shift the moving toy-shop of their heart;
> Where wigs with wigs, with sword-knots sword-knots strive,
> Beaux banish beaux, and coaches coaches drive.

A virgin's honor is not only fragile but, like the sylphs with which Pope equates it, insubstantial and silly. The implication that the

23 *The Spectator*, No. 92, I, 287.

honor about which women make so much stir is only the appearance of virtue, that they care for public opinion rather than chastity, is made clear when belligerent Thalestris exhorts Belinda:
"Honour forbid! at whose unrivall'd shrine / Ease, pleasure, *virtue*, all our sex resign" (my italics). Women should practice good
sense, of course: as Clarissa says, attractive arts are vain "Unless
good sense preserve what beauty gains." But the poem clearly implies that they are by nature inclined rather to folly than to solid
sense or virtue.

This implication is made clear by Pope's treatment of the Spleen,
the typically feminine hypochondria or melancholy which destroys
good sense and good humor alike. It is this, not reason, which rules
"the sex to fifty from fifteen." The Spleen is:

> Parent of vapours, and of female wit,
> Who give th'hysteric or poetic fit;
> On various tempers act by various ways,
> Make some take physic, others scribble plays;
> Who cause the proud their visits to delay,
> And send the godly in a pet to pray.

Thus Pope referred all unconventional female behavior, from creative efforts to temper tantrums, to neurotic folly — too trivial for
censure, but an irresistible subject for ridicule. Women, like the
sylphs, are exceedingly charming, but not to be taken seriously.
Of course, all the characters in *The Rape of the Lock* are silly,
but the emphasis is definitely on the ladies.

The sparkling belittlement of women implied in *The Rape of
the Lock* is made explicit in Pope's only formal satire on women,
Epistle II of the *Moral Essays* (1735). "Most women have no characters at all," he started out; they are so shallow and changeable
that they can be distinguished better by their coloring than by what
passes for their character. Yet this does not detract from their
charm, since they are "Fine by defect, and delicately weak." Pa-
pillia is typical of the irrational, inconsistent creatures whom Pope
went on to describe:

> Papillia, wedded to her amorous spark,
> Sighs for the shades — "How charming is a park!"
> A park is purchased, but the fair he sees
> All bathed in tears — "Oh odious, odious trees!"

Yet although women appear to change constantly, without reason or rule, they are actually all governed by one of two ruling passions: coquetry and vanity, "The love of pleasure and the love of sway."[24] The second motive echoes the old medieval conviction of woman's craving for sovereignty; "the love of pleasure" might refer to the equally old charge of lust, but is more likely to mean woman's alleged delight in being courted without loving in return. The numerous contemporary attacks on the coquette show the eighteenth-century preoccupation with this traditional charge.[25]

George Farquhar's characterization of a fine lady in *Sir Harry Wildair* (1701), similar to Pope's of Belinda, is more obviously disparaging. As one character describes the type — correctly, it seems, since this is exactly the behavior of the fine lady in this play:

She's all Sail, and no Ballast. . . . A fine Lady can laugh at the Death of her Husband, and cry for the loss of a Lap Dog. A fine Lady is angry without a Cause, and pleas'd without a Reason . . . has the Vapours all the Morning, and the Chollick all the Afternoon. The Pride of a fine Lady is above the merit of an understanding Head; yet her Vanity will stoop to the Adoration of a Peruke. And in fine, a fine Lady goes to Church for fashion's sake, and to the Basset-Table with Devotion; and her passion for Gaming exceeds her vanity of being thought Vertuous, or the desire of acting the contrary.

To the extent that they exhorted women against debasing their minds with folly, eighteenth-century writers at least credited them with being potentially rational. But many implicitly or explicitly revealed their belief that women are by nature prone to folly, that

[24] Alexander Pope, *Collected Poems* (London: J. M. Dent, 1951), pp. 79, 80, 83, 90, 91, 93, 226, 227, 231.

[25] The two female types most commonly attacked during the neoclassical period were the prude and the coquette: the types were associated because both are obsessed with sex, the prude being simply a hypocritical coquette. This association is clear in Restoration drama, in Swift — e.g., "To Lord Harley," *Poems*, I, 178; *Gulliver's Travels*, in *Works*, XI, 248; and his poem "The Progress of Love" — and in John Gay's third "Town Eclogue," "The Tea-Table." In this poem, which is directed mainly against scandal-mongering, a female vice constantly attacked during this period, Doris and Melanthe dissect the characters of a loose coquette and a prude; immediately afterward they greet these ladies with the utmost cordiality. As the eighteenth century became increasingly refined, emphasis shifted from the lustful prude to the heartless coquette, as in *Spectator*, Nos. 281, 515, etc.

their sex is particularly frail in terms of the great eighteenth-century ideal of Reason. The good wife in Farquhar's play says,

We [women] are but Babies at best, and must have our Play-things, our Longings, our Vapours, our Frights, our Monkeys, our China, our Fashions, our Washes, our Patches, our Waters, our Tattle, and Impertinence; therefore I say 'tis better to let a Woman play the Fool, than provoke her to play the Devil.[26]

The same view was flatly stated by the Earl of Chesterfield, who unfolded female psychology while telling his sixteen-year-old son how to manage women: they "are only children of a larger growth; they have an entertaining tattle, and sometimes wit; but for solid reasoning, good sense, I never knew in my life one that had it, or who reasoned or acted consequentially for four-and-twenty hours together." Any trivial slight or pique can overturn their best resolutions and most considered plans. Therefore,

A man of sense only trifles with them, plays with them, humours and flatters them, as he does with a sprightly, forward child; but he neither consults them about, nor trusts them with serious matters; though he often makes them believe that he does both; which is the thing in the world that they are proud of; for they love mightily to be dabbling in business (which, by the way, they always spoil).[27]

Although Richard Steele would have been horrified by this cynicism — he prided himself on being "a Friend to Women" and a "Guardian to the Fair" — his estimate of female capacity was not significantly higher than Chesterfield's. On the whole, of course, his criticism of women was eminently constructive: he exhorted them to behave more rationally so as to deserve the esteem of men of sense, and showed genuine concern about their lessening this esteem by trifling away their time "and gratifying only their eyes and ears, instead of their reason and understanding." But in several papers he revealed that patronage underlay his friendly guardianship: he assumed that women are inferior to men and should be dependent on and subject to them. All too often the self-

[26] George Farquhar, *The Complete Works*, ed. Charles Stonehill (London: Nonesuch Press, 1930), I, 165–66, 210.

[27] *The Letters of Lord Chesterfield to His Son*, ed. C. Strachey (New York: G. P. Putnam's, 1927), I, 261–62.

styled protector of women protects them mainly to demonstrate their weakness, to boost his own masculine ego at their expense.

Steele's ideal woman had "gentle Softness, tender Fear, and all those parts of Life, which distinguish her from the other Sex; with some Subordination to it, but such an Inferiority that makes her still more lovely." He deplored the fact that women in his day were revealing ambition in their own right: "for their own Happiness and Comfort, as well as that of those for whom they were born" (that is, men), they ought to consider themselves "no other than an additional Part of the Species," made to adorn their fathers, husbands, brothers, or children. Steele's ideal wife writes to a friend that she has "no other Concern but to please the Man I love: he's the End of every Care I have; if I dress 'tis for him, if I read a Poem or a Play 'tis to qualify my self for a Conversation agreeable to his Taste: He's almost the End of my Devotions, half my Prayers are for his Happiness."

The disparagement of women which Steele generally concealed under sentimental eulogies of the fair sex finally emerged in *Spectator* Number 510. From an apparently harmless remark on the powerful effects of beauty on men he proceeded: "It is *common* with Women to destroy the good Effects a Man's following his own Way and Inclination might have upon his Honour and Fortune, by interposing their Power over him in Matters wherein they cannot influence him, but to his Loss and Disparagement" (my italics). It is next to impossible for a man to resist the importunities, tears, sullen looks, or even constrained affection of a woman whom he loves. After quoting with approval a harshly misogynistic passage from Sir Walter Raleigh on man's "Impotence to resist the Wiles of Women," he recommended that the safest course was to determine what should be done and to execute it before saying anything to your wife, since argument is useless "with one whose Looks and Gestures are more prevalent with you, than your Reason and Argument can be with her." If you wish to make your wife a present, well and good; but you must on no account buy anything for her because she entreats for it. If you allow your wife to determine your course of action, "you are no longer her Guardian and Protector, as you were designed by Nature; but, in Compliance to her

Weaknesses, you have disabled your self from avoiding the Misfortunes into which they will lead you both, and you are," like Milton's Adam, "to see the Hour in which you are to be reproached by her self for that very Complaisance to her."[28] In his assumption that women are immune to reason, Steele disparaged them as much as Chesterfield did; and his recommendation that men scrupulously avoid consulting their wives is reminiscent of the most severe Puritan views.

4

Steele's outburst is extraordinary among his own writings and those of his contemporaries. But his dislike of ambition in women and insistence on their domesticity and subordination were often expressed, most explicitly in attacks on the learned lady. Although some women continued to be educated by their male relatives and friends, as Stella was by Swift, learning for women was not so generally approved at this time as it had been in the sixteenth and early seventeenth centuries. Despite neoclassical exhortations to reason, the woman who aspired to shine in any intellectual field was a stock butt in comedy from the later seventeenth century on. Conventional writers of the period, usually more interested in keeping women properly subordinate than in developing their minds to the greatest possible extent, maintained that wit intoxicates a woman's feeble brain (George, Lord Lyttelton, "Advice to a Lady"), or that "The Dressing-Room, not the Study is the Lady's Province — and a Woman makes as ridiculous a Figure, poring over Globes, or thro' a Telescope, as a Man would with a pair of *Preservers* mending Lace" (James Miller, *The Humours of Oxford*, 1730).[29]

Most of the learned ladies in drama are not only odious for their unwomanliness but ridiculous for their gullibility, their pride in nonexistent learning, and their belief that women are mentally capable of studying philosophy or writing plays. As the influence

---

[28] *The Spectator*, Nos. 199, 423, II, 91, III, 312 and *passim; The Tatler*, No. 109, in *The British Essayists*, ed. A. Chalmers (New York: E. Sergeant, 1809), III, 156; *The Spectator*, No. 144, I, 436; No. 342, III, 71; No. 254, II, 256; No. 510, IV, 109–11. Addison's views were like Steele's, but more conservative.

[29] George, Lord Lyttelton, *The Works* (Dublin: G. Faulkner, 1774), II, 617; James Miller, *The Humours of Oxford* (London: J. Watts, 1730), p. 79. Lady Science in this play is the typical learned lady of drama.

of Molière became important in England, characterizations of the learned lady multiplied and became stereotyped, many of the plays falling into a pattern set by *Les Femmes Savantes* (1659): a sensible but henpecked husband and his attractive, right-minded daughter suffer from the pretensions of his self-styled intellectual wife and her daughter. The cast of Thomas Wright's *The Female Vertuoso's* (1693) includes Lady Meanwell, "An imperious Wife; great Pretender to Wit"; Lovewitt, her daughter, "an Admirer of Platonick Love, yet in Love with Clerimont" (who loves her right-minded sister, Mariana); and Catchat, her sister, "a stale Virgin, who fancies every Man in love with her."

These ladies plan to open an academy which will eclipse the Royal Society, although they will generously admit some of its ablest mathematicians, so that they "may penetrate together into such dark Secrets of Nature, as have hitherto been deem'd unfathomable by humane Capacity." They propose to pass irrevocable judgment on "all Books that come out: No Authors shall write well, but those we approve of; and no body pretend to Wit, but we, and our Friends." Lady Meanwell has a project to keep London streets clean and dry by blowing the clouds away with bellows; Lovewitt, to extract with a limbeck the wit from all extant plays and sell it to contemporary poets; and Catchat, to teach a flea to sing. The philosophic virtue to which the ladies pretend is as much a sham as their intellect: Lady Meanwell has a vile temper, and Lovewitt, who scorns carnal love, is jealous of her sister. Sir Maurice Meanwell contends, rightly but vainly, that a wife's whole study and philosophy should be to perform her domestic duties. In the end, his brother discomfits Lady Meanwell and then exhorts Sir Maurice: "Let not therefore an impertinent Female Wit Usurp again so unreasonable an Empire over you." [30]

In Thomas Shadwell's *Bury Fair* (1689), Lady Fantast, Mrs. (i.e., Miss) Fantast, and Gertrude fill the roles of Wright's Lady Meanwell, Lovewitt, and Mariana. The Fantasts pride themselves on their wit and breeding, which as Gertrude rightly points out are nothing but folly and affectation, and are completely taken in by

---

[30] Thomas Wright, *The Female Vertuoso's* (London: J. Wilde, 1693), pp. 16, 23, 25, 51.

a French barber disguised as a count. Gertrude, who as a sensible woman sees through the "Count" with no difficulty, presents the correct view of woman's function — to look after the household and obey her husband. She tells her fiancé at the end of the play: "I can obey, as well as e'er a meek, simpering milksop of 'em all; and have ever held non-resistance a doctrine fit for all wives, though for nobody else." [31] (Milton, as Samuel Johnson pointed out, had maintained the same position — a typical Whiggish-Puritan one.) [32]

Colley Cibber's *The Refusal* (1721) is yet another variation of the same pattern, this time directed particularly against Platonic ladies. Both "Female Philosophic Saints" in the play, Lady Wrangle and Sophronia, are intensely vain and susceptible to sexual jealousy; and the moment Sophronia is courted she melts into her suitor's bosom "with all the yielding Fondness of a Milk-maid." Although she is unusually intelligent for a woman, any man can easily delude her. The suitor of Charlotte, the nice normal girl in the play, declares the proper limits of female learning: as Charlotte "does not read *Aristotle*, *Plato*, *Plutarch*, or *Seneca*, she is neither romantic nor vain of her Pedantry; and as her Learning never went higher than *Bickerstaff's Tatlers*, her Manners are consequently natural, modest, and agreeable." [33]

Although the dramatists who satirized learned ladies were typically hack writers trying to succeed by appealing to popular prejudice, Pope, John Gay, and John Arbuthnot, in their *Three Hours after Marriage* (1717), made use of the same comic butt in the character of Phoebe Clinket. Her uncle says of this busy authoress:

[31] *Thomas Shadwell*, ed. G. Saintsbury (London: T. Fisher Unwin, n.d.), pp. 375, 378–79, 456–57.

[32] Samuel Johnson, *Lives of the English Poets* (London: J. M. Dent, 1954), I, 93.

[33] Colley Cibber, *The Dramatic Works* (London: J. Rivington, 1777), IV, 67, 93. Cf. Hortentia in John Vanbrugh's *Aesop*. For further information, see Jean Elisabeth Gagen, *The New Woman: Her Emergence in English Drama 1600–1730* (New York: Twayne, 1954). Gagen also shows how the independent heroine declined in favor as the eighteenth century progressed. The virtuous heroine of Steele's *The Funeral* rejoices in woman's helpless dependence on man. Gay's *Beggar's Opera* recalls Restoration drama in its frequent references to woman's guileful, seductive, and mercenary nature (as well as its rake hero), but these are softened by the humorous tone of the play and the genuine amiability of the heroine.

". . . alas, the poor Girl has a Procidence of the Pineal Gland, which has occasioned a Rupture in her Understanding. I took her into my House to regulate my Oeconomy; but instead of Puddings, she makes Pastorals; or when she should be raising Paste, is raising some Ghost in a new Tragedy." Phoebe, who makes her maid carry about a writing desk on her back so she will not lose any valuable thoughts, is first seen in the throes of composing a ludicrous tragedy on the Deluge. When she reads her play to the actors, they naturally mince it to bits. Then her uncle comes in and throws her papers into the fire, while she bitterly laments. The other characters inquire what is wrong:

Plotwell: Has he burnt any Bank-Bills, or a new *Mechlen* Head-Dress?
Clinket: My Works! my Works!
First Player: Has he destroy'd the Writings of an Estate, or your Billet-doux?
Clinket: A Pindarick Ode! five Similes! and half an Epilogue!
Second Player: Has he thrown a new Fan, or your Pearl Necklace into the Flames?
Clinket: Worse, worse! The tag of the Acts of a new Comedy! a Prologue sent by a Person of Quality! three Copies of recommendatory Verses! and two Greek Mottoes![34]

The implied contrast, of course, is between Clinket's works and things that are really worth something — and what should be worth something to a woman is her billet-doux or a new fan. The fact that this scene was imitated from *The Female Vertuoso's* and was in turn imitated in *The Refusal* illustrates the triteness of much of this satire on the learned lady.

Edward Young, who could never be accused of originality, devoted most of his two satires on women (*The Universal Passion*, 1725–28, Satires V, VI) to criticism of learned or otherwise "masculine" ladies. There is lovely Daphne, who pronounces on wit and, after giving her opinions, "Fully convinces all the town — she's fair." Sophronia prefers astronomy to love, but with typically feminine inconsequentiality:

[34] Alexander Pope, John Gay, and John Arbuthnot, *Three Hours after Marriage* (London: Bernard Lintot, 1717), pp. 3–4, 25. Phoebe has been variously identified as a caricature of Anne, Countess of Winchilsea, or of the very different Susannah Centlivre.

> But tho to-day this rage of science reigns,
> (O fickle sex!) soon end her learned pains.
> Lo! Pug from Jupiter her heart has got,
> Turns out the stars, and Newton is a sot.

What angels female theologians would be if they could only sew! Satire V closes with an exhortation to women not to attempt to distinguish themselves in any field: "Your sex's glory 'tis, to shine unknown."

Tullia, whose brain has evidently been "intoxicated" by her wit, illustrates what happens when this quality lodges in a feeble female:

> If Tullia had been blest with half her sense,
> None could too much admire her excellence:
> But since she can make error shine so bright,
> She thinks it vulgar to defend the right.
> With understanding she is quite o'errun;
> And by too great accomplishments undone:
> With skill she vibrates her eternal tongue,
> For ever most divinely in the wrong.

Even were her wit grounded on good sense, however, a woman should "veil her very wit with modesty." All of these pretenders to wit, wisdom, or learning are satirized not primarily because they are pretenders, actually foolish and ignorant, but because women have no business to aspire to these qualities: they cannot possibly attain them, and it would be unseemly if they could: "Their prudence in a share of folly lies: / Why will they be so weak, as to be wise?" [35]

---

[35] Edward Young, *The Poetical Works* (London: Bell and Daldy, n.d.), II, 100, 106, 107, 113, 117, 120. Young's contemporary Edward Moore, in his fable "The Owl and the Nightingale" (*Fables for the Female Sex*, 1744), drew a pathetic picture of the household presided over by an intellectual woman:

> At home, superior wit she vaunts,
> And twits her husband with his wants.
> Her ragged offspring, all around,
> Like pigs, are wall'wing on the ground,
> Impatient ever of controul,
> She knows no order, but of soul.

She utterly scorns a gentle soul skilled in housewifery, whose only concern is to keep her family happy. Cf. his fable of "The Lawyer and the Justice," *Fables* (Paris: P. Theophilus Barrois, 1782), pp. 27, 46.

Henry Fielding's Mrs. Western in *Tom Jones* and Mrs. Atkinson in *Amelia*

5

In the latter half of the eighteenth century, although men like Samuel Johnson continued to maintain the neoclassical ideal that women should be rational as men should be, gentle assertions of patriarchy became definitely the rule. Oliver Goldsmith, in an essay in *The Ladies' Magazine,* declared that women who stray beyond "the narrow limits of domestic offices" "move eccentrically, and consequently without grace." Self-styled intellectuals who consider themselves superior to the trifles which preoccupy the rest of their sex actually only make bores or fools of themselves, since genuine reason or knowledge are beyond the reach of women. While he condemned the "affectation" of superior intelligence in women, he would by no means deprive them "of their genteel little terrors, antipathies, and affections. The alternate panics of thieves, spiders, ghosts, and thunder are allowable to youth and beauty, provided they survive them." Since women must "act their own natural parts," feminine "imperfections will become them better than the borrowed perfections" of men. What a comfort and delight a woman may be to everyone around her if she acts as a woman, "but how are they changed, and how shocking do they become, when the rage of ambition, or the pride of learning, agitates and swells those breasts, where only love, friendship, and tender care should dwell!" They should model themselves on Flavia, who is "never misled by fancy or vanity, but guided singly by reason," who carefully conceals any superiority she may have to other women.[36] It is amusing to see that even in this sentimental production, reason remains the standard by which behavior is to be judged.

Some very influential manuals of female conduct which appeared

---

are rather mild treatments of the learned lady; his ideal women, Sophia and Amelia, are explicitly not pretenders to wit and wisdom. Francis Coventry ridiculed Lady Sophister, a female theologian, in *The History of Pompey the Little.* *The Athenian Mercury,* a magazine otherwise favorable to women, disapproved of learning for women on the grounds that it would make them "prouder and more unsupportable than before," that the resulting self-esteem would be "inconsistent with the Obedience they are designed for," and that Eve "by the bare desire of Knowledge destroyed all." *The Athenian Oracle* (selections from *The Athenian Mercury*), ed. John Underhill (London: Walter Scott, 1892), p. 227.

[36] Oliver Goldsmith, *The Works,* ed. Peter Cunningham (London: John Murray, 1854), III, 335–37.

in the later eighteenth century express the same attitude as Goldsmith did: combining polite insistence on woman's capacity to cheer and comfort men with equally polite insistence on the limitations of her sphere and her abilities. Their essential position is that of *The Ladies Calling*, although, in accordance with the contemporary cult of sensibility, they lay more emphasis on delicacy and further soften their manner of insisting on female subjection. James Fordyce, in his *Sermons to Young Women* (1766), warned that most sensible men would not think of marrying a witty woman, fearing to find, instead of "a soft friend," "a perpetual satirist, or a self-sufficient prattler." "Men of sensibility," he declared, desire soft prettiness, fragility, and tearfulness in women, as well as cowardice: ". . . an intrepid female seems to renounce our aid, and in some respect to invade our province. We turn away, and leave her to herself." He described very sweetly the protected helplessness of women, but this state was not so idyllic as it might appear since, as he revealed near the end of his work, it required them constantly to practice submissive arts to win protection. Thus he attributed much marital unhappiness "to the Turbulent Passions, or Uncomplying Humours" of wives: women must exert the utmost attention, mildness, and complaisance to persuade their husbands to tolerate marriage.[37]

Dr. John Gregory's *A Father's Legacy to His Daughters* (1774), while kindly and not illiberal, presents about the same picture of the ideal woman. She may not even assert herself to the point of recognizing that she loves a man: "A woman of . . . taste and delicacy" marries a man because she esteems him and he has chosen her. Like Fordyce, Goldsmith, Young, and even Pope, he encouraged women to display the inferiority that would keep them safely subject to men. Hence he considered wit "the most dangerous talent" a woman can have, as it is seldom united with softness and delicacy and is "so flattering to vanity, that they who possess it become intoxicated, and lose all self-command." She must be cautious of displaying her good sense or learning lest she be criticized for assuming superiority, and conceal humor and even good health as incompatible with proper feminine delicacy. It is safer for

[37] James Fordyce, *Sermons to Young Women* (London: T. Cadell, 1814), I, 147–48, II, 175–76, 207.

women to direct their attention to dress than to books, since "The love of dress is natural" to them, "and therefore it is proper and reasonable." [38]

This emphasis on reason seems to be the most constant element in the prevailing attitude toward women, which otherwise changed considerably from the Restoration to the later eighteenth century. The Restoration wits liked to expose women to the blazing light of reason and find them wanting. The more destructive eighteenth-century critics likewise exhibited women's deviations from rational behavior; the more constructive ones exhorted them to eschew folly and triviality as inappropriate to reasonable beings. Even an attack on extreme fashions was directed against the senselessness of their wearers rather than the lust, vanity, or extravagance which would have been emphasized in earlier periods. "The Modern Belle," a satire on women's fashions which appeared in the *Universal Magazine* in 1776, describes its subject as "Void of talents, sense, and art." The poet asks his muse to "Sing her large terrific head," referring to the enormous, overembellished wigs of the period:

> Nor the many things disguise,
> That produce its mighty size;
> And let nothing be forgot,
> Carrots, turnips, and what not;
> Curls and cushions for imprimis,
> Wool and powder for the finis.

"What a quantity of brain" must the beholder "think such heads contain!" But alas, no; for the contents are — literally and figuratively — only feathers.[39]

From the Restoration to the end of the eighteenth century, there is a gradual softening of the prevalent attitude to women, combined with an increasing tendency toward polite disparagement. The savage exposure of women in the Restoration, which went along with an implicit recognition of their equality, yielded — with the increasing propriety of the eighteenth century — to gentle criticism; but writers who felt they must abstain from harsh attacks on women

[38] Dr. John Gregory, *A Father's Legacy to His Daughters* (London: W. Strahan, 1774), pp. 30–31, 50, 55, 67, 83.

[39] *Satirical Songs and Poems on Costume*, ed. F. W. Fairholt (London: Percy Society [27], 1849), pp. 256–57.

often compensated by patronizing them. Swift showed a reversion to Restoration tough-mindedness, in his conviction that women should be as strong and rational as men as well as in the savagery of his attacks on those who failed to meet his standards. (The latter, of course, were sharpened by his personal hostility to women as sexual objects.) Steele, more typical of his period in his scrupulous chivalry and his lower estimate of female capacity, still exhorted women to be rational. Although the appeal to reason continued to be used throughout the eighteenth century, it gradually came to lose its meaning. For Gregory, who considered the love of dress reasonable in women and the love of books not, the word "rational" must have meant "proper." Propriety, in fact, was becoming the major ideal for women, who were encouraged to be weak, dependent, and unthinking. Overt literary attacks on women ceased to be acceptable, but the insidious belittlement which replaced them was hardly less destructive.

Chapter VI ❧ THE DROOPING LILY: THE NINETEENTH CENTURY

1

THE NINETEENTH century, as its writers never tired of repeating, was the era of women's apotheosis: they were the nobler half of humanity, whose role was to elevate men's sentiments and inspire their higher impulses. Women were purer than men, more religious, more altruistic, more devoted. As members of the delicate sex, they were absolutely entitled to chivalrous protection; no decent man would even criticize them harshly. As the objects of virtuous love — as sweethearts, wives, sisters, mothers, daughters — women were largely responsible for the loftiness of English Christian civilization. Charles Kingsley, in *Yeast* (1848), drew an allegorical picture of the "Triumph of Woman" in which Woman, moving through a desert in which flowers spring up beneath her steps, inspires intelligence and tenderness in everyone who sees her. For her heart "enshrines the priceless pearl of womanhood . . . before which gross man can only inquire and adore."[1]

The obvious corollaries to this affecting picture, however, are that woman must be protected because she is by nature incapable of looking after herself, and that her vocation is self-sacrifice, devotion of her life to ministering to men. If woman is naturally weak, it clearly follows that any attempts she may make at independence are foredoomed to failure, that she must resign herself to a dependent and therefore subordinate role, which is, of course

---

[1] Charles Kingsley, *Yeast* (London: Macmillan, 1908), pp. 124, 127–28. Keats's comparison of woman to "a milk-white lamb that bleats / For man's protection" (*Poetical Works*, ed. H. Buxton Forman [London: Oxford University Press, 1908], p. 23) is a good example of the overprotective attitude characteristic of the nineteenth century.

(according to nineteenth-century theory), her mission in any case. In fact, many nineteenth-century writers insisted quite as firmly on female subjection as the Puritans had, although they tactfully attributed St. Paul's strictures on women to his concern for their welfare rather than for their punishment and needful restraint.

The Reverend J. F. Stearns preached in 1837 that "no virtuous and delicate female . . . would desire to abate one jot or tittle from the seeming restrictions imposed upon her conduct" by St. Paul, since "They are designed, not to *degrade*, but to *elevate*, her character, — not to cramp, but to afford a *salutary* freedom. . . . Let woman throw off her feminine character, and her power to benefit society is *lost*; her loveliness, her dignity, her own chief protection is *lost*." To sacrifice her "almost magic power" over men in the hope of attaining fame, or "a fancied equality with men," or independence, or even of doing "good more extensively" would be "unworthy of a wise and virtuous woman's ambition."[2] Women were no longer reproached for the sin of Eve, no longer reviled for empty-headedness or vicious passions; but the painstaking tolerance which replaced the harsh criticism of previous centuries was insidiously destructive: by belittling women, men could express subtle, covert hostility at a time when open expressions were avoided as shocking. Insistence on women's weakness and the sweetness of submission was a gentle way of keeping them in subjection, and in subjection, of course, they were prevented from doing harm.

Alfred, Lord Tennyson's *The Princess* (1847) shows the typical early nineteenth-century attitude toward enterprising women — not harsh, but patronizing. Although Tennyson treated his feminist

[2] Jonathan F. Stearns, *A Discourse on Female Influence, and the True Christian Mode of Its Exercise* (Newburyport, Mass.: John Tilton, 1837), pp. 17–18. I cannot resist quoting from George Fitzhugh's *Sociology for the South* (Richmond, Va.: A. Morris, 1854), a book which aptly combines defense of slavery for Negroes and for women: "The generous sentiments of slaveholders are sufficient guarantee of the rights of woman, all the world over" (p. 216). An illuminating remark by Coleridge shows how the overt depreciation of women in earlier times became covert belittlement in the nineteenth century: " 'Most women have no character at all,' said Pope, and meant it for satire. Shakspeare, who knew man and woman much better, saw that it, in fact, was the perfection of woman to be characterless." (*Table Talk*, in *Complete Works*, ed. W. G. T. Shedd [New York: Harper and Bros., 1884], VI, 349.)

ladies with some sympathy (except for Lady Blanche, with her dyed hair, who has evidently taken up women's rights out of contempt for her husband), he made clear that they are much misguided. The young woman who starts the story by exclaiming against the masculine conventions which keep women children is "A rosebud set with little wilful thorns." So, apparently, is the Princess, a noble and sincere woman who has broken her engagement and vowed celibacy in order to set up a university in which to develop women's true potentialities. She aspires to train women so that they are in every way the equals of men, and at the same time to purge them of the traditional feminine failings "of emptiness, gossip and spite." She disparages children in favor of "great deeds" and has only contempt for romantic love. She wants women to be regarded not as "vassals to be beat, nor pretty babes / To be dandled," but as "living wills, and sphered / Whole in ourselves and owed to none."

Ultimately the Princess is cured of her folly, first by the physical conquest of her university by the men, symbolizing apparently the nature of things, and secondly by her own finer feelings as, seeing the Prince wounded on the battlefield, she understands "all the foolish work / Of Fancy" and her noble heart melts in her breast. The Prince, however, does not triumph in his victory, but concludes with a moderate program for female development: let women learn to become "All that not harms distinctive womanhood"; let there be no talk of equality between men and women, since

> . . . in true marriage lies
> Nor equal, nor unequal: each fulfills
> Defect in each.[3]

So vague a doctrine would be hard to dispute, but it could obviously be used to suffocate women's aspirations to change their condition: who is to say what learning does not harm "distinctive womanhood"? If mentioning equality in marriage is mean and low, how can woman claim a just share in the perfect whole that it is supposed to form? Woman gets her usual nineteenth-century glorification in the end of the Prince's speech, where he explains that he learned his wisdom from the best possible source, a good woman,

[3] Alfred, Lord Tennyson, *Poems*, ed. M. Bozman (London: J. M. Dent, 1949), I, 197, 206, 220, 226, 249, 261–62.

his mother. The Princess herself would never have wandered into error had her mother been alive.

Kingsley, in *Yeast*, praised *The Princess* for showing that woman, "when she takes her stand on the false masculine ground of intellect," destroys her heart and "falls from pride to sternness, from sternness to sheer inhumanity" (just like Spenser's Radigund). His portrait of Argemone, the heroine, reveals more explicitly than *The Princess* the belittlement which underlies the typical nineteenth-century exaltation of women. (Kingsley, although progressive with regard to religion and social reform, was a thorough traditionalist in his attitude toward women.) Argemone, an intelligent and high-minded young woman, is bent on intellectual self-fulfillment, although, of course, such an enterprise in a female is intrinsically ridiculous:

She had four new manias every year; her last winter's one had been that bottle-and-squirt mania, miscalled chemistry; her spring madness was for the Greek drama. She had devoured Schlegel's lectures, and thought them divine; and now she was hard at work on Sophocles, with a little help from translations, and thought she understood him every word.

Only after she falls in love with the hero, Lancelot, does she realize her proper mission as a woman: "I will study no more, except the human heart, and only that to purify and ennoble it." Although, believing in woman's independence and enfranchisement, she has resolved "to live like the angels, single and self-sustained," she is utterly incapable of resisting Lancelot's proposal: "What was her womanhood, that it could stand against the energy of his manly will!" Argemone's moral aspirations are as misguided as her intellectual ones. In her search for spiritual fulfillment, she considers joining a sort of Anglican convent, instead of following, as she should, "the good old English plan of district visiting, by which ladies can have mercy on the bodies and souls of those below them, without casting off the holy discipline which a home, even the most ungenial, alone supplies." Kingsley believed that a woman could not be trusted to pursue the most altruistic career on her own; even self-abnegation, unless it occurs under male supervision within the family, is merely a "lust for singularity and self-glorification." [4]

⁴ Kingsley, *Yeast*, pp. 18, 22, 31, 130, 131, 133, 141. Could it be significant,

John Ruskin, like Kingsley, coupled a high-flown vision of woman's role with an insistence on "true wifely subjection" in the form of continuous self-abnegation. To fulfill her function, a wife "must be enduringly, incorruptibly good; instinctively, infallibly wise — wise, not for self-development, but for self-renunciation . . . not with the narrowness of insolent and loveless pride, but with the passionate gentleness of an infinitely variable, because infinitely applicable, modesty of service."[5] Girls should be carefully educated, but *only* in order to sympathize better with their husbands and to feel uneasy any place but at home. Ruskin regarded the women's rights movement with incredulous contempt: ". . . there has not been so low a level of thought reached by any race, since they grew to be male and female out of starfish." Women who claim justice for themselves, rather than love and fellowship, are simply mad.[6]

Complete self-abnegation is the leading characteristic of most of the good women of nineteenth-century literature: Lord Byron's Haidee and Medora, apparently mindless naturals who expect nothing from their lords and languish whenever they are not present, and Charles Dickens' Little Dorrit and Esther Summerson, who never venture even to think of wishes of their own, are obvious examples. The typical virtuous heroine of the Victorian novel is a softened version of Grisilde — rewarded for exploitation by being venerated as a saint. Women, it is implied, are wonderfully angelic and superior to men for giving up their lives to male happiness — but there is no question that this is what they should do.

Generally, the subjection of the Victorian heroine was veiled by the worshipful aura with which she was surrounded. But in John Cordy Jeaffreson's popular novel *A Woman in Spite of Herself* (1872), it is baldly exposed. The protagonist, a heroic and strong-minded woman, was forced by circumstances to masquerade as a man for some years. When a young man proposed to her (after

---

in view of the fact that Argemone is recognized as a portrait of Kingsley's wife, that he killed her off at the end of the novel?

[5] John Ruskin, *Sesame and Lilies* (1865), ed. R. K. Root (New York: Henry Holt, 1901), pp. 82, 84.

[6] John Ruskin, *Fors Clavigera* (1871–74) (Boston: Dana Estes and Co., n.d.), I, 59, 71; II, 72.

she revealed her sex), she rhetorically asked how she could show her love's

depth and greatness, its overwhelming force and passionate vehemence? Not by words, or kisses, and caresses, — but by my whole life; by the joyful subordination of all my powers of mind, heart, soul, to your will; by the natural demonstrations of the never-ceasing, ever active delight that a true woman feels in being the loyal comrade, watchful ministrant, enthusiastic slave of the man to whom she has given her heart.

When he came to see her the next day, she sank "to the floor at the feet of her lover, and throwing her arms around his knees, she exulted in her sense of subjection to masculine government. 'I am a woman again — a woman!' she ejaculated, 'at your feet — at your feet!' " [7] The lady's submission is extreme, but only a logical extension of that recommended by Ruskin.

2

The nineteenth-century idealization of self-sacrificing woman-hood provided a vehicle for covert misogyny insofar as it assumed the subjection of women and demanded self-renunciation from them. But some misogynistic feeling, requiring a more direct outlet, took the form of attacks on female types who could be considered "un-feminine" and therefore legitimate game: the domineering wife, the old maid, and the bluestocking. Wives as a class were seldom attacked in this period because of the supposed sanctity of virtuous womanhood, although Lord Byron, Thomas Moore, and Oscar Wilde did occasionally indulge in jokes at their expense. Byron especially — with his unhappy conjugal experience, his affinity for neoclassical cynicism, and his aristocratic contempt for bourgeois respectability — peppered his satiric poems with jibes against marriage.[8] But most nineteenth-century writers attacked marriage only

[7] J. C. Jeaffreson, *A Woman in Spite of Herself* (Leipzig: B. Tauchnitz, 1872), II, 285, 288–89. Even so supposedly objective a source as the *Encyclopedia Britannica* stated that woman should be subject to man and had no right to choose her prospective master, but only "barely to consent or refuse" a proposed match: see the 1842 edition under "Love."

[8] See George Gordon, Lord Byron, *Don Juan*, in *Don Juan and Other Satirical Poems*, ed. Louis Bredvold (New York: Odyssey Press, 1935), pp. 209, 452, etc. and a letter to his publisher, John Murray, quoted in Leslie A. Marchand, *Byron: A Biography* (New York: Knopf, 1957), II, 902. Cf. Thomas Moore's

covertly, by presenting satiric portraits of bad wives. The significance of these characters is not the fact that they exist, since of course an author can draw vexatious women straight from life, but the numbers in which they exist.

It has often been remarked that the adorable girls of Victorian fiction are more likely than not to turn into trying matrons — particularly in the novels of Charles Dickens, whose satire was no doubt sharpened by his own unhappy marriage. Not only did Dickens constantly rely on the henpecking wife as a source of humor, but he was apt to draw her not from life but from the misogynistic stock pile, as if he could not resist adding a bad wife to a novel even when inspiration was lacking. Mrs. Joe Gargery of *Great Expectations* (1860–61), for example, is both intrinsically improbable — surely even Joe would not be soft enough to permit her habitually to knock his head against the wall — and more crudely characterized than any other major character in the novel. She is hardly successful as a comic figure: judged as a literary character, she is too trite to be funny; considered as a real woman, she is too destructive, blighting the lives of a good man and a helpless child. Yet Dickens wrote to John Forster that he intended the Gargery family situation to be "exceedingly droll." I suggest that he over-estimated its drollery because he found this subject so congenial and because he was using humor as a camouflage for hostility toward dominant women. This maneuver was particularly common in the Victorian period.[9]

Occasionally, however, the odious wives in Dickens are charac-

---

"Love and Marriage," *Complete Poetical Works* (New York: Thomas Y. Crowell, 1895), and "The Rabbinical Origin of Women," *The Poetical Works* (New York: P. F. Collier, n.d.), mentioned in Note 4, Chapter III. Evidently considering the latter poem too nasty, Moore suppressed it in his own collection of his poems. Cf. Oscar Wilde, *The Plays* (Boston: John W. Luce, 1905), I, *Lady Windermere's Fan*, p. 56; *A Woman of No Importance*, p. 26.

[9] I do not maintain that Mrs. Joe is entirely a stock character — her worship of respectability, for example, is not part of the ordinary caricature — but only that she is markedly less original, less humorous, and less acutely observed than most of Dickens' characters, especially in this book. Dickens' extensive series of conventionally drawn shrews includes Mrs. Raddle in *Pickwick Papers*, Mrs. Sowerberry and Mrs. Corney in *Oliver Twist*, and Mrs. Snagsby in *Bleak House*. His letter to Forster is found in John Forster, *The Life of Charles Dickens* (London: Chapman and Hall, 1874), III, 362.

terized with the penetration worthy of a great novelist. Mrs. Varden, in *Barnaby Rudge* (1841), is a telling picture of the apparently ideal wife who actually manages to torment her entire household, her good-natured and inoffensive husband in particular, by her whining and perversity. In all superficial aspects she is a model wife: a good-looking woman, a devout Protestant, a fanatical house-keeper whose cleaning proceeds from Monday morning through Saturday afternoon. Far from violently opposing her husband, she protests — continually — that she is a martyr to his perversity and callousness. Since he is a kindly and devoted man, she can control him by adopting always the contrary mood to his, by falling into frequent hysterical fits, by assiduous reading of the Protestant Manual (to give her the spiritual strength to bear her marriage) when he tries to reason with her, and by lugubrious protests that his occasional innocent visits to the Maypole Inn are ruining the family. In a typical scene, Joe Willet, son of the keeper of the Maypole and her daughter's suitor, comes to call. First she throws out the flowers he has painstakingly gathered for her daughter, having decided that their odor makes her feel faint. She then reproaches Joe because his father sells liquor, turning respectable tradesmen into sots like Varden [*sic*], and complains resignedly how she suffers waiting up for him at home. Having so brightened the scene, she says to the men: "I'm sorry to see that you don't take your tea, Varden, and that you don't take yours, Mr. Joseph; though of course it would be foolish of me to expect that anything that can be had at home, and in the company of females, would please *you*." Finally she takes herself off, making them feel guilty for driving her away.

On another occasion, when Varden finally starts to defend himself after a lengthy lecture on his drinking, she cuts him off: ". . . such discussions as these between married people are much better left alone. Therefore, if you please, Varden, we'll drop the subject. I have no wish to pursue it. I could. I might say a great deal. But I would rather not. Pray don't say any more." She will not contradict him, she continues. "I know my duty. I need know it, I am sure. I am often obliged to bear it in mind, when my inclination perhaps would be for the moment to forget it." And so, Dickens concluded, "with a mighty show of humility and forgiveness, she folded her hands, and looked round again, with a smile which plainly said,

'If you desire to see the first and foremost among female martyrs, here she is, on view!' " [10]

Her daughter, Dolly, is — and this is unusual in the Victorian novel — a realistic portrayal of a younger Mrs. Varden. Although Dolly is more attractive than her mother — being young, very pretty, and still good-humored — she has the same selfishness, shallowness, and perverse determination to show her power by tormenting the man who loves her; she will surely grow up just like her mother. In the end, Dickens did make a concession to Victorian sentimentality by reforming both women; but, despite their implausible conversions, the two characters graphically demonstrate the ways in which women torment men.

Mrs. Caudle's Curtain Lectures, written by Douglas Jerrold and

[10] Charles Dickens, *Barnaby Rudge* (London: Thomas Nelson, 1900), pp. 109–13, 152. In the semiautobiographical *David Copperfield*, Dickens made a point of showing how women fail their male relatives: David's foolish, inadequate mother and first wife are not quite counterbalanced by the unrealistic Agnes Wickfield. Dickens' treatment of women in his works is the natural result of his relationships with them in life, which were almost all unsatisfactory: his thoughtless mother, his coquettish first love, his inadequate wife, and his cold-hearted mistress all caused him pain. For further information see Edgar Johnson, *Charles Dickens: His Tragedy and Triumph* (New York: Simon and Schuster, 1952).

Some critics maintain that the novels of Dickens' great contemporary William Makepeace Thackeray also show a bias against women, but it seems to me that their case depends on overemphasizing a few misogynistic elements while ignoring the general trend of his work. Biographically the parallel is tempting: like Dickens, Thackeray suffered from a series of painful relationships with women — his mother was possessive and masterful, his wife was inadequate always and soon became an utter burden on him, and (as he saw it) his friend Mrs. Brookfield coldly frustrated him for years. There is a highly significant difference, however, in that Thackeray's relationship with his mother was basically good; she was an admirable woman who deeply loved her son, as distinct from Dickens' mother, whom he felt had rejected him. Accordingly, none of the mothers in Thackeray's fiction fails her son so culpably as Clara Copperfield fails hers. Children in Thackeray are generally provided with the security of maternal love; children in Dickens are typically orphans.

It is true that there is a recurring pattern in Thackeray's novels of paired female types: the artful, selfish, cold-blooded exploiters like Becky Sharp, Blanche Amory, and Beatrix Esmond; and the clinging, possessive ladies who live only to love and pray yet who also in a way exploit their men, such as Amelia Sedley, Helen Pendennis, and Lady Rachel Castlewood. While it might seem that Thackeray was indicting all womankind through these predominant types, suggesting that if a woman does not torment her man by being too cold-

published serially in *Punch* in 1845, further show the widespread popularity of the henpecking wife as a source of humor during the Victorian period. No submission from Job Caudle, an utterly inoffensive tradesman, can still his wife's nightly eloquence. For thirty years of marriage, and thirty-five long lectures, Mrs. Caudle dilates

> upon the joys, griefs, duties, and vicissitudes comprised within that seemingly small circle — the wedding-ring. . . . A lemon-hearted cynic might liken the wedding-ring to an ancient Circus, in which wild animals clawed one another for the sport of lookers-on. Perish the hyperbole! We would rather compare it to an elfin ring, in which dancing fairies made the sweetest music for infirm humanity.

This preface sets the tone for the book, which, however jocular, demonstrates that a man has far more to lose than to gain by marriage, and that a typical wife, besides making her husband's home

---

blooded to return his love she torments him by jealously brooding over him, one should not neglect Thackeray's strong emphasis on the positive effects of woman's love. His panegyrics on maternal devotion, as in Chapter 2 of *Pendennis* (Chiswick ed.; London: J. M. Dent, n.d.), I, 28, seem mawkishly sentimental today; but that does not mean that they are insincere. There is every reason to suppose that the pure devotion given to male characters like Arthur Pendennis by the good women around them contributes a great deal to their ultimate virtue and happiness. See, e.g., *Pendennis*, II, 24–25 (Chapter 28); III, 158 (Chapter 61); *Henry Esmond* (New York: Holt, Rinehart and Winston, 1962), pp. 5–6 (Book I, Chapter 1), 220–21 (Book II, Chapter 6), 491–92 (Book III, Chapter 13); *The Newcomes* (New York: A. L. Burt Co., n.d.), II, 126 (Chapter 11), 205 (Chapter 19). Thackeray saw, with a penetration unusual in his time, that the empedestaled Victorian ideal — a woman of the greatest conceivable piety, purity, and seemingly altruistic devotion — can in fact harm the object of her love by uncritical devotion, clinging dependency, and subtle domineering. He even saw the element of sexual jealousy in "pure" maternal love. Nevertheless, Thackeray's possessively loving women are far more good than bad: they are sweet, gentle, altruistic, unworldly, dutiful, and faithful; and their effects on those around them are predominantly beneficial. Helen's influence on her son, for example, is clearly better than the "wiser" influence of Major Pendennis. Thackeray constantly emphasized the importance of maternal love in forming a happy, secure person.

In part, Thackeray's presentation of good women developed from his apparent division of humanity into people who were clever, selfish, and cold-blooded and those who were foolish, loving, and completely controlled by emotion. Although the second type is generally represented by women, one male character — Colonel Newcome of *The Newcomes* — fits it exactly. Indeed, despite his great love and excellent intentions, Colonel Newcome harms his son more than any of the doting mothers do theirs — disparaging his vocation and pushing him into a wretched marriage.

life as miserable as possible, jealously does all she can to prevent his finding any happiness with male friends outside. Jerrold made it plain, in an obviously ironic postscript, that Mrs. Caudle was supposed to be typical: "During the progress of these Lectures, it has very often pained us . . . excessively, to hear from unthinking, inexperienced men — bachelors, of course — that every woman, no matter how divinely composed, has . . . one drop of Caudle. . . . It may be so; still be it our pride never to believe it. NEVER!" The popularity of this work indicates that the Victorians themselves had some misgivings about the home they idealized, although they were loath to admit that women as well as men had a right to occasional freedom from it.

In her first lecture, occasioned by Mr. Caudle's lending £5 to a

---

The overtly bad women in Thackeray's novels are surely no worse than comparable male characters, and they are often treated sympathetically: his liking for Becky Sharp is obvious, and he occasionally gave admiration and sympathy even to less engaging characters like Beatrix Esmond. They are presented not as types of womanhood but as individuals who display the selfishness, deceitfulness, and ruthless ambition which Thackeray found in so many of his fellow humans. In noting Thackeray's emphasis on selfishness in almost all his women and his tendency to divide women into two types which are both open to criticism, one must remember that he was a satirist with an appropriately cynical view of both sexes. He made everyone selfish in *Vanity Fair* (except Dobbin), and even in the more sentimental *Pendennis* he explicitly pointed out the selfishness of all his characters (III, 72 [Chapter 56]). It may be true that Thackeray had a particular animus against mothers-in-law, based presumably on his own unhappy experience and shown in a succession of characters of which Mrs. Mackenzie in *The Newcomes* is the most famous example. But the mother-in-law had long been a stock butt, and Thackeray's animus was by no means obsessive, as the horrible mothers-in-law appear only occasionally in his novels.

One may well be suspicious of Thackeray's exaggerated panegyrics on self-sacrificing women like Helen Pendennis, since they are often so extreme as to suggest denial of an underlying hostility. Doubtless Thackeray did feel and attempt to smother hostility toward his possessive, dominating mother, his unresponsive idol Mrs. Brookfield, and the wife who blighted his domestic life; and this process may be discerned in his presentation of the fictional characters he based on them. But one must not be oversubtle: I believe that by and large Thackeray meant what he said about his good women, that they are what they appear to be — loving, unselfish, and beneficial to man. Considering the wretched failure of his marriage, Thackeray laid surprisingly little emphasis on bad wives: Rosey Mackenzie Newcome in *The Newcomes* is utterly inadequate, but is more than counterbalanced by Ethel Newcome, as Dora is not by Agnes in *David Copperfield*.

Although Thackeray was unusually sensitive to the misery which Victorian

friend, Mrs. Caudle reveals her stinginess with regard to her husband's desires, her lavishness with regard to her own, her jealousy
of his life outside the home, and her whining pretense that her only
motive is concern for her family, neglected by their unfeeling father:

I've wanted a black satin gown these three years, and that £5 would have
entirely bought it. But it's no matter how I go, — not at all. Everybody
says I don't dress as becomes your wife — and I don't; but what's that to
you, Mr. Caudle? Nothing. Oh no! you can have fine feelings for everybody
but those belonging to you. I wish people knew you, as I do — that's all.
You like to be called liberal, and your poor family pays for it.

Half £5 would have bought your daughters bonnets, but now they
must go without. Now we cannot mend Jack's broken window, and
if he dies of cold, "his death will be upon his father's head." Nor
can we pay the fire insurance, so your wife and children will be
burned in their beds; nor can we go to Margate this summer, so
little Caroline will die of consumption; nor can we fix Mary Anne's
teeth, so she will die an unwanted old maid; nor can we mend the
shutter, nor sweep the chimney, nor trap the mice, nor buy a lock
for the back door. In other lectures she berates Mr. Caudle for
joining a social club, for bringing home a friend for dinner, for
spending an occasional few hours at the tavern; like Mrs. Varden,
she insists on waiting up for him and then complains of fatigue.

When Caudle mildly protests about a meager dinner, she retorts:

There's nothing proper, now — nothing at all. Better get somebody else to
keep the house I think. I can't do it now, it seems; I'm only in the way here:
I'd better take the children, and go. . . . I *shall* speak, sir. It isn't often I
open my mouth, Heaven knows! But you like to hear nobody talk but yourself. You ought to have married a negro slave, and not any respectable
woman.

Perhaps other people do have pudding with cold mutton, but other
people become bankrupts also. "I'll do my duty as a wife to you,

---

mores compelled women to undergo, he did seem to accept the patronizing Victorian view of women as creatures designed to immolate themselves for men.
See, e.g., *Vanity Fair* (Boston: Houghton Mifflin, 1963), p. 169 (Chapter 18);
Pendennis, III, 69 (Chapter 56); *Henry Esmond*, p. 467 (Book III, Chapter
11); *The Newcomes*, II, 20 (Chapter 2). It is also true that all his women with
enterprise, convincing intelligence, and ideas of their own are bad women. However, one cannot call a man misogynistic simply because he shared the prejudices of his time.

Mr. Caudle: you shall never have it to say that it was *my* housekeeping that brought you to beggary." Later, when she is sweetly trying to persuade him to ask her dear mother to live with them, she tempts him with the delicious puddings Mother would make for him to have with cold meat — but he is wise enough to draw the line at Mother. Yet, when Mrs. Caudle finally dies, her husband, in the strange tradition of the henpecked, persists in believing that he has lost a saint, speaking of her always as "that angel now in heaven."[11] Washington Irving's Dame Van Winkle is another expert in curtain lectures, although indeed her "torrent of household eloquence" seems to flow all day as well. The main point of "Rip Van Winkle" (1820) is that the henpecking wife is the worst of evils, escape from a wife the greatest of blessings. While Dickens' Mrs. Varden may have been drawn from hard personal experience, Mrs. Gargery, Mrs. Caudle, and Dame Van Winkle are expressions of a convention. The persistence of this convention shows that Victorian men must have felt some rebellion against marriage despite the general glorification of the institution, releasing their consequent hostility against a permissible butt, the henpecking wife.

3

The old maid provided an even more convenient butt for hostility against women, since she did not justify her existence by being a wife and mother. Hence she was often depicted as a figure of fun, stripped of the sentimental chivalry with which other women were swathed, caricatured as ugly, disagreeable, and relentlessly in pursuit of men. Of course, in a society that offered virtually no role to the single woman, spinsters were apt to be soured by frustration

[11] Douglas Jerrold, *Mrs. Caudle's Curtain Lectures*, in *The Works* (Philadelphia: J. B. Lippincott, n.d.), III, 4, 7–9, 20, 103. That Jerrold's picture of marriage was not entirely the result of convention is suggested by some extremely unkind remarks he made publicly about his wife, quoted by Gordon N. Ray in *Thackeray: The Uses of Adversity* (New York: McGraw-Hill, 1955), p. 355. *Punch* seems to have specialized in jibes against marriage: its most famous joke was "Advice to persons about to marry,— don't." Quoted by Ray, p. 357.

Anthony Trollope's Mrs. Proudie, who stalks through the Barsetshire novels, is an entertaining if traditional incarnation of the domineering wife. Introduced as a purely comic figure in *Barchester Towers* (1857), she becomes more stupidly wrong-headed and malicious in *The Last Chronicle of Barset* (1867).

and to show an unseemly avidity for marriage, any marriage. Often unpleasant characteristics fostered by social conditions facilitate literary stereotyping, which in turn perhaps discourages any change in the social conditions.

While the full stereotype of the old maid was not established until the later eighteenth century (since which time it has persisted to the present, despite social changes that have made it obsolete), the satire directed against her was not altogether new: ridicule of an undesirable woman in hot pursuit of every man in sight is as ancient as Aristophanes. Women who want men more than men want them have always existed and always been irresistibly comic to men, although old maids, properly speaking — permanently unmarried women (except nuns) — were so rare in society that they scarcely appear in literature until well into the eighteenth century. In Restoration comedy the superannuated coquette, usually a widow trying to remarry, is a stock figure. Lady Wishfort, in William Congreve's *The Way of the World* (1700), is perhaps the best example. Although she "publishes her detestation of mankind; and full of the vigour of fifty-five, declares for a friend and ratafia; and let posterity shift for itself, she'll breed no more," she would actually "marry anything that resembled a man, though 'twere no more than what a butler could pinch out of a napkin." [12]

By the eighteenth century, Lady Wishfort's unattractiveness and eagerness, as well as a disposition soured by lifelong frustration, were generally attached to the old maid, who was often treated with disproportionate harshness. In 1723 Daniel Defoe described gossiping old maids as "a Furious and Voracious kind of Females; nay, even a kind of Amazonian Cannibals, that not only Subdued, but Devoured those that had the Misfortune to fall into their Hands." "If an OLD-MAID should bite any body," he went on, "it would certainly be as Mortal, as the Bite of a Mad-Dog." [13] Tobias Smollett, a specialist in caricature, created the first fully developed old maids in fiction. Grizzle Pickle of *Peregrine Pickle* (1751) and Tabitha

[12] William Congreve, *Complete Plays*, ed. Alexander Ewald (New York: Hill and Wang, 1956), pp. 298, 317. Cf. Etherege's Lady Cockwood (*She Would If She Could*), Wycherley's Lady Flippant (*Love in a Wood*), etc.

[13] *Applebee's Journal*, April 6, 1723, in William Lee, *Daniel Defoe: His Life, and Recently Discovered Writings* (London: J. C. Hotten, 1869), III, 127.

Bramble of *Humphry Clinker* (1771), having failed to marry because of their extreme unattractiveness, continue hotly to pursue men, meanwhile making everyone miserable by their extreme ill-nature. Tabitha is particularly conspicuous because she is the only character in a genial comic novel toward whom no sympathy is directed. Smollett not only made her ridiculous by showing her in avid pursuit of every bachelor in sight, but he made her odious by endowing her with all the qualities traditionally charged to old maids — avarice, selfishness, prurience, and spite.

As a woman who did not fit into the social pattern, who was nobody's wife and nobody's mother, the old maid remained fair game even in the nineteenth century, when most women were treated with painstaking indulgence. She appeared regularly in the Savoy Operas, from the "rich attorney's elderly, ugly daughter" in *Trial by Jury* (1875) through Dame Carruthers in *The Yeomen of the Guard* (1888). It is unfair to blame W. S. Gilbert for exceptional callousness in his recurrent caricatures of old maids trying desperately to attach themselves to attractive young men, since he was merely exploiting a dependable, if well-worn, source of humor. On the other hand, he did develop the type with notable persistence and harshness. His crude ridicule of Katisha and the rest contrasts strongly with the general innocuousness of his satire. Lady Jane in *Patience* (1881) is perhaps the best drawn and most human of the group. The only one of the Rapturous Maidens who does not desert Bunthorne for Grosvenor, she pursues him with relentless fidelity. But, she soliloquizes, he must make haste to enjoy her charms, which are ripe — indeed, she has to admit, overripe:

> Silvered is the raven hair,
>   Spreading is the parting straight,
> Mottled the complexion fair,
>   Halting is the youthful gait,
> Hollow is the laughter free,
>   Spectacled the limpid eye —
> Little will be left of me
>   In the coming by and by!
>
> Fading is the taper waist,
>   Shapeless grows the shapely limb,
> And although severely laced,
>   Spreading is the figure trim!

> Stouter than I used to be,
> Still more corpulent grow I —
> There will be too much of me
> In the coming by and by! [14]

The farcical setting of this verse — Jane accompanies herself on the cello as she sings — softens its impact somewhat, but the words themselves are savage. Gilbert's realistically detailed description of woman's decay (which occurs equally in the most virtuous and sensible of the sex), his methodical stripping away of the beauty which woman so prizes and for which she is idealized, is surely sadistic, especially as he makes the woman fully aware of her own ruin.

The other female type against whom nineteenth-century writers could acceptably release misogynistic feelings was the bluestocking: that is, the lady who refused to conform to the intellectual restrictions laid upon her sex, who studied Greek and theology, who wrote and published, who worked for public causes, or — worst of all, when she made her appearance later in the century — who pursued a career. Byron, for example, focused his hostility against women particularly on bluestockings. (The term, rather complimentary in the eighteenth century, had become thoroughly pejorative by his time.) Donna Inez in *Don Juan* (1819), in large part a portrait of Byron's intellectual wife, is a brilliant, cutting, and unfair version of the pretentious female intellectual. Byron introduced her as

> . . . a learned lady, famed
> For every branch of every science known —
> In every Christian language ever named,
> With virtues equall'd by her wit alone.

Then he promptly exposed these lines as ironical, showing the contrast between her pretensions and her actual knowledge. Like the

[14] W. S. Gilbert, *The Complete Plays of Gilbert and Sullivan* (New York: The Modern Library, n.d.), pp. 214–15. Dorothy Yost Deegan, in *The Stereotype of the Single Woman in American Novels* (New York: King's Crown Press, 1951), discusses Nathaniel Hawthorne's Hepzibah Pyncheon, Mark Twain's Miss Watson, and other old maids in nineteenth- and early twentieth-century American fiction; her study includes the hostile stereotype of the career woman in the later novels.

so-called learned ladies of the eighteenth century, she knew less than a schoolboy: "She knew the Latin — that is, 'the Lord's prayer,' / And Greek — the alphabet — I'm nearly sure." Since she lacked wit as well as knowledge, her ostentatious learning did no more than render her a barely comprehensible bore:

> Her wit (she sometimes tried at wit) was Attic all,
> Her serious sayings darken'd to sublimity;
>
> . . . .
>
> Her thoughts were theorems, her words a problem,
> As if she deem'd that mystery would ennoble 'em.

Intellectual ladies are not only tiresome, Byron claimed, but also invariably henpeck their husbands. This means, apparently, that they refuse to display the meek pliancy appropriate to women and disturb their husbands by challenging their patriarchal complacency. Despite his jocular tone, Byron's dislike of the faultless woman recalls Juvenal's: "To others' share let 'female errors fall,' / For she had not even one — the worst of all." In a diary of this period, Byron condemned the education and emancipation of women as "artificial and unnatural. They ought to mind home — and be well fed and clothed — but not mixed in society." They should "read neither poetry nor politics — nothing but books of piety and cookery." Although Byron did sometimes enjoy the company of intelligent women, the diary entry shows that he disliked female intellectuality in general and probably satirized Donna Inez for this more than for the pretentiousness and hypocrisy which made her a legitimate satiric butt.

Donna Inez' moral pretensions are as vast as her intellectual, and equally false: "Some women use their tongues — she *look'd* a lecture, / Each eye a sermon, and her brow a homily." Yet with all her "magnanimity" she ruined her husband and Donna Julia. Although she expurgated Juan's classical reading and refused to let him see the earthy medieval illustrations in the family missal, she had no objections to his being kept by the aging Empress Catherine of Russia. And thus she typified the hypocrisy which Byron so loathed in English society and which he traced to the influence of English women. A man cannot be too circumspect in England: he must "wear the newest mantle of hypocrisy, / On pain of much displeasing the gynocracy."[15]

Annoyed by the pretensions of the female pseudo-intellectuals whom he had met at Holland House, in particular their enthusiasm for the fourth-rate in poetry, Byron tossed off "The Blues" (1821), a skit in which Inkel and Tracy (Byron and, probably, his friend Thomas Moore) ridiculed them. Moore was equally fond of satirizing bluestockings, although — unlike Byron, whose satire on them probably expresses personal misogyny — he seems to have used them mainly as a convenient and acceptable satiric butt. His comic opera *M. P. or, The Blue-Stocking* (1811) features in old Lady Bab Blue a throwback to the learned ladies of previous centuries. Her father, as a kindly old gentleman in the play explains,

was a man of erudition himself, and, having no son to inherit his learning, was resolved to lay out every syllable of it upon his daughter, and accordingly stuffed her head with all that was legible and illegible, without once considering that the female intellect may possibly be too weak for such an experiment, and that, if guns were made of glass, we should be but idly employed in charging them.

Lady Bab is the usual bluestocking, a would-be chemist who is writing a poem upon sal ammoniac and eagerly devours learned books, although they are "about as useful to her ladyship as an opera glass to a south sea islander." Typical of his century, Moore advocated overprotective chivalry at the same time that he ridiculed the learned and therefore "unwomanly" woman. He had a virtuous young man in the play conceal from his mother the fact that they were penniless, on the grounds that "women should be like those temples of old, from which words of ill omen were carefully kept away."

[15] Byron, *Don Juan and Other Satirical Poems*, pp. 167–69, 171, 526–27, 698. The diary entry is found in *Byron: Selections from Poetry, Letters & Journals*, ed. Peter Quennell (London: Nonesuch Press, 1949), p. 754. Byron's hostility to women, conspicuous in his life and his works, may be traced to painful childhood experience with his hysterical mother, who was callously neglectful and possessive by turns, and with a nursemaid who, it is believed, prematurely initiated him into sex. Rightly or wrongly, Byron considered himself a victim of women all his life — in his unhappy marriage as well as other relationships with women. The leading characteristics of Donna Inez, intellectual pretensions and hypocritical self-righteousness, show that she is a caricature of Byron's wife.

In an epilogue Moore imagined an imp named Bas-Bleu boasting how he inspires the ladies: for him young Camilla shrinks from her beaux "and *thinks* she's thinking" and Miss Indigo attends lectures on memory, although she can never recollect the name of her professor. In "A Blue Love-Song" a lover invites his mistress to "Come wed" with him and write "from morn to night," so as to produce "smiling rows / Of chubby duodecimos" instead of the more usual "vulgar progeny." [16]

While Moore made fun of the woman who prefers a career to a family, Dickens elaborately condemned her. The lady philanthropists in *Bleak House* (1853) are unloving wives, incompetent housekeepers, and callously neglectful mothers. Mrs. Jellyby, the most conspicuous of the group,

is a lady of very remarkable strength of character, who devotes herself entirely to the public. She has devoted herself to an extensive variety of public subjects, at various times, and is at present (until something else attracts her) devoted to the subject of Africa; with a view to the general cultivation of the coffee berry — *and* the natives — and the happy settlement, on the banks of the African rivers, of our superabundant home population.

Mr. Jellyby cannot be described better than as "the husband of Mrs. Jellyby," since he is "Merged — in the more shining qualities of his wife." While Mrs. Jellyby calmly pursues the affairs of Borrio-boola-Gha on the left bank of the Niger, her household is in chaos: her unwashed children bump downstairs on their heads, her own dress gapes open up the back, there is no hot water because the boiler is out of order and the kettle not to be found, codfish is served for dinner half raw. When the child who has most recently fallen downstairs interrupts her correspondence by coming in to exhibit his wounded knees, on which one "did not know which to pity most — the bruises or the dirt," Mrs. Jellyby serenely brushes him off with "Go along, you naughty Peepy!" and fixes "her fine eyes on Africa again." Esther Summerson voices Dickens' judgment on her: "It is right to begin with the obligations of home . . .

[16] Thomas Moore, *M. P. or, The Blue-Stocking: A Comic Opera* (New York: T. Longworths, 1812), pp. 14, 39, 64. Thomas Moore, *Complete Poetical Works* (New York: Thomas Y. Crowell, 1895), pp. 313, 638.

and . . . perhaps, while those are overlooked and neglected, no other duties can possibly be substituted for them."

Mrs. Jellyby is surrounded by a group of equally misguided philanthropists. Mrs. Pardiggle, who does not neglect her children but reduces them to reluctant auxiliaries in her self-styled charitable endeavors, has succeeded only in antagonizing the poor and turning her own children into a pack of hostile urchins. There is also Miss Wisk, who absurdly maintains "that the idea of woman's mission lying chiefly in the narrow sphere of Home was an outrageous slander on the part of her Tyrant Man," and that the only practical thing for the world is the emancipation of Woman from the thralldom of her Tyrant. In the end, when the Borrioboolan scheme turns out "a failure in consequence of the King of Borrioboola wanting to sell everybody — who survived the climate — for Rum," Mrs. Jellyby too takes "up with the rights of women to sit in Parliament . . . a mission involving more correspondence than the old one."[17] That all these missions — including, for Dickens, women's rights — are intrinsically silly, as well as blameworthy because the women are shirking their proper obligations, is a suggestion that women cannot strike out on their own without making fools of themselves.

Defenders of Dickens' satire on emancipated women have pointed out that Mrs. Jellyby and her colleagues are indeed selfish and foolish. Of course they are, but that is not the point. Dickens has presented them as typical, attacking through them all women with interests outside the home. All his female philanthropists pursue ridiculous objectives, and all — as Mrs. Jellyby's casual change of cause implies — are interested more in selfish ambition than in their missions. The positive standard offered for women is not pursuit of a worthy cause with proper attention to all their responsibilities, but the homebody self-abnegation of Esther Summerson. What about women who cannot find fulfillment in housewifery? Mrs. Jellyby sits by while Esther and her daughter make plans for the latter's wedding, "occasionally shaking her head at us with a half-reproachful smile, like a superior spirit who could just bear with our trifling."[18] Obviously, a mother should find time to take

[17] Charles Dickens, *Bleak House*, ed. Morton Zabel (Boston: Houghton Mifflin, 1956), pp. 26, 29, 49, 322, 664.
[18] *Ibid.*, p. 319.

an interest in her daughter's marriage, but does this mean — as Dickens' whole treatment of woman's role seems to imply — that she must devote her life to the routine details of housekeeping, as Esther does? Many of these details are legitimately trifling to an intelligent woman. Surely Dickens was unfair in representing women with interests outside the home exclusively by odious and exaggerated examples. He was satirizing in the same spirit as a contemporary magazine writer who could not see why women authors — women like Charlotte Brontë — should not find total fulfillment in boiling dumplings and embroidering suspenders.[19]

4

As women started increasingly to demand equality with men — the right to vote, to own property, to enter the universities and the professions — male objections to competition from women took a sharper edge. Tactful disparagement often gave way to outright censure, and implications of female inferiority to flat declarations. Persuasion gave way to threat: instead of simply recommending soft weakness and dependence as endearing and appropriate feminine qualities, men told women that they would cease to be women and thus forfeit all masculine love and respect if they aspired to strength of body or mind, and that such aspirations would be further disastrous because women *are* weak — physically, mentally, and morally.

The Saturday Review shows clearly the shift from covert to overt hostility toward women as they became more emancipated and therefore more able to compete with men. This magazine, despite its Liberal politics and intellectual tone, was benightedly conservative in its policy on the position of women. During its first sixty-five years, when women fought for and largely achieved equality with men, *The Saturday Review* attacked each feminist movement that appeared with every argument that could be dredged up. Its first move was against an apparently innocuous scheme for a series of lectures to working-class women on domestic management and child care, on the basis that "anything which draws women

19 "Vivian," "A Gentle Hint to Writing-Women," *The Leader*, I (May 18, 1850), 189.

away from their own firesides" will "in the end, be more productive of harm than good." They can, as St. Paul said, learn best from their husbands (even domestic management). The writer evidently would prefer to leave a woman uninstructed, even in essential matters such as child care, than to let her glimpse horizons wider than the home (December 15, 1855).

The first major feminist struggle in the nineteenth century was for a married woman's right to her own property and income, since at that time a husband was legally entitled to all his wife owned and anything she might earn. This agitation moved *The Saturday Review* to barely controllable mirth. "The Ecclesiazusae of the Midland Counties . . . takes up a good solid grievance — it urges a large patent injustice — it complains of a wrong 6000 years old, and co-extensive with the human race." One "gentle dame" actually advocates such an extravagant "revision of the marriage laws as that women should have control over their own homes, and not be liable to have their share of the income and of the household abused and misapplied by unworthy and profligate husbands." Married women, if they knew their own interest, would "let well alone"; otherwise they might find themselves working as hard as men do. (The writer conveniently ignored the situation of working-class housewives at this time.) Furthermore — and this is the crucial point — the idea of financial independence for wives carries "a smack of selfish independence . . . which rather jars with poetical notions of wedlock" (May 3, May 24, 1856). This argument was put more bluntly later, in an article that attacked separation by mutual consent in cases of incompatibility as an absurd and immoral idea: "No woman ought to be encouraged in the belief that she has separate interests or separate duties. God and Nature have merged her existence in that of her husband" (February 14, 1857).

After the battle against the Married Women's Property Bill had subsided, *The Saturday Review* turned to "the modern Ecclesiazusae" Barbara Leigh Smith and Bessie Parkes, who were working for widened professional and educational opportunities for women — a ridiculous enterprise because of woman's natural mental inferiority to man. The evidence is simple: "Men have too much experience of the sex's charming ways ever to trust them with government or political economy, or moral philosophy, or oratory, or science."

In government, "one of the few intellectual employments in which women have been thoroughly tried [*sic*]," they have almost invariably proven themselves fools or monsters or both. Queen Elizabeth's admittedly wise political acts were probably the work of her ministers, while in her private life, "she was as silly as any nursery-maid." "All the nobler avenues of intellectual distinction" are closed to women "not by the tyranny of man, but by Nature's stern decree," since they are "fatally deficient in the power of close consecutive thought," and hence are incapable of following an argument. The writer soon ceased his attack in favor of the patronizing flippancy generally considered appropriate to the woman question, as he wished Miss Parkes's educational project "all the success it deserves" (September 12, 1857).

Later, the unsupported statements of women's mental inferiority were replaced by a more solid argument, an almost naked appeal to male self-interest. Since woman's profession is marriage, it is wrong to train her for any other career.

Men do not like, and would not seek, to mate with an independent factor, who at any time could quit — or who at all times would be tempted to neglect — the tedious duties of training and bringing up children, and keeping the tradesmen's bills, and mending the linen, for the more lucrative returns of the desk or counter. It is not the interest of States, and it is not therefore true social policy, to encourage the existence . . . of women who are other than entirely dependent on man as well for subsistence as for protection and love.

First women were told that they were better off enjoying a life of idleness in the home, then (February 21, 1857) that they could have quite as full a life in the home as outside it, and finally (November 12, 1859) that they would be forcibly kept in the home, however irksome its duties might be. Seldom, in the polite nineteenth century, does there appear so bald a statement of the righteousness of female subjection.

The whole laborious campaign to get women admitted into the universities (only fully won in 1947) was fought at every step by *The Saturday Review*. Any proposal to admit ladies to university degrees really means "that sex is a mistake," and only an old maid could fail to see its absurdity (June 14, 1862). Furthermore, any scheme for educating women beyond excellence in domestic management actually hurts rather than helps them, since it impairs their chances of marriage; for *The Saturday Review*, while insisting that marriage was woman's only proper career, took grim pleasure in insisting that men were becoming increasingly reluctant to marry (July 23, 1864). Another writer drew a ludicrous picture of what goes on in ladies' colleges — what must necessarily go on, it is implied. The poor professor is forced, instead of discoursing on philosophical principles, to compose his lecture of "Anecdotes, pretty stories, snatches of poetical quotation." Even so, he is apt to find that his lecture has "been most carefully listened to and reproduced in the note-books, but with the trifling substitution in every instance of the word 'Phoenician' for 'Venetian.'" The writer went on to make fun of the earnestness of female students, the ambitiousness of their attempts to learn, and the fact that these coexisted with woeful ignorance of spelling and grammar. The whole attempt is misguided anyway, because ignorance is one of the greatest of female charms, both before and after marriage. Since husbands find great pleasure in demonstrating their mental superiority by discoursing on politics to their wives, a well-informed wife would deprive the poor man of much innocent domestic enjoyment: ". . . his lecture would be reduced to discussion, and to discussion in which he might be defeated. To rob him of his oracular infallibility might greatly improve the husband, but it would revolutionize the character of the home" (December 28, 1867). (The possibility that this might be a good thing was not considered.)

While no one would wish a completely brainless wife, another writer pointed out, an intellectual wife is an even worse affliction. For, like many antifeminists, he was sure that intellectuality in women was inevitably associated with domestic ineptitude and disagreeable disposition.

What good is there in one's wife being an accomplished mathematician, a sound scholar, a first-rate musician, a deeply-read theologian, if she cannot keep the accounts square, knows nothing of the management of children, lets herself be cheated by the servants and the tradespeople, has not her eyes opened to dirt and disorder, and gives way to a fretful temper on the smallest provocation? (September 5, 1868)

More insidiously, it was argued that opening higher education and the professions to women would destroy their purity; since preserving the purity of a man's wife and daughter appears self-evidently desirable, this was a convenient way of begging the question. For example, although *The Saturday Review* professed to have no objections to single women's practicing medicine, it was horrified by their attempts to study in the same schools with men. (How otherwise they were to qualify was conveniently left vague.) The seven women who tried to attend the medical school of the University of Edinburgh were actually depriving young men of their educational opportunities, since coeducational medical classes would be corrupting to both sexes and no decent-minded professor could discuss medical questions thoroughly before women. The ladies' wish to practice in the wards of the Royal Infirmary of Edinburgh along with male students aroused the writer's "amazement and disgust." Such coeducation would reduce "hospitals and medical schools to the condition of the shrines of certain Oriental deities." The writer concluded, drawing on the ancient fallacy that intellectual ambition is correlated with lechery in women: "There are other places besides dissecting-rooms [unlikely places for exciting sexual desire] and hospitals where these ladies may relieve themselves of the modesty which they find so troublesome. But fathers naturally object to this being done at their sons' expense" (November 26, 1870).

Studying for the entrance examinations at Cambridge was also supposed gravely to imperil female morality. Although "It is not often that the British matron says anything worth listening to," *The Saturday Review* agreed entirely with a mother alarmed by her daughter's preparation for this examination, for which she was required to read books on population control, the dissolubility of marriage, Darwinian theory, and Hume's arguments against the existence of miracles. Far from being encouraged to think about such inflammatory topics, women should be taught unquestioning obedience to law and orthodox religion; for their unassisted reasoning powers are too meager to support their virtue. Here, even in the nineteenth century, is the old idea that women have weaker self-control than men and stronger passions. Being incapable of calculating consequences and naturally prone to reckless excess, women "are to be kept straight only through their affections" or through law; and the recent decline in women's reverence for parents, trust in male superiority, and desire for children proves that affection is no longer an adequate checkrein. (*The Saturday Review* condemned women's wish to limit the number of their children as arrant selfishness — a common patriarchal expedient for keeping women rooted in the home [September 9, 1871].) Obviously, if it is unwomanly to study freely, women must never aspire to become intellectually equal to men or to enter a learned profession.

The campaign for woman suffrage provoked innumerable articles in *The Saturday Review*, since this struggle went on for over fifty years. At first the writers treated it as a joke, only restraining their merriment long enough to point out that first, women habitually substitute personal loyalty or sentimental sympathy for reason; and secondly, the rowdy field of politics is no place for the purer sex (June 16, 1866). These two arguments, the soft, that woman is too pure to vote, and the hard, that she is too stupid, recur constantly in antisuffrage writers. Gradually *The Saturday Review* came to realize that the suffragette was a more potent adversary than it had thought. She is like a bluebottle fly, which despite appearances is "a formidable antagonist." It would seem ridiculous to fight a fly seriously, so one only flicks it off from time to time. "Its importunity is thus encouraged, and next day the tainted larder shows that the troublesome insect has not neglected its opportunities" (April 11, 1874). In order to protect the larder, *The Saturday Review* found it necessary to declare that women are not mentally capable of voting, being deficient in nearly all the requisite faculties. This belief, the writer blandly asserted, is "perfectly compatible" with admiration, respect, and affection for women (June 5, 1875).

By 1895, with a series of articles on the New Woman called "Dies Dominae," *The Saturday Review* began to relent in its misogynistic campaigns, although it never definitely approved any change in woman's traditional subordinate position. However, the final enactment of woman suffrage at the end of World War I elicited a furious outburst: "While the men of England were abroad dying by the hundreds of thousands for the preservation of England," Parliament "handed over the government of England to the women of England who were living at home in ease. Surely valour and suffering and death never had a poorer reward." Now the only hope for England is the House of Lords (July 24, 1920). On the passing of the woman suffrage amendment in America, *The Saturday Review* lamented that the suffrage

is man's last stand against the subversion of his rights of virility by a tyranny which, unless we are much mistaken, will prove to be at once humiliating and dangerous. Humiliating, because it is the submission of the superior to the inferior sex. Dangerous, because, if it be pushed beyond a certain point, it will be overthrown by an appeal to physical force.

But the hopeful possibility remains "that the men will resort to the weapons with which Nature has furnished them, and that the argument of the black eye, while it may disfigure temporarily the daughters of Eve, will be the only means of recovering the lost Rights of Man" (August 28, 1920).

And yet, at the same time that it attacked the New Woman with every possible weapon, *The Saturday Review* derided the traditional woman idealized by the Victorians, such as the proper British matron who seldom "says anything worth listening to." "Man and his Disenchanter," an attack on the pure, unspoiled girl, comes as close as the nineteenth century ever did to outright misogyny. In this venomous description of a honeymoon, women as a sex are revealed as dull and petulant, and romantic exaltation of womanhood is deliberately ripped apart. Now that the compulsory good behavior of the courtship period is over, the bride joyfully finds "herself free to live her natural little life of pouting and petting. And so she brings to the paradise of expected bliss the frowns and the sulks of the nursery." Her poor husband is only too relieved to fetch novels from the lending library "after a week of idealism," for:

Conversation is difficult in the case of a refined creature who is as ignorant as a Hottentot. He begins with the new Miltonic poem, and finds she has never looked into *Paradise Lost*. He plunges into the Reform Bill, but she knows nothing of politics, and has never read a leading article in her life. He tries music, and she kindles a little at the thought of hearing Nilsson again next season, at least if there is a royal princess in the house. Then she tries her hand in turn, and floods him with the dead chat of town, and oceans of family tattle. He finds himself shut up for weeks with a creature who takes interest in nothing but Uncle Crosspatch's temper and the scandal about Lady X. Little by little in the fatal honeymoon the absolute pettiness, the dense dulness, of woman's life breaks on the disenchanted devotee. His deity is without occupation, without thought, without resource.

Yet "He still takes her love of caresses as a sign of an affection passing the love of men, and he unfolds to her his hope that a year or two may give him the chance of a retreat into the country and a quiet life of conjugal happiness." Startled into interest at last, the bride reveals that "she has not escaped from the dulness of the nursery to plunge into the dulness of home." She has taken "from mamma a series of practical instructions in the great art of managing a husband," and, frivolous and indolent as she is, will waste "the patience and skill of a diplomatist in wheedling her husband out of his season on the moors." By the end of the honeymoon "the poetic nature" is considering:

The exact proportion in which [her husband's] old acquaintance may be encouraged to relieve him of the sense of boredom at home without detaching him absolutely from it, the precise bounds within which his taste for a good dinner may be satisfied without detriment to that little bill at the milliner's.

Here are the old inconsistencies that although woman is weak and stupid she somehow manages to ruin man's life by making him do what she wants, and that although home is so delightful that woman is wickedly foolish to try to leave it, for a man it is a prison in which his wife selfishly schemes to keep him. Finally, the poor man "finds himself floating whichever way he is guided; wheedled, managed, the husband — as women tell him — of an admirable wife. He does his weary round of work, pumping up the means for carrying out her admirable projects of social existence." But alas for "the dreams, the romance, the poetry, the sentiment" (August 22, 1868).[20] This is a reincarnation of *The Batchelars Banquet*, given added venom by continual ironic references to romantic idealization of woman. The attack on women's fashionable empty-headedness may have been justified, but it must be compared with *The Saturday Review*'s censures of women who had serious intellectual,

[20] *The Saturday Review of Politics, Literature, Science, and Art* (London), I (Dec. 15, 1855), 116; II (May 3, 1856), 5; II (May 24, 1856), 78; III (Feb. 14, 1857), 148; IV (Sept. 12, 1857), 238–39; VIII (Nov. 12, 1859), 576; XIII (June 14, 1862), 680; XVIII (July 23, 1864), 112; XXIV (Dec. 28, 1867), 807; XXVI (Sept. 5, 1868), 319; XXX (Nov. 26, 1870), 682–83; XXXII (Sept. 9, 1871), 335; XXI (June 16, 1866), 715–16; XXXVII (April 11, 1874), 454; XXXIX (June 5, 1875), 713; CXXX (July 24, 1920), 69; CXXX (Aug. 28, 1920), 172; XXVI (Aug. 22, 1868), 254.

political, or esthetic interests. How can a woman not be petty and dull if she is denied education and forbidden to look outside her home? The satirical butt in this article is the inevitable product of those traditional restrictions on women's education which the magazine consistently endorsed. Berating the New Woman for mannishness and the traditional woman for childishness, *The Saturday Review* plainly revealed its misogyny by disapproving of women whatever they did.

Henry A. Jones's *The Case of Rebellious Susan* (1894) puts many of *The Saturday Review*'s arguments into dramatic form. The main plot of this play pokes fun at a woman's rebellion against the double standard: Lady Susan horrifies everybody by her determination to leave her husband when she discovers that he has been unfaithful; but in the end she is persuaded into common sense, that is, to forget about his adultery. A minor character, Elaine, is a typical New Woman, raucous, selfish, and ridiculous. She tyrannizes over Mr. Pybus, her weakling husband, and disdains housekeeping in favor of organizing the women of Clapham to fight for their rights. When Sir Richard, her sensible and experienced guardian, questions her, she assures him she is in earnest.

Sir Richard: About what?

Elaine: About re-organising society.

Sir Richard: I don't quite follow — how will wrecking Clapham post-office re-organise society?

Elaine: We must make a start somewhere.

Sir Richard: Begin at home, in your own lives. There's no other way of re-organising society. Go back to the Nest, and give Mr. Pybus a nice comfortable dinner.

Elaine: No man shall receive dinner from me while the present inequalities between the sexes remain unredressed.

Sir Richard (to Pybus) : We shall all starve.

Elaine: Please be serious. Do you deny that Woman has been most shamefully treated by Man?

Sir Richard: It isn't Man that's ungallant to Woman. It's Nature that is so ungallant and unkind to your sex.

Elaine: We will correct nature.

Sir Richard: . . . *What do you want?*

Elaine: We want freedom to develop our real selves.

Sir Richard: Hum — sounds like a deadly dull, unwholesome process.

Elaine: . . . There is an immense future for Woman —

Sir Richard (interrupting) : At her own fireside. There is an immense future for women as wives and mothers, and a very limited future for them in any other capacity. While you ladies without passions — or with distorted and defeated passions — are raving and trumpeting all over the country, that wise, grim, old grandmother of us all, Dame Nature, is simply laughing up her sleeve and snapping her fingers at you and your new epochs and new movements. Go home! . . . Nature's darling woman is a stay-at-home woman, a woman who wants to be a good wife and a good mother, and cares very little for anything else. . . . Go home! go home, and don't worry the world any longer about this tiresome sexual business, for . . . it was settled once for all in the Garden of Eden, and there's no more to be said about it. Go home! [21]

The conversation ends when Elaine is taken off, apprehended for inciting riots. Although Sir Richard is a Queen's Counsel, she insists on conducting her own defense, which means she will get the maximum sentence of five years instead of the minimum of eighteen months. She is delighted at the prospect of martyrdom, and her husband equally delighted to see her go. In this short scene appear almost all the clichés of the opponents of women's rights: the feminists have no constructive, or even specific, aims; they disdain the work they should be doing in favor of meaningless activity; they fly in the face of Nature; they love trouble for its own sake and glory in pointless martyrdom.

5

As the movement for woman suffrage gained strength and men began really to fear that it might become law, they published a spate of impassioned books, expressing the arguments already given by *The Saturday Review* as well as some ingenious new ones. The more chivalrous opponents of woman suffrage claimed that participation in political life would necessarily sully the purity of womanhood and that — since women already ruled men by sweetness and submission — they would only endanger their present position by insisting on overt competition with them (in which, it was always implied, they would be sure to lose). If these arguments failed to prove convincing, the antisuffragists bluntly stated that women were mentally unqualified to vote: they lacked essential

[21] Henry A. Jones, *Representative Plays*, ed. C. Hamilton (Boston: Little, Brown, 1925), II, 349–50.

qualities such as justice, their physical inferiority to men necessarily entailed mental inferiority, their brains were smaller or less convoluted, their earlier maturation placed them closer than men to the lower animals, they were periodically incapacitated by menstruation and childbearing. These points were supported by anything from simple assertion to pseudo-statistics. Occasionally, the old Biblical arguments were used, and it was often stated that normal women had no interest in the suffrage: the movement consisted exclusively of frigid or sex-starved women, along with a few male weaklings.

Generally the statements of female inferiority took the form of mere assertions, supposedly so obvious that they did not require evidence. James McGrigor Allan, in a paper "On the Real Differences in the Minds of Men and Women" presented to the Anthropological Society in 1869, declared that if a woman educated "to the utmost of her capacity" and an uneducated man were presented with "a problem in Euclid, the mechanism of a steam-engine, or any other study requiring reason; the man's views [would] be more profound, broad, and luminous than those of the woman." Echoing medieval misogynists, he believed that the only talents in which woman excels man are dissimulation and lying, which come naturally to her. She has "no method of knowing right from wrong, but by implicitly receiving man's dogmatic *dicta* on every question of religion, morals, and the practical conduct of life"; nor can she give any "reason for her belief, or the principles which regulate her life." Allan's evidence consists of an assertion that every woman in Europe and America implicitly follows the directives of a male relative, a clergyman, or man-made public opinion. "Mentally and morally, the female is prostrate before the male sex, although the meek idolater often adores a brazen god!"[22] In his more popular work, *Woman Suffrage Wrong in Principle and Practice* (1890), Allan maintained, as did most of the antisuffragists, that women are hopelessly incapable of practicing or even comprehending "the highest human mental quality, where man approaches nearest Deity — *Justice*," since they lack the requisite deliberation and analytic

---

[22] James McGrigor Allan, "On the Real Differences in the Minds of Men and Women," *Journal of the Anthropological Society*, VII (1869), cxcvii, ccix, ccxi–ccxii.

capacity and are inevitably prejudiced in favor of themselves or those whom they love.[23]

In the peroration of "The Real Differences," Allan gave vent to a tirade disturbingly inappropriate in a scientific paper, declaring that the woman who imitates man becomes

a monster more horrible than that created by Frankenstein. Is it possible to conceive a more contemptible and deplorable spectacle than that of the female (I will not profane the beautiful name of *woman* [we are still in the nineteenth century!]) who . . . deliberately neglects and abdicates the sacred duties and privileges of wife and mother to make herself ridiculous by meddling in and muddling man's work?

Actually, this is no more unfair than the allegedly scientific arguments which were brought forth to demonstrate male superiority. Never since Aristotle had biology been so misused in defense of patriarchy. Allan, who practically made a career of opposing woman suffrage, was particularly unscrupulous in his use of quasi-biological arguments. He alleged that during menstruation women "suffer under a languor and depression which disqualify them for thought or action, and render it extremely doubtful how far they can be considered responsible beings while the crisis lasts." Doubtless the disturbing effects of menstruation account for "the inconsequent conduct of women, their petulance, caprice . . . irritability" and cruelty. Indeed, "Every woman is . . . always more or less an invalid. Therefore, no woman can pursue uninterrupted physical or mental labour." Pregnant and nursing women, especially, cannot compete in male activities or even read difficult books. In *Woman Suffrage Wrong* Allan enforced this point with a singularly unscrupulous argument: if a pregnant woman insists on making speeches, taking "undue mental or bodily exercise," or exposing "herself to excitement, and violent emotions," it is only in accordance with natural law if her child is stillborn or idiotic "or otherwise marked with some monstrous imperfection signally testifying to the culpable indiscretion of its mother."[24]

[23] James McGrigor Allan, *Woman Suffrage Wrong in Principle and Practice* (London: Remington and Co., 1890), p. 124. Allan also made use of the old Biblical arguments for the subjection of women (pp. 7–23).

[24] Allan, "The Real Differences," cxcviii–cc, ccxii; Allan, *Woman Suffrage Wrong*, p. 132. In "The Real Differences" he also used the physiological argument

A twentieth-century reader wonders at the passion in these protests against woman suffrage until he realizes the movement's symbolic importance to people at the time: to the alarmed patriarchs, woman suffrage meant that women, especially wives, would cease to exist in and for their husbands, but rather would claim the right to think and act for themselves. This in turn aroused the old fear that unrestricted woman would become dangerously uncontrollable. If woman gets the vote, Allan warned in *Woman Suffrage Wrong*, the husband will become a nonentity and the wife will be "practically absolved from her solemn promise to love, cherish, and obey." This means that the marriage institution will be abolished, "For no rational man will commit his happiness, his honour, his very *life* to the keeping of a wife not amenable to her husband's authority." Here, of course, Allan revealed the misogynistic conviction of woman's natural viciousness which is typical of the embattled patriarch: woman can be trusted only if she is forcibly prevented from doing wrong. Finally he gave way to hysteria altogether: "I anticipate the social revolution, disruption of domestic ties, desecration of marriage, destruction of the household gods, dissolution of the family — which would result from the political enfranchisement of married women." [25]

---

that woman is mentally inferior because her brain is smaller than man's and the shape of her head closer to that of infants or the "lower races." Allan's other works against women include *The Intellectual Severance of Men and Women* and *A Protest Against Woman's Demand for the Privileges of Both Sexes.*

[25] Allan, *Woman Suffrage Wrong*, pp. 254, 269. Perhaps the most notorious attack on the movement is *The Unexpurgated Case Against Woman Suffrage* (London: Constable and Co., 1913) by Sir Almroth E. Wright, a physician and Fellow of the Royal Society. He repeated the usual arguments, with particular emphasis on one which, despite its absurdity, was popular at the time: since voting symbolically represents physical force (voters elect officials who make and enforce the laws), and women are less physically strong than men, it is illogical for women to vote. He asserted that, since women's mental images are "over-intimately linked up with emotional responses," it is literally painful for them to pause for intellectual analysis or considered judgment. This limitation and also an incapacity for interest in "any abstract moral ideal" "appear to be secondary sexual characteristics of woman" (pp. 36, 45, 63). In E. Belfort Bax's *The Fraud of Feminism* (London: Grant Richards, Ltd., 1913) the opposition to feminism takes on a paranoid note: on the evidence of an act which forbade the flogging of criminals and the Divorce Act of 1857, which enabled women to get divorces for desertion or physical brutality, Bax declared that

T. W. H. Crosland, a popular humorist of the turn of the century, published a number of barbs at New Women, like the frowzy suffragette scrawling on the sidewalk her demand for a vote or the earnest lady medical student who "wonders fiercely" where the patient's liver is.[26] In *Lovely Woman* (1903) he contemptuously dismissed "the vociferous ladies who babble about the emancipation of their kind" on the grounds that "women can do nothing really well." And anyway, they cannot possibly be happy without men, although men can get along very well without women. Turn out first-class pies, he told women, "and you will have done something with your intellect and your life."

A home, a fireside, a husband, children, a little church-going, a little reading of innocuous writers, thirty years of small joys and small sorrows, thirty years of faithful love and careful housewifery, may mean a commonplace and undistinguished life. On the other hand, all the wisdom, and all the philosophy in the world, can suggest no better, or nobler, or more satisfying life for a woman.

This is what men had been saying all through the nineteenth century in opposition to any signs of self-assertion from women, although it is more openly contemptuous. However, the book as a whole nakedly reveals the misogyny that was usually concealed under gentle disparagement. Not only did Crosland express fears of women's increasing power and a horrified conviction that, despite their brainlessness, they already control men; but he unrolled a comprehensive attack on them which recalls older works like *The Batchelars Banquet* and anticipates the antiromantic reaction of this century. While the masculinized New Woman is detestable, conventionally feminine women are equally bad. The tone is set on the first page:

What is woman but the less edifying part of humanity? She came to man smiling, with sorrow in both hands. She smiled, and smiled, and smiled, as she still smiles; and he who might have been a god, and walked the earth in joy, rakes straws, and groans in pits. The whole trend of experience goes

"the whole power of the State is practically at the disposal of woman to coerce and oppress men" (p. 17).

[26] T. W. H. Crosland, "Votes for Women," "The 'Student,'" *Sonnets* (London: At the Marygold, 1915), pp. 6, 13.

to show that the man whose house is infested by a woman is the weaker and the less happy on that account. His liberty, his courage, his temper, his views, his ambitions, are all touched, and hurtfully touched, by such a presence.

The semijocular exaggeration here and throughout the book does not much mitigate the misogynistic charges and attitudes presented. In the good old days, Crosland went on, men knew how to manage women: they kept a whip. But woman "has been out of hand for centuries, and . . . to-day she is out of hand to an almost irremediable extent." She is, for example, responsible for modern money-madness: "The best of everything, the dearest of everything, blazes at you from behind interminable plate glass, and all for woman. . . . Meanwhile man sprints breathlessly after the cash."

Even at ten, woman is "faithless, spiteful, greedy, merciless, vindictive, impudent, unreasonable, unruly, and illogical. At twenty she is the same girl, only more cunning and a trifle more commercial." She cannot even lay just claim to beauty, which is solely a product of male infatuation. Although girls may sometimes have "a suggestion of prettiness," this is soon lost "either in the vinegar of spinsterhood or the obese complacency of wifehood." "Woman without her clothes is about as pretty as a plucked bird of paradise. Dress her, and, metaphorically speaking, she becomes more or less presentable." "As a maker of trouble and a general purveyor of unpleasantness, the modern wife may be reckoned absolutely without rival." She cannot even keep house; if a man wants his home run with decent efficiency and economy, he should hire male servants, making them responsible to himself alone. Mamma is at least well-intentioned, but, being a fool, generally ruins her son, whose career she controls. All he can do to protect himself is to try to unlearn all she has taught him.

After a chapter of such novel sayings as "Men have many faults, women have but two; there's nothing good they say, and nothing right they do," Crosland concluded:

Less freedom, less pin money, less incense, less deference, less power in the household, a less frequent appearance in public places, fewer dresses, fewer jewels, fewer compliments, might bring the enemy to whatever small senses she possesses. I do not quite know who is going to bell the cat, but I implore all able-bodied men to purchase a bell, even if they have not the pluck to take it home.[27]

This statement, apparently, was offered as a sober solution to a serious problem. It seems clear that Crosland's jokes stem from both contempt and fear of women.

Only toward the end of the nineteenth century, in Crosland and other opponents of female emancipation, did hostility toward women become overt. Before that, the nineteenth-century emphasis on propriety generally prevented open expressions of misogyny. For example, the ambivalence traditional in erotic literature, the detraction which is normally found counterbalancing undue idealization of women, was largely suppressed during the nineteenth century; it appears only in muted form as gentle insistence on their mental limitations and helpless dependence on men.[28]

I believe that some hostility lay beneath the syrupy patronage the Victorians lavished on women: patronage presupposes belittlement and that implies contempt, which is an expression of hostility. It is mainly a matter of emphasis whether the weaknesses ascribed to woman make her all the more endearing or merely consign her to hopeless inferiority to man, whether she is considered a lovable child who must be kept in the home for her own good or a not-so-

[27] T. W. H. Crosland, *Lovely Woman* (London: Grant Richards, Ltd., 1903), pp. 9–13, 18, 23–24, 29, 31–32, 45, 100, 129, 156–57, 193, 200.

[28] It may appear also in the sado-masochism so evident in nineteenth-century erotic literature, a characteristic which Mario Praz traced in *The Romantic Agony* (London: Oxford University Press, 1933). It seems to me, however, that this sado-masochism resulted from the Romantics' exaltation of suffering from passion, together with their interest in abnormal psychology, rather than from a desire to torture women or to represent women destroying men. In any case, sado-masochism was not conspicuous in the romantic literature of England and America. One should mention, however, that Edgar Allan Poe considered the death of a beautiful woman "the most poetical topic in the world" (*Poems and Miscellanies*, ed. R. B. Johnson [London: Oxford University Press, 1927], p. 197) and constantly presented this topic, and that Algernon Charles Swinburne's typical heroine is a "mystical rose of the mire," who meditates for her lovers "tortures undreamt of, unheard of, / Unwritten, unknown" ("Dolores," *The Poems* [New York: Harper and Bros., 1904], I, 166–75). In the last decadence of Romanticism, Arthur O'Shaughnessy produced in "An Epic of Women" a catalogue of *femmes fatales* almost in the medieval tradition. Cf. Keats's "La Belle Dame Sans Merci," Walter Pater's description of Mona Lisa, etc.

lovable child who must forcibly be kept where she will do a minimum of harm. Moreover, although the nineteenth-century attacks on obnoxious female types were relatively mild, they continued to be written and appreciated. The frequent appearance of antifeminism in popular magazines — "Mrs. Caudle's Curtain Lectures" in *Punch* and numerous contemptuous articles in *The Saturday Review* — show that idealization of womanhood was by no means universal in Victorian England.

Through the nineteenth century women were striving for equality in a generally unsympathetic atmosphere, but only in the later decades did men feel sufficiently threatened to express their fearful hostility openly. While some defenders of the patriarchal status quo may have been motivated solely by dislike of change, the exceptionally bitter opponents of women's rights — those who, like *The Saturday Review*, fought every attempt to improve woman's position or, like Allan, twisted biology to prove her inferiority — were surely using social conservatism as a mask for misogyny. This appears plainly in *The Saturday Review*'s suggestion that the baneful effects of woman suffrage be counteracted by a return to wife-beating.

Meanwhile, partly because women were approaching equality with men, it was becoming harder to maintain chivalrous illusions about them. Already *The Saturday Review* and Crosland, in *Lovely Woman,* had attacked Victorian idealization of romance and domestic bliss, and these attacks were to become more open, savage, and widespread in the twentieth century.

THE TWENTIETH CENTURY

1

WITH THE outspoken iconoclasm of the twentieth century, the eighteenth- and nineteenth-century disguises of misogyny could in large part be discarded. Again the misogynist could make his appearance without a blush. While Jerrold merely insinuated that Mrs. Caudle was a typical wife, H. L. Mencken flatly stated: "No man, examining his marriage intelligently, can fail to observe that it is compounded, at least in part, of slavery, and that he is the slave." [1] Mencken and his colleague George Jean Nathan never tired of attacking romantic idealization of women as a delusion. "To enjoy women at all," Nathan claimed, "one must manufacture an illusion and envelop them with it, otherwise they would not be endurable. . . . Without this deceptive illusory chicane woman is found to be simply a third-rate man; with it, she is found to be charming, amusing, desirable, lovely." [2] Mencken, puncturing the delusion of love, did not grant women even physical attractiveness. Although "The most effective lure that a woman can hold out to a man is the lure of what he fatuously conceives to be her beauty":

The female body, even at its best, is very defective in form; it has harsh curves and very clumsily distributed masses; compared to it the average milk-jug, or even cuspidor, is a thing of intelligent and gratifying design. . . . Below the neck by the bow and below the waist astern there are two masses that simply refuse to fit into a balanced composition. Viewed from

[1] H. L. Mencken, *Prejudices: Fourth Series* (1924), in *A Mencken Chrestomathy*, ed. by the Author (New York: Knopf, 1956), p. 48.

[2] George Jean Nathan, *Monks Are Monks* (1929), in *The World of George Jean Nathan*, ed. C. Angoff (New York: Knopf, 1952), p. 151.

the side, a woman presents an exaggerated S bisected by an imperfect straight line, and so she inevitably suggests a drunken dollar-mark.

(The comparison implies the greed traditionally attributed to women.) The average woman, moreover, fails even to display "the modest sightliness that her sex is theoretically capable of," since she is "ungraceful, misshapen, badly calved and crudely articulated, even for a woman." Yet men, being the self-deluded dolts they are, do not demand real beauty and habitually mistake pancake make-up for a perfect natural complexion. Many a man "never really sees his wife — that is, as our Heavenly Father is supposed to see her, and as the embalmer will see her — until they have been married for years."[3] Mencken's attack on the female body is almost Swiftian, though it is less effective because less concretely detailed than, say, "A Beautiful Young Nymph Going to Bed." Obviously it is far lighter in tone, the product of frivolous iconoclasm rather than moral conviction. But the very fact that it was written as popular entertainment shows how widespread nowadays is the impulse to degrade romance. And it is significant that for Mencken the "real" woman is not a healthy unadorned nude but a corpse, as Swift's "real" woman is an aging syphilitic prostitute.

Although women encourage romantic illusions in men, Mencken declared, they themselves are coldly free of them. They do not value beauty or showy talents in men, but only practical efficiency; for this is what "guarantees security, position, a livelihood; it is a commodity that is merchantable."[4] Mencken professed to admire female practicality in this matter, but many American novelists of the early twentieth century were to use the same charge as evidence of women's crass heartlessness. With unmistakable seriousness, they presented the modern middle-class wife as a cold, selfish creature who mercilessly drives her husband to fulfill her own materialistic ends. She derides any idealistic impulses he may have and at the

[3] H. L. Mencken, *In Defense of Women* (1918), in *A Mencken Chrestomathy*, pp. 37–38. The modern degradation of romance appears even in frivolous verse, as in Richard Armour's "What You Don't Know Won't Hurt You Till Later," a treatment of the lady's dressing room in which he represents the "true view" of one's "true love" as being ungirdled, cold-creamed, or runny-nosed (*Light Armour*, 1954).

[4] Mencken, *In Defense of Women* (New York: Knopf, 1918), pp. 49–50

same time belittles him for being a mere businessman. It never occurs to her to justify her existence by making herself useful to her husband, her children, or anybody else. And yet, with that mysterious power which is generally attributed to bad women, she makes her husband worship her and serve her gladly. The theme of Robert Herrick's *Together* (1908) is the unsatisfactoriness of modern American marriage, which he blamed primarily on the egotism of modern women. The book bristles with spoiled, dissatisfied, useless wives. The heroine, Isabelle, although basically a good and intelligent woman, had been misled by the modern feminist ambition for self-fulfillment. Thus she resented having a child, even though her husband wanted one, since it would interfere with her pursuit of a "large, full life" for herself. She took no interest in her husband's business, which was his life, and, having consigned her only child to hired help, hardly knew and did not really like her. The solution Herrick recommended is to abandon the "dray-horse interpretation of marriage," in which a husband makes a point of considering his wife's aims and wishes. A woman has no "right to her own life as distinct from her husband's life, or the family life." In a perfect marriage, the climax of the wife's day "is her hot supper laid before her lord."[5]

In *Waste* (1924) Herrick blamed women even more explicitly for the ills of modern American life. The hero, Thornton, an unusually talented and altruistic man, suffered all his life from a series of women who failed him, beginning with his nagging, materialistic mother. Early in his scientific career a brilliant teacher warned him against women — not poor, harmless prostitutes, but good women, who expect to become mothers of families, who would make him take some good job: "If you want to do anything in science, keep clear of the women!" Men who cannot do without women must "make pack-horses of themselves for their families." The teacher fearfully anticipated "the rule of women in this country. As if they didn't rule us now, make our ideas for us, and keep us at work in the way they want." But, being conventional sheep, "they can't make our ideals for us, that's one thing they haven't the brain to do, though

[5] Robert Herrick, *Together* (New York: Grosset and Dunlap, 1908), pp. 93, 182, 203, 491.

they'd like to well enough." Herrick's suggestion that the respectable middle-class woman is more dangerous than the humble whore, because more demanding, which is voiced by the teacher and borne out by the plot of the book, was to be further developed by Ernest Hemingway and Somerset Maugham.

Thornton precisely realized the teacher's warning, as he was victimized by a series of materialistic women incapable of comprehending his ideals. First his scientific career was impeded by his having to support his mother and sister in luxury; then it was ruined because he was forced into business when a girl seduced him and claimed as a right that he marry her and support her in style. After driving him into worry and debt by her irresponsible extravagance, she left him, expecting him to support her for the rest of her life: "Thornton sent her every dollar that he could spare above what he gave his mother and sister, and what he must spend to live, in a grimy enough fashion." He then had an affair with a married woman, but she soon disillusioned him by her conventionality, materialism, and craving for dominance.

Finally Thornton found a mate who seemed eminently satisfactory: Cynthia was charming, intelligent, responsive, and congenial. But their affair also soured as she revealed the typical feminine weaknesses. She too was incorrigibly materialistic and exploitative, and she also revealed the inability to comprehend justice with which nineteenth-century writers had constantly charged women. When her spoiled son killed a young Mexican, her only thought was to elude justice, causing Thornton to moralize on "the abyss that this mother-passion, so romantically extolled throughout the ages, could create in a soul as deep and strong and healthy as Cynthia's." Mother-love is very rare in Herrick, and when it does appear, it is a base and corrupting thing. Far from exempting women from the charge of selfishness, mother-love is "in essence the exaltation of the woman's ego," behind which shelter "all other egoisms"; and it is used to justify "any cruelty, any blindness — the return to primitive will." At best, it is "Sacrifice of self for self." [6] This is one of the first overt attacks on Mother, which were to become in-

[6] Robert Herrick, *Waste* (New York: Harcourt, Brace, 1924), pp. 55–56, 76, 122, 428, 431–32.

creasingly common in this century. Herrick's novels illustrate a shift characteristic of the past half century, from attacks on women for being insufficiently maternal—part of the campaign against the New Woman—to attacks on them for being too passionately maternal—part of the reaction against nineteenth-century idealization.

Sinclair Lewis, equally convinced of the materialism, conventionality, and pernicious dominance of the American wife, indicted her most fully in Fran Dodsworth. *Dodsworth* (1929) also demonstrates the recurrent antifeminist jibe that "The woman most eager to jump out of her petticoat to assert her rights is first to jump back into it when threatened with a switching for misusing them."[7] Fran, an angelic-looking blonde, appears ten years younger than she is, while Sam, her husband, has prematurely aged with the strain of supporting her in luxury. She maintains an air of utter superiority to her businessman husband, although in fact she is inferior to him in mind, in character, and even in capacity to appreciate art. Despite her superficial cleverness and sophistication, she lacks judgment, integrity, responsibility, and love for either husband or children. Like Mrs. Varden, she glories in nonexistent martyrdom and controls her husband by unpredictability. She keeps him so consistently uncomfortable that "To him, always, the best talk was no brilliance of his own, but conversation that amused Fran and drew her out of her silken sulkiness." Eventually Lewis expressed what had been implicit all along: Fran is "simply a clever child," who, with all her insistence on independence, is incapable of looking after herself and has to call on her husband to save her from the results of her own folly.[8] Nevertheless, although Fran remains her bitchy self to the end, Dodsworth can only partially break away from her.

Jinny, the young heroine of *Cass Timberlane* (1945), although a far more likable figure than Fran, is also a clever child, lacking the solid "masculine" virtues of common sense, self-control, loyalty, and responsibility. Jinny, too, enjoys tormenting her devoted hus-

[7] Ambrose Bierce, *The Devil's Dictionary* (1911), in *The Collected Writings* (New York: Citadel Press, 1946), p. 369. Bierce's writings show a cynicism about women much like Mencken's. He was especially fond of the Widow of Ephesus story, of which he told four variants.

[8] Sinclair Lewis, *Dodsworth* (New York: Dell Publishing Co., 1957), pp. 47, 227.

band and apparently does not love him; she elopes to Darien with a smooth young cad who does not really care for her and has to be rescued by her loyal husband. The grim picture of modern American marriage drawn in "Adventures of Husbands and Wives," chapters interpolated through *Cass Timberlane*, lays particular stress on the tyranny of wives over husbands.

Jinny's footling ambitions to become an artist or actress occasion a number of jibes at the career woman, ultimately inspired, I suspect, by Lewis' hostility to his former wife Dorothy Thompson. Through Cass, Lewis expressed his fear that careers for wives would destroy the home and suggested that they have a sinister connection with adultery.[9] But his real attack on the career woman appears in *Gideon Planish* (1943), which features a libelous caricature of Dorothy Thompson as Winifred Homeward, "the Talking Woman." Winifred is very close to the seventeenth-century stereotype of the learned lady — noisy, pretentious, lacking equally in brains and knowledge — and, like Jonson's female intellectuals, is sexually loose as well as mentally unrestrained. Married to a pleasant, negligible man, she indulged in unlimited promiscuity. With no genuine talent, she was prominent only because her doting father was a financial genius. She edited *Attention!*, a feminist weekly financed by her father, which lacked "nothing but circulation and the possibility of anyone's ever reading through an entire paragraph." She saw "Any throng of more than two persons" as a lecture audience, "and at sight of them she . . . started a fervent address of imaginary information about Conditions and Situations that lasted till the audience had sneaked out — or a little longer." She was so powerful a talker

that she could convince anyone at all of the exact opposite of whatever she maintained, including the man from whom she had lifted her ideas in the first place. . . . Winifred held forth about Hitler's nastiness so ferociously that . . . all present . . . became stubbornly certain that Hitler was a fine, fat, jolly, drinking fellow, who loved girls and sausages and beer and stories about pandas; as she talked on, they longed to sit with Hitler in a couple of rocking chairs on the front porch at good old Berchtesgaden. . . . There might have been a dangerous crop of Fascists grown that evening, except that presently, still hurdling over all interruptions, Winifred stated violently

[9] Sinclair Lewis, *Cass Timberlane* (New York: Random House, 1945), pp. 316–17.

that all American young people were slatternly and impertinent, so that a considerable degree of trust in Young America was instantly restored around the table. She also had a few pronouncements to make upon the movies, the immorality of symphony music, the coal business and how to decorate a twenty-dollar-a-month flat. She had a remarkable number of opinions, and she thought highly of all of them.

Lewis presented Winifred as typical of "the American woman careerist," and made her inhumanly odious.[10]

Lewis' ridicule of career women rests on the assumption that it is absurd for women to compete with men professionally, since they lack the necessary mental equipment — judgment, common sense, rationality. His disparagement of the female mind and character comes from the nineteenth-century antisuffragists. But, since women have definitely won the right to vote, Lewis and most other modern antifeminists have shifted their attack from woman suffrage to women's right to pursue careers. The idea that women are intellectually inferior to men is still held by a vocal minority, although their declarations are generally masked either as mere sportiveness or as a panacea for the present ills of both sexes. Women's alleged incapacity to deal with practical affairs remains an ever-popular joke, and elderly academics profess to find the female doctor or professor irresistibly comic.[11]

Moss Hart, in his musical *Lady in the Dark* (1944), did not attack the career woman, but pointed out that she cannot be truly

[10] Sinclair Lewis, *Gideon Planish* (New York: Random House, 1943), pp. 320, 322, 336. Lewis continued his attack on American wives, especially would-be career women, in a series of magazine stories in *Cosmopolitan* in the 1940's: "All Wives Are Angels" (February, 1943), "Nothing to Write About" (July, 1943), "Green Eyes" (September, 1943), "You Seem to Forget" (January, 1944). "Harri," a similar story in *Good Housekeeping* (August — September, 1943), was plotted by Lewis although rewritten by another author. A few of his earlier novels, of course, present sympathetic female protagonists, such as Carol Kennicott in *Main Street* (1920) and Ann Vickers in *Ann Vickers* (1933). It seems that Lewis' attitude toward women fluctuated with the happiness of his own married life. But generally speaking his relations with women were not happy, and his attitude toward them was not favorable, especially in his last years, after his marriage with Dorothy Thompson ended. For Lewis' relations with women, see Mark Schorer's biography.

[11] See, for example, Waverley Root, "Women Are Intellectually Inferior," *The American Mercury*, LXIX, No. 310 (October, 1949), 407–14 (a repetition of nineteenth-century arguments); Eric F. Goldman, "Party of One: Our American Woman," *Holiday*, XXIX (May, 1961), 11–15 (the emancipated

happy unless she is subject to a man. The heroine, editor of the most successful fashion magazine in the country, follows her profession mainly because, as the result of a childhood trauma, she fears she cannot compete sexually with other women. As the play opens she is on the point of a nervous breakdown because she has been repressing her true womanhood. Two of her three possible suitors would not interfere with her career, but she rejects them because they are weak. The third, a genuinely virile man, has been skirmishing with her constantly because he resents her career and especially the fact that she is his boss; but in the end she realizes that he is the best man for her, practically proposes to him, and hands over to him the editorship of the magazine.

A recent novel, Herbert Lobsenz' *Vangel Griffin* (1960), attacks the American career woman by contrasting her unfavorably with a promiscuous Spanish girl whose lifework is building up the male ego. At the beginning of the book the hero has decided to commit suicide because of a generally unsatisfactory life, of which his wife is the most conspicuous element. She is a frigid copywriter: ". . . the very essence of the New American female, enlightened and emancipated, a college graduate, with flat voice, blank face and dark spectacles, knowing how to drive and ski but not to cook, with one year of philosophy, three of psychology, a month and a half in Europe and suffrage." The Spanish girl, on the other hand, sleeps with him, cooks for him, washes his dishes, lets him make all decisions, and does not concern herself with intellectual topics. In the end, rehabilitated by the girl and life in Spain, the hero returns to America to do good: that is, "to turn America into a democracy again . . . to repeal suffrage for women . . . to pull down all prejudices and ignorance and persuade men to live a rational life." [12] The attack on woman suffrage lends a quaint archaic note to this otherwise conventional work.

George Jean Nathan, a bachelor, developed more explicitly the

---

woman is unhappy, the female professor unnatural and ridiculous) ; Herman Wouk, *Marjorie Morningstar* (Garden City, N.Y.: Doubleday and Co., 1955), pp. 435–36 (women can be happy only as housewives) ; Franklin P. Adams, *The Column Book of F.P.A.* (Garden City, N.Y.: Doubleday, Doran & Co., 1928), pp. 152–56 (women can't even arrange a date for lunch).

[12] Herbert Lobsenz, *Vangel Griffin* (New York: Harper and Bros., 1960), pp. 66, 370.

idea that the emancipated equal female is jeopardizing modern marriage. His attitude was unblushingly identical with that of *The Saturday Review* sixty years before:

A man . . . is always happiest with a woman who is deferentially his inferior. It is the equality of woman to man in the Anglo-Saxon countries . . . that is the cause of man's frequent dissatisfaction with his married lot and of the consequent alarming increase in the divorce rate. A marriage in which the wife knows the difference between a sonata and a *Geburtslied* . . . the relative eminence of George Eliot and George Barr McCutcheon, and the batting average of Babe Ruth, is always on its way to consult a shyster lawyer. The most successful marriage is ever the one in which the wife believes the husband to be a compendium of all the refinements of wisdom and understanding, however depressing an ass the husband may really be.

This deference is not only expedient but right, since, outside of the conflict of sex, "the best woman is the inferior of the second-best man. Women's intelligence is emotional intelligence: it is showy, appealing, moving, and generally gains its ends"; but it is not sound or rational. Nathan agreed with Nietzsche that "woman is and always has been primarily a plaything." The only woman who might possibly deny this is one "so unprepossessing that no man wants her for a plaything."[13] As late as 1961 an American doctor devoted a book to the unabashed proclamation that all women are irrational, untruthful, and senselessly extravagant; that they care for nothing beyond their own families; that they are incapable of running their own lives; that they can find true happiness only in subjection to their Lord and Master; and that they derive more satisfaction from washing dishes than from pursuing a career.[14]

2

The twentieth century's debunking of romantic idealization of women and its perpetuation of the nineteenth-century prejudices against them would doubtless have occurred in any case: there is always a reaction after a period of exaggerated respect, and always a temptation to cling to old views which build up self-esteem. But,

[13] Nathan, *World of George Jean Nathan*, pp. 121–22, 131, 141, 145.
[14] Joseph Peck, M.D., *Life with Women and How to Survive It* (Englewood Cliffs, N.J.: Prentice-Hall, 1961).

in addition, the twentieth-century attitude toward women was profoundly influenced by one man: Sigmund Freud. His theories have further undermined romantic idealization, given what appears to be scientific support to prejudices inherited from the nineteenth century, and supplied a distinctively modern form for the dread of the omnipotent female. Freud scarcely knew whether he was "to believe seriously in the power of which poets talk so much and with such enthusiasm but which cannot be further dissected analytically"; his own analytic dissection of female sexuality and the male's regular overestimation of his love object are obviously antipathetic to Victorian exaltation of womanhood and love.

And yet, despite the revolutionary originality of his theories, Freud clung to the traditional nineteenth-century view of woman's limitations. He believed that woman's particularly complex sexual development exhausts her potentialities, leaving her an almost purely sexual being and therefore hardly capable of rational or moral development, and that her late and incomplete resolution of the Oedipus complex provides her with a less strong and independent superego (conscience) than man's.[15] He constantly equated femininity with passivity, and his emphasis on penis envy of course implies that the female is inferior, a defective male as Aristotle said. On this basis Freud scientifically rationalized many misogynistic opinions of his day: women are especially prone to neurosis;[16] they have "little sense of justice" because of "the predominance of envy in their mental life" (the result of the original penis envy); they are "weaker in their social interests" and have "less capacity for sublimating their instincts than men"; it is penis envy, that is, a feeling of sexual inadequacy, that impels them to strive for independence or mental achievement; and women who do not fit the soft passive stereotype are simply displaying masculine characteristics. Freud's concession that woman's nature is not *altogether* determined by her sexual function and "that an individual woman may be a human being in other respects"[17] barely conceals his contempt

---

[15] Sigmund Freud, *New Introductory Lectures on Psycho-Analysis* (1933), in *The Standard Edition of the Complete Psychological Works*, ed. and trans. James Strachey (London: The Hogarth Press, 1964), XXII, 119, 129.

[16] Freud, *Three Essays on the Theory of Sexuality* (1905), in *Works*, VII, 221.

[17] Freud, *New Introductory Lectures*, pp. 116–17, 134, 135. A more explicit

for women and femininity. In *Civilization and Its Discontents* (1930) he explicitly charged that woman is hostile to man's higher development:

. . . women soon come into opposition to civilization and display their retarding and restraining influence. . . . Women represent the interests of the family and of sexual life. The work of civilization has become increasingly the business of men, it confronts them with ever more difficult tasks and compels them to carry out instinctual sublimations of which women are little capable.

What libido a man "employs for cultural aims he to a great extent withdraws from women and sexual life. . . . Thus the woman finds herself forced into the background by the claims of civilization and she adopts a hostile attitude toward it." [18] Freud's espousal of ideas of this sort gave valuable support to contemporary writers of similar sympathies, who probably felt that views sanctioned by Freud could not be branded reactionary. In *Lady in the Dark* Moss Hart modernized his reactionary view of the career woman with a psychoanalytic explanation for her unhappiness, given not only in the play itself but in its preface, supposedly written by a psychiatrist who is one of the characters.

Although misogynists had long chafed against the power of women, it was Freud who directed attention to "a mother's importance, unique, without parallel, established unalterably for a whole lifetime as the first and strongest love-object and as the prototype of all later love-relations." [19] The mother's enormous influence, re-

---

statement that women's ambitions outside the home are reducible to penis envy is found in an article by Freud's disciple Karl Abraham, "Manifestations of the Female Castration Complex," *International Journal of Psycho-Analysis*, III (1922), 1–29.

[18] Freud, *Works*, XXI, 103–4. Of course, many psychoanalysts, such as Karen Horney, have sharply opposed Freud's theories about women. George Bernard Shaw's representation in *Man and Superman* (1903) of the mother-woman in ruthless opposition to the artist-man strikingly anticipates Freud's picture of the relationship between the sexes in *Civilization and Its Discontents*. Probably both derive from a combination of persistence of certain nineteenth-century views and a rebellion against Victorian sentimentalizing. Shaw's attitude toward women was more sympathetic than Freud's, however; he supported the feminist movement and genuinely appreciated intelligent women. For a contrasting view, see Lizbeth J. Sachs and Bernard H. Stern, "Bernard Shaw and his women," *British Journal of Medical Psychology*, XXXVII (December, 1964), 343–50.

[19] Freud, *An Outline of Psycho-Analysis* (1940), in *Works*, XXIII, 188.

sulting first from her infant's absolute dependence upon her, is intensified in the little boy by the Oedipus complex, which causes him to fall in love with her. Since great power implies great capacity to do harm, many contemporary writers have dwelt on the ways that women can ruin their sons: those who are seeking the possibilities of maternal destructiveness can easily deduce them from Freud's writings. Of course, the devouring wife continues to appear, as in Ernest Hemingway's fiction; but she is now often fused with or replaced by the devouring mother.[20] The acute fear of female domination which appears in several major modern authors has been intensified and given shape by Freud's emphasis on maternal power — "the supreme primal uterus," as William Faulkner was to describe it.

While Freudian influence upon the major twentieth-century writers cannot be conclusively established, it seems evident that these men were sufficiently aware of Freud's theories to make use of them. D. H. Lawrence, for example, is said to have known Freudian theory, although he had not read Freud's books. Certainly Lawrence's insistence that there is an unbridgeable difference between the sexes, that femininity is (or should be) passive, and that the female is an exclusively sexual being, hostile to man's sublimated aims, is very Freudian. His awareness of the power of motherhood and the erotic bond between mother and son was undoubtedly clarified by Freud's theories.

Lawrence's basically reactionary attitude on the subordination

---

Philip Rieff discusses Freud's misogyny in *Freud: The Mind of the Moralist* (New York: Viking Press, 1959), pp. 174–85.

[20] E.g., James Thurber's domineering wives often act like castrating mothers. Some critics maintain that Henry James also saw women as devourers of men. It is true that he frequently represented women as stronger than men. The Marquise de Bellegarde, the evil matriarch in *The American*, controls her whole family. Maggie Verver, an ostensibly good woman, has virtually bought her husband at the beginning, and has spiritually mastered him by the end of *The Golden Bowl*; and sometimes James explicitly hints at the sinister effects of her all-embracing love upon him, as in Chapter 9 of *The Golden Bowl* (New York: Grove Press, 1905), p. 113. Over and over James represented male protagonists who shy away from passionate involvement with women. Although some of these characters are represented unfavorably, like Winterbourne in "Daisy Miller" and Marcher in "The Beast in the Jungle," some are very sympathetic, like Strether in *The Ambassadors*. Strether not only fears his fiancée, Mrs. Newsome, whom everyone finds formidable (he compares her to a "particularly large

of women is somewhat disguised by mystical terminology: instead of stating flatly that a wife should obey her husband because God created her inferior, Lawrence proclaimed that man must, to be saved, stand for a deep purpose — "the god in him" — and woman believe in that purpose because it is his and then follow him. This view is really the same as Milton's "Hee for God only, shee for God in him." Lawrence stated his position most clearly in *Fantasia of the Unconscious* (1922), where he insisted that equality between men and women is impossible because the sexes are as different mentally as they are physically. They cannot even truly communicate: ". . . *whatever* a man says, his meaning is something quite different and changed when it passes through a woman's ears. . . . The *apparent* mutual understanding, in companionship between a man and a woman, is always an illusion, and always breaks down in the end." Since Lawrence agreed with Freud that woman is inevitably limited by her sexuality, he insisted that she cannot truly devote herself to intellectual or social aims and is naturally hostile to the pursuit of these aims by men. Her mission is almost purely biological — to solace her mate and to breed children; any other aims she may have are perversions of her true nature and will inevitably bring her to despair. Her "deepest consciousness is in the loins and belly." If you "pervert this, and make a false flow upwards, to the breast and head," "you get a race of 'intelligent' women, delightful companions, tricky courtesans, clever

---

iceberg" in Book XI, Chapter 2 of *The Ambassadors* [Boston: Houghton Mifflin, 1960], p. 316), but he shrinks from marrying the seemingly innocuous Maria Gostrey; and even the adorable Mme. de Vionnet inspires in him the thought that to deal with women "was to walk on water" (p. 340 [Book XII, Chapter 2]). Furthermore, the facts of James's life suggest an autobiographical element in these characters. His mother, although doting and apparently selfless, was stronger than his father and seems to have inspired in him a lifelong fear of controlling women. James, of course, remained celibate, apparently fearing female domination or sexual involvement or both, and recoiled in horrified embarrassment from women who made intense emotional appeals to him. (For further detail see Leon Edel's biography of James. Edel emphasizes James's "sense of the feminine sex as a destructive force." [*Henry James: The Conquest of London* (Philadelphia: J. B. Lippincott, 1962), p. 206. Cf. pp. 345–46].)

It seems to me that all these implications are too subtle and ambiguous to use as evidence that James was a misogynist. There is no indication that the Marquise de Bellegarde is a typical mother, and her elder son is as evil as she

prostitutes, noble idealists, devoted friends, interesting mistresses, efficient workers, brilliant managers." But then, "The moment woman has got man's ideals and tricks drilled into her, the moment she is competent in the manly world," she has had enough: her sexuality bursts out uncontrollably, and usually turns to destruction. In conclusion Lawrence exhorted men, in unnecessarily sadistic terms:

Fight for your life, men. Fight your wife out of her own self-conscious preoccupation with herself. Batter her out of it till she's stunned. Drive her back into her own true mode. Rip all her nice superimposed modern-woman and wonderful-creature garb off her. Reduce her once more to a naked Eve, and send the apple flying. Make her yield to her own real unconscious self, and absolutely stamp on the self that she's got in her head. . . . And then you've got a harder thing still to do. Stop her from looking on you as her 'lover' . . . make her know she's got to believe in you again, and in the deep purpose you stand for.

It is the man's problem, Lawrence admitted, to find this deep purpose; a man cannot expect a woman to follow him if he is aimless

---

is. Maggie's conquest of the Prince might be construed as the triumph of the castrating female, but is not definitely indicated to be any such thing. Strether's fear of women is at least as likely to be his own personal limitation as a comment on the female sex. It is probable that James intended Mrs. Newsome to represent a prevalent type of American matron, but clearly this is not the feminine type that predominates in the novel.

More important, any hints of misogyny in James's fiction are greatly outweighed by favorable representation of women. In *The Golden Bowl* James insisted on Maggie's purity, generosity, selflessness, and love; her excess of innocence is hardly a major flaw. Mme. de Vionnet, the outstanding female character in *The Ambassadors*, is an exquisite and amiable human being who has unstintingly given great benefits to her lover and allowed herself to be exploited by him. Turning to the heroines of other major novels, such as Isabel Archer in *The Portrait of a Lady* and Milly Theale in *The Wings of the Dove*, one finds an even less ambiguous picture of feminine intelligence, sensitivity, honor, unselfishness, and love.

Leon Edel has pointed out James's fondness for the vampire theme (*Henry James: The Untried Years* [Philadelphia: J. B. Lippincott, 1953], pp. 54–55, 256–58; introduction to *The Sacred Fount* [London: Rupert Hart-Davis, 1959], pp. 9–11), which he inherited from the Romantics (see above, Chapter VI, Note 28). This theme appears most conspicuously in *The Sacred Fount*, where Grace Brissenden, another of James's formidable ladies, grows young and blooming while her chronologically younger husband withers away. However, James did not represent the vampirism as sexually one-sided: he stated that a man

himself. The man's role is to "go on alone, ahead of the woman, to break a way through the old world into the new." [21]

Like the Victorians, Lawrence wished to evade the question of women's rights altogether: "All this talk of equality between the sexes is merely an expression of sex-hate. / Men and women should learn tenderness to each other." [22] His ideal wife was one who had "at last learned to hold her tongue and not to bother about rights and wrongs: her own particularly." [23] In *Lady Chatterley's Lover* (1928) he deplored that "endless assertion of her own will, which is one of the signs of insanity in modern woman." Connie Chatterley, Lawrence's feminine ideal, is happily submissive when she meets a strong man and rejoices to be "free of the dominion of *other women*," whom she considers "awful." Her sister, Hilda, who asserts herself against men and proclaims her independence from them, who is getting a divorce and dislikes sex, is a far less attractive figure. She seems to be an example of the typical modern girl, "all tough rubber-goods and platinum." [24]

Fantasia of the Unconscious, despite its uninhibited style and

might be equally apt to gain at his wife's expense (*Sacred Fount*, p. 34 [Chapter 2]), and he paired the Brissendens with another couple in which a dull man absorbs the cleverness of his mistress, who correspondingly becomes dull. Although James represented Mrs. Brissenden as rather frightening and repellent — she is "bloated" with undeserved well-being, blandly unaware that she is devouring her husband, and impregnable in her complacent egoism — I do not believe she should be expanded into an attack on womankind. The crucial fact is that neither in *The Sacred Fount* nor elsewhere did James represent all or most of his vampires as women: the vampirism could go either way. It seems to me that he recurred to this theme as an allegory, not of the destructiveness of women, but of the dangers of giving oneself up to a passionate relationship.

[21] D. H. Lawrence, *Fantasia of the Unconscious* (New York: Albert and Charles Boni, 1930), pp. 279–81, 284–85. Cf. Lawrence's articles "Give Her a Pattern," "Matriarchy," "Cocksure Women and Hensure Men," "Enslaved by Civilisation," and a book by his friend John Middleton Murry, *Adam and Eve: An Essay towards a New and Better Society* (London: Andrew Dakers, Ltd., 1944), pp. 101, 217–21. However, in *Son of Woman: The Story of D. H. Lawrence* (New York: Jonathan Cape & Harrison Smith, 1931) Murry called attention to and disagreed with some aspects of Lawrence's misogyny.

[22] D. H. Lawrence, "Men and Women," *The Complete Poems* (London: Heinemann, 1957), III, 49.

[23] Lawrence, *Fantasia*, pp. 197–98.

[24] D. H. Lawrence, *Lady Chatterley's Lover* (New York: Grove Press, 1959), pp. 113, 140, 304–5.

its occasional hints at woman's destructive capacities, presents an essentially nineteenth-century view of the relationship between the sexes. But in other works Lawrence was more modern, attacking Victorian sentimental idealization of the lady, the mother, the good woman. In *Aaron's Rod* (1922) he explicitly protested against "this great and ignominious dogma of the sacred priority of women," the belief "that all that is productive, all that is fine and sensitive and most essentially noble, is woman." [25]

Annable, the misogynistic gamekeeper in *The White Peacock* (1911), has a particular hatred for ladies. While Annable's views cannot be identified with Lawrence's own, they are presented rather sympathetically: he is clearly the most virile figure in the book, and Cyril, the character who does represent Lawrence, admires him greatly. Annable has become a misogynist because women have failed him. His first wife, a lady, tormented him by asserting her own will and finally by denying him sexually. Then he left her (the first of many male characters in Lawrence to be justified in deserting his family) and married a servant. He treats his new wife with brutal lack of consideration, never bothers to talk to her, but impregnates her regularly. (Despite this maltreatment, she worships him.) He has made his little girl a doll, "a hideous carven caricature of a woman," and given her some red chalk to rouge its face and make it "like a lady." Looking at a peacock — a male bird, one may note — perched on a monumental angel, Annable exclaims: "That's the very soul of a lady . . . I should like to wring its neck." After he drives it off, he cries, "Just look! . . . the miserable brute has dirtied that angel. A woman to the end, I tell you, all vanity and screech and defilement." [26] Probably Annable is an exaggeration of one side of Lawrence himself; certainly Mellors, the gamekeeper in *Lady Chatterley's Lover*, is. He too is disgusted with women, wanting above all not to come in contact with one again; he has left his wife and even lives apart from his mother and daughter. From his previous experience with women — the first two with whom he was involved were frigid; the third, his wife, wanted

[25] D. H. Lawrence, *Aaron's Rod* (New York: Albert and Charles Boni, 1930), pp. 186–87.

[26] D. H. Lawrence, *The White Peacock* (London: J. M. Dent, 1935), pp. 149–50, 165.

"to be the active party" — he concludes that all are sexually unsatisfactory, except black women, who are "a bit like mud." He can enjoy Connie only when he can "forget the rest."[27]

Presumably the speaker in *Look! We Have Come Through!* (1917), Lawrence's poetic account of his romance with his future wife, is voicing Lawrence's own views when he protests against the lady's feeling of superiority — as a lady and as an object of courtship. He tells her that he has no use for an "Angel in disguise" who expects him to be "Smitten with reverent surprise." Rather, she should put on ashes and sackcloth "And learn to serve . . . as a woman should, / Implicitly." What has woman to pride herself on anyway, he continues, as a woman or a mother? What is there in herself, or the fruit of her womb either? In the end it will be nothing but dust, just like the apples of Sodom, which looked beautiful but turned to ashes in the mouth.[28] Thus Lawrence sadistically dragged the lady down from her Victorian pedestal, not only as a wife, but as a mother. For he sensed women's pride in motherhood and found it deeply troubling to his male ego. He was envious — first of the woman, because she has the primary role in reproduction; secondly of the baby, because it is more important to the woman than the man is. To compensate for his feeling of inferiority, he revived the old contention that somehow, despite the evidence, the father is more important to his child than the mother is: "The father, from his distance, supports, protects, nourishes his child, and it is ultimately on the remote but powerful father-love that the infant rests, in a rest which is beyond mother-love."[29]

More often, Lawrence simply expressed resentment of women's pride and absorption in motherhood — most openly in his first novel, *The White Peacock*, which is also his most crudely misogynistic work. Cyril, Lawrence's spokesman in the book, describes a mother and child as "very calm, very complete and triumphant together." Their completeness makes him "feel alone and ineffectual. A woman who has her child in her arms is a tower of strength, a

[27] Lawrence, *Lady Chatterley's Lover*, pp. 243–44.
[28] D. H. Lawrence, "Lady Wife," *Look! We Have Come Through!* (London: Chatto and Windus, 1917), pp. 84–86.
[29] Lawrence, *Fantasia*, p. 54. Freud also undervalued motherhood, theorizing that women have babies as substitutes for the penises which they do not have.

beautiful, unassailable tower of strength that may in its turn stand quietly dealing death." In the end, "weary of babies," Cyril longs "for a place where they would be obsolete, and young, arrogant, impervious mothers might be a forgotten tradition." [30] This fear of a mother's power and resentment of her self-sufficient pride undoubtedly derive from Lawrence's perception of his own mother, who possessed her sons and overwhelmed her husband — partly by superiority of mind, character, and class, partly by using his children against him.

Later Lawrence found his revenge: his most virile figures voluntarily abstain from fatherhood, thus depriving the female of what she most wants. His own inability to beget children no doubt contributed to his sterile ideal of virility, but his protagonists are purposely sterile, so as to prevent the female from triumphing. Lilly in *Aaron's Rod*, who represents Lawrence, is glad that he has no children, although his wife wants them badly; for it is "against his instinct" to add to the mass of children in the world. Besides, he is jealous: ". . . when a woman has got children, she thinks the world wags only for them and her. . . . Sacred children, and sacred motherhood, I'm absolutely fed stiff by it." He is thankful his wife "can't come it over me there." "Men have got to stand up to the fact that manhood is more than childhood — and then force women to admit it. . . . But the rotten whiners, they're all grovelling before a baby's napkin and a woman's petticoat." [31] When the virile, bearded groom in "St. Mawr" (1925) is asked why the magnificent stallion St. Mawr never gets foals, he answers, "Doesn't want to, I should think. Same as me." [32] Frustration of the most powerful of female instincts represents the ultimate triumph of male will. Lawrence is getting back at Mother, indeed!

Lawrence condemned all self-assertion in women as destructive. even in the sphere of sexual relations. Although he often showed women failing their men by being frigid, he detested the vigorously sexual female — the woman who, like Mellors' wife, seeks sexual satisfaction for herself. The woman is to be infinitely receptive to

[30] Lawrence, *White Peacock*, pp. 325–26, 350.

[31] Lawrence, *Aaron's Rod*, pp. 116–17.

[32] D. H. Lawrence, *The Short Novels* (London: Heinemann, 1956), II, 30.

the man, but not to have desires of her own. It is mainly because of female self-assertion that lovers in Lawrence's fiction are typically in conflict and marriages so often fail. (Lawrence and his wife, although they loved each other, quarreled savagely; and it appears that Mrs. Lawrence was unfaithful.) In his early novels wives almost always dominate their husbands and undermine their virility. As George, a leading character in *The White Peacock*, put it: "I think . . . marriage is more of a duel than a duet. One party wins and takes the other captive, slave, servant — what you like. . . . In the marital duel Meg is winning. The woman generally does; she has the children on her side." [33] At the end of the book George was a useless alcoholic; his degradation had been started by the first woman he loved and completed by Meg, his wife. In Lawrence's later fiction there are characters like Pauline Attenborough, the "Lovely Lady" who enslaved her sons by female fascination, and Rachel Bodoin, whose constant pastime was puncturing male self-esteem. Pauline "put a sucker into one's soul and sucked up one's essential life," and Rachel, with "the health and muscular equipment of the Sphinx," "would live for ever, seeking whom she might devour, and devouring him." "Women, very often . . . proceed gently to wring the neck of the man they think they are loving with all their hearts." [34]

Yet, despite his theoretical conviction of male superiority and his fear of female destructiveness, Lawrence found himself irresistibly dependent on women. The resulting humiliation led him to protest, in "Tortoises" (1920–22), against the sexual nature of man, which drives him helplessly to women. Projecting his feelings onto the reptile world, Lawrence pities a male tortoise in desperate pursuit of a female, a female stronger and more stolid than he. Though "Born to walk alone" as a fore-runner, he is "Now suddenly distracted" into "This awkward, harrowing pursuit." "Crucified into sex" in his adolescence, he is now "Doomed to make an intolerable fool of himself / In his effort toward completion again." After the courtship is consummated, Lawrence asks indignantly:

[33] Lawrence, *White Peacock*, p. 335.
[34] D. H. Lawrence, "The Lovely Lady," "Mother and Daughter," in *The Complete Short Stories* (London: Heinemann, 1955), III, 778, 806.

Why were we crucified into sex?
Why were we not left rounded off, and finished in ourselves,
As we began.[35]

If only we could dispense with the female altogether, as Hippolytus
and Posthumus wished!

In *Aaron's Rod* Lawrence wishfully projected a situation in which
men did dispense with women. At the beginning of the book, Aaron
deserts his wife and daughters, an action presented as perfectly
unexceptionable; and all the relationships between men and women
in the book are shown to be unsatisfactory, since women persist in
exerting their will against men — their diabolical, enticing, snakelike female will.[36] Masculine friendship, such as that between Aaron
and Lilly, remains the only hope. While Lilly's wife is away,
Aaron falls ill and comes to stay with his friend. Lilly looks after
him with a more than wifely tenderness, effecting his cure by rub-
bing his body with oil as a mother rubs her baby: a man does not
neglect his mate in favor of a child! The scene closes with Lilly's
declaration that men must assert their superior importance to women
and children.

Although Lawrence later discarded his belief that the only satisfactory human relationship was between a male leader and a male
follower, his dread of the diabolical, snakelike female will persisted. In *Fantasia of the Unconscious* he had insisted on the subjection of women ostensibly for the good of both sexes. In his
interpretation of *The Scarlet Letter* in *Studies in Classic American
Literature* (1923), however, Lawrence revealed that he believed
subjection of women to be necessary for male self-preservation. He
saw *The Scarlet Letter* as a great allegory of woman's destruction of
spiritual man — Lawrence himself, of course, was a spiritual man.
He assumed as an obvious fact that Hester seduced Dimmesdale —
a point on which there is no evidence in the book — and that she
took intense delight in destroying his integrity:

The greatest triumph a woman can have, especially an American woman,
is the triumph of seducing a man: especially if he is pure. . . . Because the
greatest thrill in life is to bring down the Sacred Saint with a flop into the
mud [as the peacock dirtied the angel in *The White Peacock*]. Then when

[35] Lawrence, *Poems*, II, 91–94.
[36] Lawrence, *Aaron's Rod*, p. 185.

you've brought him down, humbly wipe off the mud with your hair, another Magdalen. And then go home and dance a witch's jig of triumph, and stitch yourself a Scarlet Letter with gold thread, as duchesses used to stitch themselves coronets. And then stand meek on the scaffold and fool the world.

Dimmesdale had lost his spiritual integrity to Hester; she, Lawrence obviously assumed, had none to lose, only biological drives and instinctive hostility to the spiritual.

Because of women's lack of moral purpose or standards, of anything within themselves to believe in, they must be kept subject. Lawrence said, echoing nineteenth-century arguments: ". . . unless a woman is held, by man, safe within the bounds of belief, she becomes inevitably a destructive force." For unless she believes in a man, "she believes, essentially, in nothing," which means that "she becomes subtly diabolic. The colossal evil of the united spirit of Woman. WOMAN, German woman or American woman, or every other sort of woman, in the last war, was something frightening. As every *man* knows." "When the subconscious soul of woman recoils from its creative union with man" — in plain terms, when she tries to be anything other than the junior partner in a sexual union — "it becomes a destructive force." Lawrence's meaning seems to be that if a woman asserts herself at all, she is undermining her man's self-esteem and therefore his virility. Lawrence's anxiety about man's precarious supremacy is traditionally patriarchal, but was no doubt sharpened by his mother's destructive influence on his father and himself. Even the most altruistic motives cannot neutralize the destructiveness of women who throw off their yoke of subjection to men, Lawrence went on:

The very women who are most busy saving the bodies of men, and saving the children: these women-doctors, these nurses, these educationalists, these public-spirited women, these female saviours: they are all, from the inside, sending out waves of destructive malevolence which eat out the inner life of a man, like a cancer. It is so, it will be so, till men realize it and react to save themselves.

Lawrence looked forward hopefully to the time when, after generations and generations "of nurses and political women and salvationists," there will be "the dark erection of the images of sex-worship once more," and women will *choose* to experience again the great submission."

Pearl, who has not sinned and whose name connotes purity, inspires an even more indignant tirade — Lawrence's simultaneous attack on the emancipated modern woman and the sinless woman idealized by the Victorians. Since children are "either devils or sons with gods in them," her character is only to be expected from the fact that she is female. Her rejection of fatherly authority, that is, her rebellion against man-made law, means that she cannot sin because she has no god to sin against. Hence, her sinlessness becomes a ghastly sham: "These dear Pearls, they do anything they like, and remain pure. . . . But they can't stop themselves from going rotten inside. . . . Their *souls* smell, because their souls are putrefying inside them." And gradually they will rot from within, and decompose into madness.[37] The "pure" woman is even worse than the sinner — for she is not only female but invulnerable because sinless; she is doubly destructive because harder to keep in subjection.

This is Lawrence's most impassioned declaration of his consistent attitude toward woman: only if she implicitly follows man's direction, giving up all assertive wishes of her own, even wishes for sensual satisfaction and motherhood, will she be harmless. Otherwise man must fight her in order to protect himself. Lawrence's reactionary insistence on the subjection of women, his deliberate attacks on feminine ideals, his hostility to the distinctively female function of motherhood, his yearning for independence from women, his conviction of their destructiveness, and his belief in their natural antipathy to the spiritual, place him clearly in the misogynistic tradition. While in part he covered his misogyny in the nineteenth-century manner, by insisting that women would be happier following men than leading independent lives, his main concern was obviously dread of the female.

3

Ernest Hemingway was never so explicit as Lawrence, but his fear of the female was equally strong. It was expressed mainly through his preference for undemanding primitives over emanci-

[37] D. H. Lawrence, *Studies in Classic American Literature* (Garden City, N.Y.: Doubleday and Co., 1951), pp. 98–99, 102–5, 107, 114.

pated Anglo-Saxon women. His ideal women, like Maria in *For Whom the Bell Tolls* (1940), resemble more the creations of erotic fantasy than real people; his realistically depicted women are generally engaged in destroying the men around them. In the relationship between Robert Jordan and his "little rabbit" Maria, which Hemingway himself suggested is like an adolescent fantasy, the woman offers the man submissive devotion without limit, everything he could possibly wish. Maria, who has suffered multiple abuse in the Spanish Civil War, lives only to serve her man, her sole anxiety being that she cannot please him enough. "I will do anything for thee that thou should wish . . . understand always that I will do what you wish. But thou must tell me for I have great ignorance." [38] On the other hand Jordan, although he loves Maria, sends her off when he has anything important to discuss.

Another Hemingway hero, Nick Adams, who put himself to sleep by recalling his fishing trips, once tried thinking instead of all the girls he had known and what sort of wives they would make. But he soon "went back to trout-fishing," for he found fishing streams much more interesting and individualized than girls, who "blurred and I could not call them into my mind and finally they all blurred and all became rather the same and I gave up thinking about them almost altogether." [39] At the end of the story he had not yet bothered to marry—partly because he remembered his parents' marriage, partly, it would appear, because women are not important to a genuinely virile man. It seems fair to regard these heroes as representative of Hemingway himself, since in his work heroes of the same type constantly recur, their opinions are neither explicitly nor implicitly criticized, and there is no favorable presentation of a love relationship in which the man and woman meet on equal terms.

In Hemingway's play *The Fifth Column* (1938) again the hero is too virile to remain seriously involved with a woman. And again there is a suggestion of adolescent fantasy in the woman's abject

[38] Ernest Hemingway, *For Whom the Bell Tolls* (New York: Charles Scribner's Sons, 1945), pp. 137, 349. In general outline my discussion of Hemingway's attitude toward women follows Edmund Wilson's in *The Wound and the Bow* (Boston: Houghton Mifflin, 1941), pp. 237–40.

[39] Ernest Hemingway, "Now I Lay Me," in *Men Without Women* (Cleveland, Ohio: World Publishing Co., 1946), p. 164.

devotion to the hero, no matter how brutally he treats her. Unlike Maria, however, Dorothy is a middle-class American, a Vassar graduate and a war correspondent — and therefore, Hemingway implies, by definition lazy, spoiled, and aggressive, however inoffensive she might appear. Though she loves the hero, Philip, he sneers at her continually and ultimately breaks with her as brutally as he can. Habitually he tells her at night that he loves and wants to marry her, but in the daytime he ridicules her dream of a comfortable domestic life with children. In the end he escapes from Dorothy by devoting himself altogether to the Communist cause, and he invites a comrade to watch him break off the affair, for he is proud of his technique. After describing to Dorothy all the wonderful places they will go together, he tells her flatly they will not go anyplace. Nor will he take her along with him into the Communist cause, "Because you're useless, really. You're uneducated, you're useless, you're a fool and you're lazy." Dorothy answers meekly, "Maybe the others. But I'm not useless," meaning that she can provide sexual pleasure.[40] At last she is provoked to insult him, but as he is about to go he kisses her good-by, which so excites her that she begs him to have intercourse with her. He spurns her, but even at the end she loves him. Clearly, the author, like his character, is reveling in sadism, triumphing over the woman who cannot resist him; he is provoked by the mere fact that she has sufficient status to think herself entitled to some consideration from the man.

A look at Hemingway's portrayals of women who have succeeded in gaining the upper hand reveals why he thought it so important to keep them in subjection. When the woman is not subservient, she is destructive (as in Lawrence). In "The Doctor and the Doctor's Wife," Nick Adams' mother, a Christian Scientist, gently but relentlessly probes into her doctor husband's quarrel with an Indian, in which he has betrayed his lack of virility. The poor man's only defense is to busy himself cleaning a shotgun, and finally to escape into the woods. Dr. Adams meets Nick and tells him that his mother wants to see him, but Nick answers, "I want to go with you." So they escape together. On another occasion, described in "Now I Lay Me,"

---

[40] Ernest Hemingway, *The Fifth Column and the First Forty-Nine Stories* (New York: P. F. Collier, 1938), pp. 98–99.

Mrs. Adams gets even with her husband for going on a hunting trip by burning his cherished Indian collection. The doctor says nothing to his wife, but her son remembers the episode, which in part accounts for his reluctance to marry. Most of Hemingway's protagonists dislike their mothers, although few are so violent as the bullfighter in "The Mother of a Queen," who jokes when his mother's body is dug up and dumped on the public bone heap.

Lady Brett Ashley of *The Sun Also Rises* (1926), Hemingway's most fully developed picture of the emancipated modern woman, illustrates the destructiveness of the type. Her sexual looseness is only the most conspicuous aspect of her general freedom from internal and external restraint; she is conspicuously boyish, calling herself a "chap" and refusing to let her hair grow long. Irresistibly she attracts all the men in the book, and almost inevitably she destroys them, although she does spare a young bullfighter by breaking off their affair; with much effort, she can abstain from being a bitch. The implication seems to be that only the traditional woman, the ignorant, unpretentious one who knows her place, is harmless. Brett is attractive and almost sympathetically presented, but she is nevertheless a destructive force which needs to be restrained.

Later in his career, in "The Short Happy Life of Francis Macomber" (1938), Hemingway made explicit what he had implied about women in *The Sun Also Rises*: he viewed his destructive heroine with simple fear and condemnation. Mrs. Macomber, who as an American comes closer to Hemingway's personal feelings than the English Brett, is presented as a typical American wife. Her attacks on her husband's ego recall Fran Dodsworth's, although in Hemingway the emphasis is overtly sexual. Watching Mrs. Macomber's treatment of her husband, the guide, Wilson, reflected that American women are "the hardest in the world; the hardest, the cruelest, the most predatory and the most attractive and their men have softened or gone to pieces nervously as they have hardened." Perhaps women must be cruel to govern their men, as Hemingway assumed they do; but Wilson had "seen enough of their damn terrorism." And terrorism was exactly what Mrs. Macomber inflicted on her husband — she had somehow paralyzed him into utter inability to resist her. When he went to pieces on being faced by his first wounded lion, she needled him without mercy and then deliberately removed her hand from his and kissed Wilson, with whom she went to bed that night.

But the next day, when Macomber suddenly found courage, became at last a mature man, and faced a wounded buffalo very bravely, his wife could not stand it and "accidentally" shot him, supposedly to save him from the charging beast. Although she methodically destroyed her husband's manhood — first psychologically and then physically — she and her kind were irresistibly attracted to Wilson, the virile professional hunter, who despised women and could do without them very well. He slept with women only because it was expected as part of his job, "although he liked some of them well enough at the time."[41] The implication is plain, here as in most of Hemingway's work: the truly virile man, and the one women love, keeps them well under control and regards them as no more than a pleasant pastime. A man who regards woman as anything more allows her to gain the upper hand, and a woman who gains the upper hand necessarily destroys the man. The mysteriously all-powerful bitch-heroine, usually an angelic-appearing blonde, remains a popular heroine in novels to this day. Sally Marcherson in Anton Myrer's *The Violent Shore* (1962), for example, goes to diabolical lengths to ruin her three lovers, escaping unscathed at the end to victimize more men.

4

Nathanael West's *The Day of the Locust* (1939) presents a burlesque version of this destructive-female theme which, despite its farcical exaggeration, seems to express genuine feeling. His heroine,

[41] *Ibid.*, pp. 107, 109, 125. Although Nicole Diver, a blonde who looks like an angel, does much to destroy her man in *Tender Is the Night*, I believe that F. Scott Fitzgerald was concerned with the effects of mental illness on both parties rather than the destructiveness of the female. Somerset Maugham resembled Hemingway in his preference for totally undemanding women over emancipated middle-class Anglo-Saxons: see *The Moon and Sixpence* (the Polynesian girl Ata), *Of Human Bondage* (Sally and the opinions of her father, Athelny), "The Fall of Edward Barnard," etc. Like Herrick and Lewis, he considered the modern middle-class wife selfish and spoiled: see Margery in *The Bread-Winner*, Mrs. Strickland in *The Moon and Sixpence*, etc. Mildred Rogers in *Of Human Bondage* seems to me an odious individual rather than an odious type of womanhood.

Faye Greener, a mindless, heartless movie extra and call girl, is beautifully blonde and avidly desired by all men. Her invitation, however, is not to pleasure,

but to struggle, hard and sharp, closer to murder than to love. If you threw yourself on her, it would be like throwing yourself from the parapet of a skyscraper. You would do it with a scream. You couldn't expect to rise again. Your teeth would be driven into your skull like nails into a pine board and your back would be broken.

As the hero pretends to listen to her endless, mindless daydreams, he thinks how he would like to rape her: "Nothing less violent than rape would do." He fantasies holding her in his hand like an egg: "It was her completeness, her egglike self-sufficiency, that made him want to crush her." Yet, sadistic as she makes men feel, she is never in danger: "Nothing could hurt her. She was like a cork. No matter how rough the sea got, she would go dancing over the same waves that sank iron ships and tore away piers of reinforced concrete."[42] Although West expressed these sentiments with exceptionally crude sadism, they are common in the misogynistic tradition: woman is mindless and heartless, but all-powerful; sexual involvement with her is irresistible, but dreadfully dangerous; man had better defend himself by attacking her before she attacks him; yet, no matter what he does, she will survive him because of her animal insensitivity and unawareness of morals. William Faulkner presented these ideas seriously and in almost as extreme form as West did.

Like Hemingway, Faulkner split womankind into self-assertive, masterful ladies and mindless female animals, and like West he distrusted even the latter type. While Lena Grove of *Light in August* (1932) is sweetly and innocuously retarded, Belle Mitchell, a similar type in *Sartoris* (1929), enveloped her man "like a rich and fatal drug, like a motionless and cloying sea in which he watched himself drown."[43] Jenny in *Mosquitoes* (1927) and Eula Varner in *The Hamlet* (1940), equally irresistible to everything male, do no actual harm, although Eula is described as "another mortal natural

[42] Nathanael West, *The Complete Works* (New York: Farrar, Straus and Cudahy, 1957), pp. 271, 320, 406.

[43] William Faulkner, *Sartoris* (New York: New American Library, 1953), p. 223.

enemy of the masculine race." None of these women is quite human in mind or character: Jenny is "an utterly mindless rifeness of young, pink flesh," although, ironically, she looks like an angel.[44] Eula, constantly swarmed over like the queen bee, tranquilly abrogates "the whole long sum of human thinking and suffering which is called knowledge, education, wisdom, at once supremely unchaste and inviolable." Even as a child she was equipped with "too much of mammalian female meat," and at eight years old she brought into the schoolroom "a pagan triumphal prostration before the supreme primal uterus." Inevitably she drew every male in the room, even the boys just entering puberty, making them spring "into embattled rivalry, importunate each for precedence in immolation." At twelve she forced the schoolmaster to flee her "to escape destruction": he was afraid of what he might do to her — not for her sake, for no man could hurt her, but for his own.[45] All these women are mysteriously invulnerable. Even Lena Grove, an unusually decent example of the Faulknerian female animal, deserves no protection because woman has natural advantages over man; though she has just given birth to a child whose father has deserted her, she can very well, somehow, look after herself.

If the richly physical traditional female is not quite human, the delicate, emancipated New Woman is corrupt and even more dangerous. Temple Drake of *Sanctuary* (1931) is a good example. A seventeen-year-old coed at the University of Mississippi, she had a boyish figure and a boy's name, was typically engaged in drinking or painting her face, indulged in promiscuous necking, and in general did whatever she liked, regardless of law or tradition. Although she was on probation for slipping out at night with the town boys, she lacked feeling for anyone: she kept her numerous dates "written down in her Latin 'pony,' so she didn't have to bother about who it was. She'd just dress, and after a while somebody would call for her."

At the same time, Temple is an attack on the lady — an expression of Faulkner's reaction against nineteenth-century idealization,

[44] William Faulkner, *Mosquitoes* (New York: Liveright Publishing Corp., 1927), p. 104.

[45] William Faulkner, *The Hamlet* (New York: Random House, 1940), pp. 113, 129–32, 136, 171 ("mortal enemy").

which of course was especially strong in the South. As Leslie Fiedler points out, the very title *Sanctuary* ironically suggests that Faulkner set out to degrade something once held sacred. Temple was a lady by social position, being a judge's daughter, and by nature: like the ultrarefined heroine of the novel of sensibility, she was fragile in body and constitution, with tiny feet that could not support her for a long walk; she discreetly abstained from giving men sexual satisfaction; and she was incapable of independent action, of extricating herself from painful situations. Faulkner methodically conducted her through the standard perils of the ladylike romantic heroine: the den of brutal men (the bootlegger's house), the sexual assault (from Popeye), the imprisonment in a brothel. But, far from showing any sympathy for her, he treated her with cold derision. Even when she was still bleeding from the corncob rape, he represented her as contemptible rather than pitiable. Moreover, after the rape, Faulkner pushed Temple into a degradation unbelievable in view of his original presentation of her character. From an empty-headed and cold-hearted but not abnormal college student, he turned her into a creature who voluntarily remained in a brothel to perform sexual intercourse for a whinnying spectator and who went up to a man in a restaurant, writhed her loins against him, and begged, "Let's hurry. Anywhere. . . . Please. Please. Please. Please. Don't make me wait. I'm burning up."[46] And yet at the end of the book Temple is again self-possessed, unhurt and apparently untouched by her frightful experiences.

Temple's series of ordeals seems almost to have been designed

[46] William Faulkner, *Sanctuary* (New York: Random House, 1932), pp. 182, 287–88. Leslie Fiedler, *Love and Death in the American Novel* (New York: Criterion Books, 1960), p. 312. Fiedler describes Faulkner's double attack on the female animal and the lady or New Woman, which he sees as typical of American fiction. His thesis, briefly, is that American novelists "rather shy away from permitting in their fictions the presence of any full-fledged, mature women, giving us instead monsters of virtue or bitchery, symbols of the rejection or fear of sexuality" (p. xix), with the result that they practically equate sexual love with death and constantly celebrate men's escape from women. While Fiedler makes many interesting and valid points, it seems to me that he sometimes makes too much of his evidence and that he overemphasizes the influence of nationality on the misogyny he describes: the attitudes of Lawrence and Osborne are similar to those of contemporary American writers, and all were influenced by the traditions of a common culture.

to debase the ideal of the attractive, self-assured, properly controlled lady. Faulkner was exposing through her the so-called purity
of the traditional lady, implying that it is no more than a professed
horror of sexual intercourse, a selfish refusal to give men what
they have paid for, and that it masks depths of concealed lechery.
He made it clear that Temple had unconsciously wanted to be raped
all along. The discrepancy between Faulkner's original presentation
of Temple on the one hand, and the harsh punishment he meted out
to her and implausible degradation to which he brought her on the
other, reveals his misogynistic animus against her and her type.
Furthermore, he represented Temple as typical of University of
Mississippi coeds and therefore, presumably, of upper-class twentieth-century American girlhood.

Apart from his recurrent horrifying female types, Faulkner included in his novels many remarks disparaging women as a sex,
which range from cynical commonplaces to declarations of woman's
evil nature and physical loathsomeness recalling those of the early
Christian ascetics. More often than not, he put these remarks into the
mouths of characters who were obviously speaking for him, such as
the group of clever artists in *Mosquitoes*, who are the only intelligent
characters in the book and who agree unanimously on the nature
and function of woman. A sculptor says that his marble statue of
a female torso represents his "feminine ideal: a virgin with no legs
to leave me, no arms to hold me, no head to talk to me." The novelist agrees that women who have more intelligence than they need to
move and eat and stay alive "become nuisances sooner or later." He
insists that "Women are never stupid," because "their mental equipment is too sublimely sufficient to do what little directing their
bodies require"; and he has no objection to their blind conventionality: "After all they are merely articulated genital organs with
a kind of aptitude for spending whatever money you have; so when
they get themselves up to look exactly like all the other ones, you can
give all your attention to their bodies." Asked whether he believes
women have souls, another man answers, in what reads almost like
a sketch for Eula Varner, "Certainly. If they are not born with
them, it's a poor creature indeed who can't get one from some man
by the time she's eleven years old." The same man dismisses romantic love as nothing more than "a rather dreadful mixture of

jealousy and thwarted desires and interference with that man's world which after all, we all prefer, and nagging and maybe a little pleasure like a drug."[47]

This flow of misogynistic commonplaces did not appear in Faulkner's later, more distinctive, and less conversational novels, although the same view of women is implied in characters like Eula Varner. Furthermore, in the later novels it is more difficult to determine whether characters are speaking for Faulkner, since those who are moral and intelligent enough to be probable spokesmen have been exposed to searing experiences with women which may have biased their views. Of course, the recurrence of such experiences in Faulkner's fiction is in itself significant: the Reverend Hightower's career and life were ruined by the outrageous behavior of his wife; Quentin Compson's mental illness and ultimate suicide were precipitated by the wantonness of his beloved sister; and Joe Christmas was started on his career of self-destruction by the sins of his mother and the dietician at his orphanage. The opinions of the first two of these characters, moreover, seem to be independent of their particular situations. Hightower declares that "No woman who has a child is ever betrayed; the husband of a mother, whether he be the father or not, is already a cuckold. . . . There have been good women who were martyrs to brutes, in their cups and such. But what woman, good or bad, has ever suffered from any brute as men have suffered from good women?"[48] This remark definitely pertains to good women like Lena Grove; it has nothing to do with women like his wife. I believe Faulkner was using Hightower to say, as Lawrence did, that women are culpable for neglecting their husbands in favor of their children, and that the best-intentioned destroy the souls of their men.

Similarly, certain observations by the Compson men in *The Sound and the Fury* seem intended to have general validity, despite the fact that Mrs. Compson would be enough to sour anyone on women. If the Compsons thought about the miseries of marriage,

[47] Faulkner, *Mosquitoes*, pp. 26, 229, 240–41.
[48] William Faulkner, *Light in August* (Modern Readers Series, 1932), pp. 298–99. Joe Christmas is more fanatically opposed to women than Hightower, but he, it seems to me, is so abnormal that he cannot be taken as a spokesman for Faulkner.

their views might be traced to their particular experience; but they are preoccupied with women's menstrual filthiness and natural proclivity to evil. Quentin Compson meditates that women "have an affinity for evil for supplying whatever the evil lacks in itself for drawing it about them instinctively as you do bedclothing in slumber fertilising the mind for it until the evil has served its purpose whether it ever existed or no." His father saw women as "Delicate equilibrium of periodical filth between two moons balanced . . . full and yellow as harvest moons her hips thighs. . . . Liquid putrefaction like drowned things floating like pale rubber flabbily filled getting the odour of honeysuckle all mixed up." [49] Grandfather Compson in *Absalom! Absalom!* (1936) speaks of "the dread and fear of females which you must have drawn in with the primary mammalian milk." [50] It seems clear that this dread, while projected onto the desperate male characters he created, was Faulkner's own. Grandfather Compson's remark shows how his fear of woman, although sometimes generalized, was typically focused on the mother, in accordance with Freud's emphasis on her power. Similarly, Belle envelops her man "like a motionless and cloying sea" (that is, the amniotic fluid), Jenny is "a supine potential fecundity," and Eula represents "the supreme primal uterus."

5

Although Faulkner expressed fear and Lawrence jealousy of woman as mother, and Hemingway's men are generally alienated from their bossy mothers, elaborate indictments of Mother emerged first in lesser writers and have gathered full virulence only in recent decades. The first extensive attack was Sidney Howard's play *The Silver Cord* (1927), which is practically a dramatization of Freud's theory of the Oedipus complex. Mrs. Phelps, a still pretty and invariably sweet woman with limited intelligence but superabundant vitality, tightly clutches her two grown sons: she continually proclaims the beauty of mother-love and whines about her sacrifices for

[49] William Faulkner, *The Sound and the Fury* (New York: Random House, 1946), pp. 115–16, 147.

[50] William Faulkner, *Absalom! Absalom!* (New York: Random House, 1936), p. 265. My discussion owes a great deal to Maxwell Geismar's chapter on Faulkner in *Writers in Crisis* (New York: Hill and Wang, 1961).

them, glories in their jealous rivalry for her affection, does all she can to destroy their relationships with younger women, and actually comes into her married son's bedroom, dressed in a fetching negligee, to try to revive the sloppy emotional bond of his youth. Finally his wife tells her what she is:

You belong to a type that's very common in this country, Mrs. Phelps — a type of self-centered, self-pitying, son-devouring tigress, with unmentionable proclivities suppressed on the side. . . . Talk about cannibals! You and your kind beat any cannibals I've ever heard of! And what makes you doubly deadly and dangerous is that people admire you and your kind. They actually admire you! You professional mothers!

In the end Mrs. Phelps fails to destroy her son's marriage, but she has broken the other son's engagement; he is "engulfed forever."[51]

Philip Wylie, in *Generation of Vipers* (1942), formalized the attack on the predatory, useless mother, as well as giving her the label of Mom. Starting with a justifiable denunciation of modern sentimental mother-worship, he proceeded to a comprehensive tirade against middle-aged American matrons. Despite a few psychoanalytic embellishments, his work recalls earlier outbursts like Swetnam's *Araignment*, not only in general content but in intemperate tone and in self-conscious ingenuity of epithet. Wylie even added the traditional unconvincing defense: ". . . only moms — or incipient moms — could imagine, after a close reading of this very chapter, that I had any other sensation for *real* women than love."

Mom, he wrote "is a middle-aged puffin with an eye like a hawk that has just seen a rabbit twitch far below." Overweight and virtually sexless, "She none the less spends several hundred dollars a year on permanents and transformations, pomades, cleansers, rouges, lipsticks, and the like — and fools nobody except herself." Her man has ulcers and colitis, since he has to worry about acquiring money; but "she has the guts of a bear," since her only worry is spending it. In the past Mom was safely occupied with heavy housework and in most cases providentially died of hard work in middle life, but now she "survives for an incredible number of years, to stamp and jibber in the midst of men, a noisy neuter by

[51] Sidney Howard, *The Silver Cord* (New York: Charles Scribner's Sons, 1927), pp. 193–94.

natural default or a scientific gelding sustained by science, all tongue and teat and razzmatazz."

Equipped with the traditional mysterious omnipotence of bad women, Mom dominates every male within reach:

Our land, subjectively mapped, would have more silver cords and apron strings crisscrossing it than railroads and telephone wires. Mom is everywhere and everything and damned near everybody, and from her depends all the rest of the U.S. . . . Men live for her and die for her, dote upon her and whisper her name as they pass away.

"The male is an attachment of the female in our civilization," which is devoted almost exclusively to ministering to her wants and whims. Furthermore, Mom is responsible for the manifold moral and political ills of modern American society, for which Wylie could see no possible cause except woman suffrage: they did not exist before woman had the vote [sic], they do exist now that she has it; the case is clear. Hence, women are responsible for "a new all-time low in political scurviness, hoodlumism, gangsterism, labor strife, monopolistic thuggery, moral degeneration, civic corruption, smuggling, bribery, theft, murder, homosexuality, drunkenness, financial depression, chaos, and war." By the same reasoning, they were responsible for World War II and McCarthyism — and, of course, for modern American materialism, even for the materialism observable in man, which results from "the femaleness within him, put there to keep women from being wholly inscrutable to him." The only salvation for America, Wylie concluded, is to put women back in the subjection where they belong: "We must face the dynasty of the dames at once, deprive them of our pocketbooks when they waste the substance in them, and take back our dreams which, without the perfidious materialism of mom, were shaping up a new and braver world." [52]

Wright Morris' novel *Man and Boy* (1951) is a far more telling attack on Mom. The heroine, whom everybody calls "Mother," has reduced her husband to a cypher and driven her only son into the Marines, where he died heroically in action. The book describes her glorious day, on which she goes to christen a ship named after

[52] Philip Wylie, *Generation of Vipers* (New York: Pocket Books, 1959), pp. 185–92, 205–7, including a note added in 1955.

her son. She has subjugated her husband through a regime of un-predictable moods, oppressive silences, and relentless sweetness; and as the book goes on she masters every other male in sight, in-cluding the entire United States Navy and a young man whom her husband meets on the train, Private Lipido, who was originally a stridently patriarchal representative of the male libido. As the book ends, every man at the ceremony rises in irresistible tribute to Mother and motherhood.

Mother seems to have all the traditional womanly virtues, but the book gradually reveals that she has turned them destructively against men. She is a compulsive housekeeper, carrying to a ludi-crous extreme the virtues of neatness and thrift, traditionally en-joined on women; but she uses these virtues not to increase her husband's comfort, but to keep him constantly uneasy in his own home. Since her womanly tenderness makes her disapprove of kill-ing anything, she terminated Christmas celebrations in the house when her husband gave her son a gun for Christmas. (Preparing for Christmas had been one of the few pleasures which man and boy had previously been permitted to enjoy.) Mother's opposition to violence, it is implied, pushed the boy to his hero's death in the Marines.

She feels no grief for her dead boy, only pride of motherhood; and, like many professional mothers in contemporary literature, she is not even biologically adequate: she was incapable of nursing her son, who as an infant refused her breast, "making a face like the milk was sour." [53] Thus it is suggested that Mother is wholly de-structive, not even productive in the narrow biological sense. This attribution of literal or symbolic sterility to the ostentatiously moth-erly woman underlines further the real destructiveness which lurks beneath her professed devotion. The sterile mother-figure may be a development of the "masculine" New Woman whom the Victorians censured for her reluctance to devote her life to breeding children: both illustrate woman's failure to meet men's exalted ideal of per-fect motherhood, though the earlier type was criticized outright, the later more subtly, by implications that her ostentatious maternity is false in every possible way.

[53] Wright Morris, *Man and Boy* (New York: Knopf, 1951), p. 49.

Edward Albee's *The American Dream* (1961) develops the falsity of Mom's motherhood with horrible explicitness. The heroine, "Mommy," is literally sterile, so she buys a baby from an adoption agency. Then she proceeds to mutilate him until he dies: first, preferring Daddy to Mommy, the baby looked only at Daddy, for which she cut out his eyes; then he masturbated, for which sexual assertion she cut off his genitals and then his hands. The mutilated baby boy develops (in the person of his identical twin) into a symbol of modern American men — "the great American boy-men," as Hemingway described them. The play as a whole is an indictment of our emasculated society and of the predatory women who are largely responsible for it. Mommy has Daddy completely under control; now and then in her deadly monologues she waits impatiently for him to make an appropriate comment to prove that he has been listening. She tells him she has a right to live off him "because I married you, and because I used to let you get on top of me and bump your uglies; and I have a right to all your money when you die." She speaks wistfully of the "absolutely adorable husband" of a friend of hers, adorable because he is permanently confined to a wheel chair.[54]

John Osborne's *Look Back in Anger* (1957) includes a typical twentieth-century attack on Mother, but recalls Jacobean drama in its tirades against women in general. The hero, Jimmy Porter, is a fervent misogynist, reviling his wife and mother-in-law, explicitly rebelling against the monstrous regiment of women. And it seems justified to consider him a spokesman, albeit an exaggerated one, for Osborne himself: he is treated sympathetically and is the most intelligent and idealistic character in the play, although his ideals have turned rancid because of modern society in general and the

---

[54] Edward Albee, *The American Dream* (New York: Coward-McCann, 1961), pp. 14, 23. Hemingway referred to "the great American boy-men" in "Francis Macomber," in *Fifth Column*, p. 132. In Albee's *Who's Afraid of Virginia Woolf*, the heroine is a merciless virago who constantly attacks her husband's manhood; it turns out that her basic motive is her own inability to have a child. The wife in the younger couple, after forcing her husband to marry her through a false pregnancy, takes contraceptive pills because she is afraid to have children. Arthur Kopit's *Oh Dad, Poor Dad, Mamma's Hung You in the Closet and I'm Feelin' So Sad* (1960) is a wild farcical development of the devouring wife-mother theme.

machinations of women in particular; and, while the other characters do register sporadic protests against his vituperation, he retains
the devotion of all. Jimmy is constantly moved to fury by his upper-
class wife's self-possession; unable to break her composure, he tells
her she needs a sorrow like the death of a child to make a human
being of her. "I want," he tells her, "to stand up in your tears, and
splash about in them, and sing. I want to be there when you grovel.
. . . I want the front seat." The only apparent motive for this wish,
which Osborne seems to present as unexceptionable, is Jimmy's
desire to weaken the woman, to subjugate her. His wife finally leaves
him, but in the end she comes back, repentant. She has had a mis-
carriage, and when she assures him that she is now groveling, they
are reconciled.

During the play Jimmy claims that women are noisy and clumsy,
which proves their fundamental insensitivity; indignantly asks
"Why, why, why, why do we let these women bleed us to death?"
even though the bleeding in the play seems to be the other way
around; and suggests that homosexuality would be a better arrangement than the " 'expense of spirit' lark" with women. He lavishes
his most vivid efforts on his wife's mother, who had opposed his
marriage:

I knew that, to protect her innocent young, she wouldn't hesitate to cheat,
lie, bully and blackmail. Threatened with me, a young man without money,
background or even looks, she'd bellow like a rhinoceros in labour —
enough to make every male rhino for miles turn white, and pledge himself
to celibacy. But even I under-estimated her strength. Mummy may look
over-fed and a bit flabby on the outside, but don't let that well-bred guzzler
fool you. Underneath all that, she's armour plated.

Then he proceeds to the familiar charge that women are instinctively
hostile to idealism: Mummy fought so hard to keep him from carrying off her daughter on his "poor old charger . . . all tricked
out and caparisoned in discredited passions and ideals!" Yet she
might have spared herself the trouble, for the poor old charger,
which could barely carry him, dropped dead under the weight of his
wife. "That old bitch should be dead," he finally concludes. "My
God, those worms will need a good dose of salts the day they get
through her! . . . Alison's mother is on the way! . . . She will

pass away, my friends, leaving a trail of worms gasping for laxatives behind her." [55] Jimmy's wish that mankind could go on without women goes back to Greek misogyny; the inclusion of misogynistic set pieces in a popular play recalls Jacobean drama; the vulgarity of the abuse and the particular animus against Mother are distinctively modern.

Casting off nineteenth-century sentimentality about woman, this century has come close to recognizing her as an equal. Although some voices still insist that woman is inferior and should therefore be kept subject, this is now definitely a minority attitude. On the other hand, with the loosening of nineteenth-century bonds of propriety, men have felt freer to express hostility toward women. This tendency has been accentuated by fears arising from women's real gains in power in recent years — in the family, in the professional world, in the American economy. On the middle-class American wife, who seems to have particularly benefited from these gains, have been focused the greed, inability to love, and antipathy to idealism of which misogynists have always accused women; she is charged with callous exploitation of her husband and made responsible for the materialism of contemporary American society. Many twentieth-century writers, including the major novelists Lawrence, Hemingway, and Faulkner, have openly expressed fear of and hostility to women. Lawrence's frantic insistence that women must be kept under control, Hemingway's representations of what happens when they are not, and Faulkner's enigmatic references to the fearsomeness and invulnerability of the mammalian female express dread alike of the emancipated modern woman and the eternal female animal.

The most significant new development of recent decades has been the undisguised attack on woman as mother. No doubt, this is in part a reaction against the Victorians' excessive idealization of motherhood (which persists today, in Mother's Day observations and so forth), the natural impulse to drag down what has been unduly elevated. This impulse has been greatly strengthened by Freud's exposition of the Oedipus complex, as, stripping away the

[55] John Osborne, *Look Back in Anger* (New York: Criterion Books, 1957), pp. 24, 35, 52–53, 59, 84.

traditional pieties surrounding the mother, he liberated hostility which had doubtless been present all along and showed specifically how women may cripple their sons. Primarily, however, the modern attacks on Mom seem to be the currently fashionable way in which fears always latent are to be expressed. The menace which earlier centuries attached to the devouring whore, ours attaches to the devouring mother.

Chapter VIII ❧ THE REASON WHY

HE FACT that certain male writers have always found some
female villain to hold up to ridicule, censure, or furious
indignation indicates the perennial desire to express hostility
against women. The whore in Jewish and classical antiquity and
again in the Renaissance, the shrewish wife in the Middle Ages, the
"unfeminine" woman in the nineteenth century, and the devouring
mother in the twentieth served the same purpose: they provide a
morally justified outlet for the expression of misogyny. Since misogyny is generally recognized as an abnormal feeling, not to be
expressed directly, it is apt to be disguised as criticism of an admittedly obnoxious type, or satire against women's failings, or statements of their mental and moral differences from men, or ostensibly
harmless jokes about the married state. The disguise is given away
by uncalled-for vehemence in the satiric attacks, blurring of the
distinction between censurable women and women in general, revelation that woman's differences from man invariably make her
inferior, and undercurrents of seriousness in the jokes.

The volume of misogyny which has poured forth in all periods
must be interpreted in the light of several modifying factors. In the
first place, the attacks on women were sometimes justified — not
only because women have their faults like everybody else, but because social conditions often encouraged the development of obnoxious female types. In Western society up to the present, women
have been dependent on men for financial support, so that a wife
who needed money — for running the household or for any other
purpose — had to get it from her husband. Men earned the income,
and, to some extent at least, women spent it. Women were often
forced to nag or cajole for money and might easily become unduly
mercenary in their attitude toward their husband or lover. It is a
short step to the greedy, exploitative wife of literature, who values

her man only as a source of income and talks to him only of the things he must buy for her. Then again, many of the early learned ladies must have been very like the literary stereotype — noisy, pretentious, superficially pedantic but truly ignorant. Such is the natural result of half-education, and true higher education was not available to women until very recent times. It might be pointed out that if women had been treated equally with men these types would not have arisen, but on the other hand the writer who is describing society looks at end products, not causation.

Secondly, a distortion is necessarily produced by confining attention to what the male says of the female: women would have expressed much of the same hostility had they written the books. When two people enter into a marriage, a lifelong intimate relationship, there are bound to be vexations and conflicts of interest. Since these have been described almost entirely from the male point of view, we have from all periods of literature a procession of selfish, exploitative, contentious, trying, bossy, unloving wives. Doubtless these are the result of human frailty on the part of both sexes: the real imperfections of women and the self-centered censoriousness of the men who wrote about them.

Furthermore, since men have written about women far more than the other way around, some of the most prominent ideals in literature are of the mistress, the wife, the mother. High ideals almost ask to be torn down — either by the idealist himself, when the real thing falls short of his expectation (as she necessarily must; no woman is really a Beatrice or a Grisilde) ; or by a cynic annoyed by undue idealization of frail humanity. Since this book is concerned with the masculine point of view, it naturally describes the tearing down of the feminine ideals which men have set up. This may not, however, be entirely a matter of who wrote the books: according to Freud, the male is more inclined than the female to overidealize his love-object; and overidealization prepares the way for disillusionment. Also, the more intense a relationship — and, by and large, men's most intense relationships are with women — the more apt it is to generate not only passionate devotion and idealization, but ambivalence.

Lastly, a man who writes against women is not necessarily moved by hatred; he may be concerned mainly with capitalizing on a perennially interesting — and therefore salable — subject. Although the medieval debate on whether woman's creation was a good thing would not be published today, a book on whether she should be confined to the home might well be a best-seller. Wylie's *Generation of Vipers* (1942), which continues to sell briskly, resuscitates ancient elements of the misogynistic tradition: woman is responsible not only for her own sins but for those committed by man; she drives her husband to ulcers while remaining healthy herself because she has nothing to do but spend his hard-earned money; the only salvation for society is to put her back in subjection. The saying that women have only two venial faults, "they neither doo, nor yet say wel," trite in *The Schole house of Women* in 1541, reappeared in Crosland's *Lovely Woman* in 1903. This persistence of the old charges illustrates the role of convention in misogynistic writing. On the other hand, even a hack writer is inclined to write on subjects congenial to him; if he does not dislike women, he will probably choose some other subject than misogyny.

Perhaps the most constant charge in the misogynistic tradition is that woman, created as a helpmate, instead hinders and vexes man as much as she can. Chaucer's Dame Alice of Bath drove five husbands to their graves. Lydgate's group of henpecked rustics petitioned the King for relief from the oppression of their idle, domineering wives. Jerrold's Mrs. Caudle destroyed her husband's sleep by constantly clamoring for money and grudging his every pleasure. Lewis' Fran Dodsworth never missed an opportunity to undermine her husband's self-respect. The characterization of bad wives has become more subtle in modern times, but their characteristics — selfishness, idleness, extravagance, perversity — have not changed much. Like Wylie's Mom, these women are generally fresh and strong after years of marriage, while their poor husbands are worn out by their nagging and the strain of supporting them in luxury. It is still commonly assumed that women gain much in marriage and give little in return. Mencken bluntly asserted that marriage is slavery, with man the slave.

Continually, in various forms, men have explained woman's failure to be helpful by charging that she is closer to the lower animals than man and is instinctively hostile to his higher aspirations. This is evident in the story of the Fall, when the serpent easily seduced

Eve through her passions and appetites, while he did not dare to approach Adam. Without woman, man might have remained forever in paradise, with his lower impulses safely subject to his reason and no obstacle to his spiritual perfection; under her influence, he allowed passion and appetite to control him and alienated himself from God. This story pervaded the early and medieval church and remained influential through the seventeenth century. Milton, for example, was much preoccupied with woman's degrading effect on man, stating that knowledge and wisdom collapse before her. The same idea reappears in secular writers of the twentieth century, as Lawrence declared that woman finds her greatest delight in dragging the spiritual man down into the mud, Faulkner described his eternal female tranquilly abrogating the whole sum of human knowledge, Wylie and Osborne blamed Mom for contemporary materialism and destruction of men's ideals.

The recurrent charge that woman is incapable of love, valuing a man only for the money he gives her, follows from her alleged insensibility to idealistic feelings. Prominent in erotic poetry from Roman times through the eighteenth century, it persists today in the middle-class wives drawn by Lewis and other novelists. The Renaissance insistence upon woman's violent and uncontrollable passions, "the unsounded sea of women's bloods," seems related to the belief that woman is less spiritual than man. She is supposed to be less capable than he of controlling lust, gluttony, anger, and greed, because these impulses are stronger in her and reason weaker. This idea, which can be traced back to the ancient Greeks, emerged occasionally even in the polite nineteenth century.

In our culture, some degree of hostility to women must be considered normal, in that it derives from a man's general cultural background rather than his personal peculiarities. Naturally a man's attitudes are affected by his culture, so that an orthodox Christian will be very aware of the Fall, a Puritan convinced of the righteousness of Pauline subjection of women, a contemporary writer alert to the baneful effects of possessive motherhood. Furthermore, convention has played an important part in writing about women, both for and against. It was expected that a Renaissance lyric poet would write a sonnet sequence and include a few hostile poems in it. We must distinguish between cultural and individual attitudes. On the other hand, it is significant what a man selects from his heterogeneous cultural inheritance: if he interprets the myth of the Fall primarily as a divine condemnation of woman, if his erotic poems are concerned mainly with woman's unworthiness as a love object, if he sees the typical mother as cannibally destructive, he is surely misogynistic.

Personal reasons for misogyny, as distinct from cultural ones, can only be sketchily suggested, since there are so many writers involved, each with an individual history which is rarely known in sufficient detail for analysis. Perhaps the most obvious reason is sexual guilt (in excess of what is normal for the society), which often leads to obsessive concern with lust, the conviction that sexual relations are degrading, and the impulse to rebel against sexual dependence on women by degrading them. This pattern is apparent in Marston, whose satires and plays are even more concerned with lust than was usual in his period and who protested with extraordinary violence against lovers' subjection to women, glowworms "That soile our soules, and dampe our reasons light." A subtle development of sexual guilt led to the paradoxical attitude shown by St. Jerome and Jonathan Swift, who combined love and genuine esteem for women friends with loathing for woman in her physical aspects, as mistress, wife, or mother. Their attitude seems to suggest the psychological conflict that Freud described as the split in male love life, which prevents a man from loving physically a woman he respects, although not from loving and admiring women he can desexualize. In men of strict morality the result is likely to be sexual repression with a consequent intense condemnation of woman as animal.

In some cases we know that a writer went through experiences that embittered his attitude toward women. Lawrence's possessive and masterful mother, described in his autobiographical novel *Sons and Lovers*, undoubtedly contributed much to his fear of the dominant female. In his own home he saw how a dominant woman can undermine her husband's virility, how even a good woman can cripple her sons. He saw the power inherent in motherhood and reacted against it with envious resentment, which he carried to the extent of wishing to deprive women of children. His mother's domination combined with his own sterility and his wife's unfaithfulness to weaken his confidence as a male: the results were outright expressions of fear of women and attempts to allay that by insisting that women be kept in subjection. Milton's painful first marriage confirmed his belief in woman's mental and moral infirmity and demonstrated to him both the humiliating sexual power she can exert and the likelihood that an apparent helpmate may turn out to be a domestic thorn. Over and over his declarations of woman's ruinous power over man echo his personal experience. Byron's wretched marriage to an intellectual undoubtedly sharpened his satire on bluestockings.

Of course, all these men were influenced by cultural as well as personal forces. Byron and, to a much greater extent, Milton were writing in accordance with a patriarchal tradition of female inferiority and subjection. Lawrence felt the influence of Freudian theory and the general twentieth-century fear that woman is gaining the upper hand. Swift's attacks on overidealization of love and women derived from the savage cynical reaction of the Restoration. St. Jerome, Marston, Swift, and perhaps even Milton were influenced by the antisexual tradition of the Christian church.

Of the cultural causes of misogyny, rejection of or guilt about sex is the most obvious. It leads naturally to degradation of woman as the sexual object and projection onto her of the lust and desire to seduce which a man must repress in himself. At the same time that he denigrates woman's sexual functions, the preoccupation with sex resulting from the attempt to repress desire is apt to make him see her exclusively as a sexual being, more lustful than man and not spiritual at all. The pernicious seductive animal described by the early Christian ascetics haunted medieval clerics and lurked behind Milton's treatment of the falls of Adam and Samson and the temptation of Christ. The attempt to repress sexual desire motivates attacks on woman's physical nature, such as Swift's nauseating descriptions of her flabby breasts and body odors. The difficulty of repressing desire, the disgusted recognition of woman's sexual power, is one reason for the misogynist's belief in her omnipotence.

Misogyny can also develop as a result of the idealization with which men have glorified women as mistresses, wives, and mothers. This has led to a natural reaction, a desire to tear down what has been raised unduly high. Realistically correcting the idealistic view that woman is more spiritual and altruistic than man, writers may be carried too far in the opposite direction and present her as less. The reaction is apparent in the traditional ambivalence of erotic poetry, where — along with worship of a woman as the embodiment of beauty, virtue, and bliss — have regularly appeared allegations of woman's falsity, greed, and incapacity for true love. There may also be an element of projection here, as an exploitative man may project his own emotional limitations on his mistress. Someone like the Earl of Oxford, who wishes to ensnare and cheat women, is apt to convince himself that they are out to cheat him.

While this erotic hostility has been present in the whole tradition, it has been especially strong in certain periods: in the Middle Ages, because of the asceticism of the Church; in the Restoration, because of the cynical impulse to tear away all illusions in the name of reason. Its virtual suppression in the nineteenth century may have intensified the twentieth-century reaction against idealization of women. Although erotic hostility does appear as attacks on romance, such as Mencken's declaration that love is fatuous illusion and the female body an ill-proportioned dollar-sign, the more significant attacks come on the ideal of mother rather than mistress (perhaps because nowadays there is less idealization of the mistress to react against). Contemporary villains are often pointedly called Mommy. The superhumanly edifying, self-sacrificing, devoted Mother of the Victorians is now seen as a cannibal who lives by castrating and possessing her sons. This vision has been clarified by modern psychological insight which has shown how subtly destructive apparent devotion can be.

The idea that Mother does not truly love her son is perhaps a more sophisticated form of the old charge that the mistress does not truly love her devoted lover. Both feelings may be traced to the Oedipus complex: the boy's first erotic object is his mother, who rejects him in favor of his father; he accordingly sees her as faithless, unresponsive to his love, a feeling which persists unless the complex is completely resolved. The resulting bitterness may remain attached to Mother, but is more apt to be transferred to other women, since a man's relationship with his mother is the prototype for all his relationships with women.

In some writers, there is a more intense reaction against lovers' idealizations than charges of falsity or coldness, in the form of exposures of the female as an object of disgust rather than attraction. Beauty, of course, is an essential element in conventional feminine ideals. Although these attacks were strongest in the Restoration, when rational exposure of illusion was at its height while an undercurrent of ascetic condemnation of sex still lingered, they derive from the Romans and have persisted into the present. Lucretius first developed the visit to the lady's dressing room as an antidote to love, indicating that one whiff would dispel an infatuation. Ovid took up the theme less seriously, as did Lyly in the sixteenth century, Gould in the seventeenth, and Mencken in the twentieth. Even Steele, who developed it very gently, represented the lover cured of love by a view of his lady as she really was. The most impressively horrid treatment is undoubtedly that of Swift, whose tour through a belle's dressing room reveals in graphic detail her ugliness, dirt, sweat, and excrement. In this case at least, the degradation of the romantic ideal must surely be connected with revulsion against sex.

The most important cause of misogyny, because the most widely and firmly entrenched in society, is patriarchal feeling, the wish to keep women subject to men. There is an obvious reason for this: the top dog naturally wishes to remain on top. Many a man would like to make all household decisions himself or would prefer not to have women competing with him in his profession.

As the real motive for patriarchy is too selfish to be admitted, the system must be justified and rejustified by rationalizations. For some time the myth of the Fall sufficed: for St. Paul and for medieval and sixteenth- and seventeenth-century preachers, it was usually enough to say that woman was placed in subjection by God as the penalty for her leading role in the Fall. Later, with the more secular approach of the eighteenth and succeeding centuries, the emphasis shifted to woman's alleged natural limitations: she was weak and timid, incapable of reasoning, insensible to abstract ideals, lacking in judgment and responsibility. These charges set up a vicious circle: the story of the Fall served to explain the subordination of women existing in ancient Jewish society, and the Christians then used the story to justify keeping women subordinate; women were supposed to be mentally and morally frail because of the subjection in which law and custom placed them, and they could not be permitted equal status because of their frailty.

Patriarchal feeling is largely responsible for the prominence of insubordination as a charge against women, since the patriarch, seeing woman merely as a helpmate to himself, resents any independent wishes she may have. Attacks on women for beating their husbands, for talking back to them, for pressing ruinous advice on them, for going off to the alehouse instead of staying home to wait on them, for spending their hard-earned money on finery, for giving away their bodies to other men — all spring from the patriarch's need to keep his wife subject. Since the patriarch's low opinion of the female mind and character prevents him from seeking friendship from his wife, he is apt, like Juvenal, to equate conjugal love with uxoriousness. Because he is overpreoccupied with keeping his wife in line — which naturally encourages her to rebel, to get away with as much as she can — he thinks of her more as an unruly domestic animal than as a companion. He often projects his own exploitative feelings onto her, as when Hesiod (who reluctantly advised marriage only as a means of getting a nurse for a man's senile illnesses and heirs to his estate) warned that a woman who is nice to a man is really after his barn. Morbidly sensitive to signs of insubordination in women, the patriarch is convinced that they are all struggling for supremacy. At the same time he believes, with Walter Map, that a disobedient wife is a man's greatest reproach. No wonder the patriarch is apt to find more pain than pleasure in marriage.

The other important manifestation of patriarchal hostility to women is opposition to their every attempt to escape from their traditional limitations: to exercise power in the household, to own property, to study academic subjects, to influence public affairs, to vote, to pursue careers. The typical patriarch indignantly condemns any such attempt as a violation both of the time-honored ways of society and of woman's basic nature. He is so attached to the idea of female inferiority that he may openly admit, as Juvenal and Byron did, that faultlessness is the worst fault a woman can have.

Unlike attacks on the insubordinate wife, which have flourished in all periods, attacks on aspiring women appear only when social conditions are appropriate: thus Juvenal was infuriated by the remarkable degree of freedom attained by the Roman matrons, Knox by the appearance of women rulers in Europe, Jonson and Shadwell by the increasing conspicuousness of the learned lady. In the nineteenth and twentieth centuries, as women have actually approached equality with men, this form of patriarchal antifeminism has been especially noticeable — in the increasingly frantic campaigns of *The Saturday Review*, for example. The tradition of associating intellectual aspirations in women with unchastity has persisted into Lewis' novels of the 1940's. It is not only an easy way to discredit female intellectuals and underline the "unwomanliness" of their activities, but an expression of the patriarch's constant worry about his rights of ownership in women. His overconcern with preserving for himself the wife he regards as his property leads him to a gnawing suspicion of her unfaithfulness.

The opinion that woman is mentally different from man and that she finds her true fulfillment in the home and no place else does not express hatred of women, and it would be absurd to consider as misogynistic a man who simply accepted this assumption from his culture. On the other hand, the man who makes a point of insisting on, even gloating over, the inferiority of woman's nature and the restrictions on her role is surely expressing hostility. Certainly he is defending a selfish attitude in which man profits at woman's expense.

Furthermore, penetration below the surface of innocuous patronage very often reveals the submerged motives of suspicion and fear of women. One would surely suppose that Steele, that ostentatious "Guardian to the Fair," was free of hostile intentions when he recommended lovely inferiority to women and told them that for their own happiness they should devote their lives to adorning their male relatives. His criticism of women is both gentle and constructive and his attitude toward the sex affectionate. Yet, in one of the last *Spectator* papers, he revealed a Miltonic conviction of woman's ruinous influence on man and man's impotence to resist her wiles, and urged that a man's only safe course is to avoid any discussion of his plans with his wife, lest her blandishments overcome his reason. An inconsistent passage in *Paradise Regained* shows more sharply how the patriarch's belittling of woman's capacities may serve as a reassuring cover for the fear that she is really much more powerful than man. After describing how successfully women seduce the best men from virtue by their "Amorous Nets," Milton hastened to declare that the truly noble are immune to women because intent "on worthier things."

The fear that the woman who is freed from restrictions will become man's master lies at the root of patriarchal insistence on her subjection. It may be traced ultimately to the mother's power over her son and more directly to the power of the wife or mistress over her husband or lover. The patriarch is particularly sensitive about this power because he is so anxious to be dominant in every way: he feels that courting a woman degrades him, and yet he must do it. Lawrence, for example, protested against man's sexual nature because it made him dependent on women. Cato's declaration, in the second century B.C., that if woman were allowed to attain equality with man she would become his master shows that he assumed she was intrinsically more powerful. This apprehension has continued to appear through the centuries, as in Walter Map's warning against "the deceit of the omnipotent female." Once having got the upper hand, the bad wives of Dekker, Jonson, Jerrold, and Lewis ruled their husbands absolutely, receiving both service and devotion, no matter how abominably they behaved.

Fear of female domination has been expressed most sharply in the present century, when it has been aggravated by woman's real gains in power. Crosland declared that she "has been out of hand for centuries, and . . . to-day she is out of hand to an almost irremediable extent." Lawrence protested that modern man grovels before "a baby's napkin and a woman's petticoat" and expressed panic at the destructiveness of woman when she is not "held, by man, safe within the bounds of belief." In the modern attacks on Mom, it seems almost as if men saw a resurgence of the matriarchy that patriarchy once managed to suppress. Wylie charged that woman has reduced man to a mere appendage in our society, which she absolutely controls; thus, she is responsible for modern gangsterism, labor strife, and World War II. (The patriarch, assuming woman's fundamental viciousness, always supposes that if unrestrained she will use her power for evil ends.) There is, of course, a factual basis for the belief in female power, since women may have quite as forceful characters as men and do exert a strong influ--

ence on their husbands and sons. But the idea that woman is more powerful than man seems to be a creation of male hostility, caused by men's alarm at *any* manifestation of strength or influence by woman and aggravated by resentment provoked by their sexual dependence on her.

The perennial attacks on bad wives can be traced both to the patriarchal spirit which has been so persistent in our culture and to the factual conditions of the institution of marriage. Conjugal experience can furnish a daily source of vexations to writers inclined to exploit it. The patriarchal structure of traditional Western culture helped to develop greed, perversity, and rebelliousness in wives. In husbands, the patriarchal attitude encourages selfish censoriousness, suspicion, and constant alertness to the ways in which women fall short as helpmates.

The idea that women are animals hostile to man's idealism derives from all three of the cultural causes of misogyny. In the first place, if sexual desire is considered degrading, the woman who excites it appears as a seducer from virtue: she hands man the apple, she soils his soul, she brings him down into the mud. The same view can result from reaction against the romantic vision of woman exalting man, of Beatrice leading Dante to the throne of God. In the antiromantic tradition woman is seen as a mercenary creature incapable of love, of high motives, or even discernment, who crassly exploits her idealistic lover. Her unworthiness may be ironically underlined by making her appear, like Rochester's Corinna or Lewis' Fran Dodsworth, to be much more spiritual than man. Finally, the patriarchal tradition has always maintained — has had to maintain, in order to justify itself — that woman is a creature weak in mind and morals who must be kept in check if society is to survive and man to progress. Just as the undue influence of Eve impaired man's spiritual nature and drove him from Paradise, the undue influence of her twentieth-century daughters is supposed to destroy man's ideals and undermine "the god in him."

Criticism of women — whether inspired by handy convention, the desire to release feelings through humor, or deep hostility — has flourished in all periods. It strikingly illustrates both the hostility that often arises in sexual relationships and the natural human tendency to stereotype the members of a different group. It is gratifying to a person's own ego to stereotype the other group as inferior. The same mechanism appears in racial, religious, or social prejudice; but women, as an ever-present group of outsiders (outsiders in the sense that most authors are men), have been subjected to more widespread and longstanding attack than any other group. Of course, the parallel must not be pushed too far: unlike the victims of racial prejudice, women have been loved and idealized much more than they have been hated and degraded, and naked expressions of misogyny have rarely been considered acceptable. And yet, misogynistic hostility has been constantly present in our culture, ranging from mild disparagement of woman's mind and character to harsh charges that she torments, exploits, and seduces man.

◄▷ INDEX

Aaron's Rod, 241, 243, 245, 275
Abraham, Karl, 236*n*
Absalom! Absalom!, 257
Absalom and Achitophel, 166
Adam, 3, 4, 9, 11, 19, 20, 22, 60, 62, 70, 72, 74, 84, 91, 92, 93*n*, 138, 143, 144, 146, 152, 154–56, 158, 166, 180, 268, 270
Adam and Eve, 240*n*
Adam and Eve, Books of, 10*n*
Adams, Franklin P., 233*n*
Addison, Joseph, 165*n*, 167, 168, 174–75, 180*n*
"Address on Vainglory and the Right Way for Parents to Bring Up Their Children," 17–18
"Advice to a Lady," 180
"Advice to an Old Gentleman Who Wished for a Young Wife," 86
"Advice to Bride and Groom," 28
The Aeneid, 29–30, 44
Aeschylus, 30–31, 41
Aesop, 182*n*
"Against Evil Women," 64–65
"Against Helvidius," 19
"Against Jovinianus," 19–20
Agathias Scholasticus, 44–45
Albee, Edward, 261
Alexis, 45*n*
Allan, James McGrigor, 219–21, 225
Allestree, Richard, 150–51
All's Well That Ends Well, 120
An Alphabet of Tales, 93*n*
The Ambassadors, 237–39*n*
Amelia, 184–85*n*
The Amending of Life, 68
The American, 237–38*n*
The American Dream, 261
The Anatomie of Absurditie, 108–9

The Anatomie of Abuses, 140
The Anatomy of Melancholy, 110
Anaxandrides, 26–27
Anaxilas, 45
The Ancren Riwle, 67, 68, 71
Andreas Capellanus, 60–61, 110
"Answer to Several Letters," 169
An Answer to . . . The Doctrine and Discipline of Divorce, 153–54
Antonio and Mellida, 128*n*
Anything for a Quiet Life, 127*n*
An Appeal to all that Doubt . . . [with] Some Animadversions upon Dr. Trap's Late Reply, 141
The Araignment of Lewde, idle, froward, and unconstant women, 105–6, 109*n*, 258
Arbuthnot, John, 182–83
Arcadia, 112
Aristophanes, 31, 35*n*, 43*n*, 202
Aristotle, 24, 31, 35–37, 41, 56–57*n*, 64, 66, 155, 182, 220, 235
Armour, Richard, 227*n*
Arnobius, 16*n*
The Art of Courtly Love, 60–61, 110
The Art of Love, 49, 50–51, 53, 61
Athanasius, 16*n*
Athenaeus, 42*n*
The Athenian Mercury, 185*n*
"At the town's end," 88, 89
Augustine, St., 10*n*, 16, 17, 20, 21*n*, 65, 142–43
Aureng-Zebe, 120*n*
The Ayenbite of Inwyt, 69, 71*n*
Aylmer, John, 137, 139

The Bacchae, 34*n*
Bansley, Charles, 102
Barchester Towers, 201*n*

"The Bargain of Judas," 71n
Barnaby Rudge, 196–97, 200, 201, 230
The Batchelars Banquet, 102–5, 127, 216, 222
"The Battle of the Books," 170
Bax, E. Belfort, 221–22n
Beaumont, Francis. See Fletcher
"A Beautiful Young Nymph Going to Bed," 169–70, 171, 227
Becon, Thomas, 136n
The Beggar's Opera, 182n
"The Beginning of Man's Life," 68–69n
"La Belle Dame Sans Merci," 224n
Belvedére, 107n
Bible, 3–11, 41, 56, 65, 70, 84, 92, 105, 106, 124, 135, 142, 158, 159, 219, 220n
— I Corinthians, 8–10, 16n, 83n
— Ecclesiastes, 6–7
— Ephesians, 10, 83n
— Esther, 11n
— Ezekiel, 7n
— Genesis, 3–4, 10, 22n, 153, 155, 158
— Isaiah, 7n, 11n
— Job, 101–2
— I Kings, 5
— Luke, 8
— Mark, 8
— Matthew, 8, 15n, 16–17n
— Nehemiah, 5
— I Peter, 10n
— Proverbs, 6–7, 11, 19–20, 124, 153
— Revelation, 7n, 8n
— I Thessalonians, 10
— I Timothy, 9, 10
Bierce, Ambrose, 230
Bleak House, 193, 195n, 207–9
"A Blue Love-Song," 207
"The Blues," 206
"The Boy and the Mantle," 59n
The Bread-Winner, 251n
A Bride-Bush, 144–45
The Bride-Womans Counsellor, 145–46
Bromyard, John, 69–70
Browne, Sir Thomas, 147–48, 159
Burns, Robert, 165n
Burton, Robert, 110
Bury Fair, 181–82

Bussy d'Ambois, 121, 268
"Bycorne and Chichevache," 85
Byron, George Gordon, Lord, 193, 194, 204–6, 270, 273

"Cadenus and Vanessa," 173
Camden, Carroll, 102n, 106n
Carey, Millicent, 90n
The Case of Rebellious Susan, 217–18
"Cassinus and Peter," 171
Cass Timberlane, 230–31
The Catholic Encyclopedia, 4
Catiline, 130–31
Cato the Elder, 37–38, 41, 275
Catullus, 46, 47
Chapman, George, 121–23, 125–26, 268
Chaucer, Geoffrey, 24, 56, 57n, 58, 62, 65, 71n, 74, 77–85, 86, 99, 267
Chesterfield, Philip Dormer Stanhope, Earl of, 178, 180
The Chester Plays, 70, 90
"Child Waters," 79n
Christian Doctrine, 153n
Christian Oeconomie, 151n
Christs Teares Over Jerusalem, 108, 173n
Cibber, Colley, 182, 183
The Citizen of the World, 123
The City Madam, 126
City of God, 16, 17n, 20
Civilization and Its Discontents, 236
Clement of Alexandria, 17n
Clement of Rome, St., 17n
"The Clerk and the Nightingale," 62
"The Clerk's Tale," 78–80
Clodia, 46, 47, 53
"Cocksure Women and Hensure Men," 240n
Colasterion, 154
Coleridge, Samuel Taylor, 190n
Colet, John, 141n
The Column Book of F. P. A., 233n
"Communitie," 115
Confessions, 16
Congreve, William, 202
Cotton, Charles, 165n
Counsel to the Husband: To the Wife Instruction, 151n
The Country Wife, 165n

Coventry, Francis, 185n
Crosland, T. W. H., 222–24, 225, 267, 275
Cymbeline, 119–20, 245
Cynthia's Revels, 127–28
Cyril of Alexandria, St., 21n

Daemonologie, 148n
David, 5, 18, 19, 22, 60, 71, 105, 147
David Copperfield, 197n, 199n
The Day of the Locust, 251–52
Deegan, Dorothy Yost, 204n
Defoe, Daniel, 202
Dekker, Thomas, 102–5, 114, 120, 124, 127, 133, 216, 222, 275
Demosthenes, 28–29n
De Nugis Curialium, 74–76
The Devil's Dictionary, 230
Dickens, Charles, 98, 193, 195–97, 199n, 200, 201, 207–9, 230
Dido, 39, 44, 57, 58
Diogenes Laertius, 26, 56, 173n
A Discourse of the Damned Art of Witchcraft, 148n
A Discourse on Female Influence, and the True Christian Mode of Its Exercise, 190
The Disobedient Child, 91n
"The Doctor and the Doctor's Wife," 249
The Doctrine and Discipline of Divorce, 153, 158n
Dodsworth, 230, 250, 267, 276
"Dolores," 224n
Don Juan, 194n, 204–6
Donne, John, 114–16, 133, 140n, 141n, 142–44, 148, 162
Drayton, Michael, 113
Dryden, John, 120n, 165–66
The Duchess of Malfi, 120–21
Dunbar, William, 62, 64–65, 86–88
D'Urfey, Thomas, 161–62, 165n

Eastward Ho!, 125–26
Ecclesiasticus, 11–13, 41, 74
The Ecclesiazusae, 35n, 210
Les Échecs amoureux, 61
Edel, Leon, 238–39n, *passim*
Elohist, 3, 152
Encyclopedia Britannica, 194n

England's Parnassus, 107
"Enslaved by Civilization," 240n
"Envoy to Bukton," 84
Epicoene, 120, 123, 127, 130, 132
"An Epic of Women," 224n
"Epigram on the Court Pucell," 128
I Esdras, 13
Etherege, George, 160, 202n
The Eumenides, 30–31
Euphues, 110–11
Euripides, 31–33, 34–35, 41, 75
Eve, 3, 4, 9, 15, 20, 22, 70, 71, 72, 76, 77, 91, 93n, 100, 101, 108, 110, 115, 143, 144, 146, 149, 152, 154–56, 158, 165, 166, 185n, 190, 239, 268, 276
Every Man Out of His Humour, 127
"Examples Against Women," 71–72
"An Exhortation to Theodore After His Fall," 18, 110
An Exposition of St. Paul's First Epistle to the Corinthians, 141n
"The Extasie," 114

Fables for the Female Sex, 184n
The Faerie Queene, 7n, 137–39, 192
"The Fall of Edward Barnard," 251n
Fantasia of the Unconscious, 238–41, 242, 245
"A Farewell to Love" (Donne), 115
"Farewell to Love" (Suckling), 117
"The Farmer's Curst Wife," 88, 165n
Farquhar, George, 177–78
A Father's Legacy to His Daughters, 186–87
Faulkner, William, 237, 252–57, 263, 268
Feltham, Owen, 142n
Female Policy Detected, 106
The Female Vertuoso's, 181, 183
Les Femmes Savantes, 181
Fiedler, Leslie, 254
Fielding, Henry, 184–85n
The Fifth Column, 248–49
The Fire of Love, 65n, 68
The First Blast of the Trumpet against the Monstrous regiment of women, 135–36
Fitzgerald, F. Scott, 251n
Fitzhugh, George, 190n
Fleetwood, William, 148–49

Fletcher, John, 92–93
Fletcher, John, and Francis Beaumont, 120, 128*n*
Follie's Anatomie, 110*n*
Fordyce, James, 186
Fors Clavigera, 193
For Whom the Bell Tolls, 248
"The Franklin's Tale," 83
The Fraud of Feminism, 221–22*n*
Freud, Sigmund, 54, 138, 235–37, 242*n*, 257, 263–64, 266, 269, 270
The Funeral, 182*n*
"The Furniture of a Woman's Mind," 166, 174*n*

Gagen, Jean Elisabeth, 182*n*
Galla, Martial's epigram on, 46, 123
"The Garden," 117*n*
Gascoigne, George, 24, 113*n*
Gataker, Thomas, 151*n*
Gawain and the Green Knight, 60
Gay, John, 177*n*, 182–83
Geismar, Maxwell, 257*n*
The Generall History of Women, 29
The Generation of Animals, 36–37
Generation of Vipers, 258–59, 267, 275
"A Gentle Hint to Writing-Women," 209
Gesta Romanorum, 95–96
Gideon Planish, 231–32
Gilbert, Allan, 153
Gilbert, W. S., 203–4
"Give Her a Pattern," 240*n*
"God gif I wer wedo now," 89*n*
"Goe and catche a falling starre," 115
The Golden Bowl, 237–39*n*
The Golden Legend, 69*n*
Goldman, Eric F., 232–33*n*
Goldsmith, Oliver, 123, 185, 186
Goodman, Christopher, 136
Gospel of the Twelve Apostles, 71*n*
Gosson, Stephen, 107*n*
Gosynhill, Edward, 101–2, 106*n*
Gould, Robert, 164, 272
Gower, John, 56
Graves, Robert, 23*n*
Great Expectations, 195, 201
Great Goddess, 23, 29, 31*n*, 46*n*
The Greek Anthology, 25*n*, 44–45, 46
Greene, Robert, 107*n*, 120, 173*n*

Gregory, Dr. John, 186–87, 188
Gregory of Nyssa, 16*n*, 18*n*
Grisilde, 77–80, 85, 193, 266
Guilpin, Everard, 110*n*
Gulliver's Travels, 169–71, 173, 174, 177*n*

Halifax, George Savile, Marquis of, 149–50
Hali Meidenhad, 65*n*
Hall, Dr. John, 117*n*
Hall, Joseph, 109*n*, 119, 141*n*
Hamlet, 113, 118–19
The Hamlet, 252–53, 255, 256, 257
Handlyng Synne, 69, 94*n*
The Happy Ascetic, 151*n*
An Harborough for faithful Subjects, 137
Hardy, Thomas, 13*n*
Hart, Moss, 232–33, 236
Hawthorne, Nathaniel, 204*n*, 245
Hemingway, Ernest, 229, 237, 247–51, 252, 257, 261, 263
Henry Esmond, 197–200*n passim*
Herrick, Robert (seventeenth century), 116–17
Herrick, Robert (twentieth century), 228–30, 251*n*
Hesiod, 13, 22–24, 28, 29, 41, 273
Heywood, John, 91*n*
Heywood, Thomas, 29*n*
Highet, Gilbert, 46*n*
Hippolytus, 32–33, 51, 119, 245
Hippolytus, 32–33
The History of Animals, 36*n*
The History of Pompey the Little, 185*n*
Histrio-Mastix, 140
Homer, 29, 30, 39
The Honest Whore, 120, 124
Hooker, Richard, 141*n*, 142
Horace, 51*n*
Horneck, Anthony, 151*n*
"How, gossip mine, gossip mine," 94
Howard, Sidney, 257–58
How Superior Powers Ought to be Obeyed, 136*n*
Hughes, Merritt Y., 158*n*
An Humble Supplication unto God, 136*n*

The Humours of Oxford, 180
Humphry Clinker, 202–3
Hutton, Henry, 110n

"If women could be fair and yet not fond," 113–14
The Iliad, 30
In Defense of Women, 226–27
Ingelend, Thomas, 91n
The Insatiate Countess, 124–25, 133
"In villa, in villa," 89n
"The Invincible Pride of Women," 108n
Irving, Washington, 201

Jahvist, 3, 4, 9, 11, 22, 152
James I, King, 148n
James, Henry, 237–40n
Jeaffreson, John Cordy, 193–94
Jean de Meun, 61
Jerome, St., 18–20, 21n, 24, 25n, 269, 270
Jerrold, Douglas, 197–201, 225, 226, 267, 275
Jezebel, 5n, 101, 136, 146
Job's wife, 3, 72, 101–2, 147
John Chrysostom, St., 16n, 17–18, 21n, 110
John of Salisbury, 24, 44n, 57, 71n, 73–74
Johnson, Edgar, 197n
Johnson, Samuel, 182, 185
Jones, Henry A., 217–18
Jonson, Ben, 98, 120, 123, 125–26, 127–31, 132, 231, 274, 275
The Journal of a Modern Lady, 167–68
"The Joys of Marriage," 165n
Jude the Obscure, 13n
Judith, 6n, 72, 137
Juvenal, 38–40, 41, 123, 127, 166, 205, 273

Keats, John, 189n, 224n
Kelso, Ruth, 131n
Killigrew, Thomas, 131–32
King Lear, 119, 121n
Kingsley, Charles, 189, 192, 193
Kitto, H. D. F., 31
Kittredge, G. L., 80n

Knox, John, 35–37, 159, 274
Kopit, Arthur, 261n
Kraemer, Henry. *See* Sprenger

The Ladies Calling, 150–51, 186
Lady Chatterley's Lover, 240, 241–42, 243
Lady in the Dark, 232–33, 236
"The Lady's Dressing Room," 169, 171
The Lady's New Year's Gift, 149–50
Lady Windermere's Fan, 195n
The Last Chronicle of Barset, 201n
Latimer, Hugh, 146
Law, William, 141
Lawrence, D. H., 237–47, 249, 254n, 256, 257, 263, 268, 269–70, 275
The Laws, 35n, 43
"Leave me ô Love," 113
The Legend of Good Women, 58, 84–85
"*A Letter from Artemisa*," 164
"Letter from Valerius to Ruffinus," 74–76, 81
"Letter to a Young Lady on Her Marriage," 167, 172, 173, 174
Lewis, Sinclair, 230–32, 250, 251n, 267, 268, 274, 275, 276
Life with Women and How to Survive It, 234
Light in August, 252, 253, 256
Lives of the English Poets, 182
The Lives of the Noble Grecians and Romans, 28
Livy, 37–38
Lobsenz, Herbert, 233
Look Back in Anger, 261–63
Look! We Have Come Through!, 242
"Love and Marriage," 195n
Love in a Wood, 165n, 202n
"The Lovely Lady," 244
Lovely Woman, 222–24, 225, 267
The Love of Fame, the Universal Passion, 169n, 183–84
"Loves Alchymie," 114–15, 133
Lucretius, 48–49, 75, 272
Ludus Coventriae, 70n
Lydgate, John, 58, 61, 62, 71–72, 75n, 85–86, 267
Lyly, John, 110–11, 114, 272
Lyndesay, Sir David, 139n

Lysistrata, 35n
Lyttelton, George, Lord, 180

The Malcontent, 128n
Malleus Maleficarum, 148n
Malory, Sir Thomas, 58–59
Man and Boy, 259–60
Man and Superman, 236n
"Manifestations of the Female Castration Complex," 236n
The Man of Mode, 160
Map, Walter, 74–76, 81, 109, 273, 275
Marchand, Leslie A., 194n
Marjorie Morningstar, 233n
Mark Twain, 204n
Marriage Duties Briefely Couched together, 151n
Marston, John, 109–10, 123, 124–26, 128n, 133, 269, 270
Martial, 46, 123
Marvell, Andrew, 117n
Massinger, Philip, 126
"Matriarchy," 240n
Maugham, Somerset, 229, 251n
"The Mechanical Operation of the Spirit," 173
Medea, 31–32, 33, 51, 108
Medea (Euripides), 31–32, 33n, 34
Medea (Seneca), 33
"Men and Women," 240
Mencken, H. L., 226–27, 267, 271, 272
"The Merchant's Tale," 80n, 83, 86
A Mery Play betwene John Johan the husband Tyb his wife and syr Jhān the preest, 91n
Messalina, 38, 101, 119
Micro-Cynicon, 110n
Middle Comedy, Greek, 26–27, 45
Middleton, Thomas, 110n, 127n
The Mikado, 203
Miller, James, 180
Milton, John, 10n, 138, 144, 151–59, 160, 170n, 180, 182, 215, 238, 268, 270, 274–75
"The Modern Belle," 187
Molière, 181
The Monarche, 139n
Monks Are Monks, 226
The Moon and Sixpence, 251n
Moore, Edward, 184n

Moore, Thomas, 106n, 194–95, 206–7
Moral Essays, 176–77, 190n
"The Moral of the Legend of Dido," 58
Morris, Wright, 259–60
Le Morte D'Arthur, 58–59
Mosquitoes, 252, 253, 255–56, 257
"Mother and Daughter," 244
"The Mother of a Queen," 250
M. P. or, The Blue-Stocking, 206
Mrs. Caudle's Curtain Lectures, 197–201, 225, 226, 267
Mulgrave, John Sheffield, Earl of, and Duke of Buckingham, 160–61
"A Mumming at Hertford," 85–86, 267
Murry, John Middleton, 240n
My Fair Lady, vii
"My Love Was False and Full of Flattery," 56n
Myrer, Anton, 251

Nashe, Thomas, 108–9, 133, 173n
Nathan, George Jean, 226, 233–34
The Nature of the Universe, 48–49
Newcastle *Noah's Ark*, 90n
New Comedy, Greek, 26–27, 45
The Newcomes, 198–200n passim
The New Inn, 127
New Introductory Lectures on Psycho-Analysis, 235
Nicomachean Ethics, 36n
Noah's wife, 89–90
Northumberland, Earl of, 111–12, 114
"Now I Lay Me," 248, 249–50
"The Nun's Priest's Tale," 83–84

"Off Ladies Bewties," 89n
Of Human Bondage, 251n
Of the Laws of Ecclesiastical Polity, 141n, 142
"Of the State of Matrimony," 142
Oh Dad, Poor Dad, Mamma's Hung You in the Closet . . ., 261n
Oliver Twist, 195n
"On Chattering in Church," 94
"On Marriage," 24–25
"On the Apparel of Women," 15
"On the Real Differences in the Minds of Men and Women," 219–21
"On the Veiling of Virgins," 15
Orlando Furioso, 120

Orpheus Brittanicus, 161–62
Osborne, John, 254*n*, 261–63, 268
O'Shaughnessy, Arthur, 224*n*
Othello, 92*n*, 120–21
"Our Goodman," 89*n*
An Outline of Psycho-Analysis, 236
Overbury, Sir Thomas, 131
Ovid, 47, 49–51, 52, 53, 56, 57, 58, 61, 76, 110, 111, 123, 171, 272
Owst, Gerald R., 69, 70, 71
Oxford, Edward de Vere, Earl of, 113–14, 271

"The Pain and Sorrow of Evil Marriage," 75*n*
Palladas of Alexandria, 25*n*
Pandora, 22–23, 29
Paradise Lost, 151–52, 154–56, 157, 170*n*, 215
Paradise Regained, 157–58, 274–75
"Paradoxes," 115–16
"A Paraphrase of the Ten Commandments," 89*n*
Parasitaster, 123
"The Parson's Tale," 65, 71*n*
The Parson's Wedding, 131–32
"Party of One: Our American Woman," 232–33*n*
Pater, Walter, 224*n*
Patience, 203–4
Paul, St., 4, 8–11, 16, 20, 21, 28, 41, 54, 65, 82–83, 135, 136, 141, 142, 147, 149, 152, 153, 158, 159, 190, 210, 268, 272
Peck, Joseph, 234
Pendennis, 197–200*n passim*
Peregrine Pickle, 202–3
Perkins, William, 148*n*, 151*n*
"The Permutation of the Proper Place," ix
Petronius, 46*n*, 51–52, 73, 97–98, 122–23, 230*n*
Phaedra, 31, 33
Phaedra, 33
Philaster, 120, 128*n*
Phillips, James E., 136–37*n*
Philobiblon, 74
Philo Judaeus, 13*n*
Pickwick Papers, 195*n*
The Plain-Dealer, 165*n*

Plato, 35, 43, 129, 182
Plautus, 27–28, 45–46*n*
Plutarch, 28, 182
Poe, Edgar Allan, 224*n*
The Poetaster, 127
The Poetics, 35–36
Policraticus, 44*n*, 57, 71*n*, 73–74
Politeuphia, 107
The Politics, 35
Ponet, John, 136
Pope, Alexander, 167, 168, 169*n*, 175–77, 182–83, 186, 190*n*
Praz, Mario, 224*n*
The Precepts of Alfred, 95, 96
Prejudices: Fourth Series, 226
A Preparative to Marriage, 146–47
The Princess, 190–92
"The Progresse of the Soule," 144
"The Progress of Beauty," 169*n*
"The Progress of Love," 177*n*
Propertius, 47–48, 54
Prynne, William, 139–40
Punch, 198, 201*n*, 225

Quinze Joyes de Mariage, 102
Quippes for Upstart Newfangled Gentlewomen, 107*n*

"The Rabbinical Origin of Women," 106*n*, 195*n*
Raleigh, Sir Walter, 179
"Ramble in St. James's Park," 163, 172, 276
The Rape of the Lock, 167, 168, 169*n*, 175–76
Ratcliff, Alexander, 161
Ray, Gordon N., 201*n*
Reason and Sensuality, 61
"The Recantation of a Lover," 113*n*
The Refusal, 182, 183
The Relative Duties of Parents and Children, Husbands and Wives . . ., 148–49
Religio Medici, 147–48, 159
"The Relique," 115
The Remedies of Love, 49–50, 53, 61, 110, 171
"The Remedy of Love," 65*n*, 93
The Republic, 35
Richard de Bury, 74

Rieff, Philip, 237*n*
"The Righteous Mammon," 141*n*
"Rip Van Winkle," 201
Robert of Brunne, 69, 94*n*
Robertson, D. W., Jr., 79*n*
"Robin Hood's Death," 59–60
Rochester, John Wilmot, Earl of, 162–64, 172, 276
Rolle, Richard, 65*n*, 68
The Romance of the Rose, 61, 85
Root, Waverley, 232*n*
Rowlands, Samuel, 107*n*
Rudyerd, Benjamin, 114*n*
Rule a Wife and Have a Wife, 93
Ruskin, John, 193, 194

Sachs, Lizbeth J., and Bernard H. Stern, 236*n*
The Sacred Fount, 239–40*n*
The Sages at Dinner, 42*n*
"St. Mawr," 243
Sallust, 130
Salomon, Louis, 113*n*
Samson, 5, 22, 60, 63, 65, 71, 72, 101, 105, 137, 147, 270
Samson Agonistes, 156–57
Sanctuary, 253–55
Sartoris, 252, 257
The Saturday Review (English), 209–17, 218, 225, 234, 274
"Satyr Against Love, and Women," 161
A Satyr Against Wooing, 164
The Satyricon, 51–52, 73
The Schole house of Women, 101–2, 106*n*, 114, 267
Schorer, Mark, 232*n*
The Scourge of Villanie, 109, 269
Second Defense of the People of England, 152*n*
The Second Shepherds' Play, 90
Semonides of Amorgos, 25*n*
Seneca, 33, 40*n*, 182
Sermons to Young Women, 186
Sesame and Lilies, 193
The Seven Sages of Rome, 96–98, 99, 123
Shadwell, Thomas, 181–82, 274
Shakespeare, William, 92, 99, 113, 118–21, 190*n*, 245

Shaw, George Bernard, 236*n*
She Would If She Could, 202*n*
Shirley, James, 117*n*
"The Short Happy Life of Francis Macomber," 250–51, 261
A Short Treatise of Politique Power, 136*n*
Sidney, Sir Philip, 111, 113
The Silver Cord, 257–58
Sir Harry Wildair, 177–78
Skelton, John, 94–95
Skialetheia, 110*n*
Sledd, James, 80*n*
Sloane, Eugene Hulse, 164*n*
Smith, Henry, 146–47
Smollett, Tobias, 202–3
Sociology for the South, 190*n*
Socrates, 20, 26, 35, 43, 56, 73, 107*n*
Soliloquies, 17
Solomon, 5, 6, 18, 19, 20, 22, 60, 63, 64, 68, 71, 105, 157, 158
Sons and Lovers, 269
Sophocles, 129, 130*n*, 192
The Sound and the Fury, 256–57
The Spectator, 165*n*, 167, 168–69, 175, 177*n*, 178–80, 274
Spenser, Edmund, 7*n*, 136*n*, 137–39, 192
Sprenger, Jacob, and Henry Kraemer, 148*n*
Sprint, John, 145–46, 148
Stearns, Jonathan F., 190
Steele, Sir Richard, 165*n*, 168–69, 174, 178–80, 182*n*, 188, 272, 274
Stenton, Doris Mary, 142
Stern, Bernard H. *See* Sachs
"Strephon and Chloe," 170–73 *passim*
Stubbes, Philip, 140
"The 'Student,' " 222
Studies in Classic American Literature, 245–47, 275
Suckling, Sir John, 117
The Summa Theologica, 65–67
The Sun Also Rises, 250
The Suppliants, 31*n*
Swetnam, Joseph, 24, 105–6, 109*n*, 114, 258
Swetnam, the Woman-hater, 105
Swift, Jonathan, 166–74, 177*n*, 180, 188, 227, 269, 270, 272

Swinburne, Algernon Charles, 224n
The Symposium, 43

Table Talk, 190n
The Taming of a Shrew, 91–92
The Taming of the Shrew, 92
The Tatler, 178–80, 182
Taylor, Jeremy, 142n
Tender Is the Night, 251n
Tennyson, Alfred, Lord, 190–92
Tertullian, 14–16, 21
The Testaments of the Twelve Patri-
  archs, 13–14
Tetrachordon, 152, 153n
Thackeray, William Makepeace, 197–
  200n
Theogony, 23
Theophrastus, 20, 24–25, 26, 73, 74,
  76, 81, 165n
The Thesmophoriazusae, 35n
Thomas Aquinas, St., 65–67
*Three Essays on the Theory of Sex-
  uality*, 235
Three Hours after Marriage, 182–83
"The Thrush and the Nightingale," 72
Thucydides, 28n
Thurber, James, 237n
Tibullus, 47, 48n
Timon of Athens, 119n
"To Fine Lady Would-Bee," 128n
Together, 228
"To his Coy Mistress," 164
"To His Friend, a Cautious Lover,"
  163
"To Lord Harley," 177n
Tom Jones, 184–85n
Tom Tyler and His Wife, 90–91
"To My Honour'd Kinsman, John
  Driden," 165–66
"Tortoises," 244–45
"To the Countesse of Huntingdon,"
  115
Tottel's Miscellany, 113n
"Town Eclogues," 177n
"To W. O. . . . upon his Offer of a
  Wife to me . . . ," 164–65
*Treatyse shewing and declaring the
  Pryde and Abuse of Women Now a
  Dayes*, 102
Trial by Jury, 203

Troilus and Criseyde, 85
Trollope, Anthony, 201n
Truculentus, 46n
"The Tunnyng of Elynour Rummyng,"
  94–95
Turbervile, George, 113n
*The Twentieth-Century Encyclopedia
  of Catholicism*, 4n, 9n
The Twin Menaechmi, 27
"The Two Married Women and the
  Widow," 86–88

*The Unexpurgated Case Against Wom-
  an Suffrage*, 221n
The Unlovelinesse of Love-Lockes,
  139–40
"Upon some women," 116–17
Utley, Francis Lee, 102n

"A Valediction: Forbidding Mourn-
  ing," 114, 142
"A Valediction: of the Booke," 115
Vanbrugh, John, 182n
Vangel Griffin, 233
Vanity Fair, 197–200n passim
*The Vertuous schole-hous of ungra-
  cious women*, 102
The Violent Shore, 251
Virgidemiarum, 109n, 119
Virgil, 29–30, 39, 44, 56–57n
Volpone, 129–30
"Votes for Women," 222

*The Wakefield Pageants in the Towne-
  ley Cycle*, 89–90
Ward, Ned, 106
War with Catiline, 130
Wasserstrom, William, 63n
Waste, 228–29
The Way of the World, 202
Webster, John, 120–21, 124
Weddirburne, 56n
West, Nathanael, 251–52
Whateley, William, 144–45, 152
"What vaileth trouth," 113
"What You Don't Know Won't Hurt
  You Till Later," 227n
The White Devil, 124
The White Peacock, 241, 242–43, 244,
  245

The Whole Duty of Man, 151n
Who's Afraid of Virginia Woolf, 261n
Widow of Ephesus, 51–52, 73, 97–98, 122–23, 230n
The Widow's Tears, 122–23
"A Wife," 131
Wife of Bath, 65, 77, 79, 80–83, 84, 85, 87, 89, 100, 133, 267
"The Wife of Bath's Prologue," 56, 80–83, 86, 98n
"The Wife of Bath's Tale," 82
"The Wife Wrapt in Wether's Skin," 89n
Wilde, Oscar, 194–95
Wilson, Edmund, 248n
The Winter's Tale, 120n
Wit and Mirth: Or Pills to Purge Melancholy, 161–62, 165n
A Woman in Spite of Herself, 193–94
A Woman of No Importance, 195n

The Woman's Prize, 93
Woman Suffrage Wrong in Principle and Practice, 219–21
"Women Are Intellectually Inferior," 232n
Wouk, Herman, 233n
Wright, Sir Almroth E., 221n
Wright, Thomas, 181, 183
Wyatt, Sir Thomas, 113
Wycherley, William, 163, 164–65, 202n
Wylie, Philip, 258–59, 267, 268, 275

Xanthippe, 20, 26, 56, 76, 107n
Xenophon, 28n

Yates, Frances A., 112n
Yeast, 189, 192
The Yeomen of the Guard, 203
The York Plays, 70n, 90
Young, Edward, 169n, 183–84, 186